THE TUDOR ROSE

Princess Mary, Henry VIII's Sister

Jennifer Kewley Draskau

STA BOOKS

Revised edition The Tudor Rose

Published by STA BOOKS 2015
www.spencerthomasassociates.com

First published by The History Press 2013
Cover image: Mary Tudor c. 1520, daughter of Henry VII
(1498-1533) sister of Henry VIII
(Photo by Hulton Archives/Getty Images)

Editor Vicki Villers

ISBN 978-0-9933957-1-0

—

For Fiona

CONTENTS

1 THE YOUNG TUDORS

A quiver of excitement ran through the chamber. Silken robes rustled as the courtiers craned for a better view. The musicians struck up a merry tune and out he strode, head high, the personification of England's hopes and dreams, handsome as a young god, the teenage King of England, leading his beautiful younger sister Princess Mary Rose, by the hand. The young King's wife, dumpy little Queen Katherine looked on, graciously smiling. After a quick glance to check that the Queen approved, the courtiers broke into spontaneous applause.

Katherine, daughter of the Catholic Kings, Ferdinand of Aragon and Isabella of Castile, knew that even her best features, her long auburn hair, her fair, healthy complexion and cool grey eyes, were outshone by her gorgeous sister-in-law. At twenty-four, Katherine's face retained a childish roundness, but her expression was serene and demure.

Katherine had long practice of smiling even in adversity. Left an impoverished widow by the death of her first husband, Prince Arthur, when her young brother-in-law and husband-to-be, Prince Henry, succeeded to the throne, nothing had been settled. Her own future was still unsure.

Now she had at last achieved her destiny, cherished from childhood: she was Queen of England, bride of the splendid new eighteen-year-old King. Tall and muscular, young Henry VIII attacked life like a lion. He moved with the easy swagger of the trained athlete. His auburn hair was cut straight in the French fashion. Despite his aquiline nose, Henry favoured the Yorks, his mother and his handsome maternal grandfather, King Edward IV, with his broad face, small, sharp eyes and sensual little mouth. Described in 1516 by a Venetian envoy as 'the handsomest prince ever seen',[1] at this early stage of his career, Henry was also idealistic, liberal and generous. The arrogance and brutality that would tarnish his later years were not apparent. Even his vanity and susceptibility to flattery were effectively masked by his natural charm and genial manner.

Katherine, by nature more reflective than these flamboyant Tudors, lacked their animation and energy. Indulgently she looked on as Mary Rose stole the show. Katherine and the Tudor Princess would remain lifelong friends.

Radiant Mary Rose revelled in the limelight, conscious of her own grace and skill. She had inherited her mother's delicate features, belying the passion, wilfulness and charisma that were the legacy of her father's Tudor ancestors. Glowing with health and high spirits, splendidly clad, jewels flashing, dipping and swaying in the rhythm of the dance, the glamorous Tudor siblings epitomised the new tide of optimism sweeping through England after the horrors of a protracted and bloody civil war. If ever, since the mythical days of King Arthur, the English court recaptured the fabled glory of Camelot, it was for those few glorious years in the early 16th century when Henry VIII came to reign.

Sir Thomas More celebrated Henry's coronation:

> Now the nobility long since at the mercy of the dregs of the population, lifts its head… and rejoices in such a King, and with good reason. Among a thousand noble companions, the King stands out the tallest and his strength fits his majestic body…There is fiery power in his eyes, beauty in his face, and the colour of twin roses in his cheeks…'[2]

More's coronation ode contains no portent of his bitter quarrel with the King that would culminate in More's death on the block.

In April 1509, Henry and Mary Rose's father, King Henry VII, worn beyond his fifty-two years by his long struggle to hold the throne, had succumbed to tuberculosis, the curse of his dynasty. Few mourned his passing. That Henry had brought peace to the land after the bitter War of the Roses was long forgotten. With the selective memory of afterword, people chose to remember the first Tudor King as tight-fisted and rapacious.

When his seventeen-year-old son was proclaimed as King Henry VIII on 22nd April, a spirit of rejoicing, powered by an outpouring of love for the charismatic young prince, swept through England. The handsome teenager appeared to embody all the knightly virtues. Surely his reign would usher in a 'golden world'. The undisputed star of young Henry's glittering court was his sister, the beautiful fourteen-year-old Mary Rose, famed throughout Europe as 'the Rose of Christendom'.

Nobody watching this radiant pair, brimming with joyous life, could have foretold that their Prince Charming would become a diseased tyrannical monster, or that the Princess would die young, and that violence and tragedy would stalk her descendants, because they had been chosen by her adoring brother to inherit the throne of England, should he fail to produce an heir. These dynastic devices would prove a lethal inheritance.

The task of a monarch was to secure the throne, through battle, genocide and fratricide if necessary, to consolidate the seat of power through a politically advantageous marriage, and then to secure the succession though the procreation of a sufficient number of male offspring to counteract the dangers of infant mortality. An heir and spare were not always sufficient. Prince Henry was the last chance the newly fledged Tudor dynasty had of surviving, even though the young Tudors' parents, Henry VII and Elizabeth of York, had embraced the important task of securing the succession and celebrating the reconciliation of their two warring houses by producing several offspring.

Henry VII, as the first Tudor King, was determined to found a dynasty where the throne of England would be passed from father to son, rather than usurped by a series of random claimants. By the time their third daughter, Princess Mary Rose, was born, the royal couple already had two promising sons, Princes Arthur and Henry.

In an age of widespread infant mortality, even the birth of a princess – a useful political bargaining chip – could invoke celebration.

However, this princess was born into a climate of intrigue and suspicion. Establishing the dynasty was a brutal business: visitors gaped at the grisly spectacle of decaying severed heads, lopped off traitors and rebels, and now adorning London Bridge.

Only Mary Rose's formidable paternal grandmother, Lady Margaret Beaufort, Countess of Richmond, recorded the birth of a new Tudor Princess in her exquisite *Book of Hours* on 18 March: 'Hodie nata Maria tertia filia Henricis VII, 1495'.[3] Not much escaped the extraordinary Lady Margaret. During their formative years, she would be a major influence on her royal grandchildren.

Tall, severe, and imposing, Lady Margaret was generally regarded as a phenomenon mysteriously elevated above the well-known weaknesses of her gender. The 'Great Chain of Being', the organizational principle of the whole western medieval and therefore the Tudor world, which originated in Aristotelian thought and was later adopted by Christian philosophers, conceived of the universe as being ordered in a strictly hierarchical linear sequence. Inanimate rocks were the lowest order; God was the pinnacle. As for women, they ranked lower on the chain than, not only men but also horses, the argument being that, whereas one could live perfectly adequately without a wife, one could certainly not live without a good horse. Until the Renaissance, this view was accepted, without question, by most educated men. According to Aristotle, women were less emotionally stable, 'more jealous, more querulous, more apt to scold and to strike[,] ... more prone to despondency and less hopeful[,] ... more void of shame or self-respect, more false of speech, more deceptive, of more retentive memory [and] ... also more wakeful; more shrinking [and] more difficult to rouse to action'.[4]

Strict, devout and cultured, and now having achieved the height of her worldly ambition as Queen Mother to the first Tudor monarch, Lady Margaret was the principal power at court. She it was who prescribed rules of conduct and enforced their observance. Margaret let no-one forget her exalted descent from King Edward III, through the illustrious John of Gaunt, Duke of Lancaster, and his illegitimate Beaufort line. This insistence on her ancestry was more than a matter of personal pride: it reinforced the Tudor claim. Unlike many of her relatives, Lady Margaret had managed to survive the brutal Wars of the Roses – a considerable achievement, in view of the fact that she had been an inveterate intriguer during the conflict, displaying a shockingly unfeminine flair for *Realpolitik*.

Now, after a turbulent personal life, she had accumulated land holdings second in importance only to those of the King. Her first husband, Edmund Tudor, Earl of Richmond, to whom she had been married off as a child, had died within a year of their nuptials. Although dynastic marriages were often contracted when the parties concerned were barely out of the cradle, it was usual to postpone consummation until the couple were mature – generally around age fourteen. But Edmund Tudor, desperate for an heir, had been reluctant to wait. Margaret, a slight twelve-year-old, was widowed and also pregnant. She struggled through the winter storms to Pembroke Castle, where Edmund's brother Jasper Tudor gave her shelter.

Not yet thirteen, little Margaret was quickly married off again, with no consideration for her own feelings. Her second husband, Henry Stafford, second son of the Duke of Buckingham, also died few years after the marriage. After his death, Margaret vowed never to admit another man to her bed. Her chastity has been ascribed by some to her piety, but it is at least equally probable that the horrors of childbirth, delivering her son when she was a mere child herself and almost dying in the process, contributed to her reluctance to engage in intimacy.

None the less, like others of her sex, Margaret had to work through men to gain her objectives. Her third marriage, to Thomas, Lord Stanley, first Earl of Derby, was a marriage of convenience. According to legend, it was Stanley who placed the crown on the head of his stepson, Henry Tudor, on Bosworth Field, having, despite his family motto 'sans changer' successfully changed sides on this and several other occasions. Thereafter, Henry was known as King Henry VII. Lord Stanley, who had once been poleaxed by one of Richard III's men, and bore the scars to his dying day, was created Earl of Derby.

Having seen her son established in his divinely ordained place as King, Lady Margaret devoted her remaining years to the very necessary task of shoring up the Tudor claim, and supervising the education of her welcome grandchildren, who had secured the Tudor succession. Her love of learning was unquestioned. A generous benefactor of scholarship, she founded both Christ's College and St

John's College and became the patroness of William Caxton. Her religious piety bordered on the ascetic. She wore a severe widow's barbe up to her chin and, next to her skin, a flesh-mortifying hair shirt.

Nevertheless, on state occasions she donned her golden coronet and, gritting her teeth against her crippling rheumatism, hobbled proudly behind her daughter-in-law, Edward IV's beautiful daughter, Elizabeth of York, whose gentle personality she overshadowed with her regal presence.

In December 1483, while still in exile in Brittany with his uncle Jasper, Henry Tudor had sworn in Rennes Cathedral to marry Elizabeth, recognising that a marriage between himself and the Yorkist Princess would resolve England's political turmoil. Most of his relatives having suffered violent deaths, Henry was the closest legitimate male claimant to the throne on the Lancastrian side. But, like Edward IV himself and many previous sovereigns, he would not accede without a bitter and bloody struggle.

On the death of Edward IV, the King's younger brother, Richard of Gloucester, [1452-1485], appointed Lord Protector of England in 1483 on behalf of his nephew, the twelve-year-old Edward V, envisaged consolidating his claim to the throne by marrying his niece Elizabeth himself. Initially prepared to face down the scandal this consanguinity would cause, he eventually dismissed the notion. Much has been made of a putative romance between Elizabeth and her uncle. His subsequent actions would appear to give the lie to the rumour. Recognising Elizabeth's dangerous potential as the focus of rebellions, he decided to neutralise the threat by marrying her off to someone sufficiently insignificant to preclude any claims on the throne. His choice fell on a young naval officer, a son of his Chancellor, Robert Stillington, Bishop of Bath and Wells, to whom Richard owed a huge favour. (The plan miscarried when the prospective bridegroom was captured by the French off the coast of Normandy, later dying in prison in Paris.)

Richard was in Bishop Stillington's debt, for he it was who had raised the crucial question of the legitimacy of young Edward V and his brother Richard, Duke of York, on the grounds that Edward IV had been betrothed, or possibly even married, to another woman, Lady Eleanor Talbot, before his unexpected and widely resented marriage to their mother, the widowed beauty, Elizabeth Woodville. On June 25, a jury declared the young Edward V illegitimate. Richard promptly had himself proclaimed king and was crowned two weeks later on 6 July. To Lady Margaret, grimly putting a good face on it, fell the honour of bearing the train of the usurper's sickly Queen, Anne Neville.

Neither the boy King Edward V, nor his younger brother Richard, were ever seen again. As discontent with Richard III's rule grew, sinister rumours that the young princes had been secretly murdered in the Tower on Richard's orders gained credence.

Learning of the darkening popular mood, Lady Margaret's son, the exiled Henry Tudor, and his allies moved in to strike. In 1485, although outnumbered, Henry, with French support and the superior ability of his superb Welsh archers, triumphed at Bosworth. Richard was the last King of England to die in battle. During the melee, Henry reputedly snatched the Crown from a thorn-bush where he discovered it hanging.

Losses on both sides were heavy; casualties included Henry's faithful standard-bearer, killed in brutal close combat, apparently at the hand of Richard himself. This standard-bearer, William Brandon, already a widower, left behind a young son. The orphaned Charles Brandon would rise to unimagined prominence; his close friendship with a monarch would gain him a dukedom. He would also win the love of a Queen.

Richard III's defeat at Bosworth effectively rang down the curtain on the bloody Wars of the Roses. Henry now implemented his plan of uniting the warring factions through his marriage to Edward IV's oldest legitimate child, Elizabeth of York – hardly an onerous duty: beautiful blonde, blue-eyed Elizabeth was celebrated as the flower of Yorkist womanhood. The marriage had the full approval of the couple's influential mothers, Elizabeth Woodville, widow of King Edward IV, and Lady Margaret. (Despite their mutual antipathy, popular opinion credited the two mothers-in-law with masterminding the whole arrangement...)

Henry wanted records to show that he had won the crown by military conquest, not by merely marrying into the Yorkist Royal family; he insisted on being crowned before wedding Elizabeth. Their marriage set the official seal on the reconciliation between the houses of York and Lancaster, even if it did not succeed in stilling all the seditious murmurings. Henry VII commissioned the collar of the Order of the Garter, in which the bride's emblem, the white rose of York, is embedded within his own, the red rose of Lancaster, symbolizing their union in the heraldic device of the Tudor Rose.

As arranged dynastic marriages went, it was surprisingly successful. Elizabeth, kind and gentle, immersed herself in her charity work and her duties as wife and mother, bearing the King several children, four of whom survived infancy. Worn out by repeated pregnancies, she died six years before her husband.

The baptism of the last of Elizabeth's children to survive infancy, her second daughter, Princess Mary Rose, in 1495, had been overshadowed by the climate of civil sedition and dissention in the country. But Lady Margaret Beaufort insisted that her grandchildren's christenings should follow traditions observed for Edward IV's many offspring, including the prescribed height of the dais on which the silver-gilt font was mounted. An impressive circular canopy was erected, but there were no curtains. Royal babies must be christened in full view of the congregation. Infant princesses were carried by a duchess, another duchess bearing the richly embroidered chrisom cloth. A countess bore the train, of cloth-of-gold furred with ermine. This depended from the infant's shoulders and was so long that the countess needed the assistance of a gentleman usher to hold up the middle section and stop it dragging on the ground.

Despite the turbulent social and political landscape of the country, Mary Rose's early years were safe and serene. News of local insurrections might create anxieties for the Court and the Council, but the reins of the royal household were held by Mary's grandmother, Lady Margaret, whose personal discipline ensured that life in the royal nursery proceeded on an even keel. The thrifty King kept a close eye on household accounts, paying for the children's upkeep from the Great Wardrobe. The Queen contributed from her own Privy Purse. But Henry was a true Tudor: when diplomacy necessitated a splash, he could put on displays of conspicuous extravagance to rival any monarch in Europe.

The young Royals wanted for nothing. There were regular consignments of soft furnishings and clothing from the Great Wardrobe, bright silk ribbons for the Princesses, new clothes to delight

Mary's older sister, vain, tempestuous Margaret. Active children like Mary fretted in the restrictive apparel decreed by the fashions of the day. Royal babies were encased head to toe in stiff garments of silk or damask. There were few concessions to infancy. By the age of three or four, the little Princess wore full-skirted, long-sleeved dresses with tight-fitting bodices, miniature versions of the gowns worn by grown women. On formal occasions, both Princesses wore close caps, with long gold chain necklaces draped around their chubby little necks. The frequent deaths of members of her family meant that Mary was often in mourning, but black suited her blonde beauty. Black, like scarlet, achieved by using the kermes beetle, was an expensive colour to produce at the time. It entailed a complicated dyeing processes, and was in consequence a popular colour with the aristocracy and adopted by people of all ages and not only in connection with mourning. At two, Mary Rose was pictured in gowns of dusky satin and velvet, trimmed with mink or ermine, and belted with heavy dark ribbon. Her wardrobe included linen smocks, black damask kirtles, hose – and a constant supply of soled shoes, testament to her passion for dancing!

At four, she appeared in purple tinsel satin and blue velvet, crimson, green or tawny kirtles. Kirtles, tunic-like garments worn by both sexes since the Middle Ages, by peasants as well as princesses, had a front-opening bodice and an unlined skirt. At eight, Mary graduated to nightgowns; before then, the list of her clothing includes only night kerchiefs. Children probably slept naked, and were often told to sleep with their mouths hanging open – a measure recommended for the sweetening of the breath.

When Mary was two, the Tudors were spending Christmas in one of the King's favourite residences, the delightful old Yorkist palace of Sheen, nine miles upriver from the Tower. This former hunting lodge, once known as the 'Shining Palace', had undergone frequent refurbishments. Mary's father, enthusiastic about his building projects, had had it repaired and enhanced, adding gardens, warrens and a deer park. Suddenly a mysterious fire broke out and most of the palace burned to the ground.

After the fire, the younger royal children, Margaret, Mary Rose and their brothers, Henry and Edmund, moved more permanently to Eltham, a moated palace in Kent, although they still occasionally stayed in other royal residences. Oarsmen liveried in the Tudor green and white rowed the Princesses in a state barge between the new palace of Richmond, with its fairy-tale turrets, and Greenwich, where the excited children could watch the bustle as the high-masted sailing vessels put to sea. On summer days the royal party were serenaded by musicians as their barge glided along the Thames. When in London, they were usually based at Baynard's Castle or the Tower, residences which their mother preferred to the cramped quarters at Westminster.

Eltham, with its royal apartments, chapel, great hall, courtyard and new tilting yard, had been rebuilt by their maternal grandfather, Edward IV. It was an ideal location for the royal nursery, convenient for London, yet set in rural surroundings away from the unhealthy city dirt and the hectic distractions of the court. Discipline here was more relaxed. Mary's grandmother's influence was visible everywhere. Lady Margaret had completed building the chapel started by Edward IV. Even the swans on the moat wore enamelled badges bearing the Beaufort insignia, lightly chained about their graceful necks.

Mary's oldest brother, Arthur, Prince of Wales, inspired universal admiration. Meeting him in 1497, the Milanese ambassador noted that Arthur, at eleven, was 'taller than his years would warrant, of remarkable beauty and grace, and very ready in speaking Latin'.[5] After Arthur acquired his own household as heir apparent, his younger brother Prince Henry, became the focus of the nursery establishment, and this suited Henry very well. Princes were encouraged to be vigorous and full of bluster, and Henry, an ebullient, forceful lad, needed no urging, strutting about and lording it over his sisters and attendants by sheer force of personality. Nobody dared rebuke him. His showing-off was regarded with smiling indulgence as a token of manliness.

The princesses were attended by ladies, but shared their brothers' tutors. Like all royal children, Mary was taught French, Latin, music and composition, also dancing and embroidery, at both of which she excelled. Her handwriting was soon better than her sister Margaret's, although when distressed she scribbled. She was given a French companion, Jane Poppincourt, before she was five and was soon chatting fluently in French, a skill that was to stand her in good stead. She was also assigned her own small entourage, including a physician, wardrobe-keeper and gentlewomen of the chamber.

The chatelaine of a great house required a grounding in household administration, and, ideally, the skill of an amateur apothecary. Lady Margaret possessed both qualifications and ensured that her granddaughters acquired the same proficiency.

A princess also needed to acquire social graces and accomplishments; she must be a competent dancer and able to participate in social activities such as card games and the performance of masques. She must be a good conversationalist, a mistress of table etiquette and manners. Some knowledge of *belles lettres* was desirable, but her sphere was the spiritual rather than the academic. As a mere female, contemporary custom denied her the opportunity to exploit her mental gifts to the full. Greater intellectual accomplishments were not required; her job was to serve her husband and bear his children. Even the enlightened Thomas More, in his *Utopia*, accepted the mediaeval view that the husband was supreme. To Renaissance theologians, women were still tainted with the frailty of Eve, *ianua diabolis,* a natural temptation. A hundred years after Mary's birth, in 1595, churchmen in Wittenberg would still be debating whether women could, in fact, be counted as human beings at all.

Although Mary would never receive the same intensive education as her nieces, Princesses Mary and Elizabeth, like all the Tudors, she was intelligent and eager to learn.

The natural brilliance of Mary's precocious brothers blossomed under the tutelage of inspiring and dedicated tutors. Prince Arthur was conversant with an exhaustive list of works by the great Classical scholars, and could quote them extensively. Prince Henry showed even greater promise. Besides Latin and French, he displayed a remarkable facility for mathematics.

In the autumn of 1499, four-year-old Mary and her prodigious siblings encountered a rising star of the humanism of the English Renaissance, the Dutch scholar Erasmus. Erasmus, on Sabbatical from his Augustinian monastery, was tutoring young Lord Mountjoy. Mountjoy had been married at eighteen to Elizabeth Say, an heiress, in 1497, but the bride, considered too immature for cohabitation, had remained at her father's home in Gloucestershire. Erasmus and Mountjoy had been planning a jaunt to Italy, but the young Lord's mother, Dame Laura, informed Mountjoy that it was high time his marriage was consummated; he was to forget Italy and get on with it. Mountjoy had also been invited to become what Erasmus called 'socius studiorum', a study companion, to Prince Henry.

Disappointed of his Italian trip, Erasmus accepted Mountjoy's invitation to stay at his house in Greenwich. Aspects of English manners struck Erasmus as delightful: he enthused to his friend the poet Andrerlini, (poet laureate to King Louis XII of France, Mary Rose's future husband):

> When you arrive anywhere you are received with kisses on all sides,
>
> and when you take your leave, they speed you on your way with kisses.
>
> The kisses are renewed when you come back.
>
> If you should happen to meet, then kisses are given profusely.
>
> In a word, wherever you turn, the world is full of kisses.[6]

When a visit to the royal nursery at Eltham was suggested by Erasmus's new acquaintance Thomas More, a clever Lincoln's Inn lawyer in his early twenties with impressive connections at Court, the Dutch scholar was prepared to be enchanted by a peek into the schoolroom. Aware that Arthur, Prince of Wales, would not be present, Erasmus was not expecting any formal reception. Consequently, when More led the way into the Great Hall, and he beheld, gathered beneath the splendid hammer-beam roof, the four youngest Royals, splendidly attired, posed among their assembled attendants in a reception committee, he was disconcerted. The centrepiece of the impressive tableau was eight-year-old Prince Henry, probably, with his already well-developed notion of his own importance, posing beneath a canopy of state.

On his right stood ten-year-old Margaret. Although golden-haired Margaret was as vain and headstrong as her brother Henry, there was as yet no hint of the outrageous behaviour that would cause notorious scandal. Four-year-old Mary Rose was preoccupied with some childish game. But decades later, Erasmus, in 1523, complimented Mary's prospective bridegroom, Prince Charles of Castile, on being 'thrice blessed to acquire such a bride. Nature never formed anything more beautiful, and she exceeds no less in goodness and wisdom.'[7]

Now that the situation in England appeared more settled, the Spanish sovereigns, Ferdinand and Isabella, felt it was safe to proceed with the plans for their daughter Katherine's marriage to the English heir apparent. Hoping to engineer a lasting peace between Henry VII and James IV, they despatched a new ambassador to Scotland, tasked with progressing the plans for the marriage of Princess Margaret and the King of Scots. This union had been under discussion since Margaret was six, but negotiations had been intermittently disrupted by various rebellions.

Despite his mission as a peacemaker, the new Spanish Ambassador to Scotland, Don Pedro de Ayala, first sought to ingratiate himself with the King of Scots by accompanying him on a border raid against England. Writing to their Catholic Majesties, he dismissed this engagement as a skirmish, but noted with some alarm the warlike spirit of the twenty-five-year-old King of Scots. James, reckless and charismatic, relished hunting, amorous dalliance and combat. Don Pedro complained that he had had to drag the King back from the fray by clinging to his skirts.

The Scots pressed to have Margaret sent as a bride without delay but Margaret, at nine, was small for her age, and delicate. Both her mother and grandmother warned King Henry she should not be forced into a physical union too early. Henry confided their concern to Don Pedro, man to man: 'They fear the King of Scotland would not wait, but injure her and endanger her health'. [8] He spared the ambassador's blushes, and respected his own mother's privacy, by refraining to mention something that was common knowledge, although never openly discussed. Although Lady Margaret had been married three times, Henry VII was her only child. In giving birth to him in extreme youth, she had been 'spoyled' and could have no more children.

Neither Lady Margaret nor the Queen would countenance Margaret's being sent to Scotland until she was more mature. Their doubts were reinforced by rumours of King James's numerous and flagrant amours.

Margaret's siblings were also involved in various matrimonial projects from babyhood. Formal negotiations for the marriage of Prince Arthur to Catherine of Aragon had been on-going since March 1488. Eleven years later, the proxy marriage finally took place on 19 May at Bewdley in Worcestershire. King Henry VII and King Ferdinand spent the next few months haggling over the dowry.

Katherine was expected to arrive in England during the summer of 1500, when her bridegroom was almost fourteen, but various obstacles, notably the market-trader bartering between the monarchs, delayed her departure for another year.

Meanwhile, the death of her youngest brother Edmund in 1500 was five-year-old Mary's first direct experience of death. The Eltham household was plunged into mourning. Even Mary's schoolmaster and Jane Poppincourt had black garments ordered for them.

By early October 1501, the mood lifted when the ships of Mary's long-awaited sister-in-law were sighted off Plymouth Sound. Katherine landed to a thunderous welcome. Her progress was slow: [9]Jubilation greeted her at every staging post along her route through the West Country. People thronged the streets, quaffing the free wine and gaping at the foreign dignitaries, the gorgeous costumes and the impressive decorations. At Elthamstead, Prince Arthur joined them, heading a procession of splendidly attired noblemen.

There now occurred the first head-on clash between Spanish and English protocol.

Don Pedro de Ayala intercepted the King's procession and explained that both the Archbishop of Santiago and Doña Elvira Manuel, the Princess's duenna, insisted that the Princess must neither converse with the King nor meet her bridegroom before her wedding day. Such was the old Castilian custom.

Henry immediately made it clear that he cared not a fig for the old Castilian custom. Without bothering to dismount from his horse, he summoned an impromptu council meeting right there on the field. It was decided that, since Katherine was already betrothed to Arthur, she was now Henry's subject, so the laws and formal customs of Old Castile were irrelevant. Henry pressed on, determined to meet the Princess. Informed she was resting, he retorted that he didn't care if she was still in her bed, he had come to see her, and he intended to do so. Scandalised, Doña Elvira was forced to back down.

Princess Katherine was undismayed, and was soon exchanging pleasantries with the King of England. Later, to Doña Elvira's dismay, once the travellers had changed out of their riding clothes, the Princess and her bridegroom met. Both Henry and Arthur were impressed: pretty Katherine appeared well-mannered and biddable. They conversed in a mixture of Spanish and Latin, with a bishop acting as interpreter. Although the Queen and Lady Margaret had urged Katherine to learn French, she had found it hard going. (Lady Margaret had also advised Katherine to get used to drinking wine, because, she said, the water in England was undrinkable, and anyway, one could not drink water in England because of the climate.)[10]

Henry and Arthur rode back to join the Queen at Richmond. At St George's fields Katherine first met her new brother-in-law, Prince Henry. The ten-year-old Prince displayed the self-confidence Erasmus had noted two years earlier, prancing about the town at the head of his own company, two hundred men in blue and tawny livery. Katherine was accommodated in the Bishop of London's Palace, which had been expensively reglazed in her honour.[11]

Her entry into London was a riot of colourful pageantry. The streets were festooned with draperies of cloth-of-gold and silver, velvets and gleaming satins. Triumphal arches adorned with the arms of England and the pomegranates of Spain had been erected, and from the fountains red wine flowed. Mary, a wide-eyed child of six, gazed in wonder at the foreign fashions and at the Spanish Princess who would become her friend. Katherine was riding a mule, Spanish style, richly gowned, with a 'little hat fashioned like a Cardinal's,' secured in place with a golden lace.

The young Princesses, waiting at Baynard's Castle, had been excitedly trying on their new dresses. Mary had two new velvet gowns for the occasion, one russet, the other crimson, fur-trimmed, with a green satin kirtle and matching sleeves. She chose the crimson one. Margaret, six years Mary's senior, as the betrothed of a King, preened in gorgeous cloth-of-gold, fully aware that she would be subjected to close scrutiny by the Scottish ambassadors.

On November 14 the wedding of Prince Arthur and Princess Katherine was magnificently solemnised at St Paul's. There was more spectacle to delight a curious child. After the Nuptial Mass, celebrated by the bishops, trumpets blared and carillons rang out. Enlivened by free wine, Londoners cheered the handsome bridal couple all the way back to Baynard's castle. The sumptuous wedding banquet was followed by the formal bedding. The Earl of Oxford led the way to the bedchamber. He tried the bed first on the side where the Prince would lie, then on the Princess's side. The Princess was then positioned in the bed, next to the Prince, and the bishops blessed both the bed and the anticipated union. The teenage couple were described by an observer as 'both lusty and amorous'.

Many years later, Arthur's gentlemen would swear that the prince emerged next morning from his chamber, flushed with triumph, announcing that he was thirsty, because 'I have been this night in the midst of Spain.'

This adolescent boast would have far-reaching consequences.

The wedding celebrations continued for days. Besides banquets and dancing, there were public games, masques, and a grand tournament. The whole affair had cost a fortune; to recoup some of the expenses, seats were offered to the common people at extortionate prices. Princess Mary Rose sat enthralled, with her new sister-in-law, the Spanish princess, along with her mother, grandmother and sister. Hundreds of attendant ladies occupied one whole side of the stands.

The vast processions and the grand tournament created a challenge for the King's new Master of the Horse, Sir Thomas Brandon. Finding stabling and fodder in London for so many extra horses was a daunting task. Himself a skilled jouster, Thomas had carved out a successful career at Court, serving the King in many capacities, as councillor, naval and military commander, and diplomat. As he watched the grand display, he could congratulate himself on another success: the advancement he had contrived for his orphaned teenage nephew, Charles, the son of his disreputable older brother William, a rascal who had only redeemed himself by his hero's death at Bosworth Field in 1485, where the Tudor crown was won. The East Anglian estates of Thomas's father, Sir William Brandon, had passed to the second son, Robert, leaving baby Charles and his sister penniless. Now, Thomas, through his contacts, had managed to obtain for young Charles a temporary position in Prince Arthur's household.

On the Friday after the tournament, a 'disguising' took place in Westminster hall, a versatile building now used to showcase Tudor wealth and status, hung with rich tapestries, sideboards piled high with gold plate. On new mobile stages lavish pageants rolled in, bearing musicians and entertainers.

One highlight of the revels was when young Henry, Duke of York, thoroughly over-excited, dancing with his sister Margaret, threw off his gown and danced in his jacket, to the delighted amusement of his parents and applause from the onlookers.

The final entertainment was calculated to appeal to the youngest princess. A pageant two stories high appeared, drawn by seahorses, and filled with singing children. From the lower storey eight knights leapt down and released baby rabbits, which scattered in panic among the guests. From the upper storey eight ladies released a flock of white doves, which flew around the hall, causing 'great laughter and disport.'[12]

At the end of November the Court moved to Windsor. Henry and his Council decided that the Prince and Princess should leave for Wales. The King, seeing Katherine's distress over bidding farewell to those Spanish attendants who had accompanied her to England but were now returning to Spain, summoned her to his library, on the pretext that he wanted to show her his books. Suddenly a jeweller, until then concealed, stepped forward and spread before Katherine an array of precious jewels. The King invited her to make her selection, and then turned to her ladies, inviting them to choose jewels for themselves.

Henry's ruse cheered Katherine and 'relieved her heaviness somewhat'.[13] Every effort was being made to cherish Katherine. As the bride of the heir apparent, she was precious. It would not always be so.

Lady Margaret Beaufort, deeply affected by Arthur's wedding, burst into tears. John Fisher, Bishop of Rochester, her confessor, fellow humanist and associate in her educational projects, found this show of emotion typical of the King's mother. 'Either she was in sorrow by reason of present adversities, or else when she was in prosperity she was in dread of the adversity to come'.

As things turned out, Lady Margaret's sense of impending doom was to prove well founded.[14]

1 **Notes**

1. Calendar of State Papers (CSP): Venetian
2. Sir Thomas More, *Coronation Ode of King Henry VIII*, 1509, BL
3. BL MS Royal 2 AXVIII, f 29, *The Beaufort Hours*

4. Aristotle, *History of Animals,* 608b, 1-14

5. Raimundo de Raimundi of Socino, to Ludovico Sforza, Duke of Milan, CSP Milan, 1497, 539

6. *Opus Epistolarum Des. Erasmi* Roterodami (Oxford, 1906) ed PS Allen vol 1 193

7. ibid vol 1 p 6

8. CSP Spanish vol 1 176

9. John Leland vol v 353ff

10. Bergeroth CSP Span I 156

11. 'Arthur, Prince of Wales (1486-1502)', *Oxford Dictionary of National Biography*. Oxford University Press, doi:10.1093/ref:odnb/705

12. H M Colvin, *The History of the King's Works*, vol III, pt 1, London, 1975, 34

13. Leland vol v p 372

14. College of Arms MS, 1 M 13, f 66r &v

2   Betrothals

Before the euphoria generated by Arthur's wedding subsided, Henry VII reopened negotiations with the Scottish ambassadors regarding the marriage of his daughter Margaret. Despite his reservations about the wild character of the King of Scotland, Henry had already taken the precaution of procuring a Papal dispensation for the marriage. This was required because King James IV and Princess Margaret Tudor were distant cousins, James I having married Joan Beaufort, whose brother John, Duke of Somerset, was Margaret's great-grandfather.

Rumour (falsely circulated by de Ayala) claimed that James IV had installed Margaret Drummond, who had been his favourite mistress since 1496, at Stirling with her daughter, one of now five acknowledged royal bastards to whom the King gave the name 'Stewart'. After each amorous adventure, James, a devout son of the church, always hastened to the shrine of St Ninian to be shriven. In 1501, Margaret Drummond, along with her sisters Eupheme and Sybilla, died of food poisoning. Suspicion of murder fell on Scottish courtiers and English agents, who feared James would never marry while Margaret lived and would, therefore, never sire a legitimate heir.

James assured Henry that he now desired 'with a pure mind' to express the affection he felt for the King of England 'by the sacred bond of matrimonial alliance'.[1]

In reality, he was desperate to get his hands on Margaret's dowry of 30,000 golden nobles.

The marriage treaty was finally signed on 24 January. Little Princess Mary Rose sat through High Mass celebrated by three archbishops and four bishops, and watched Margaret's proxy wedding at Richmond palace, which Mary would come to know so well.

The ensuing festivities were slightly marred when the realisation dawned upon young prince Henry that not only was his sister the focus of the celebrations, but that, as a Queen, she would henceforth take precedence over him. Henry, bursting into tears of fury, flew into one of his notorious tantrums.

That afternoon his attention was distracted when a recent invention, the hoisting harness designed to lift fully armed knights on to their chargers, was tested in the celebratory 'notable jousts'. The ladies, snuggling into their fur wraps against the January chill, gasped at the skill of the competitors. Next day Margaret presented the prizes to the victors. In a field of strong contenders, the third prize went to a promising newcomer, Charles Brandon, the dashing young nephew of the Master of the Horse. Brandon's brilliance in the tiltyard would play a key role in his rise to prominence.

The tournament was followed by dancing and feasting. Londoners revelled in the distribution of free wine; celebratory bonfires were lighted throughout over the city. On March 14 there followed more public celebration: it was proclaimed that peace with Scotland had been established 'for ever more.' The thistle and the rose were united at last.

But in April the Tudor rollercoaster took another plunge. In the winter of 1501-2, the country had awaited with bated breath the glad tidings from Ludlow proclaiming the pregnancy of the Princess Katherine.

On 4 April 1502, after two days of hard riding, the long-awaited messenger reached Greenwich Palace, but the news he brought was not joyful but appalling. The Prince of Wales, reputedly never as robust as his younger brother, was dead, apparently having succumbed to the sweating sickness currently ravaging the West Country. The Queen was no stranger to grief, having lost many friends and relatives during the Wars of the Roses. Of the six children she had borne the King, two had died in infancy. Overnight, the royal couple's sole surviving son, Prince Henry, became the focus of all their hopes.

Possibly Henry VII felt guilty. His Council had warned him that Arthur was not strong, although their caution was motivated less by a sense that the Prince was a weakling than that they dreaded lest he might exhaust himself in a fervour of uxorious zeal. Henry admitted to King Ferdinand that he feared he had risked his son's health because of his love for Katherine. Couples who married very young were sometimes initially kept apart so that the bridegroom might complete his education and the bride mature in readiness for childbearing, or else they were separated shortly after the wedding, lest the bridegroom in his youthful enthusiasm should overdo things. Ferdinand knew only too well what Henry meant, having before him the tragic example of his only surviving son, Katherine's brother, the darkly handsome Infante Juan, who had allegedly overexerted himself after his marriage to Margaret of Austria, dying at eighteen.

But Prince Arthur, at fifteen, and Katherine, almost sixteen, were not considered too young to consummate their marriage, with the exercise of self-restraint and moderation.

The question of the consummation of their marriage would become the cornerstone of the most famous divorce in history. Katherine always maintained that consummation never occurred, despite her bridegroom's earthy jests the next morning with the young squires of the bedchamber.

The limitations of Tudor medicine failed to explain the exact nature of Arthur's fatal illness. Victorian historians assumed he died of tuberculosis, a disease characterised by night sweats. The herald chronicler's description, when Arthur's body was being prepared for embalming, suggests that the Prince may have already been suffering from some malignant disease, possibly affecting his virility.

> The most pitiful disease and sickness that with so sore and great violence had battled and driven in the singular parts of him inward, that cruel and fervent enemy of nature the deadly corruption did utterly vanquish and overcome the pure and frendfull [healthy] blood without all manner of physical help and remedy [2]

The nephew of Katherine's Spanish doctor said that when his uncle was asked in Zaragoza to explain Katherine's allegedly intact status, 'he often said that the Prince had been denied the strength necessary to know a woman as if he was a cold piece of stone, ...because he was in the final stages of tisis' (an infectious disease, possibly pthisis, or tuberculosis).[3]

Prince Arthur's body was embalmed at Ludlow. His obsequies were prolonged and costly, amid widespread distress. Even for little Mary Rose, once more dressed in mourning black, Arthur's death cast a pall over the celebration of her sister Margaret's marriage to the King of Scotland.

It took five weeks for news of Prince Arthur's death to reach Toledo. Ferdinand and Isabella immediately despatched a special envoy, Hernan Duque de Estrada, to Henry on 12 May with a formal letter of condolence, and a peremptory demand for the return of the money already paid as the first instalment of Katherine's dowry.

The Queen, who had hoped to be equipping her daughter Margaret with a sumptuous trousseau to impress the Scots, instead found herself paying for Margaret's black velvet gown to be relined. For Mary Rose she bought a new black satin gown. Elizabeth also had to finance mourning wardrobes for her nephews and niece, the children of her beloved younger sister Katherine. Their father, Lord William Courtenay, was attainted for treason following yet another Yorkist plot involving her nephews, Edward IV's grandsons, Edward and Richard de la Pole. Elizabeth spent so much money that she had to pay off her debts of £107.10s to Henry Bryan, a London silk merchant, in instalments, after he had presented his bill several times.

Elizabeth also came to the aid of the widowed Princess Katherine, now penniless. Swallowing her Yorkist pride, the Queen resorted to the humiliating measures of pawning her plate and borrowing the sum of £320 from two gentlemen in the City.

The Catholic Kings of Spain continued their wrangle with Henry VII about Katherine's dowry for years. Ferdinand wanted his money back. At the same time, he also needed to keep his alliance with England alive, especially now that the French military campaign was storming ahead. By summer 1502, the French King Louis XII had expelled the Sforzas from Milan and set his sights on the Aragonese Kingdom of Naples. Victory here would make France the dominant European power, a situation Ferdinand was determined to prevent.

Consequently, Estrada was instructed to arrange a new marriage for Katherine with eleven-year-old Prince Henry, who would be heir to the English throne, unless Katherine turned out to be carrying his brother Arthur's child. In an age of unsophisticated gynaecology, three months was the time traditionally appointed to ascertain pregnancy.

De Puebla, the permanent Spanish envoy in London, anticipated the hopes of the Catholic Kings. As a qualified practitioner of canon law, he knew that to render Katherine's second marriage to the brother of her first husband acceptable in the eyes of the Church, a Papal dispensation from Rome would be required. According to Leviticus 20, it was forbidden for a man to marry his brother's wife. Their union would be fruitless as an expression of God's displeasure:

> 'If a man shall take his brother's wife, it is an unclean thing, he hath uncovered his brother's nakedness, they shall be childless.'

De Puebla realised that the question of the consummation of Katherine's marriage to Arthur was key to how easily a dispensation could be obtained. Accordingly, he discreetly enquired of Katherine's chaplain and confessor, her former tutor Don Alessandro Geraldini, whether the marriage was a 'true' one. Don Alessandro replied in the affirmative.

At this point there was an unexpected turn of events. Learning of the consultation between the two learned men, Katherine's fierce duenna, Doña Elvira Manuel, suddenly fired a broadside. Sexual relations in the traditional sense had never taken place between the young couple, she insisted. No blood-stained sheets had been exhibited to Doña Elvira. Thirty years later, when Henry VIII had set his heart on marrying Anne Boleyn, Doña Elvira's outburst would help change the course of history. The question of the consummation of Katherine's first marriage was the crux on which the English Reformation was based.

Virginity was a serious matter. Although ignorance was rife – a common test for pregnancy or virginity was to wave a chicken wing over the woman's abdomen – a classic internal examination was also possible. Unless Doña Elvira genuinely believed in Katherine's virginity, it was reckless of her to lie. It also reflected badly upon her, as Katherine's mentor. The marriage of Arthur and Katherine was the culmination of thirteen years of intricate negotiation. To claim non-consummation despite five months of apparently blissful cohabitation was an outrageous admission on Dona Elvira's part, implying gross negligence, and failure in her duty to her lady and to both dynasties.

If the couple had never enjoyed full marital relations, a Papal dispensation for a second marriage would be more easily obtained. On the other hand, if Katherine were still a virgin, then, on the grounds of non-consummation, she was not legally Princess of Wales -a financial disaster for Katherine personally and also for her retinue, since Henry could then claim that he was under no obligation to maintain them.

Henry, bitterly grieving for the loss of his eldest son, was affronted by the apparent aspersions cast on Arthur's manhood by Doña Elvira's assertion. On June 16 1502 the rumours reached the Spanish royal household. Katherine's horrified parents pressed Estrada to find out the truth. Ferdinand suspected that Henry feigned to believe the non-consummation story so as to wriggle out of paying Katherine's dower revenues. 'Get to the bottom of it – use all the flattering persuasions you can to prevent them from concealing it from you,' he urged Estrada.[4]

The strongest evidence used to discredit Doña Elvira's declaration was the widely-reported boast Prince Arthur made to his gentlemen the morning after his wedding night, where he called for drink, implying that he had had thirsty work of it: 'Gentlemen, I have been in the midst of Spain.' Among those who would later claim to remember the teenage bridegroom's bragging, and to have believed it, was Charles Brandon. Perhaps Brandon and others hoped to ingratiate themselves with Henry VIII, who by then was intent on discarding Katherine in order to marry Anne Boleyn.

Henry VII, predictably, pointed out that, if Katherine were still a virgin, then she was not his daughter-in-law; he had therefore no obligation to support her.

Katherine, still in mourning, was excluded from the Christmas celebrations of 1502, and the exciting plans for Margaret's wedding to the King of Scots.

Though distraught over her son Arthur's death, Elizabeth had comforted the King, assuring him that they could have more sons. She made offerings at various efficacious shrines; by early summer 1503, she was pregnant for the seventh and last time.

Autumn drew on; pheasant and venison graced the Queen's table. As her pregnancy advanced, she relaxed, enjoying music-making with her daughters and her ladies. The family spent Christmas at Richmond, the King's new showpiece, built after the fire at Sheen. Cynics referred to the ambitious new palace as 'Riche mount', a pun on Henry's title, Earl of Richmond, hinting at his talent for heaping up riches. Glazed, paved, lavishly ornamented with gold leaf, the royal apartments exuded luxury. The gardens were embellished with stone statues of heraldic beasts. Henry, unlike his sons, lacked the advantages of cultural education, but he had expensive tastes. Although miserly in other respects, he spent freely on buildings, jewels, ostentatious hospitality and clothes. All these were rapidly becoming renaissance status symbols, with the new emphasis on culture.

Mary grew up surrounded by fine things. 'There is no country in the world where Queens live with greater pomp than in England' remarked De Puebla. Calling unexpectedly on Mary's mother, he expressed his surprise at finding 32 ladies 'all very magnificent and in splendid style' in attendance. Elizabeth's seamstresses worked tirelessly on the hangings for the Queen's great bed of state, using yards of costly gold twist and silk. In January, Elizabeth was rowed to the Tower for her lying-in. On February 2, she gave birth to a girl, christened Katherine, after her favourite younger sister, Lady Courtenay. Elizabeth had made many generous gifts to Katherine, including satin to cover her saddle. Nine days after giving birth, on her thirty-seventh birthday, Elizabeth of York died. Her baby daughter did not long survive her.

The King was devastated. All England mourned. In London alone 636 Masses were said for the repose of the Queen's soul. At Cheapside groups of thirty-seven virgins with chaplets of green and white held vigil, bearing lighted tapers. 3,000 torches lighted the stretch from Mark Lane to temple Bar; candles burned in all the parish churches. The hearse was emblazoned with the Queen's motto, 'humble et reverente.'

Bewildered little Mary donned mourning again, like everyone. But within four months she was back in colours, wearing blue damask with velvet edgings, white stockings and tawny silk ribbons. She was nearly eight. Prospective suitors had already been sniffing around for five years. Life had to go on.

Despite his private grief, Henry's life was dominated by intrigue powered by dynastic ambition. He appreciated the importance of astute alliances and political marriages. The Austrian Habsburgs were reputed to have won more land and power through marriage than through conquest. At forty-six, despite declining health, Henry felt himself still capable of siring sons. With only one surviving male heir, he briefly considered remarriage, his eye falling first on his daughter-in-law Katherine, now seventeen. Queen Isabella reacted sharply, denouncing this notion as barbarous. She suggested Henry transfer his attentions to her niece, young Joanna, Queen of Naples.

Henry declared that he would consider Queen Joanna only if she was beautiful. De Puebla, through whom negotiations were conducted, confided to Ferdinand that the English King, although himself neither prepossessing nor a spring chicken, was obsessed by physical appearances. Henry despatched three ambassadors to investigate Joanna's charms.[5] Armed with a detailed questionnaire, they were to report back on her age, weight, mannerisms and personality, the colour of her hair and eyebrows, the state of her teeth and skin, the shape of her fingers, neck, breasts 'whether they be big or small', 'the favour of her visage, whether she be painted or not, and whether it be fat or lean, sharp or round, and whether her countenance be cheerful and amiable, frowning or melancholy, stedfast or light, or blushing in communication,' whether she had hair on her upper lip, and, most importantly, her fortune. The ambassadors described Joanna as amiable and presentable, sweet-breathed, with passionate lips and a pretty neck, 'having a noble gravity and not too bold, but somewhat shamefacedly womanly, a good feeder, and eateth well her meat twice on a day.' They told the king that Joanna's breasts 'be somewhat great & fully, and in as much as that they were trussed somewhat high after the manner of (the) country, which causes her Grace for to seem much the fuller and her neck to be the shorter.'

Henry, still not satisfied, commissioned a portrait of Queen Joanna for his scrutiny. But the young Queen of Naples, irritated, refused to co-operate. She had had enough.

On 30 September 1503 the treaty for a marriage between Katherine and Prince Henry was ratified. It took another year for the dispensation to reach England. Queen Isabella saw a copy a few days before she died, in her great fortress of Medina del Campo in the heart of Castile, where she had reigned as king in her own right.

The succession of Castile passed to Katherine's older sister, the beautiful, fragile Joanna. In the tangled web of European dynastic politics, tragic Joanna's fortunes were to directly influence the fate of Princess Mary Rose.

In 1496, Joanna had been married at seventeen to the Archduke Philip, son of the Emperor Maximilian. 'Philip the Handsome' was a conceited popinjay. Joanna fell passionately in love with him. Philip had been ordered to remain in Flanders, but he cherished ambitions to control Castile. On 26 November 1504, when Isabella died, Joanna being still in Flanders, her father, King Ferdinand, announced that he intended to represent her as 'Governor and Administrator' of Castile, despite his unpopularity with Castilian separatists. The idea was approved by the Cortes, the region's ancient council but it enraged Philip. Already Lord of the Netherlands and Burgundy, by virtue of his wife, Philip promptly declared himself King of Castile and prepared to fight his father-in-law.

Distress over her adored Philip's incorrigible philandering, and the strain of repeated pregnancies, had affected Joanna's nerves. As soon as her instability manifested itself, her husband treated her henceforth as an incompetent lunatic. Rumours were spread that Joanna was mad; her husband would rule Castile as her proxy.

Much of what Isabella had achieved began to unravel with her death. Trade treaties favourable to the English were now decreed to have lapsed. In August 1505, 800 English merchants had returned to London from Seville 'lost and ruined'.

Ferdinand had still not sent the next instalment of Katherine's dowry, despite her pathetic appeals to her father, in which she described the humiliation of living on the charity of the King of England. The Queen, who had often helped her, was dead.

Katherine and Prince Henry, six years her junior, were betrothed in 1503, but on 27 June 1505, in a ploy intended to force Ferdinand into paying up, Prince Henry was made to revoke the contract on the grounds that it had been entered into during the time of his minority.

In the autumn of 1505, Ferdinand set the seal on the new hostile relationship with both Archduke Philip and with England by signing the Treaty of Blois with the old enemy, Louis XII. This effectively meant that Philip would not now be able to cross through Europe to reach Castile. Accordingly, in January 1506 Philip set sail with an army, vowing to se Castile by force of arms. When news of his audacity reached Ferdinand, such was the monarch's fury that he allegedly threatened to throw himself upon Philip with *'capa y espada'*, the toreador's mantle and sword.

Fortunately, such dramatic measures were not required, for fate intervened. Philip's Armada was blown off course by a ferocious gale in the English Channel. His ships were tossed for forty-eight hours and then scattered; Philip himself landed at Melcombe Regis in Dorset on 13 January 1506. He immediately sent a plaintive message to Henry.

Henry welcomed Philip's fortuitous stranding on his shores as a God-given opportunity to revive the old Anglo-Burgundian alliance. Sir Thomas Brandon was despatched to conduct the royal guests to Windsor. Queen Joanna, shaken by her ordeal, rested until Henry, now Prince of Wales and in his fourteenth year, arrived accompanied by gorgeously dressed nobles, to extend an official welcome. The King, with a great procession, rode out to greet his guests personally on 31 January. As they trotted into the castle through the main gate side by side, so neither should assume precedence, trumpeters sounded a rousing fanfare. Henry VII lacked a natural talent for convivial hospitality, but he had a gift for the spectacular.

There followed weeks of bargaining. Philip, despite his impatience to get his ships repaired and proceed to Castile, was seduced by Henry's lavish hospitality. On 1 February, the Princesses Katherine and Mary Rose arrived, thrilled by the prospect of enjoying the 'great cheer' brought about by the influx of distinguished guests. Mellow with hospitality and captivated by beauty, Philip kissed the royal ladies and all their gentlewomen, one by one. Entertainments were laid on in the King's dining chamber; Katherine and her ladies performed Spanish dances; Mary Rose danced too, and displayed her skill on the lute and clavicle, and was rewarded with an extra kiss from the Archduke. She was not quite eleven years old, golden-haired, exquisite, a competent musician; above all, she behaved like a princess, enchanting everyone, including Philip.

Despite the ten years' age difference, Katherine and Mary had grown close; their mutual affection would last a lifetime. Katherine, at twenty-one, widowed, prematurely grave, kindly and dignified, found a foil in young Mary's light-hearted spontaneity.

Servants were sent to fetch Mary Rose to Croydon, where some of Philip's suite were accommodated at the Archbishop of Canterbury's palace, so that she might be serenaded by the Flemish musicians. Again, her beauty, sweetness and poise won all hearts. With her irresistible charm, Mary was launched on her long career in subtle state diplomacy behind the scenes and dazzling public relations centre stage.

Henry involved Philip in hunting in the park and games of tennis. On 9 February, he made Philip a member of the Order of the Garter. Philip, not to be outdone, bestowed on the new Prince of Wales the illustrious Golden Fleece, an ancient Burgundian order of knighthood. They signed a treaty according to which Henry would provide military assistance in Castile if required; Philip would offer support against French incursions. Both would hand over any rebels who sought refuge in their domains. This promise was especially relevant from Henry's point of view, because Philip promised to give up the last Yorkist White Rose pretender, Edmund de la Pole, the self-styled Duke of Suffolk, who had sought asylum in the Netherlands and had been prowling around Europe since 1498 soliciting support for his dynastic ambitions. After eliciting the promise, Henry detained the Archduke with relentless banquets and entertainments until Edmund de la Pole had been duly handed over and deposited in the Tower.

Desperate times called for desperate measures: De la Pole's cousin, the unfortunate Earl of Warwick, had been executed just before Katherine's arrival, to secure the safety of the realm.

The next week Queen Joanna, much restored, arrived at Windsor, where she was welcomed by Henry and Mary and reunited with her own sister, Katherine. Windsor was the ancient seat of the English kings, but Henry was determined that his royal guests should also admire his own crowning architectural achievement, Richmond, where more hawking, hunting, feasting and dancing were planned. Katherine and Mary were sent on ahead to make sure all was in readiness for the royal visitors. Even Philip, who prided himself on his own showpiece, the palace of Beau Regard, declared himself impressed by Richmond.

On the Saturday before Philip departed, perhaps much later than he had intended, after 97 days as Henry's guest, Henry escorted him on a visit to Eton, where the schoolboys lined the churchyard, waving and cheering.

Henry VII was well content. He knew he had made good political use of the Archduke's visit. In their discussions, Henry had laid out the foundations of his dynastic master plan: he himself would marry Philip's sister, Margaret. His son Prince Henry was loosely promised to Philip's daughter Eleanor. His daughter Mary Rose would marry Philip and Joanna's son, Prince Charles of Castile, also heir to the Burgundian lands.

This fine scheme soon fell apart. That very autumn, 1506, Philip died. The European political landscape changed again. To safeguard his plan for Mary's marriage, Henry now needed the co-operation of Charles of Castile's grandfather, the slippery Emperor Maximilian.

The deaths of Philip and of her older siblings had left twenty-five-year-old Joanna Europe's most eligible widow, heiress to the entire Spanish empire. Her reputation as a madwoman had allowed her father Ferdinand to step in as regent of Castile in the name of her son Charles. At fifty-four, and an unwelcome regent in Castile, Ferdinand knew an energetic son-in-law could be crucial. For Henry, this represented a great opportunity to ensure that the marriage of Mary Rose and Charles would certainly take place, and also to increase the likelihood of a marriage between his heir, Prince Henry, and Katherine.

Known to her contemporaries, as to history, as Juana la Loca, the severity of Joanna's condition was almost certainly exaggerated by her family for political reasons. But the death of her beloved husband cast Joanna into a morbid depression. She refused to allow his burial to proceed. Instead, persuading herself that his resurrection was imminent, she kept his embalmed corpse in her bedchamber, frequently embracing it, and then dragged it around Europe with her in a leaden coffin wherever she went, in case she missed this glorious event. (A soothsayer had once told Philip he would travel further after his death than he would do in his lifetime. His prophecy was eerily realised.)

For Henry, Joanna's madness was irrelevant: he aimed to gain control of her kingdom, and hoped she was still capable of bearing children. He directed Katherine to write to her father in support of his suit, stressing his affection for her sister. De Puebla, acting for both parties, told Ferdinand in the spring of 1507 that Joanna would soon recover her reason if she were wedded to the King of England, because nobody in the world would make her such a good husband.

He added that it wouldn't much matter if she was mad, if she lived in England. Nobody there would care, as long as she could breed.

Joanna's condition deteriorated, however, and English diplomacy embraced closer links with Germany and the Low countries. Negotiations with Spain collapsed in favour of a general European coalition, the Treaty of Cambrai.

Even while courting Joanna, Henry had continued to toy with his long-held notion of a double wedding with the Burgundians. Impecunious Maximilian and mercenary Henry, despite their mutual distrust, recognised the advantages of such an alliance. The stumbling block to the male rulers' ambitions was Maximilian's daughter, Margaret of Austria, Archduchess of Savoy. Twice widowed, Regent of the Netherlands in her own right, Margaret had no intention of becoming a pawn in her father's political games again. Motherless, she had been betrothed at the age of three to Charles, Dauphin of France. Her father Maximilian, delighted with the connection, despatched his little daughter to Amboise to spend her childhood being groomed to become Queen of France .

Ten years later, she was ignominiously repudiated in favour of 'la petite Brette', Anne of Brittany, who at fourteen had been briefly married by proxy to Margaret's own father, Maximilian. Margaret was sent home in disgrace. She did, however, acquire a throne, for she was quickly married off to the priapic Infante Juan, that Prince of Castile whose unrestrained enjoyment of his marital rights allegedly hastened his demise. Despite warnings, his mother Queen Isabella refused to counsel restraint, declaring it was God's will. Evil tongues whispered that the Queen of Castile's desire for an heir outweighed her concern for her son's health. So debilitated was his constitution by his lack of moderation that Juan was unable to resist the pestilence a few months later, and succumbed.

The baby girl Margaret carried did not survive. In 1501 she married

Philibert II, Duke of Savoy. At 24 she was widowed again, and returned to Brabant, establishing a distinguished court at Malines, where she devoted herself to ruling the Low Countries and bringing up her nephew Charles and his three sisters.

Margaret was a woman who knew her own mind. She resisted pressure from her father Maximilian and from Henry to marry the King of England.

Henry sent two embassies to the Netherlands in 1508. In the first of these, Thomas Wolsey excelled himself, accomplishing the whole mission there and back in under seventy hours, displaying the ruthless efficiency which would be his ground-note. His first foray into diplomacy was an eye opener for Wolsey; he noted the inconstancy, mutability, and total disregard of promises on the part of those with whom he had been sent to negotiate. He might not approve of vacillation and deceitfulness, but he understood that such qualities could be exploited to achieve his own and his royal master's ends.

Henry, impatient for an answer, commanded Wolsey to press for Margaret's response to his suit. But Margaret remained adamant in her refusal.

Henry's prime objective was not so much obtaining Margaret's hand in marriage for himself, as ensuring fulfilment of the longstanding agreement for the marriage of Charles of Castile and Princess Mary Rose. Maximilian was desperate to stop England from forming an alliance with France or Spain. A treaty was signed at Calais in December 1507. This provided for mutual aid in the event of war, and clinched Mary's betrothal, scheduled for the following Easter, and the solemnization of her marriage forty days after Prince Charles's fourteenth birthday.

Henry greeted the news of the signing of the marriage contract with 'great contentment'. On Christmas day he ordered general celebrations – the usual clamour of bells, lighting of bonfires and distribution of free hogsheads of wine. The citizens, enlivened by the prospect of free drink and cheered by the news that the valuable traditional trading links with the Low Countries were now restored, joined in the general rejoicing.

At last this 'great and honourable marriage' now appeared imminent. So confident was Henry of its success that he announced that he had built a 'wall of brass' around his kingdom, with on every side 'mighty princes our good sons, friends, confederates and allies.'

But Maximilian, ever devious, continued his flirtation with the French; the treaty remained unconfirmed. Henry grew impatient. However, he knew Maximilian. As a sweetener he loaned the chronically impecunious Emperor 100,000 crowns. This tipped the balance in England's favour and in December 1508, after eight years of negotiations, the Emperor's ambassadors finally arrived for Mary's betrothal.

The distinguished emissaries were led by the Sieur de Berghes, one of the great lords of Northern Brabant and the Emperor's chamberlain, who was to act as proxy for eight-year-old Prince Charles. Underlining the significance of the occasion, the Governor of Bresse came in person, as did the President of the Council of Flanders. King Henry's Latin secretary, Pietro Carmeliano, and the London printer Pynson were stumped by the difficult name of Dr Pflug, the legal expert, and recorded it in the printed souvenir record of the event as 'Dr Splonke'.

The Imperial party were overwhelmed by their rapturous welcome; they were showered with lavish gifts. The King received them at Greenwich seated beneath a golden canopy of state, flanked by the Archbishop of Canterbury and Prince Henry.

Next day, the legalities were completed. Mary's dowry was set at 250,000 gold crowns. Her jointure would include all the lands which had once belonged to her great-aunt Margaret of Austria.

The formalities concluded, the ambassadors were welcomed to Richmond. In view of the couple's youth, heavy bonds were exchanged and penalty clauses inserted, to guarantee the fulfilment of the contract. Consummation of the union was to be postponed for another four years, when the Princess was to be taken to her husband at the court of his aunt Margaret, Regent of the Netherlands. Mary would spend the next four years preparing for her new life.

The espousal contract used in the ceremony was a covenant of betrothal, with marriage to follow. Recognised by both church and state, it took the form of a public exchange of vows known as 'hand-fasting', in which the couple joined hands and sealed the contract with a kiss. In the case of royal marriages, it was quite usual to employ a proxy. Two types of contract were recognised, *per verb de futuro* and *per verba de praesenti*. In the first case, wedlock was pledged by saying 'I will' or 'I shall take thee to be my wedded wife or husband', but fulfilment of these vows was not obligatory. Such an announcement made in public was a statement of future intent. This form was used when the parties concerned were so young that the date of consummation could not be definitively established. But the *de praesenti* contract was more binding. In both cases, cohabitation sealed the deal.

The initial mistrust on the part of the English court, disillusioned after the many vicissitudes of the negotiations, had been replaced by enthusiasm. In the streets of London preparations went ahead for the popular celebrations

Ten days later, Mary Rose took her place on a high dais beneath a glittering canopy of cloth-of-gold at Richmond for her betrothal to Prince Charles. Slender Mary appeared young and vulnerable for her thirteen years, but she displayed extraordinary poise and dignity. The Archbishop of Canterbury delivered a solemn discourse in Latin on the dignity of holy matrimony and the significance of this promising union. The President of Flanders, Jean de Sauvaige, responded. The Sieur de Berghes, acting as proxy for the Prince, took Mary's hand, and recited the words of matrimony, promising the loyalty and undying affection of the absent bridegroom, and formally reciting his authority to represent the prince in the marriage vows. He repeated the formula, *per verba de praesenti.*

Mary unhesitatingly took his hand and declared her vows, giving a long speech in French. Her delivery never faltered. The poet and royal official Pietro Carmelianius observed that some of the audience were moved to tears by their young Princess's grace and composure.[6]

The proxy then placed a gold ring on Mary's middle finger and kissed her respectfully. The trumpets sounded a fanfare; the minstrels struck up; Mary was now married, to a child she had never seen. The company proceeded to the royal chapel to hear Mass said by the Bishop of London, followed by a banquet, and three days of feasting, music, dancing and jousting. From a richly appointed gallery, the new bride and her companions could admire, criticise, gasp or giggle or laugh at the feats and outfits of the contestants. The highlight of the event was a grand tournament on the third day, celebrated with bonfires and bell-ringing.

At the Emperor's request, the absent Prince Charles was honoured by membership of the order of the Garter, as his father had been, as a gesture of Henry's good will. Early 16th century diplomacy was becoming a game in which the rules increased in formality as Renaissance ceremonial became increasingly ritualised and elaborate. From the Netherlands came a stilted letter in Charles's name, formally expressing his satisfaction with his new bride, accompanied by three jewels, presented to Mary Rose in the course of a formal banquet: a balas ruby, pale rose red and set among pearls, from Margaret; a brooch containing one large diamond and an oriental ruby surmounted by pearls from Maximilian. From Charles, a more personal ornament, a ring bearing the monogram 'K' for 'Karolus' surrounded by diamonds and pearls, with the Biblical Latin inscription: *'Maria optimum partem elegit que non auferetur ab ea'*.

Pynson's record of the occasion featured a Latin poem by a dazzled Carmelianus:

> '... what delicate and sumptuous meals, what diversity
> of pleasant wines, what plate of gold and silver-gilt the
> King had, no dish or saucer but it was gilded, and as
> bright as gold.'[7]

Carmelianus's account was circulated in 1508 in Latin and reprinted in English the following year. A copy, translated into Castilian Spanish, reached Charles's other grandfather, the King of Aragon; the English ambassador to Spain reported that Ferdinand was 'sore displeased' by the marriage.

Their mission accomplished, laden with gifts, the Imperial ambassadors departed. Maximilian had secured his loan; Henry had engineered the Habsburg alliance he had long desired. Carmelianus regarded the outcome as a triumph of English diplomacy:

'Rejoice, England, and to thy most noble victorious and fortunate sovereign lord and King give honour, praise and thanks... all Christian regions shall hereafter be united and allied unto thee, which honour till now thou never couldst attain.'

Now, as Princess of Castile, Mary took precedence over her friend and sister-in-law, the Dowager Princess of Wales, but Mary loved Katherine, and was not one to flaunt her advantage. Nonetheless, writing again to beseech her father for money to pay her household, the humiliated Katherine of Aragon wept for shame.

Mary Rose's betrothal to Charles of Castile did not last. Over the next twenty years, Charles would woo and jilt ten different ladies, before finally wedding Isabella of Portugal.

2 - **Notes**.

1. *The Reference of the Great Seal of Scotland*, ed. J Balfour Paul, Edinburgh, 1882, 1602, 553

2. ibid, 67v

3. *Real Academia de Historia*, MS 9-4674, Veruela.

4. *Reference of the Great Seal of Scotland*, 271

5. Francis Bacon's 1622 biography, *The Historie of the Raigne of King Henry the Seventh*, mentions Henry's list of questions and the responses. A document containing the questions and answers was published in London in 1761 by T. Becket and P.A. De Hondt, *Instructions given by King Henry the Seventh, to his embassadors, When he intended to marry the young Queen of Naples: together with the answers of the embassadors.*

6. Carmelianus, Petrus, 2013, 36-7. *The Spousells of the Princess Mary, Daughter of Henry VII, to Charles Prince of Castile, 1508*. London: Forgotten Books. (Original work published 1894)

7. Pynson's Tract: '*The Solemnities and triumphs doon and made at the spousells of the King's daughter*', printed by The Roxburghe Club, Donee MSS, No 198 Bodleian; Carmeliani Carmen, Grenville Library, BM

3   CHARLES BRANDON

Young Mary Rose, as Princess of Castile, had acquired a new significance in court society. Now, after the shadowy years of humiliation, the situation of Mary's friend the Dowager Princess of Wales also improved dramatically. Although Katherine and Prince Henry had been betrothed since 1503, Henry VII had treated his widowed daughter-in-law shabbily, keeping her in penury and prevaricating about allowing the marriage – which would solve the problem of her status as well as her financial difficulties – to take place. His motives were mercenary and political rather than personal – he was sufficiently fond of young Katherine to entertain thoughts of marrying her himself at one point, after the death of his Queen, Elizabeth of York. But Henry VII was piqued at King Ferdinand's persistent failure to pay out the remainder of his daughter's dowry. Henry VII also hoped for a more prestigious and politically advantageous match for Prince Henry, his last surviving son and heir. As a sixteen-year-old childless widow in a strange land, Katherine of Aragon had endured a difficult time, with straightened finances and an uncertain future.

Once Henry VII was finally laid to rest, the young royals were able to enjoy their privileged positions to the full; they gave their teenage zest for living free rein in a Court newly fired with *joie de vivre* and devoted to the pursuit of pleasure.

For Henry, his father's death meant liberty from oppression.

For the past year, Henry VII had kept his son under such close supervision that, as the Spanish Ambassador remarked, the prince might have been a young girl. Henry, unlike his late brother Arthur, was given neither royal responsibilities nor training in kingship, apart from a random history tutorial when his father could spare the time from his political intrigues and architectural ambitions.

Prince Henry was forbidden to leave the palace except by a private door leading into the park, and even then only in the company of specially appointed companions. His person was surrounded by an almost superstitious cloud of anxiety. Henry VII's motives for his tyrannical treatment of his son during this last year appear complex. Possibly, having lost his other three sons, the King, obsessed by the fear that some catastrophe might befall his only surviving male heir, scarcely dared to believe the succession was secure and that the prince, apparently so indestructible, would really live to succeed him as monarch. Preparing young Henry for his future role might be tempting fate.

Or perhaps the King had detected in his son's character potentially dangerous flaws: the Tudor tendency to tantrums, excessive cravings, obsessional competitiveness. Scholars have claimed that he banned from his son's environment anything likely to encourage depravity: all the talk in Henry's presence was to be of 'virtue, honour, cunning, wisdom and deeds of worship, of nothing that shall move him to vice.' Yet this reference applies not to Henry VIII but to the uncrowned King Edward V, the 'disappeared' son of Edward IV. Edward IV drew up ordinances for the regulation of his son's daily life in 1473.[1]

Under the vigilant surveillance of his father and his faithful retainers, the prince's life was now rigorously regimented. His cousin, Reginald Pole, observing the strict hand the King bore upon his only surviving heir, speculated that in reality the King loathed his son, 'having no affection or fancy unto him'.[2] During the year which preceded his death, the King once quarrelled so violently with the young Prince that it appeared to horrified observers 'as if he sought to kill him'.[3]

Nobody dared approach Henry or instigate a conversation with him. He spent most of his time secluded in his chamber, which led off his father's bedchamber. When he did appear in public, he seemed 'so subjected that he does not speak a word except in response to what the king asks him'.[4]

This is not the usual view of Henry VIII favoured by posterity. But it is small wonder that, released from his father's repressive regime, the young Prince threw himself into living with furious enthusiasm.

Notwithstanding, during the last weeks of the old King's life, Henry had played the part of the dutiful son, remaining at his father's bedside at Richmond. Henry would later claim that his father had reiterated to him on his deathbed his last wish: Henry was to wed his brother's widow, Princess Katherine of Aragon, and establish a line of male heirs.

Whatever his personal feelings for his father, Henry VIII gave him a worthy send-off, digging deep into the apparently bottomless coffers he had inherited to provide a magnificent funeral. For his sister, Mary Rose, four new mantelets were ordered from Paris. Her saddle, pillion and the coverings of her horse required 17s worth of black velvet. The palfreys ridden by Princess Katherine and her ladies in the cortege were similarly caparisoned.

On the evening of May 8 1509, the body of Henry VII was brought from Richmond where it had lain in state, to the City for the formal services and burial. At London Bridge a great crowd gathered excitedly. They were not disappointed: the funeral cortège was a magnificent spectacle. Torches and lighted candles flickered on the canopy of cloth-of-gold beneath which the King's effigy, in full regalia, with sceptre and crown, reposed upon the coffin. Five horses decked in black velvet drew the chariot. Behind it rode the Master of the Horse, noblemen, and the whole Guard.

Finally, on 10 May, in the final ritual, the staves of the late King's household were ceremoniously broken and Henry VII was laid to rest in the splendid chapel at Westminster Abbey, where his Queen, Elizabeth of York, already lay entombed. Here, in the imposing tomb designed by Pietro Torrigiano, people who chose to remember the late monarch as a miser murmured that Henry VII dwelt more richly dead in his monument than he had in life, in Richmond or any of his other palaces.

Two weeks after the King's death, the whole country seemed to breathe a sigh of relief when the long mourning vigil was brought to a close. Only a month later, on June 11, two weeks before the date set for Henry VIII's coronation, the young heir to the throne and the Princess Katherine, his brother's widow, would be married quietly at the Franciscan oratory near Greenwich.

As Henry VII's funeral cortège clattered through the crowded streets of London, many an eye had lingered upon a large athletic figure riding among the 93 esquires of the body. Men regarded him with envy, women sighed. Charles Brandon was tall, dark and strikingly handsome, his bearing impressive; but few of those who rode alongside him or watched awestruck from the side-lines could imagine that within five years, royal favour would elevate the dashing young esquire to a Dukedom.

There were four Esquires of the Body, proficient knights who guarded and attended the king night and day, helped him dress, and informed the Lord Chamberlain 'if anything lack for his person or pleasaunce'.[5] Theirs was a highly confidential position.

Charles Brandon was the ideal companion for the new King. Such was their physical resemblance that he was sometimes taken for the King's bastard brother. Handsome, brave, charming and extrovert, Brandon shared Henry's devotion to competitive and often dangerous sports. Brandon was destined to become the most successful courtier of the Tudor age. Remarkably, he owed his success neither to exalted birth, exceptional intelligence or ruthless ambition, but to his personal charm, loyalty, and superb physical prowess, in the service of a monarch who valued these qualities above all. Brandon was instinctive: though not skilled in the subtleties of high-level diplomacy, the law and economics, or the arcane mysteries of strategy and military tactics, he achieved success in both diplomacy and generalship thanks to his common sense and ability to work with people.

After his meteoric rise, he would successfully survive another thirty-one years at Henry VIII's court, that insidious hotbed of gossip, warring factions, raw ambition and lethal intrigue. At his death he would leave his family amongst the greatest in the realm, with claims on the throne of England. For many of his descendants, this distinguished legacy would prove a poisoned chalice.

Brandon's elevation to prominence was so rapid that it stunned his contemporaries, and later writers devised imaginative fables to account for it; in these romantic myths, Brandon either saved the King's life, or the two gallant young men, so similar in many respects, squabbled over a maiden, who made them swear eternal friendship. Preposterous fictions though these stories were, they did capture some aspects of the emotional bond that bound Henry VIII and Charles Brandon – chivalrous rivalry, courtly love, brotherhood in arms, a passion for sport and for the chase.

But Brandon's success owed less to random happenstance than might appear. He was reaping the rewards of two generations of a family who had possessed the foresight and good fortune to throw in their lot with the winning side, and had in consequence won honourable places at Court.

Nonetheless, at the time of Henry VII's funeral, there was little to suggest that the lives of Charles Brandon, Esquire of the Body, and the dead king's beautiful younger daughter would be inexorably intertwined. Brandon, already the veteran of complex and unsavoury matrimonial entanglements, was married to his long-suffering wife, Anne Browne.

Princess Mary Rose, for her part, was betrothed to Prince Charles of Castile. Henry VII's will had stipulated that Mary Rose was to have £50,000 for her dot and marriage, over and above her plate and wardrobe, jewels and accoutrements, and the cost of transporting her to Flanders to take up life as the bride of Prince Charles. Canny to the end, the old King, conscious of the pitfalls which might beset dynastic marriage contracts, determined that, should the Habsburg alliance founder, the money was to be used to finance an alternative marriage for the Princess, to a bridegroom selected for her by her brother, Henry VIII, and his Council. He expressed the hope that the princess might be married abroad, 'to some noble Prince out of this our realm.' An English marriage was not envisaged. Certainly not a union with an upstart like Charles Brandon.

Brandon, although a close companion and confidant of Mary's brother the new King, had no immediate prospect of advancement which would make him a suitable applicant for the hand of a Princess. He belonged to the large, ill-defined class of the gentry – some 1500 -2,000 families – but not to the more exclusive, tightly knit superior circle of the nobility. He was a familiar figure at court in an honourable but relatively menial capacity, having since 1503 been a sewer for the board's end, waiting on Henry VII at table. Between 1505 and 1509, when he was appointed an Esquire of the Body, Brandon had been serving as Master of the Horse to the Earl of Essex, himself a leading courtier as well as a renowned military leader. In this post, Brandon gained invaluable experience which would stand him in good stead when he was appointed Master of the King's Horse.

Brandon and Henry were friends, but the King possessed precocious mental gifts, fostered by a rigorous education from an early age by skilled and scholarly tutors. Charles Brandon could not pretend to equal him intellectually. The foundations of their friendship lay elsewhere. Brandon was a valiant partner in the lists, one of the few who could give the physically brave and superbly athletic king a run for his money. He became a successful military leader, courtier and diplomat thanks to his personal charisma, amiability and candour, rather than to bullishness or guile.

Most importantly, Brandon was the King's man, so loyal that he would not, and did not shrink from mildly compromising his own integrity if it were in his master's interests. Along with the King's other closest friends, he was a gentleman of the Privy Chamber, a group of dashing gallants with whom the King enjoyed jousting, hunting, play-acting, gambling and making merry. The King delighted in their company and showered them with gifts. As his favourite, Brandon was rewarded for his service with lucrative appointments including stewardships, receiverships, wardships and licences. In1513, Henry VIII made him a Knight of the Garter.

Even after he had quarrelled disastrously with many former friends and allies, Henry VIII remained conscious of Brandon's qualities. Unlike many of his contemporaries, Brandon retained Henry's affection until the day of his death. It could have been very different: Brandon's antecedents, and some aspects of his own life, were in many respects highly dubious.

Brandon's father, the hero of Bosworth, had previously enjoyed a sleazy reputation. Writing in 1478, Sir John Paston, a Norfolk neighbour of the Brandons, recorded how young William Brandon had 'by force ravished and swived an old gentlewoman, and yet was not therewith satisfied, but swived her oldest daughter, and then would have swived the other sister both; wherefore men say foul of him, declaring that he would have not only the hen but all her chickens as well.'[7]

William, a ward of the King, added to his iniquities by marrying a widow without paying the accustomed fee, a crime which in the eyes of his contemporaries was more heinous than rape. At the time, people said he was lucky to escape the hangman's noose.

His son Charles Brandon was a *bon viveur* rather than a villain, but he too boasted a lively and somewhat unsavoury reputation with the ladies. He left a trail of complicated marriage contracts behind him. Around 1503, while still in his teens, he had become pre-contracted per *verba de praesenti* to one of Elizabeth of York's ladies-in-waiting, Anne Browne, the daughter of Sir Anthony Browne, later Governor of Calais. In 1503, Brandon admitted to Walter Devereux that he was 'in love and resorted muche to the company of …Anne Browne'. [8] Fond of Anne he probably was, but she was also quite a catch: her father had married the well-connected Lady Lucy Neville, daughter of John Neville, Marquis of Montagu and Earl of Northumberland.

De praesenti contracts were recognised by canon law in England, but a formal church ceremony was supposed to follow. Often, however, this never happened, making it possible for men to wriggle out of their obligations. Since English practice accepted the husband's testimony rather than the wife's, a man could easily repudiate his publicly acknowledged spouse without fear of reprisals or disgrace.

In 1506, Brandon rather callously abandoned the pregnant Anne in order to enter a more advantageous marriage with her wealthy widowed aunt, Dame Margaret Mortimer. At forty-three, more than twenty years his senior, Dame Margaret was well born, the third daughter of John Neville. Margaret was a considerable heiress; she had inherited a fortune, and was childless.

Brandon's grandmother had been the sister of John Mortimer's father; thus he was a cousin of Margaret's former husband, placing Brandon and Margaret within the second and third degrees of relationship prohibited by canon law. The marriage therefore required a papal dispensation.

Shortly after Brandon's desertion, Anne bore him a daughter, Anne, the future Lady Powys. (Since Brandon's bigamous alliance would have rendered Lady Powys illegitimate, her friends and supporters would later claim that Anne Browne had miscarried her first child from shock at Brandon's betrayal, and that Lady Powys was not born until several years later.)

Within two years, possibly because Brandon was suffering pangs of conscience about Anne, Brandon and Dame Margaret were divorced on the grounds of consanguinity. The dispensation was revoked and the marriage declared null and void by the Archdeacon's court in London. Even before the conclusion of the negotiations with Dame Margaret's representatives, Brandon and his mates galloped off into Essex, where they abducted the long-suffering Anne Browne, whom

Brandon then married in secret in Stepney Church in early 1508. Brandon's employer, the Earl of Essex, and Anne's family, 'fearing that the said Charles wold use her as he dyd before', insisted that Brandon make a proper job of it this time and so the couple underwent a public ceremony in St Michael's, Cornhill, in the presence of 'a great nombre of worshypfull people.' Brandon put a good face on it, appearing resplendent in a russet velvet gown faced with martens and joined with beaver, alongside Anne, once again heavily pregnant. She would not long survive the birth of her second daughter, Mary.

At the time, Brandon's scandalous marital history had little effect on his career. It would, however, come back to haunt his descendants.

The congregation at Brandon's marriage to Anne included members of the exclusive group who would become the intimate circle of Henry VIII during the first years of his reign, men such as Edward Howard and Edward Guildford, son of Sir Richard, who also stood godfathers to Brandon's first two daughters by Anne. The circle was close-knit and the relationships within it complex. Thomas Knyvet and Brandon owed money together to Henry VII in 1508; Brandon and Howard were granted a joint ward-ship in 1509, and early in the reign of Henry VIII Brandon, Knyvet and Howard twice joined Edward Guildford in trading ventures.

Henry had greatly enjoyed the jousts organised by these friends in May and June 1507, before his accession. Now, as monarch, he showed his appreciation by showering them with favours and lucrative patronage. Brandon and Guildford, in particular, often received gifts of clothing. Over the next two years, Brandon, Knyvet and Howard would take part in more jousts, masques, pageants and tourneys than any other courtiers except Edward Neville.

Brandon, although not by nature devious or manipulative, was probably sufficiently astute to make sure he retained the King's favour by beating everyone else and then allowing the King to best him, thus emerging as overall champion.

Brandon was living with his wife Anne in that heady

summer of 1509, when he excelled in the jousts and tourneys which celebrated the coronation of his friend and patron, Henry VIII. On 24 June, Midsummer's Day, two weeks after their quiet wedding and six weeks after the funeral of Henry VII, Henry VIII and Katherine of Aragon were crowned. The day before, the teenage Princess Mary Rose had watched the traditional procession through the streets of London with her grandmother from the window of a house in Cheapside. Lady Margaret, overcome with emotion, again burst into tears as Henry left the Tower, escorted by his Knights, dressed in white damask and cloth-of-gold. Katherine followed in a litter, reclining on white damask cushions under a canopy lined with white silk and adorned with golden ribbons. She wore a kirtle of white damask and cloth of gold, furred with miniver – fine squirrel pelts, exclusively worn by the nobility. Her fair hair hung down her back beneath a golden circlet set with pearls and gems. Her attendants followed, resplendent in doublets of crimson satin and gowns of blue velvet. Her ladies, in blue velvet trimmed with crimson, followed, riding matching palfreys.

Sir Andrew Windsor, Master of the Great Wardrobe, and Sir Thomas Lovell, Keeper of the Great Wardrobe of the Household, had sent their staff out to scour London and Flanders for 1,641 yards of scarlet cloth and 2,040 yards of crimson cloth to deck the streets and dress the courtiers. When the cost of the Queen's 'silks and necessaries' for herself and her household, and those of the fourteen-year-old Mary Rose, Princess of Castile, and her ladies were added, the total expenditure came to £4,748 6s 3d. Tailors, embroiderers and goldsmiths earned a fortune creating coronation robes for the nobility. On Midsummer's Day, the court in their fur-trimmed scarlet robes processed from the Palace of Westminster to the Abbey along a striped carpet. As soon as Henry entered the church, the crowd surged forward and hacked up the carpet he had trodden on, bearing off the pieces for souvenirs.

In a lengthy, dignified ceremony, Archbishop William Warham blessed the crown of St Edward. The King and Queen prostrated themselves before the high altar, and were then crowned and anointed with holy oil. Warham asked the congregation whether they took Henry for their King. The congregation shouted their assent. The massed choir burst into the *Te Deum*. The crowds cheered, the organ thundered, trumpets blared, bells pealed, all signifying that Henry VIII had been 'gloriously crowned to the comfort of all the land.' Thus, on a high tide of euphoria, began the reign of King Henry VIII.

Thomas More's coronation ode echoes the Easter hymns of joy:

> This happy day consecrates a young man who is the everlasting glory of our age, a king worthy to rule the entire world, who will wipe the tears from every eye and banish our long distress with joy. Now the people, liberated, run before their king with bright faces.[9]

The King and Queen then returned to Westminster Hall for a magnificent banquet 'greater than any Caesar had known.' The Duke of Buckingham and the Earl of Shrewsbury entered on horseback to lead in the procession of dishes of 'sumptuous, fine and delicate meats [in] plentiful abundance.'[10] After the guests had enjoyed the second course, they watched the traditional ritual challenge of the King's Champion. Riding up and down the Hall in full armour on his courser, the Champion, Sir Robert Dymmocke, threw down his gauntlet in challenge to any who questioned Henry's right to rule, proclaiming that he was willing to defend it. No such challenge being forthcoming from the assembled persons, he then approached Henry, claiming a drink. He was offered wine in a golden goblet, which he drained, and then rode off with, as reward for his services. Originally a simple mediaeval expression of homage and fealty by a knight to his liege lord, this ritual was now a symbol of the whole nation's acknowledgement of their sovereign.

When the company had feasted to repletion, a tournament was held, lasting until midnight. The celebrations continued for several days and were only brought to an abrupt end on June 29, the day before the King attained his majority, by the death of the King's grandmother, Lady Margaret Beaufort. Lady Margaret had recovered sufficiently from her emotional response to the coronation of her grandson to gorge herself on a dish of cygnet at the subsequent banquet, with fatal consequences. The King ordered the church bells to toll her passing for six days.

The loss of Lady Margaret was a grave blow. But the celebrations had been unparalleled. Mary Rose and other royal spectators had watched the jousting in the grounds of the palace of Westminster from a specially constructed pavilion hung with tapestries and rich Arras cloth. Heralded by fanfares, young gallants and noblemen took the field, all splendidly attired and accoutred.

The tournament played a crucial role in Henry's ambition to be what he regarded as a real King. It was the ultimate theatre of chivalry, attended by lavish pageantry and allegory. Jousts were held in honour of the ladies, who presented favours such as scarves or handkerchiefs to their chosen knights. The champion of the day received his accolade from the Queen or the highest-ranking lady present.

Achieving honour in the joust was almost as prestigious as winning glory on the battlefield. Tournaments were a dangerous business; men and horses were injured and occasionally killed. In 'barriers', the challengers ran at each other down opposite sides of a wooden barrier, aiming to shatter their lance on their opponent or, if they were really lucky, tip him up. The tourney was fought on horseback with swords; in the dramatic tilt or joust, mounted knights with lances thundered towards each other at the lumbering gallop of huge chargers sturdy enough to transport a large man in full armour, with the aim of unhorsing the opponent. In the tilt, competitors fought in pairs. In the joust, each man competed alone. The lances, although solid, could be splintered fairly easily by a robust strike at full tilt against a fully armoured breastplate. Hitting the target required a good eye; often knights missed one another completely, causing gasps, jeers and laughter from the spectators.

Besides an opportunity to demonstrate courage and prowess, tournaments served a useful purpose, in that they kept fighting men in shape. The King was 'not minded to see young gentlemen inexpert in martial feats'. This meant, on the domestic scene, excelling in the knightly pastime of jousting in preparation for service abroad, and military victories. The nobility played a key role in this process. They furnished the King with the worthiest challengers in the lists and, in a country without a standing army, they provided both the military leadership and the troops for warfare.

Henry's coronation tourney was organised by Lord Thomas Howard, heir to the Earl of Surrey; his brother, Admiral Sir Edward Howard; Lord Richard Grey; Sir Edmund Howard; Sir Thomas Knyvet[t], and, the only esquire among them, owing his position to his skill at jousting, Charles Brandon. Brandon, wearing a complete gilt armour, revelled in the opportunity to display his skill. The young Princess of Castile could not fail to notice him. Brandon was pitted at barriers against a massive German challenger, whom he 'so pummelled about the head' that his nose bled and he was led away defeated.[11]

The reign of Henry VIII had now been formally launched on its glorious course, and along with it the flourishing careers of his most notable servants, the Howards, born into the nobility, and the parvenu Charles Brandon.

3 - Notes

1. 'Letters of Edward IV to Earl Rivers and the Bishop of Rochester', 1473, in *Readings in English Social History*, Cambridge University Press, 1921, 205-8

2. L&P

3. CSP Span

4. Correspondencia de Gutierre Gomez de Fuensalida, embajador en Alemania, Flandes é Inglaterra (1496-1509) Duke of Berwick and Alba, ed, 1907, Madrid, 449

5. L&P

6. Samuel Pegge, *Curalia, Or an Historical Account of some branches of the Royal Household*, John Nichols, ed, London, 1782, 13

7.   James Gairdner, *John Paston's Letter. The Paston Letters, A. D. 1422-1509*. London: Chatto & Windus, 1904, 6

8.   Deposition of Walter Devereux, Viscount Hereford, 1552

9.   Sir Thomas More, *Coronation Ode of King Henry VIII*, 150

10.   Holinshed's *Chronicles of England, Scotland and Ireland*, vol 1 11 London, 1808, 549

11. This exact same statement is made about a giant hooded German Challenger who was introduced surreptitiously into the competition by the Dauphin Francis in the jousts held in Paris to celebrate the marriage of Princess Mary Rose to King Louis xii of France.

4 FROM ESQUIRE TO DUKE

The riotous self-indulgence of the new reign continued relentlessly for the next couple of years. In addition to the feast and the chase, the King indulged his boyish delight in impromptu disguising and other merry japes. In January 1510 he and eleven companions, dressed as Robin Hood and his Merry Men, in short green coats, hoods concealing their features, burst into the Queen's chamber, brandishing bows and arrows and swords. Queen Katherine, heavily pregnant, and her ladies, although much 'abashed', consented to dance with the intruding ruffians. Afterwards the King threw back his hood and revealed his identity, to the great 'astonishment' of the ladies. Katherine smilingly indulged the childish fantasies of her young husband.

The headstrong young monarch's next prank, a few days later, on January 12, horrified Court and Council. Desperate to put into practice his years of training, Henry made the first-ever public appearance in the tiltyard by an English monarch. He later pursued a glorious jousting career, ignoring the dismal mutterings of the 'ancient fathers' about the terrible risks he was running. As a token effort to allay their fears, Henry consented to use hollow lances to reduce impact, but he still courted danger, 'having no respect or fear of anyone in the world', and on at least two occasions narrowly escaped death. But his obsession with jousting persisted. His favourite opponent was

Charles Brandon, the only man with a physique and courage to equal his own. Brandon soon became his regular sparring partner; the King ordered jousting outfits to be made for Brandon which exactly matched his own.

The only cloud on the horizon was Queen Katherine's failure to deliver a living heir. In January 1510, during the Robin Hood episode, the King was exultant, eagerly anticipating the birth of a son. He had already ordered a magnificent cradle of estate padded with crimson cloth-of-gold embroidered with the royal arms, and a 'groaning chair' for the birth, with a cut-away seat, upholstered in cloth-of-gold, and a copper-gilt bowl intended to receive the blood and placenta. But all was in vain. After hours of agony, during which Katherine vowed to send her richest headdress to the shrine of St Peter the Martyr in Spain, she was delivered of a stillborn daughter. Katherine was distraught; four months would pass before she could bring herself to inform her father King Ferdinand of her humiliating 'failure'.

Henry put a brave face on his disappointment. On Shrove Tuesday he set another new precedent, astounding his court by personally taking part in a revel: at a banquet for foreign ambassadors Henry and his courtiers dressed up as scimitar-wielding Turks, attended by blacked-up torch-bearers. Henry later reappeared, having changed into a short doublet of blue and crimson slashed with cloth of gold, and led the dancing, partnered once again by his sister, Mary Rose.

By September the Queen was pregnant again. Again, her confinement followed the rules established by Lady Margaret Beaufort. Throughout her grandson's reign these would be strictly adhered to. The delivery chamber was shrouded in rich cloth of Arras except for one window. The tapestries adorning the chamber portrayed suitably innocuous images, lest the Queen or the infant should be 'affrighted by figures which gloomily stare.'[1] The chamber contained an altar and a cupboard for the birthing equipment. In case the child was weakly and immediate baptism was necessary, the 'rich font of Canterbury' stood ready. To this chamber Katherine retired about six weeks before her time, after Mass and a banquet. During the weeks of her lying-in, she would see no man, not even the King.

On New Year's Day, 1511, to great jubilation, Katherine was delivered of a prince. The King, overjoyed, lavished gifts on Katherine's attendants and there were general celebrations. Having appointed forty attendants for the prince, Henry embarked on a pilgrimage to the Priory of Our Lady of Walsingham in Norfolk to give thanks. Dismounting a mile from the Priory, in the Slipper Chapel, he removed his shoes and trudged barefoot to the Virgin's shrine, where he lit a candle and offered an expensive necklace.

In February, the King staged a dazzling tournament at Westminster in honour of the Queen. That night, at a banquet in the White Hall, the revels featured a pageant, the Garden of Pleasure, in which the King appeared as 'Coeur Loyal', Sir Loyal Heart, attired in purple satin adorned with gold Hs and Ks. When guests, including the Spanish ambassador, refused to believe that Henry's ornaments were real gold, Henry invited them to tug them off and examine them.

Unfortunately, the common people, admitted to gape at their glorious monarch and the aristocratic capers of their betters, took this as an open invitation to strip the King and his courtiers of their finery as a form of largesse. They surged forward, grabbing whatever items they could lay their hands on, tearing people's clothing in their excitement. Even the King was stripped down to his doublet and hose, while poor Sir Thomas Knyvet was stripped naked and was obliged to shin up a pillar to escape. When the mob turned their attention to the court ladies, the King's guard intervened, driving them back. Henry passed the whole thing off as a huge joke; the evening concluded with a banquet in the presence chamber, guests making the best of it as they clutched the remnants of their tattered finery around them.[2]

In future, however, measures were taken to ensure that security surrounding public events was tightened up.

The joy was short-lived. On February 23, the baby prince died. Henry, again suppressing his own disappointment, comforted the distressed Katherine.

At Easter, Pope Julius II bestowed on Henry a Golden Rose personally blessed by himself, a sign of high favour. In 1512, this was followed by a Sword and Cap of Maintenance. These blandishments were intended to induce Henry to join the so-called Holy League, an alliance between the Papacy, Spain and Venice against Louis of France, with the intention of foiling the French monarch's aggressive ambitions in Italy. Henry joined the Holy League in October, and, impressed by the Holy Father's overtures, briefly abandoned Epicurean hedonism for sober austerity. He ordered the court to curb their extravagance, and abandoned his habitual finery for a long grey cloth gown cut in the Hungarian fashion.

Unsurprisingly, Henry's ascetic phase was not of long duration. By Christmas, he was again seeking distractions. On Twelfth Night 1512, the Court were startled by an outrageous Continental innovation: the Italian masque. The King and his gentlemen, disguised, ignored considerations of formal precedence and invited the most attractive ladies, the ones they fancied, to dance. Many ladies refused, scandalised by the breach of etiquette, but Mary Rose cheerfully joined in. She shared her brother's delight in the novel and the bizarre, participating enthusiastically in his conceits, happy to dress up as a rustic maiden or an African princess.

Henry's banquets were once again Gargantuan gastronomic extravaganzas: one meal might comprise 240 dishes: beef, pork, veal, venison, mutton, game, fish, cheese, jellies, fruit, nuts, pastries and sweets, accompanied by wines from all over Europe. Servants staggered under heaped solid gold platters. Before retiring, the overfed guests might be offered a 'voidee of spices'. Those accustomed to the restraint of Henry VII's court were appalled by the extravagance. But senior courtiers welcomed it as a return to the grand old glory days of Yorkist rule.

Meanwhile, still with no sign of a viable heir, Henry indulged his young sister, 'our well-beloved sister the Lady Mary', lavishing gifts of jewels and fine apparel upon her, and insisting on her presence at Court. Mary was only too glad to comply; she shared his love of music, and delighted in the dancing, pageants and disguisings. The two were rarely apart. When Mary was staying away from court at one of the royal manors, Henry constantly sent her little gifts, entreating her to return to court. Here, she was automatically drawn into her brother's intimate circle, and the company of his favourite, Charles Brandon.

Despite rumblings of discontent, the surface of domestic affairs was unruffled. The major threat to serenity of mind was the plague, which periodically swept in from the Continent, spreading terror and death. Then Henry, Mary and their companions made a hasty mass exodus to the country until the danger had passed.

Although Mary's marriage to Prince Charles of Castile was not due for consummation for five years, plans for her wedding were under annual review. In 1510, Henry had sent an Embassy to the Emperor Maximilian in an attempt to progress matters. Henry was discovering for himself an unpleasant truth long apparent to everyone else: Maximilian's promises were worthless. In 1512, alarmed by reports that Maximilian was dallying with 'amity' with the King of France, Henry again despatched special envoys to Germany, hoping for a definite response that would bring the marriage forward or at least reconfirm the Imperial intent. Since the Emperor was not only shifty by nature but was constantly on the move, Henry's ambassadors had to work mostly through Maximilian's daughter Margaret, now Archduchess and Regent of the Netherlands. Margaret, for her part, was making every effort to advance the marriage between her nephew Charles and Mary Rose.

Before the end of 1509, there had been plans for Mary to visit the Low Countries and become acquainted with their fashions and life style. The Emperor had appointed her a gentleman in waiting in 1512, and the next autumn, his daughter, the Archduchess Margaret, sent a Fleming to attend on her. Mary had been sent patterns showing the style of dress fashionable at the court of the Netherlands. She wrote in French to thank her 'bonne tante', and said that she hoped to introduce Flemish fashions to the English court. Some historians have criticised Mary's French spelling. But orthography in both French and English was relatively unstable and unstandardised at the time.

No firm date was set for Mary's visit, though there was some suggestion that Henry would deliver his sister personally when he launched his French campaigns. Henry took the contract seriously; he supported the Archduchess in her war with the Duke of Guelders, sending 1500 soldiers, thus placing Burgundy in his debt, and also demonstrating English military power. The Archduchess was mortified by her father's shilly-shallying.

Soon, Henry and his favourite, Brandon, would cause poor Margaret even greater agonies of embarrassment.

Brandon's wife Anne Browne died in the summer of 1510, within a fortnight of the birth of their second daughter, Mary. Brandon had obtained the lucrative offices of Chamberlain of the Principality of Wales and Marshal of the King's Bench, a position formerly held by his uncle. A year later, in November 1511, Brandon was granted, together with Sir John Carew, the marshalship of the King's household. This entailed keeping the Southwark prison, an influential quasi-sinecure with little work but the potential for profit, and close involvement with the King's safety. He was created ranger of the New Forest, an appointment he would retain all his life, entitling him to take a number of bucks and fell a quota of forest trees annually. Craftily, he appointed as his deputy a local man, Robert Hussey, who had often been in trouble for felling trees in the royal forest, and would henceforth have to pay handsomely for the privilege of doing so legally.

In March 1512 Pope Julius II withdrew from Louis XII the title of 'Most Christian King' and declared that, as far as the Church was concerned, France belonged to Henry, if he could win it back. A campaign was mounted in June under Thomas Grey, the 2nd Marquis of Dorset. Thomas was the grandson of Elizabeth Woodville, King Henry's grandmother. Henry's favourite courtiers all stepped forward to assume military commands. The war would cost Brandon the loss of good friends; yet, as usual in such cases, their deaths would open the door to dramatic advancement. Together with Sir Henry Guildford, Brandon was given the command of elite troops aboard a large, newly refitted vessel.

His first taste of real warfare that summer was bitter. In the naval campaign, through either misfortune or misjudgement, his command failed to support Sir Thomas Knyvet as he grappled with a French warship. The French vessel exploded; both ships burned to the waterline before the horrified eyes of helpless onlookers. Knyvet died, along with most of his crew. This tragedy put Brandon off maritime campaigns forever. He never went to sea again. Sir Edward Howard was so appalled by Knyvet's terrible fate that he swore he would never again look the King in the face until he had avenged Knyvet. Howard obsessively sought battle with the French until, in a fit of foolhardy heroism, he was killed in April 1513.

With Knyvet and Howard dead, of the leaders of the King's intimate circle Brandon alone survived. From 1512 to 1514, he played an increasingly important part in the King's life. Often, they again took to appearing wearing the identical outfits that distinguished them from other members of the court.

In the short term, the death of Edward Howard, Brandon's closest friend, the only man who consistently outshone him, opened up new military opportunities for Brandon; the long-term effects were even more important. Howard bequeathed to Brandon, 'his special trusty friend', the chain on which his admiral's whistle hung, and also the lucrative ward-ship of whichever of his two illegitimate sons the King did not choose to raise.

Brandon and Howard were elected to the Order of the Garter on 23 April 1513, but Howard was dead before the ceremony itself. In October 1512, Brandon assumed his uncle's old office as Master of the Horse, gaining complete control over the royal stable, the travelling arrangements of the royal household, and the King's own hunters and warhorses. The King's horses played a huge part in the young monarch's life, dedicated as he was to hunting, jousting, splendid processions and dreams of leading his cavalry in a succession of resounding military triumphs. Under Edward IV, annual expenditure on the stables had been less than £380, with 45 staff employed. Under Brandon, annual expenditure grew to £1,500, and 137 personnel were employed.

Brandon had long been dominant in the jousts, but on 1 June 1512 he and the King challenged alone together for the first time, and this set the pattern for the next two years. Brandon, the best jouster in the country, had the good sense never to outperform the monarch, while succeeding against every other opponent, thus highlighting the King's own skill. As Master of the Horse, Brandon was also the King's esquire. When the King rode out to meet his ally the Emperor Maximilian and again to meet his grandson, Prince Charles, Brandon rode immediately behind him, leading the spare horse. On these occasions Brandon was attired in great splendour, and was often mistaken for a member of the royal family.

Brandon enjoyed the King's favour and his finances had improved in consequence; but his status needed enhancement. Even before the death of Thomas Knyvet's widow, Muriel, Lady Lisle, in December 1512, Brandon had acquired the ward-ship of Knyvet's eight-year-old step-daughter Elizabeth. Aristocratic families customarily sent a child to live with a well-connected family. This tradition linked the parents as political allies and the children as friends. The resultant contacts were often useful in the arrangement of future marriages. Little Elizabeth, Baroness Lisle in her own right, was the heiress to substantial estates. Brandon obtained her ward-ship on very easy terms – £1,400 payable over 7 years. As her lands brought in almost £800 a year, and Brandon could expect to hold them for at least six years, this was a sound investment.

On Lady Muriel's death, Brandon contracted to marry little Elizabeth when she came of age. This enabled the King to create him Viscount Lisle in virtue of his future wife on May 15, at the same time granting him an annuity of 40 marks. The new title meant a slight increase in income and a higher rank. Usefully so, since Brandon would soon be in command of men who outranked him.

His first major command was in the raid conceived by the King in May 1513 to avenge the death of Sir Edward Howard. Edward's elder brother, Sir Thomas Howard, was appointed admiral in his dead brother's place, while Brandon was to lead a landing party in a co-ordinated operation, intended to destroy the French fleet in its Breton ports. The King was very enthusiastic about the raid, planning to travel secretly to observe its execution. But experienced officers warned that Brandon's force of 4,000 was inadequate, the time scale was unrealistic, and would seriously disrupt Henry's main project, the glorious invasion he planned to lead in person. Nevertheless, their advice was ignored and arrangements went ahead. German mercenaries arrived in Southampton, and artillery was sent from London. But the logistics were disastrous: victualling remained problematic, despite the best efforts of Brandon's staff. The diversion of troops from the Kent ports to Southampton caused chaos, and time was running out. By 21 May most of the invading force had been assembled two days' march from the port, to avoid pressure on the food supplies. Brandon had arrived, but Admiral Howard was still detained in Portsmouth by unfavourable winds. The victuallers' ships from London and Sandwich were nowhere to be seen. Now reports were coming in that their quarry, the French fleet, had dispersed from Brest.

The enterprise was doomed to failure. Under intolerable pressure, Brandon and Howard quarrelled. The raid never took place. But for Brandon, the affair had important consequences. Firstly, it initiated a decade of difficult relations with Howard, soon to be Earl of Surrey. On the other hand, Brandon's appointment to such a significant command, to which he was entitled neither by rank nor experience, clearly demonstrated the high favour he enjoyed with the King. It was true that he had been placed in command over men of higher rank. However, most of them had participated in the previous summer's disastrous expedition to Guyenne: Brandon, untried but with an untarnished reputation, was appointed high marshal of the army for Henry's invasion of France.

Henry had been itching for action ever since the League of Cambrai gave way to the Holy League in October 1511, but had hitherto heeded his advisers' counsels to withhold English support and continue his father's policy of peaceful neutrality, avoiding the waste and expense of belligerence. But the Papal prompting, the Spanish connection, and above all his own hankering after military glory, tipped the scales. Henry ached for a great victory to rival Agincourt. Of the great Plantagenet empire, only Calais and its Pale remained. By the spring of 1513, Henry, in a ferment of excitement, prepared a huge invasion force against France.

The Emperor Maximilian had at long last concluded a treaty, Henry advancing him 25,000 crowns, most of which was to be used to bribe the Swiss. Henry promised to invade France with a force of 30,000 men. The Emperor, sweetened by English gold, graciously offered to lead a division under Henry's command. England, Germany, Spain and the Papacy were pledged to declare war on France within thirty days, and attack a month later.

Thousands of suits of armour had been ordered from Italy and Spain; a dozen new cannon, nicknamed the 'twelve apostles', were on their way from Germany. Henry, in a fever of anticipation, hastened to the docks every day to inspect his pride and joy, his navy. Transport vessels were being equipped to convey a force of 40,000 men across the Channel. The pride of his fleet, the 1,500ton *Great Harry*, was almost ready for launching. The young men of the King's Chamber enthusiastically supported the King's new venture, fired by notions of chivalry, valour and glorious military pageantry. His new efficient servant, the upstart butcher's son, Thomas Wolsey, was demonstrating his invaluable flair for administration and organisation.

In 1508, the last year of Henry VII's reign, Wolsey, newly returned from an embassy to Scotland, had been despatched by the King on a mission to Flanders. Wolsey left Richmond at noon, took a barge from London to Gravesend, travelled on by post horse to Dover, sailed for Calais within three hours and by the next day had reached the Emperor's court and completed his mission. Returning immediately to Richmond by the same route, he encountered the King on his way to early Mass only three days after he had been sent out. The King, supposing he had tarried, reproved him sharply for delaying on his errand. Learning to his astonishment that Wolsey already been and come back, he created him Dean of Lincoln on the spot.

By the beginning of Henry VIII's reign, Wolsey had advanced to the post of Royal Almoner. Henry was young and too self-indulgent for the serious work of government. Wolsey, noting this, 'took upon him therefore to disburden the King of so weighty a charge and troublesome business', so that he was not forced to 'spare any time from his pleasure.'[3] The young Royals trusted him. To Mary, only fourteen when her father died, Wolsey virtually became a father figure.

Henry left Greenwich for Dover, accompanied by the Queen, who was to act as regent in his absence, and an entourage of twenty-one peers, the Duke of Buckingham, Bishop Foxe, Wolsey, heralds, musicians, trumpeters, the choir of the Chapel Royal, six hundred archers of the yeomen of the guard, and three hundred household servants. He also took along his bed of estate, several suits of armour, and a collection of gaudy tents and pavilions. On 30 June, the King, his great army and his copious impedimenta, set sail for France.

On 24 July, Henry and his ally, the Emperor Maximilian, laid siege to the town of Thérouanne. On 16 August the French were routed at the Battle of the Spurs – so called because of the haste with which the French cavalry, arriving to relieve the town, retreated, overawed by the sight of the allied forces encamped around. Thérouanne fell. It was England's first victory in France since 1453. Henry's jubilation knew no bounds.

Brandon commanded the vanguard of the King's ward, some 3,000 men. Though he took little part in the military decisions of the campaign, and at first saw little action, as High Marshal, and especially since the King had commissioned him lieutenant of the whole army, he had found himself in command of dukes, earls and veteran warriors. Although the effective victualling of the army was in reality Wolsey's achievement, Brandon acquitted himself honourably of his command, earning great recognition.

After their triumphal entry into Thérouanne, Henry and his entourage made a forty-mile detour to Lille, where they were lavishly entertained by Maximilian's daughter, the alluring Archduchess Margaret. Brandon had cut a fine figure at the siege of Thérouanne. Margaret's agent had described Brandon to her as 'a second King'. The Burgundian nobility flocked to the Archduchess's court to be presented to Henry, whom they were pleased to find 'merry, handsome, well-spoken, popular and intelligent'. Officially enjoying rest and recuperation, his energy astonished everyone. In a hastily assembled tiltyard constructed from planks, he displayed his skill before the Archduchess and her nephew, Prince Charles, his sister's young fiancé, running numerous courses against Brandon and against the Emperor's champion. The Milanese ambassador, amazed at his stamina, reported: 'He was fresher after this awful exertion than before. I do not know how he can stand it.' [4]One tournament was held indoors in a hall with a black marble floor. The horses wore felt shoes to prevent them damaging it. The King also demonstrated his skill at archery, and in the evenings entertained the company by playing various musical instruments and as the night wore on by dancing 'magnificently in the French style' with Margaret and her ladies, at one point becoming so hot he had to discard his doublet and hose, earning even more approbation than he had done when as a child he threw off his jacket to dance at his parents' court. The jousts were a useful showcase for English military prowess.

After three days of lavish feasting, the English proceeded to besiege the wealthy town of Tournai. On 25 September, the King was handed the keys of the city, and also a great quantity of *vin de Beaune*. Tournai became his headquarters throughout October; while he and his nobles were still celebrating their triumphs, the Emperor Maximilian, the Archduchess Margaret and Prince Charles of Castile arrived. They had come in person to discuss the Prince's forthcoming marriage with Princess Mary Rose.

The atmosphere was cordial. Henry, flushed with success, was disposed to find Charles charming, while the Emperor, still grateful for English gold and military assistance, declared that he loved Henry more than a son. The two exchanged gifts, a jewel and a great ox. By 15 October, they had signed two treaties: a military one, for a joint invasion of France with Spanish support, by June 1514. The second contract was for the consummation of the marriage between Mary and Charles by mid-May 1514.

One secret clause in the marriage treaty reflects the cunning of its chief author, the Archduchess. She extracted an oral promise from Henry that, lacking male heirs, he would settle the succession on his sister Mary and her descendants. Margaret would later remind Henry of this pledge, urging him to obtain Parliamentary sanction, but no action was taken until the third Succession act of 1543, which empowered the King to dispose of the crown at will. Henry's will would be publicised a decade later, in the summer of 1553, in connection with Northumberland's plot to secure the throne for his family. It would reveal the King's clear preference for the descendants of his sister Mary Rose, thus placing them in mortal danger, costing some of them their freedom and others their lives.

The campaigning season was ending. His triumphs and celebrations on the Continent completed, and the desired treaties signed, Henry was now keen to consolidate his alliance with the Emperor, and return home to devote himself to his next exciting project: organising the grandest of weddings for his beloved sister – a marriage he knew would bring him massive prestige in Europe, equalling his recent triumphs on the battlefield.

When the army reached Calais, there was a shortage of hay for the horses. Henry noted that this situation must be rectified next spring, when Charles and Mary were to meet there, and he would be there too, accompanied by his army. He envisaged a stunning double event comprising nuptials and military campaign. On 22 October, Henry returned to England in triumph.

Between Henry's accession in 1509 and June 1513, over a million pounds had flowed out of the treasury, two-thirds of it having been used to finance the war with France. Ten years later, Wolsey's protégé Thomas Cromwell would remark that the winning of Thérouanne cost his Highness 'more than twenty such ungracious dog-holes could be worth to him'[5]

The whole campaign had in fact been quite unnecessary, since the French King had already made peace with the new Pope, Leo X, even before Henry and his forces embarked.

But Henry, still revelling in his conquest, rewarded those who had served him well during the campaigns of 1513. At Candlemas 1514, while still convalescing from small pox, in a move deplored by many members of his court, he elevated his faithful commander and companion, the charming upstart Charles Brandon, to a dukedom.

4 - Notes

1. John Leland, *Collectanea, Collection of Ordinances*, Trinity College Dublin MSS

2. Hall, *The Union of the Two Noble and Illustre Families of York & Lancaster*, ed. H Ellis, London 1809

3. George Cavendish, *The Life of Cardinal Wolsey*, ed. Samuel Weller, London, 1825, 81

4. Paolo da Laude, Milanese Ambassador to the Emperor, L&P I ii, 2389, 2359; CSP Milan 1385-1618, 669

5. L&P Hen VIII 1523 2958

5 'THAT NEW DUKE'

Henry VIII was busy rewarding his faithful servants, especially those who had acquitted themselves honourably on the battlefield. On 2 February 1514, Thomas Howard, Earl of Surrey, was restored to the Dukedom of Norfolk in recognition of his defeat of the Scots at Flodden. (A permanent, if gory, inset into the Earl's family coat of arms was an image of the Scottish lion, chopped in two, with an arrow down its throat).

The King's cousin and Lord Chamberlain, Charles Somerset, Lord Herbert, was created Earl of Worcester. Charles, the bastard son of the last Beaufort Earl of Somerset, had performed valiantly in the French campaign.

But the greatest upset among Henry's courtiers was caused by the King's elevation of the upstart Charles Brandon to the Dukedom of Suffolk. Brandon's rise to prominence had been breath-taking and, to some people, profoundly annoying: knighted on 30 March 1512, before 14 months had passed he was a viscount, and a mere nine months later, he had been made a Duke. The Dukes of Norfolk and Suffolk had to be created separately, there being insufficient peers of comparable status to accompany them both at once. The Marquis of Dorset obliged; the Duke of Buckingham sulked.

The ceremony of ennoblement, which took place after High Mass in the great chamber at Lambeth Palace, followed the procedure established in the 14th century when Edward III had raised his sons to the peerage. Each Duke received a crimson robe and cap of estate, a coronet and sword, and a golden rod. Henceforth, Brandon had the right to be styled 'the right high and mighty Prince'; he was usually more simply addressed as 'Your Grace'.

The ceremony was watched by the Queen and her ladies, a crowd of peers up in London for the parliamentary sittings, and also by Louis d'Orléans, the Duc de Longueville, the most prominent of the noble hostages taken in accordance with the rules of mediaeval warfare, to ensure that the defeated French government honoured the terms of the truce. During his time in France and the Low Countries, Henry had been impressed by the sophisticated culture of the Franco-Flemish Renaissance. The cessation of hostilities heralded a new craze for French style, etiquette, fashion, food and art, architecture and entertainment in England. The King himself initiated the trend, which would last for most of his reign. The French language, banned during the war, now once again became the fashionable mode of communication among the upper classes.

The Duc de Longueville was lodged in considerable comfort in the Tower with six attendants. He and Henry had become so friendly that Henry impulsively offered to pay half of the Duc's ransom out of his own pocket. The Duc became a popular figure at court, and, although he had a wife back in France, embarked upon a prolonged romance with one of Mary Rose's ladies, her childhood companion, the Frenchwoman Jane Poppincourt.

The Duc would also soon come to play a brief but memorable role in Princess Mary's life.

The elevation of Brandon infuriated the older nobility, who were resentful of his influence over the King, and suspicious of his ambition. The family of the Duke of Norfolk were lying in wait for the opportunity to destroy him. Buckingham, who since 1503 had been the only Duke in England, was so outraged by Henry's ennoblement of Brandon that he had boycotted the ceremony. It was Buckingham's rival, Wolsey, who had recommended that the King should raise his friend to the peerage, perhaps with the specific intention of reducing the influence on the Council of the new Duke of Norfolk.

Henry's reasons for elevating Brandon were complex. Brandon was his trusted friend and boon companion. He wanted to honour those who had contributed to his own modest success in France, signalling that this victory, bought at such enormous cost, was truly momentous and of much greater significance than it really was. But bestowing on Brandon the title of Suffolk, formerly held by the royal Yorkist de la Pole family, also fulfilled Henry's political agenda. Divesting the de la Poles of the title deprived the last major Yorkist claimants to the throne of their final chance of restoration. Edmund, the last Earl in the de la Pole line of Dukes and Earls of Suffolk, which stretched back to 1385, had fled England in 1501. Five years later, he was forcibly repatriated, attainted and executed in 1513 by Henry. This left at large on the Continent his brother Richard, who styled himself Duke of Suffolk, served the French as a general, and canvassed French support to claim the throne of England.

In Europe, Brandon's new Dukedom kindled immediate speculation; it fuelled the rumour, current by early 1514, that Brandon and the King had hatched some extraordinary plot to marry Brandon off to the Archduchess Margaret, and that Henry had ennobled Brandon expressly to facilitate such a union.

In early 1514, Henry had half-jokingly envisaged this unlikely fairy-tale romance between lowly esquire and Emperor's daughter as one of the three pillars of one of his favourite notions, a triple marital edifice designed to cement European alliances. Three marriages would bolster this structure: the unlikely concept of a marriage between Archduchess Margaret and the new Duke of Suffolk - a far-fetched notion plucked from the realms of fantasy; the already-contracted dynastic marriage between Mary Rose and Charles of Castile; and a possible marriage between Henry's older sister Margaret, recently left a widow by the death of James IV of Scotland at the battle of Flodden, and the Emperor Maximilian himself. But Maximilian, at 54, found Margaret's younger sister more to his taste, confiding to his daughter the Archduchess Margaret his intention of forcing his grandson Charles to repudiate Mary Rose so he could marry her himself. However, six months later, he abandoned the notion, announcing dramatically that he would never go near another woman again as long as he lived.

The gossiping about a possible romance between herself and Brandon would upset Archduchess Margaret, and offend her father, Emperor Maximilian, but despite the aggravation Margaret retained a soft spot for Brandon, causing speculation bolstered by some of her discreet but revealing correspondence that they had in reality either been lovers, or had certainly enjoyed a romantic attachment. Margaret was not only distressed by the scandal but detested having to treat Brandon coolly and distantly to preserve face.

Brandon had rescued little Magdalen Rochester, the eight-year-old daughter of an English resident of Calais, from drowning, and subsequently adopted her. He entrusted Magdalen to Margaret's care, and later sent his older daughter Anne Brandon to be educated at the court at Malines on the Dyle, at the palace built for the Archduchess. Both girls remained under Margaret's tutelage for 2 years. This great concession by the Archduchess Margaret fired more speculation about a potential match. The rumour that Brandon had one or more wives living only added spice to the gossip. Writing to Venice from London, at the end of July 1514, the Venetian Andrea Badoer [Badoaro] spoke of it as a fact, adding 'The Duke is a very handsome man, may have had more than three wives and she more than one husband.'* Whether the King of England envisaged the match as a genuine possibility, or even seriously actively promoted it, or whether he was appalled by the rumours, as he pretended to be, it is difficult to ascertain. Elevating Brandon to a Dukedom was certainly a radical step. When Henry granted Brandon the former de la Pole estates, this made him at one stroke immediately wealthier and therefore more powerful than most of the landed aristocracy. The former Master of the Horse took it all in his stride. A Venetian observer assured the Senate that 'no one ever bore so vast a rise with so easy a dignity.' Brandon was now 'the chief nobleman in England, a liberal and magnificent Lord'. Brandon was indubitably magnificent. But not everyone experienced him as liberal: Sir Edward Baynton, Anne Boleyn's vice- chamberlain, wrote: 'My Lord of Suffolk is loath to let fall a noble unless he took up a royal for it'.[1]

Brandon was not the only man of humble origins to be honoured. On 6 February, Wolsey, the Ipswich butcher's son, who had worked so hard to ensure the success of the French campaign, was created Bishop of Lincoln. The base-born cleric had been plucked from obscurity when his brilliance was recognised by Richard Foxe, Bishop of Winchester, the ablest of the Councillors whom Henry had inherited from his father. His career was already set on its remarkable trajectory as one promotion succeeded the next: in quick succession he was made Archbishop of York, Chancellor of England, and Cardinal. Wolsey was to prove his worth yet again when in March Henry, still a political innocent, received a nasty shock.

Preparations for the wedding between Mary Rose and Charles of Castile, scheduled, according to the terms of the contract, to take place at Calais before 15 May, were already far advanced. Charles would be fourteen, the age of majority for boys. Mary had already approved the list submitted to her of temporary attendants for her Flemish household; her betrothed had sent her a pompous letter from Mechlin, addressing her as 'my good wife'. The letter was signed, in a childish hand, 'votre bon mari', but had been written by a secretary. Charles was a cold fish. Even his grandfather, the Emperor Maximilian, admitted the lad was 'as cold and immovable as an idol.'

England was in the throes of wedding fever. Henry, still fretfully convalescing from smallpox at Lambeth Palace, Westminster having been damaged by fire, energetically dictated memoranda planning next season's military campaign and despatched envoys to the Netherlands, bombarding Archduchess Margaret with queries about his sister's wedding: the precise number of riders in the three cavalcades that would

74

escort the Emperor, the Prince and the Archduchess: would there be enough hay for his horses this time? Was the provision of hangings and furniture for the Burgundian contingent to be his responsibility? Was the marriage to be solemnised in a private chapel or a parish church? He assumed that the principal royal visitors would bring their own beds with them, but he needed a detailed guest list. Since he proposed to march off to war immediately after the wedding, he needed to know what VIPs would be staying on in Calais and what provision he would need to make for their accommodation in England's last Continental possession.

At home, proud of his sister's beauty, celebrated throughout Europe, he personally supervised her trousseau. Charles was a lucky man: he was getting a jewel beyond price. Erasmus had told the Abbot of St Berthin that Prince Charles was blessed because his bride was a real beauty, a model of goodness and wisdom; Peter Martyr wrote that her deportment in dancing and conversation was as pleasing as anyone could desire. He added approvingly that her legendary complexion was achieved without the aid of cosmetics. Henry wanted to ensure that such loveliness was enshrined in the most fitting way possible. Impressed with Archduchess Margaret's good taste, he sent her swatches of fabric by royal courier, asking Margaret to 'devise all things' so that Mary's apparel would be 'Queenly and honourable.' The King wanted his sister to honour the Burgundian fashion, but, knowing her tastes and her colouring, he wished to select the materials himself. Margaret received a complete list of the Princess's retinue of 101 persons, which included two ladies in waiting, five gentlewomen, twelve gentlemen of the chamber, chamberers, chaplains, an almoner, several grooms and yeomen. Her officers included a tall sturdy doorkeeper whose job was to drive beggars away from her door.

For travelling Mary had a rich litter of cloth of gold lined with satin or damask, chariots, three wardrobe cars to transport her clothing, and splendid caparisons for her palfreys and horses. The Archduchess's advice was solicited on every aspect of her wardrobe and equipment.

In the ferment of preparation, the teenage bride allegedly carried about with her a miniature of her unknown bridegroom, 'sighing dutifully', as required. But Mary's time and energy were chiefly taken up with the delightful practical tasks of selecting and assembling her magnificent trousseau. The inventory of her plate and jewels ran to eleven pages, every item meticulously selected, down to the tiny silver-plated scales for weighing spices, and a little pot for ginger, with a fork. [2] Henry intended no expense to be spared. Besides jewels, Mary had dresses and robes, bonnets, mirrors, gold necklaces and chains, ornate girdles, and a golden coronet studded with gems to wear on her wedding day. Her chambers and stables were expensively equipped. Her gold and silver plate filled four coffers. The two gentlewomen who were to sleep in her chamber would be provided with pallet beds and fustian sheets, while Mary was to have a featherbed of fine down, with linen sheets, a bolster and two pillows. Her chapel was to have a silver crucifix, a private pew, vestments of purple and crimson, candlesticks, and a missal of fair print. Her household larder, buttery, almonry, scullery, chandlery, spicery, bakehouse and pantry were all set up. Hundreds of people, including the whole Court, were involved. Excitement was at fever pitch. Everyone was eagerly awaiting the summons to the Netherlands for the ceremony.

It never came.

The groom's government prevaricated, issuing one excuse after the other. Charles was ill; he was feeble, unfit to enter an early marriage; there was an outbreak of plague in Calais; Mary was too old for Charles, he needed a wife, not a mother [in England the nineteen-year-old Princess was officially being passed off as sixteen, perhaps anticipating this objection.] The seamstresses were still finishing Mary's gowns, when international politics intervened.

Henry's trusted ally, his father-in-law Ferdinand of Aragon, joined forces with Maximilian behind his back and signed another pact with Louis XII. Ferdinand, who, according to the

English Ambassador in Spain, was working against the marriage of Charles and Mary, announced a year's truce with France, while still protesting his good faith to England.

Louis seized on this as the thin end of the wedge leading to peace and quickly capitalised on it in hopes of breaking up the Holy League. He was confident that Spain would make a defensive alliance with France, offered the right inducement. He felt sure he had just the right lure: the hand of his three-year-old daughter, Renée, for the ten-year-old Infante Ferdinand. Renée would bring as her dowry Milan, Genoa and the other territories Louis and his armies had conquered.

Little Renée was to become the most frequently engaged Princess in Europe.

Louis then turned the pressure on Maximilian, who was caught in a dilemma, urged by France and Spain to join their alliance, and on the other hand, by Henry to continue the war and proceed with the marriage of Mary and Charles. Louis, with two marriageable daughters and now the backing of Spain, pressed his negotiations hard. Charles of Castile could have his pick of the two French princesses, little Renée or her older sister Claude, who, according to the Spanish ambassador, was lame and deformed.

The personal defects and intimate state of health of royal personages was under constant scrutiny. It attracted gossip, criticism and speculation. Whatever was said of Mary Rose, nobody denied that she was beautiful, sweet, and accomplished. Feted as the fairest Princess in Europe, her splendid trousseau poised for transport to the Continent, she had now been betrothed to Charles for six years. The Archduchess Margaret wrote urgently to her father the Emperor, stressing the importance of proceeding with the English marriage forthwith, for the safety of the Low Countries. She also pointed out that the treaty he had signed the previous year contained heavy penalty clauses. Towns, nobles and burgesses would have to foot the bill, if the nuptials were not celebrated before the end of May. Aware of her father's cupidity, she also reminded the Emperor that Henry was to pay £100,000 of Mary's dowry at Bruges.

Henry sent to Flanders urging them to get a move on with the nuptials, but again he was fobbed off. He was becoming angry and disillusioned. For Mary, it was disappointment and humiliation.

When Ferdinand deserted the Holy League to make peace with Louis XII, Maximilian quickly followed suit.

Henry, outraged by this betrayal by allies he had trusted, rose from his sickbed, fired with rage against Louis and disappointed and furious with Ferdinand. Peter Martyr wrote: 'The King of England bites his lips.'[4] Henry was now spoiling for another fight. His appetite for military campaigns had replaced his obsession with jousting; war was the real thing, and he wanted more of it. He had planned to arrive in Calais with his sister, see her wed to the Prince of Castile in a blaze of glory, and then continue his own valiant and warlike deeds against the French. Now, the wedding with Maximilian's grandson was clearly off.

Young and hot-headed, Henry cast around for a scapegoat. Poor Queen Katherine bore the brunt of his rage. Had the Spanish Princess not failed to provide him with an heir? Was she not the daughter of the treacherous Ferdinand? This sowed the first seeds of discord between the royal couple. Suddenly, Katherine's success in rallying the troops during Henry's absence and achieving victory at Flodden against the Scots – a feat of greater significance than any of Henry's much-trumpeted but essentially petty triumphs in France - faded into insignificance. The Queen was no longer his most trusted adviser. There were even rumours in Rome that year that divorce was on the cards.

The worst aspect of the betrayal by Ferdinand and Maximilian was that Mary was betrothed to the Prince of Castile, heir to both monarchs. Henry, outraged by their duplicity, declared he would attack France, even if the only support he could look for came from the Swiss. From this rash enterprise he was dissuaded by Pope Leo X, and by the combined efforts of Foxe and Wolsey. Wolsey, who had lived in Calais and remained strongly pro-French, advocated making peace with France. As he found himself obliged to deal with increasingly complex matters of national importance, the young King had begun to rely on Wolsey's judgment and advice even more than on Brandon's. While relations between Brandon and Wolsey remained superficially cordial, lacking the open animosity displayed by the Howards and Buckingham for the King's new Councillor, privately Brandon was discomfited by Wolsey's growing influence over the King. But Brandon would soon have cause to be eternally grateful to Wolsey. On one occasion, when he did forget how much he owed to the wily cleric, Wolsey quickly and sharply reminded him.

Leaving Wolsey to negotiate peace with France, Henry concentrated on another of his projects. He began building the first of his recreational complexes at Greenwich. The new larger tiltyard may have been completed in time for the tournament held in May 1514, when the King and Brandon appeared disguised as hermits, Henry in white velvet habit with a cloak of overlapping pieces of leather and a hat of cloth of silver, Brandon in black velvet. Before the violent joust began, both champions threw off their disguises and tossed them to the Queen and their ladies as largesse, as modern sporting celebrities throw their shirts. Now Henry was seen to be dressed all in black and Brandon in white. Both bore pennants with the motto: 'Who can hold that will away?' This was interpreted by the avid gossips as a reference to the notional romance between the Archduchess Margaret and Brandon.

Erasmus, who besides being a great thinker was an incorrigible newsmonger, wrote to his friend Gonnell: 'Rumour has it that Maximilian's daughter Margaret is to marry that new Duke, whom the King has recently turned from a stable-boy into a nobleman'.[5] This incautious remark was expurgated from the published edition of Erasmus's *Letters* printed in Basel five years later.

The story had to be quashed. Despite his feigned ignorance, Henry was well aware of the particular incident that had generated it; he also knew that it was largely his own fault. During his French campaign, he and Brandon had been frequent guests at the court of the Archduchess. As early as October 1513, Brandon's supposed flirtation with the Archduchess had set tongues wagging. Margaret was highly eligible. Intelligent and attractive, having buried two young husbands, she was only a little older than Brandon himself. Brandon was already contracted to his child ward, Elizabeth Grey, Baroness Lisle, now aged ten, and bore his title of Viscount Lisle by virtue of her right to it. Margaret feasted the King and his company lavishly, and Henry spent a fortune on gifts for her.

There prevailed an air of celebratory informality at the Archduchess's court; it was a hotbed of courtly love, where amorous dalliance was an acceptable part of the Continental tradition. Henry himself indulged in a courtly romance with a Flemish lady-in-waiting, Etienne de la Baume. According to a letter she wrote to him later, they laughed and joked together, and he called her 'his page'. Henry promised her a dowry of 10,000 crowns if she found a husband. In that highly charged atmosphere, gallant after-dinner flirtations were the order of the day.

Matters got out of hand: Henry's half-jocular suggestion of a possible marriage between the Archduchess and Brandon caused major embarrassment. Marshal of the Army and celebrated throughout England as a star of the tournament though he was, in the eyes of Continental aristocracy Brandon was merely a jumped-up East Anglian squire, certainly no match for the daughter of an Emperor. Later, Margaret reminded Henry exactly how the 'misunderstanding', as Henry and Margaret hastened to describe it when others began to take it seriously, arose. At Tournai Brandon had knelt before her, drawn a ring from her finger and tried it on his own; his clowning had made her fall about with laughter. Margaret spoke no English, and Brandon was pretending not to speak French. When Margaret could not get him to return her ring, after trying in French and then in Flemish, Henry stepped in as interpreter. Up till then, the jocularity had been within acceptable bounds, Brandon promising to be her 'rygthe humble servant', Margaret swearing 'to do unto hym alle honneur and plesure'.

Henry then urged her to take Brandon as a husband, as he had done on other occasions, saying she was too young to remain single. He told her that in England ladies remarried when they were fifty or sixty years old. Margaret firmly told him she had no such desire. Her experience of husbands had been less than favourable but he refused to believe her.

Margaret later tactfully noted that Henry, probably in his fondness for Brandon, over interpreted his desires. Henry and Brandon were probably flushed with wine and military conquest, relaxing in an atmosphere of mirth and conviviality, and showing off before the attractive Archduchess and her ladies. There was certainly a mutual attraction, if nothing more, between the handsome thirty-three-year-old Archduchess and the English Duke.

The tale of a budding romance spread until bets were being taken in London on the likelihood of a marriage. Margaret's enemies began to promote discreditable rumours. Crucially, the story reached the ears of Margaret's father, the Emperor Maximilian. Things had gone too far. Margaret assured her shocked father that it was a fabrication: she would rather die than entertain notions of such a mésalliance. Margaret idolised her nephew, Charles, and was reluctant to jeopardise his chance of marrying the King of England's sister.

Henry, knowing he was to blame, overreacted, setting in motion a major investigation into the source of the rumours, and threatening with death the rumourmongers themselves. He fired off letters of apology to Margaret and Maximilian, wondering disingenuously how such an idea could ever have entered people's heads.

Margaret asked him not to send Brandon back to Flanders to raise troops for next year's war, and Henry meekly agreed. He did, however, draw the line at commanding Brandon to marry little Lady Lisle, which would have scotched the scandal once and for all, and redeemed Margaret's reputation. Henry was not willing to sacrifice his friend's happiness on the altar of Anglo-

Imperial amity.

In any event, as Wolsey's efforts had borne fruit and the possibility of peace with France was becoming a reality, the need for an Anglo-Imperial alliance was less urgent. Henry demanded Thérouanne, Boulogne and St Quentin, plus 1½ million gold crowns, this sum to include arrears of pensions due from the Kings of France to the Kings of England since the 15th century. Wolsey had avenged the King's honour by out-tricking the tricksters.

As a final incentive in the peace negotiations, Henry threw into the deal the hand of one or other of his sisters as a bride for the ageing King Louis XII. If the King agreed to accept Margaret, the widowed Queen of Scots, Henry declared he could have her at a knock-down price; he was prepared to settle for a lower annual payment of 100,000 crowns. But Louis was not tempted by Margaret, even as a bargain. He had already seen Mary's portrait. Although the bride-price was higher, it was on beautiful Mary that the French King had set his heart.

Consequently, Mary was informed that, instead of being sent to the Netherlands as the bride of a sulky teenager, she was now to be despatched to Paris to become the cosseted bride of an elderly monarch.

5 - Notes

*As Pollard points out, 'Badoaro', whose name was anglicised in the Venetian Calendar, was not the author of the work attributed to him by Froude. The volume he cites is an anonymous, mutilated and pirated edition of Raviglio Rosso's *Historia*.

1. L & P Hen VIII vol 1 pt 22656
2. NA SP1/76 f195 (stamped f 168)
3. BL MS Cotton Vitellius CXI F52
4. L&P For&Dom Hen VIII vol 1 E5372697
5. *Complete Works of Erasmus*, 287

6   QUEEN OF FRANCE

Pock-marked, ailing and well beyond the first flush of youth, King Louis XII, like other male sovereigns of his time, was quite unabashed by his own lack of personal attractions and convinced that he could marry any lady he chose. Accordingly, before he settled on Mary Rose, he drew up a short list of five potential candidates and made a cool appraisal of their qualifications. First on the list was the Archduchess Margaret, who had been rejected by Louis' cousin, Charles VIII, in a daring bid for an advantageous political marriage with Anne of Brittany, despite the fact that Anne was already betrothed to Margaret's father, the Habsburg Holy Roman Emperor Maximilian. The marriage contract between Charles and Anne stated that if Anne should fail to provide the necessary male heir, she was bound to marry the King's successor. Anne, at fourteen, showed so little enthusiasm for the arranged marriage that her retainers arrived bearing two beds when she came to marry Charles and the couple lived apart much of the time. Even so, their cohabitation was sufficiently fruitful for Anne to spend most of her married life pregnant. The ceremony of dubious legal validity which sealed the union of Charles and

Anne, created the union of France and Brittany and enabled France to escape being encircled by Habsburg territories.

When, in 1498, Charles VIII struck his skull on a door lintel and died leaving no male heir, Louis, his cousin, had succeeded to the throne. His rebellions against Charles in the Foolish War had been forgiven, and he now cemented the vital union with Brittany by renouncing his wife, with alacrity and no regrets, and marrying his cousin's widow, Anne of Brittany. Described at fourteen by contemporaries at the time of her reluctant marriage to Charles as slight, brown-haired, with a limp and an air of cunning beyond her years, Anne had never been a beauty, but was said to be charming and to possess a certain air of nobility. By the time she married Louis, she was a shadow of her former self. From her seven pregnancies with Charles, no children had survived. She went on to become pregnant at least seven times by her new husband, Louis, but only two daughters, Claude and Renée, survived. When she died in 1514 at the age of thirty-six, the intelligent, cultured and strong-minded Anne was wan and exhausted.

Newly single, the King now considered the potential candidates for his hand. There was the Archduchess Margaret, her two nieces, Eleanor, sixteen, and Isabella, thirteen, and Henry VIII's two sisters, Margaret and Mary Rose Tudor. It was rumoured that the Archduchess was incapable of producing a live heir; Isabella was rather too young and her older sister Eleanor too slight and, more importantly, unattractive. King Ferdinand attempted to reassure Louis, telling him that thin women conceived more easily and were better breeders. But the King still found Eleanor unappealing.

There remained the Tudor sisters. Although the widowed Margaret Tudor had recently produced a male heir, thereby proving her fertility, France had no political need to woo Scotland. Scots help against England could always be depended upon. Besides, reports claimed that Margaret, at twenty-five, was growing stout and starting to lose her bloom.

That left Mary Rose. Tempted by reports of the younger Tudor Princess's legendary beauty, Louis listened attentively to accounts of her grace and vivacity. Crucially, the girl appeared healthy enough to breed successfully. Louis decided young Mary might suit him very well.

Peace negotiations between France and England had been encouraged by the Papal Nuncio who had arrived in London in January 1514. These had been further advanced behind the scenes by the Duc de Longueville who, although officially a hostage, was unofficially an envoy of the French King. By June, it was becoming clear that peace would soon be sealed.

Ferdinand made a last-ditch effort to salvage what he could: his envoy was instructed, if it were true that Louis was contractually bound to Mary, to press for the marriage of Princess Renée, the younger surviving child of Louis and Anne of Brittany, to the Infante Ferdinand; if Louis were not yet committed to Mary, then he must be persuaded to choose Eleanor instead.

On 30 July 1514, in a formal ceremony at Wanstead in Essex, Mary repudiated her contract to marry Charles of Castile. In a rehearsed speech, she renounced her marriage vows, charging her fiancé with breach of faith, and declaring that malicious gossip and evil counsel had turned him against her. Thus humiliated, she was no longer willing to keep her part of the bargain, so the contract was null and void. Disclaiming any wifely affection for the Prince, she swore before Wolsey, Norfolk and Suffolk that she was acting of her own volition, and was 'in all things ever ready to obey the King's good pleasure.'[1]

One week later, on 7 August, the treaty of peace and friendship between France and England was signed. But its public proclamation a few days later prompted no general rejoicing. There was no great love for the French among the people of England, and much bad blood. Londoners received the news in glum silence. There were no celebratory fanfares or ringing of bells. The mood throughout the country was far from conciliatory; the memory of recent hostile exchanges was too raw. Prior John, the freebooting French admiral from Rhodes, discovering that his Levantine galleys could out-manoeuvre any other vessel in the Mediterranean, had used them to harry

British vessels at every opportunity. In May 1514 he went even further, landing at Brighton, then a small hamlet on the Sussex coast. Before the watch were alerted, he and his men had set fire to the town and made off with 'such poor goods as he found'. When the alarm sounded, six battle-ready English archers chased the invaders back to their boat, wounding several, their arrows flying so thick and fast that they grazed Prior John's face.

When Edward Howard, the commander of Henry's fleet, heard of the outrage, with the King's encouragement, he commanded Sir John Wallop to sail to Normandy, where the English perpetrated fierce reprisals, burning 21 small towns and villages and destroying a number of French ships. Wallop's name has since become synonymous with a severe beating. Henry also sent Sir Thomas Lovell to strengthen the defences at Calais.

However, despite the resentment it caused in both countries and an armistice with the traditional enemy, the peace would be sealed by the projected marriage between the two royal families. Louis, having selected his bride, was now impatient to secure Mary Rose's hand without delay.

Accordingly, on 12 August 1514, Henry VIII wrote to inform the Pope of the change of plan. His sister, he explained, had been engaged to Prince Charles of Castile for six years. During this time, the Emperor and his government had prevaricated, reneged on their word and offered one specious excuse after the other, until the situation had become both humiliating and untenable. In consequence, to seal the new peace, the Princess Mary would now marry the King of France.

The negotiations were supposed to be secret, but news of the betrothal soon spread like wildfire. Horrified, the Archduchess Margaret, who had worked for so long to bring about the marriage between Mary and her nephew Charles, sent envoys to London to find out if it were true. When she learned that it was, she burst into tears. Prince Charles, when informed by his councillors, bitterly accused everyone of breaking their promises and disrespecting him because of his youth. In an unpleasant episode which indicates something of the character of Prince Charles, and suggests Mary may have had a lucky escape, he gave a cruel and graphic symbolic response when his councillors told him that he was young, whereas the King of France, as the first King in Christendom, had the pick of princesses. Thrown into a furious sulk, the prince turned to stare out of his window. His eye fell upon a man with a hawk on his wrist. He sent one of his courtiers to buy the bird. The courtier reported back that, apparently, the hawk was young and not fully trained, so not a sporting bird fit for a prince. Charles stormed out, thrust some coins at the man and seized the unfortunate bird himself. Returning to his council chamber with the hawk perched on his fist, he began before their startled eyes to pluck out its feathers one by one. To their appalled murmurs, he announced: 'You asked me why I plucked this hawk; he is young, you see, and because he is young he is held in small account, and because I am young, you have plucked me at your good pleasure; and because I was young, I knew not how to complain.' He added with scorn 'Bear in mind that for the future I shall pluck you.'[2]

While England's former European allies speculated wildly, the proxy wedding of the French King and the English Princess was arranged for Sunday 13 August. Mary dutifully set about learning more about her prospective bridegroom.

Louis XII, third Duc d'Orléans, born around 1462, was the son and heir of Charles d'Orléans, the poet prince captured at the battle of Agincourt, who spent 25 years in England. His mother was the delightful Mary of Cleves who presided over the lively and cultured court of Blois, which throughout Louis's life became his favourite bolthole, where he relaxed from the stresses of kingship. In his youth, Louis was athletic and physically impressive, excelling at various sports. This 'lusty and beautiful' young man was forced at the age of fourteen, for dynastic reasons, into a marriage with his unfortunate cousin Princess Jeanne.

Jeanne's congenital deformity was such that her own callous father, 'Spider Louis', King Louis XI, vilified her as the most hideous thing imaginable. She was frail, hunchbacked and lame, and suffered from a number of incurable conditions. She had little hope of ever bearing children. Poor little Jeanne was only eight when the travesty of a marriage was celebrated and the cousins were pronounced man and wife. Jeanne bore her afflictions patiently and even grew to care for her husband, although Louis made no secret of his disgust at being tied to this pathetic figure. He could hardly swallow his repugnance when in her presence and for most of the twenty-two years of their grotesque sham of a marriage they lived apart. Louis, angry and frustrated, sought adventure, both romantic and political, wherever he could

His father in law, Spider Louis, died in 1483 and was succeeded by Jeanne's thirteen-year-old brother Charles VIII, who was as deformed in body as his sister, and, although nicknamed 'The Affable', much less intelligent. Louis, recognising the inadequacy of Charles, made a bid for the Regency, leading to the 'Foolish War'; he spent three years in prison for his recklessness.

When, in 1498, he finally inherited the throne of France at the age of thirty-six, Louis had lived a hard life and his physique and health had suffered: the former sportsman was a broken down old man. Anne of Brittany, his predecessor's widow, was under contract to marry him. She agreed to honour the obligation on condition that Louis obtained an annulment of his marriage to Jeanne within a year. He immediately set wheels in motion, proclaiming as grounds that Jeanne was infertile, despite her protestations to the contrary. The current Pope was the accommodating and politically astute Alexander VII. Alexander needed French military aid in Italy; in return for this, plus a title, a fief and a French bride for his son, the infamous Cesare Borgia, he granted the annulment. Tragic Jeanne, 'given to God because she was not good enough for man', retired to a convent, where she died six years later. She founded the monastic order of the Sisters of the annunciation of Mary, and was canonised in May 1950 as St Joan of Valois.

Having repudiated Jeanne in the most humiliating way

possible, including public descriptions of her alleged physical deformities, rather than adopting the gentlemanly path of pleading consanguinity as grounds for annulment – the usual excuse at the time, and one to which many persons would have been willing and able to bear witness in the case of Louis and Jeanne, through various marriage contracts – in 1499 Louis acquired a bride more to his taste. The Dowager Queen Anne of Brittany, the widow of his cousin and brother-in-law, Charles VIII, had excellent prospects, and was hopefully capable of bearing him an heir. As heiress to the rich feudatory province of Brittany, the one large quasi-independent state that 'Spider' Louis XI had failed to integrate into his empire, ambitious suitors had competed for Anne's hand since her early childhood. At the age of five she had been betrothed to the Emperor Maximilian. When her father, Francis II of Brittany, died in 1488 without male issue, the pledge was reinforced by a proxy marriage which was never consummated – the couple never actually met – and Anne was married off to Charles VIII in 1491. This marriage could easily have been as disastrous as that of Louis XII and Jeanne, but, despite Anne's initial reluctance, and the fact that her husband forbade her to use her title of Duchess, it turned out quite well. France acquired Brittany, and Charles got a wife who grew to accept his physical and mental challenges.

Anne was a fairly small woman whose beauty was never exalted even in an age when the physical attractions of queens and princesses were habitually exaggerated, and she was lame. Yet, although Louis had reacted with queasy inhumanity to his first wife's disabilities, despite her imperfect physique, he adored 'his Bretonne'. Anne proved a helpful Queen and a pleasant companion. Her court at Blois retained its reputation for culture and education.

In only one respect did she fail Louis, but that failure was crucial. Providing a male heir was a wife's first duty. Lack of heirs, and the unfortunate gender of female children, was always blamed on the woman.

Anne gave Louis several children, but they were not what he

required: stillborn sons, and two surviving children who were mere girls. Under Salic law, Princess Claude, the first-born, could not inherit the throne of France, but she would have Brittany. Anne had insisted in her marriage contract that the duchy should revert to the second son or, failing male issue, a daughter could inherit. She knew in her heart that betrothing Claude to her husband's son-in-law, François d'Angoulême, a great-great-grandson of King Charles V, was the sensible thing to do, but she fought against it tooth and nail, her opposition fuelled by her dislike of Francis's scheming mother, Louise of Savoy. Louis, conscious of his own failing health, pushed for the match, to ensure France's continued possession of Brittany. The last year of their marriage was not harmonious. Louis got his way over the betrothal, but he was embittered over his Queen's determined opposition to it. It also rankled that, when she thought he was on his deathbed, Anne attempted to salvage whatever she could by sending off boatloads of plate, jewels and the best of the royal furniture to her own château at Nantes.

However, as it happened, Louis recovered, and outlived her by almost a year. Anne died on January 9 1514, 'wonderfully lamented;' she was accorded a royal burial in Paris and entombed in the church of St Denis. As she had wished, her heart was removed and placed in a raised enamel gold reliquary, to be sent to Nantes where it was placed in the tomb of her parents.

Now in his fifties, Louis's health was far from robust, yet he proposed to embark on matrimony for this third time, with Princess Mary Rose, from dynastic as well as diplomatic motives. He had been plagued by premonitions of death since the demise of his beloved Anne. 'Before the year is out, I shall be with her, to keep her company', he had sobbed over her coffin. Having only daughters, he desperately needed a son and heir, otherwise his throne would pass to his son-in-law François d'Angoulême, whose betrothal to Princess Claude when she was seven was consummated with their marriage in May 1514. Louis dreaded that Francis, with his extravagant Renaissance ideas, would ruin France.

Louis, formerly rash and improvident, had grown cautious and thrifty. He was paying the physical price for his years of prodigality and over-indulgence, and for the debilitation exacerbated by his spell in prison. He suffered from gout and a skin condition. People who saw him in later years referred to him as infirm and diseased. On at least two occasions, he had in fact been given up for dead. The previous summer, in 1513, when he led his troops against Henry's English forces, the comment had been made that the King's heart was stronger than his legs. That autumn, he had to be carried to the battlefield in a carriage. In the English Parliament the following January, his increasing infirmities were contrasted with the robust vigour of Henry VIII, 'who is like the rising sun, that grows brighter and stronger each day.'[3]

France, on the other hand, was thriving under his governance. Even the Italian wars, fostering the Valois dream of an empire beyond the Alps, did not affect growing domestic prosperity or prevent the administrative reforms that were improving conditions for the populace. His chief minister, Cardinal d'Amboise, was responsible for the financial measures, but Louis got both the credit and the blame. He settled down to become a good and caring King, earning the epithet 'the father of his people'. Life at the French court, previously brimming with gaiety and characterised by conspicuous over-indulgence, was quieter. When courtiers grumbled at the frugality of the royal household, Louis replied that he preferred listening to their sneers at his parsimoniousness to hearing the groans of the people labouring under the yoke of their Sovereign's extravagance.

Now a royal wedding to a, with attendant sumptuous festivities and lavish feasting, raised everyone's spirits. An official at the Venetian Embassy, Nicolo di Favri – the same Favri who had repeated the distressing story of Charles of Castile and the unfortunate young hawk to his friend Francesco Gradenigo – joined the guests as the court foregathered in the great banqueting hall at Greenwich. Everyone was in a ferment of excitement to see Princess Mary married to the King of

France. Resplendent in cloth-of-gold and rich silks, wearing heavy gold chains about their necks, the Dukes of Norfolk and Suffolk, Dorset and Buckingham, and the principal nobles assembled early in the morning in the hall, which had been decked with arras of cloth-of-gold, bordered with unembroidered frieze emblazoned with the royal arms of France and England.

The buzz of pleasantries was hushed when, three hours later, the King and Queen arrived – Katherine, in silvery satin with a little gold Venetian cap on her head, visibly and joyfully pregnant again, closely followed by Mary Rose, bedecked with jewels, wearing a kirtle of silver-grey satin under a purple and gold chequered gown which matched, as French tradition demanded, the robes of the French King's representative, the Duc de Longueville. Mary looked stunning and appeared composed. Such was her innocent radiance that di Favri thought she looked sixteen, not nineteen. After a Latin sermon by Archbishop Warham, Archbishop of Canterbury, vows in French, rings, and a kiss were exchanged. After the nuptial Mass, there followed a banquet. Two hours of energetic dancing were led by the King and Buckingham, who removed their long gowns and danced informally in their doublets, even older dignitaries energetically following suit.

The dancing concluded, a frisson of anticipation ran through the company as they proceeded to the official bedding, a symbolic act which supposedly represented consummation and thereby rendered the union irrevocable. In an adjacent chamber a great bed had been prepared for the bridal couple. Mary, who had now changed from her wedding gown into a magnificent déshabille, lay down on the bed, with one leg bared to the thigh. The Duc de Longueville, having removed his red hose, also bared a leg, with which he touched the bride. Warham then declared the marriage consummated, at which the 'King of England made much rejoicing.'[4] Later the legal documents were drawn up and signed in de Longueville's chamber. His ransom paid, the noble hostage returned home next day with ten horses and a cart weighed down with two thousand pounds' worth of gifts, one of which was the splendid gown worn by the King the previous evening. This garment alone was valued at three hundred ducats.

In some quarters the marriage caused outrage. Resentful that Mary was not, after all, to come to the Netherlands, the Dutch 'spake shamefully of this marriage, that a feeble, old and pocky man should marry so fair a lady'[5]. From Valladolid Peter Martyr expressed the Spanish view that 'an old valetudinarian'[6] should not consort with a handsome girl of eighteen. She would be the death of him. To Queen Katherine's chagrin, the Spanish ambassador boycotted the wedding and left London.[7]

Yet if Mary herself had objections, she kept them to herself. There has been some speculation that Mary, wearied and humiliated by the Charles of Castile fiasco, almost welcomed the prospect of becoming Queen of France, preferring to marry an aged monarch rather than a shilly-shallying adolescent with a Habsburg lantern jaw and jutting lip. Marrying Louis was a matter of politics; Mary had little choice. Her own motto, 'To do God's will is enough for me', was an ironic summary of her position. Her brother had appealed to her sense of patriotism and duty, mentioning 'the peace of Christendom'. The French King had no male heir. If Mary could manage to put aside her personal feelings and any revulsion inspired by his geriatric fumblings, and eventually produce the longed-for Dauphin, thereby ousting Francois d'Angoulême from the succession, she would establish herself and her brother at the head of the most powerful alliance in Europe.

What puzzled the Venetian ambassador Badoer was the air of exultation the Princess radiated as she tripped down the aisle. Surely mere satisfaction that she was fulfilling a patriotic and dynastic duty could not account for it. He could only assume she was dazzled by the realization of her august new status. In his report to the Signory, he commented: 'The Queen [Princess Mary] does not mind that the King [of France] is a gouty old man…and she herself a young and beautiful damsel…so great is her satisfaction at being Queen of France.'[8]

Few realised that there were very different reasons for Mary's serene and blissful aspect.

What buoyed Mary's spirits on her wedding day and throughout the remainder of 1514 was the knowledge of the secret bargain she had managed to make with her brother the King. Between her repudiation of Charles of Castile on 30 July and the drafting of the meticulous French marriage treaty, signed in its final form on 14 September, she had somehow succeeded in extracting from Henry a promise which he had probably made on the spur of the moment, and had little real intention of fulfilling, his sole aim being to get the French marriage accomplished quickly, with as little protest from the bride as possible. Whether his heart was in the promise or not, Mary was quietly determined to hold Henry to his word.

Historians have suggested this shows a crafty and calculating side to Mary's usually sunny character.

But we should reflect, perhaps, on the limited scope of women's options. In the Tudor taxonomy of world order, woman was an inferior creature, in thrall to man. Even a Princess was relatively powerless, a mere pawn in the political game, with little room to manoeuvre and few possibilities open to her other than to manipulate men and exploit every twist of fate. This required a certain opportunistic sleight-of-hand, even on the part of women not by nature scheming or underhand. Mary, already deeply in love, had the strongest possible motivation to find the courage to force Henry into striking a deal. She certainly must have been reluctant to leave home to be married off to an ailing monarch thirty-four years her senior whom she had never met. She was already infatuated with Charles Brandon.

The letters that passed between Mary, Brandon and Wolsey in 1515 reveal that not only was the King aware of his sister's feelings, but that she had only 'consented to his request, and for the peace of Christendom, to marry Lewis of France, though he was very aged and sickly',[9] on condition that, if she survived him, she should marry whom she liked. Mary played her trump card skilfully.

In the light of that bargain, the more ailing and sickly her husband appeared, the better, for the sooner would she be united with the man she loved.

Hugging this secret knowledge, small wonder that Mary appeared overjoyed.

6 - Notes

1. L&P Hen VIII vol 1 pt 2 3139
2. CSP Ven vol II505
3. L&P Hen VIII vol 1 18
4. CSP: Ven
5. Hall 569
6. L&P Hen VIII vol 1 pt 2 3334
7. L&P Hen VIII vol 1 E5372697
8. Marino Sanuto, *Diarii*, vol xix
9. L&P Hen VIII vol 1 75

7   LA ROSE VERMEILLE

Louis, exhilarated by the prospect of acquiring a beautiful young bride and impatient to see for himself what he was getting, despatched to England the French portrait painter Jehan Perréal, with orders to capture a good likeness of the princess. Perréal was probably the artist to whom the task of designing the reliquary for the heart of the French King's last Queen, Anne of Brittany, had been entrusted. Louis had confidence in Perréal's taste. The English were not famous for their dress sense, so the artist was also tasked with helping the Princess design a trousseau in keeping with the latest Paris fashions. Clearly, the splendid wardrobe prepared in England for Mary's planned marriage to the Prince of Castile would not suffice for a Queen of France, although Mary's dressmakers found that some small economies were achievable. It was found possible to remodel some gowns, and the insignia of Castile was speedily unpicked from the more valuable items, and then embroidered over with the fleur-de-lis.

Otherwise, expense was not shunned. Henry again raided his coffers, determined to send his sister off in style. She would arrive in Paris, sumptuously attired, with an array of gorgeous gowns in the English and Milanese styles, with matching hats, in cloth-of-gold, silks, rich brocades and crimson velvet. He supplemented her already considerable store of jewellery with sapphires, rubies and diamonds in settings representing the Tudor rose and the fleur-de-lis, and extended her inventory of luxurious furnishings. Once completed, the magnificent trousseau was loaded on elegant closed carts, emblazoned with Mary's coat of arms and with her new rightful emblem, the fleur-de-lis. Goldsmith's work embellished her saddlecloths, chapel hangings and bed curtains. It had been a mammoth task, everyone working at top speed under pressure. It was therefore perhaps with a touch of irony that Henry added to Mary's massive impedimenta a set of seven superb tapestries depicting the labours of Hercules...[1]

In contrast to the wavering indifference and stilted formality displayed by her youthful Habsburg suitor, Charles of Castile, Mary now found herself an old man's darling; her doting elderly bridegroom bombarded her with letters and gifts. The Sieur de Marigny, who accompanied Jehan Perréal to London, brought along two coffers crammed with jewellery, so heavy that they had to be carried into the Presence Chamber on a sturdy white horse. With a flourish, de Marigny presented Mary with the crowning glory of the gem collection, the legendary pearl-and-diamond pendant known as the 'Mirror of Naples', which had belonged to the father of Anne of Brittany. Henry, impressed in spite of himself, quickly sent the pendant off to be valued by the 'jewellers of the Row.' Awestruck, Lorenzo Pasqualio, an Italian merchant resident in London, described it as a diamond as big as a finger, surmounting a pearl the size of a pigeon's egg. He estimated its value at 60,000 crowns.[2]

Meanwhile, Henry sent the Earl of Worcester to France to final the paperwork for both the peace treaty and the marriage. Worcester reported back that the marriage was proving very popular with the French. Mary's jointure was to comprise the traditional lands and revenues enjoyed by a Queen of France. Like her predecessor, Anne of Brittany, she was to have the town of La Rochelle, the county of Saintonge, Chinon with its fine castle and the revenues from Rochefort, Pezenas, Montigny,

Cessenon and Cabrières, in addition to dues from Montpellier and rents and taxes from other estates scattered all over France, to the tune of 10,000 'livres tournois'.[3] According to the Venetians, Henry was also hoping she would be granted the Duchy of Milan. Louis was to pay Henry the million crowns stipulated in the peace treaty.

Mary's dowry would be 40,000 gold crowns, including her plate and jewellery. However, Henry's advisers, mindful of Louis's poor health, ensured that the contract included a proviso guaranteeing the return of Mary's personal property, if the King should die. Once the contracts were signed and sealed, Louis underwent a proxy betrothal ceremony. Mary was represented by the Earl of Worcester. The French, bamboozled by his name, recorded it as 'Nonshere'.

Thankfully, this ceremony, unlike that held in England, dispensed with the symbolic 'bedding' and the touching of naked legs...

Mary's retinue would include, as Mother of the Maids, Lady Guildford, the widow of Sir Richard Guildford, Controller of the Household to Henry VII. Lady Guildford had been a lady-in-waiting to both Mary's grandmothers, Elizabeth Woodville and Margaret Beaufort. She would be Lady of the Bedchamber, chaperone and mentor to the young Queen, offering guidance and advice to both Mary Rose and the younger, dizzier members of her suite. She had been especially chosen for this delicate appointment by Henry, Wolsey and Katherine. Of unimpeachable English descent and forthright character, she spoke French well. Despite Perréal's interference, she ensured that English milliners received their share of the lucrative orders for the Princess's trousseau and the apparel of her entourage. By 12 September, over £76 had been spent in London on hats alone.[4] The wedding had benefited the London garment trade. In appreciation of her custom, before Mary left for France, drapers, mercers and haberdashers, many of them from abroad, foregathered to bid her godspeed. Mary wore a costly gown in the French fashion, of woven gold, and graciously gave her hand to each. To the general delight, she made a brief speech of thanks in French, which she had been practising with her tutor, John Palsgrave. Everyone hoping for a place in Mary's entourage had been polishing up their language skills. Pasqualigo noted that 'the whole court now speaks both French and English, as in the time of the late King'.

Golden-haired[5] Mary was now a major celebrity: her appearance and demeanour were scrutinised and analysed by commentators both at home and abroad. Peter Martyr praised her dancing and conversation. Pasqualigo described Mary as 'very beautiful, tall, fair, of a light complexion with a colour, and most affable and graceful. She wore a gown in the French fashion, of wove gold, very costly'. Mesmerised by Mary's beauty, Pasqualigo called her 'a 'nymph from heaven, a paradise'.[6]

The agents of the Archduchess Margaret, aunt of Charles, Mary's former betrothed, reported that Mary was lovely, and, contrary to malicious rumour, she could not be described as 'oversized.' This probably referred to her height, rather than her weight.

Philip Sieur de Brégilles wrote in March 1514 to the Archduchess Margaret: 'I think never man saw a more beautiful creature, nor one having so much grace and sweetness, in public and in private. There are not any so small or so sweet as she'. Ambassador Gérard de Pleine, after studying Mary carefully, informed the Archduchess: 'I think I never saw a more charming creature. She is very graceful. Her deportment in dancing and conversation is as pleasing as you could desire. There is nothing gloomy or melancholy about her... I assure you she has been very well educated'. He noted her good figure and outstanding beauty. She was less tall than he had believed, and would have been a much better match for Prince Charles than he had imagined before seeing her.[7] But Charles was the past. Now Mary was to be a Queen.

Her final preparations for the move to France complete, in August 1514, Mary joined King Henry on his summer progress. In the royal cavalcade, sister and brother rode side by side, followed by a great procession of nobles glittering in cloth-of-gold, golden chains jingling. Queen Katherine, well advanced in her fourth pregnancy, travelled in a litter. She had suffered a miscarriage the previous September. During the New Year revels of 1514 Henry embarked on an affair with Bessie Blount, Lord Mountjoy's charming teenage cousin, an interlude interrupted by Henry's attack of smallpox. No sooner had he recovered than Katherine was pregnant again.

King Louis, too, was hoping his marriage to a young, healthy and desirable Princess would produce the longed-for heir who would displace as Dauphin his daughter Princess Claude's husband, Francis, about whom the ageing monarch held grave misgivings. Francis had been brought up by his clever, fiercely ambitious mother, the widowed Louise of Savoy. Louise, widowed at nineteen, had focussed her whole life on her son. She deplored the thought that her ambitions would be dashed if this English princess provided Louis with an heir. When Louis left Paris on 22 September to meet Mary at Abbeville, Louise balefully recorded in her journal: 'The King, *very antique and feeble*, has gone to meet his *young* bride' – representing Louis as a lustful old rake drooling at the prospect of a smooth-limbed maiden.[8]

Louis, rackety in youth, had grown moralistic. When the names of Mary's permanent attendants were submitted for his approval, Louis raised only one only objection, to Mary's childhood companion Jane Poppincourt. The King had learned – probably from the Earl of Worcester – of Jane's liaison with de Longueville. The Duc was married to a Princess who would be among the guests at the royal wedding. Louis, feigning moral outrage, struck Jane's name off the list, declaring that he would rather see such an wanton female burned alive than have her anywhere near his new wife.

Mary's departure was delayed by foul weather. At last, on 2 October, she was able to take ship. At the waterside in Dover, Henry embraced her and gave her his blessing, saying: 'I betoken you to God and the fortunes of the sea, and the government of the King your husband.'[9] Mary took advantage of his evident emotion to remind Henry of the promise she had extracted from him earlier.

Escorted by the Duke of Norfolk, she then embarked for France with a fleet of fourteen ships. The plan had been for de Longueville to welcome her at Boulogne with a retinue of 200 French ladies, but the autumn storms continued to disrupt arrangements. On 4 October, ten days later than expected, the new Queen of France, pale, dishevelled and soaked to the skin, was borne through the waves to her new country by Sir Christopher Garnyshe and deposited on dry land, where she was received by the Duke of Vendôme and the Cardinal of Amboise.

She travelled on to the village of Montreuil, where she rested, tidied up and recovered from her ordeal, while her servants unpacked the gown which had been specially selected for her first meeting with her bridegroom. At 2 in the afternoon on 8 October, messengers rode post-haste to inform the King that Mary was on her way to Abbeville. Louis sent the Dauphin Francis, accompanied by the royal dukes, to escort her procession. This was part of an elaborate romantic stratagem: Renaissance custom demanded that the happy couple's first meeting should have the character of a chance encounter. Accordingly, Francis detained Mary's party at a prearranged rendezvous about two miles from Abbeville. Suddenly, as by coincidence, Louis appeared, dressed for a hawking expedition. (Somewhat belying the pretended impromptu nature of this encounter, Louis was, nonetheless, accompanied by 200 gentlemen, a guard of mounted archers and the Swiss foot guards, as well as by the Cardinals of Auch and Bayeux, and also the Duke of Albany, who, as the heir to Mary's infant nephew, James V of Scotland, was such a thorn in the flesh of Mary's older sister, Margaret).

Louis, although showing his age, cut a fine figure in a short riding dress of cloth-of-gold on crimson, mounted on his splendid Andalusian horse, Bayart, caparisoned in cloth-of-gold chequered with black satin. According to the Dauphin's best friend, the young Sieur de Fleuranges, the elderly, gout-ridden King made Bayart perform the caracole. However well trained the horse, this sideways dressage manoeuvre requires good balance and a strong seat and legs on the part of the rider. It must have delighted the crowd, who had braved the persistent Normandy drizzle to observe the historic meeting of the royal couple.

There followed a romantic pantomime in which Mary blew Louis a kiss – shocking the Venetian observers – and he gamely blew one back, then rode up and embraced her properly from the saddle. One Venetian noted that the King kissed his bride 'as kindly as if he had been five and twenty and came in this dress and on horseback the more to prove his vigour'.[10] Mary sportingly pretended to be astonished by this apparently unscheduled encounter. However, her gown of cloth-of-gold on a crimson ground had been carefully designed to match Louis's outfit perfectly, thus rather giving the game away...

The royal couple exchanged pleasantries. The King greeted Norfolk and the English lords, and then continued with his hawking expedition, while Mary made her grand entry into Abbeville, accompanied by princes and nobles in a spectacular piece of theatre. The Swiss Guard marched first, followed by the French gentlemen and then, skilfully matched and choreographed by the Master of the Horse, the French princes and English lords in pairs, dressed in gorgeous brocades, their signature gold chains looped about their necks and shoulders up to six times: one wit joked that the English milords looked like prisoners, weighed down by the shackles of their wealth.[11]

The Papal, Venetian and Florentine Ambassadors followed in the procession. Fleuranges later estimated Mary's escort at 2,000 chevaliers. Mary, mounted on a white horse, was preceded by her squires dressed in silk with heavy gold collars. Four footmen held over her a canopy of white satin, embroidered with the roses of England and two bristling porcupines, the heraldic beasts which traditionally supported the arms of France. Her hair was dressed 'in the English fashion' with gold and pearl ornaments; she wore a gown with tight-fitting sleeves, also considered to be an English fashion, but she changed en route, and when she arrived at Abbeville to a civic welcome by the dignitaries and the deafening roar of a salute from the cannon, she was wearing white and gold brocade, embroidered with jewels. She wore her crimson silk hat throughout, jauntily cocked over her left eye.[12] Two running footmen in velvet caps and black and gold chequered doublets kept pace with her palfrey. The Dauphin Francis rode at her side wearing a surcoat of silver and gold, remaining outside the canopy in order not to usurp Mary's place as the centrepiece of the glorious cavalcade.

Three carriages had been shipped over from England for the procession. The first two were covered in cloth-of-gold, drawn by horses wearing golden bridles. Each carriage transported four sumptuously attired ladies, probably including the Duchess of Norfolk, her daughter the Countess of Oxford, and Lady Guildford. Then came six ladies mounted on palfreys caparisoned in cloth-of-gold and purple velvet. Another carriage, decked in crimson velvet, was occupied by four more ladies. More ladies followed the carriages, their mounts decked in mulberry-coloured velvet, edged with silk fringing in white and light blue. After the ladies 200 archers marched in pairs, the first row wearing the Tudor livery of green and white. Their precision deeply impressed Fleuranges, himself a seasoned soldier, affectionately nicknamed by Louis 'the Young Adventurer,' a name which Fleuranges would use to describe himself when writing his Memoir.

Among the Queen's ladies rode Henry VIII's future mistress Mary Boleyn, the older daughter of Sir Thomas Boleyn, Henry's semi-permanent Ambassador in the Low Countries. The younger Boleyn sister, thirteen-year-old Anne, had been sent the previous year to the court of the Archduchess Margaret, regarded as one of the finest finishing schools in Europe. Anne was said to have taken to French and to Continental ways like a duck to water. In these days of their youth, before their mutual antipathy had deepened to loathing, Mary Rose had requested Anne Boleyn by name as one of her *demoiselles d'honneur*. Reluctantly, Margaret allowed Anne to leave. But she did not join Mary's retinue in time for the grand entry into Abbeville.

When the procession reached the town centre, Mary attended

a Mass of thanksgiving at the Church of St Vulfran before rejoining the King for a state reception. She was welcomed in the main city square by the King's elder daughter, her new step-daughter, the unattractive but worthy Claude, wife of the Dauphin Francis. Princess Claude conducted her new stepmother to her apartments in the palace, the ancient Hôtel de Gruthuse, separated by a pleasant garden from the King's apartments.

That evening a grand ball was hosted by Claude and Francis, whose talent for organising spectacular entertainments rivalled that of the Tudors. The night could easily have ended in disaster. A fire broke out in a quarter where many of the Venetians were lodging, and four houses burned down. The Venetians were saved by the river that flowed between their lodgings and the fire. The blaze could have been brought under control much earlier had it been permitted to ring the alarm bells, but this was forbidden, to avoid disturbing the King at his amusements.[13]

The Venetians reported back from the French court so assiduously, because the Venetian Signory desperately needed to know whether Louis intended to try to recapture Milan. After losing their greatest general, the brilliant Gaston de Foix, at the Battle of Ravenna two years previously, the French had been forced to retreat from Milan, leaving the Sforzas back in power. Shortly after Mary arrived in France, the Venetian Ambassador, Marco Dandolo, managed to broach the subject. The King, who but a few months previously had publicly lamented that his days were numbered, and his sole desire was to join his late wife Anne of Brittany in her coffin, was now fired with renewed optimism. He announced that not only did he intend to mount another Italian expedition, but added that Mary had begged him to show her Venice, and he intended to do so, as a conqueror.[14]

The morning after the ball, the Venetian informant reported that Mary, with the Duke of Norfolk and other lords in her entourage, had risen before daybreak. The wedding procession formed up outside the Queen's apartments in the cold October dawn. The English knights wore sumptuous, sable-lined damask, velvet, satin, and cloth-of-gold. Mary proceeded through the garden, preceded by 236 knights, 2 heralds and the royal mace-bearers, the Duke of Norfolk, as her brother's representative, at her side, her ladies following, each walking between two gentlemen, holding their caps in their hands. There was a great crush inside the palace, where the Bishops of Auch and Bayeux were to perform the marriage in a great hall hung with cloth-of-gold.

Mary entered to a fanfare of trumpets. Her golden hair flowed about her shoulders, crowned with a coronet of precious stones. Her gown was of gold brocade edged with ermine and ablaze with diamonds. The Venetians nodded in approval, finding this French design a great improvement on the Princess's English gowns. Louis, also wearing ermine-trimmed gold brocade, swept off his hat and bowed. Mary curtsied. The King raised her to her feet, kissed her, and then, taking from his Treasurer Robertet a superb necklace of rubies and pearls, he fastened it about her neck. After the nuptial Mass, Mary curtsied again gracefully and retired to her own apartments to dine with her ladies.

That evening, the royal couple co-hosted a three-day feast and ball at the Hôtel de Gruthuse. At eight o'clock, the pregnant Dauphine Claude led her stepmother to her bridal bed, which had already been officially blessed by the bishops. The Dauphin's circle, led by his mother Louise of Savoy, feigned detachment from the whole event, but were in reality agog. Louise recorded scathingly: 'On 9 October took place the *amorous* marriage of Louis XII, King of France, and Mary of England. They were married at ten in the morning and in the evening they went to bed together.'[15] To his intimates, Francis declared that his father-in-law's marriage had 'pierced his heart'. Privately, he muttered to his friend Fleuranges that the King was incapable of begetting a son.

However, next day, the King triumphantly asserted that he had 'crossed the river three times that night and would have done more had he chosen.'[16] Courtiers greeted this boast with amazement, incredulity and lewd giggles. Fleuranges for one was in no doubt. 'In the morning the King said he had performed marvels'. He added sardonically 'I certainly believe this was true, for he was most uncomfortable.'[17] Louis appeared remarkably rejuvenated. The French were euphoric, the Venetians fretful. The Venetian ambassador wrote:

> Everything is held up, politics like the rest. No one speaks of anything but fêtes. There you have the French. They always believe that what they wish for will be successful. This marriage has been a success; they see themselves already installed in Milan. They feared only England; this phantom has vanished. The King says everywhere that he will take Milan or die...no one thinks of an obstacle, which terrifies me. To amuse himself with a wife of 18 is very dangerous at his age.[18]

Possibly Louis had indeed overdone things; he promptly suffered a new attack of what was described as 'gout', a contemporary catch-all term for ailing joints. Consequently, the state entry into Paris was postponed. The court remained at Abbeville. Francis spent his time planning grand tournaments to celebrate Mary's coronation.

Perhaps illness made Louis irritable. Mary had been upset when he had objected to the appointment of Jane Poppincourt, because of her 'evil life'. Now Louis once again threw his weight about, causing the only known rift during their brief marriage. Louis, reflecting that Mary's large entourage would represent a drain on the French exchequer, remembered how his last Queen had undermined his authority by filling her household with uppity Bretons. He summarily dismissed many of Mary's suite, including Lady Guildford. Mary was dismayed. 'Mother Guildford', her former governess, known since childhood, had been a tower of strength. She was a source of comfort and a welcome link with home in Mary's demanding new situation and new country. Some authorities, noting the Venetian Ambassador's observation that the day after his wedding the elderly King of France seemed 'very jovial, gay and in love', conjecture that the wedding night had been an unexpected ordeal for the 'nymph from heaven', and that the bride had confided intimate details to the experienced Lady Guildford. Certainly, Mary dreaded the prospect of staying in France without Lady Guildford's reassuring presence. She had been deprived even of her secretary Palsgrave, her former tutor. Feeling desolate, she dictated an appeal to her 'kind and loving brother' on 12 October:

> My Good Brother,
>
> As heartily as I can I recommend me to your Grace. I marvel much that I have [not] heard from you since my departing, so often as I have sent and written to you. Now I am left post alone, in effect, for on the morn next after my marriage my Chamberlain and all other menservants were discharged and in likewise my Mother Guildford, with other my women and maidens except such as never had experience nor knowledge how to advise or give me counsel in any time of need, which is to be feared more shortly than your Grace thought at the time of my departing as my mother Guildford can more plainly show your Grace than I can write, to whom I beseech you give credence, and if it may be by any means possible, I humbly request you to cause my mother Guildford to repair hither to me again. For if any chance happen other than well, I shall not know where nor of whom to ask my good counsel to your pleasure nor yet to mine own profit.
>
> I marvel much that my good Lord of Norfolk would at all times so lightly grant everything at their requests here. I am well assured that when ye know the truth of anything as my mother Guildford can show you, ye would full little have thought I should have been thus treated. Would God my Lord of York had come with me in the room [in place of] my Lord of Norfolk. For I am sure I should have been left much more at my heartsease than I am now, and thus I bid your Grace farewell.

She signed with an urgent plea in her own hand:

> Give credence to my mother Guildford
> By your loving sister, Mary Queen of France.[20]

Conscious that Henry would be reluctant to compromise his new cordial relationship with the King of France, Mary sent an even more urgently worded letter to Wolsey, pointing out that she had been specifically told always to consult Lady Guildford. She found the Duke of Norfolk lacking in empathy, and entreated Wolsey to find some way to have Guildford reinstated:

'I have not seen in France any lady or gentlewoman so necessary for me as she is, nor yet so meet to do the King my brother service as she is. And for my part, my lord, as you love the King, my brother, and me, find the means that she may in all haste come hither again, for I had as lief lose the winning I shall have in France to lose her counsel when I shall lack it, which is not like long to be required as I am sure the noblemen and gentlemen can shew you more than becometh me to write in this matter.'[21]

Something was certainly bothering Mary. She may have found her marital duties distasteful. She certainly dropped broad hints that Lady Guildford knew everything, and would be in a position to tell both the King and Wolsey how Mary felt. Perhaps Louis' doctors had also hinted that his days were numbered. While his death could open the door to freedom – Mary always clung to her belief that her brother would honour their bargain and allow her to marry the man of her choice– she realised with alarm that as a widow, she could quite easily find herself stranded in France at the mercy of the scheming Louise of Savoy and her son the Dauphin Francis, the heir presumptive.

Her comments about the Duke of Norfolk's callousness are the first suggestion that Norfolk had ulterior motives for supporting Louis, and that he was working at cross-purposes with Wolsey, whose increasing influence at court, in politics and over the King Norfolk and other nobles increasingly resented. Norfolk had not been consulted over the selection of Mary's attendants, many of whom had been suggested by Wolsey.

Wolsey did his best to help Mary. He wrote tactfully to Louis from Eltham on 23 October, explaining in excellent French that

Lady Guildford, wise, discreet and respectable, had been specially selected for her appointment. He humbly requested that she be reinstated, pointing out that she had come out of honourable retirement specifically to serve Mary. Wolsey assured Louis that when he got to know Lady Guildford, he would esteem her for her excellent qualities.

Louis was not to be swayed. Eventually, the reason for his aversion to Lady Guildford emerged. Louis had found Guildford over-protective of the young Queen, and her forbidding presence inhibiting. He found her interference in the relationship between man and wife intolerable. He did not want 'when he would be merry with his wife to have any strange woman with her, but one that he is well acquainted withal, afore whom he durst be merry,'[22] wrote Worcester, Henry's Ambassador to France, adding that Louis swore that no husband ever doted on his wife more than he did, but rather than have a woman like that around her, he would be without her altogether.

Mary now accepted that wifely duty meant obedience and resigned herself. Louis allowed her to retain the services of several attendants and six ladies of the bedchamber, one of whom was the newly arrived Anne Boleyn. Apart from this one spat over Mary's household, the relations between the newly-weds appeared cordial. When Louis's health delayed the court's progress to Paris, courtiers suspected that Louis so delighted in Mary's company that he was using his illness as an excuse to linger in dalliance before confronting more formal occasions – the coronation and the return to Paris. As Louis reclined on his chaise longue, Mary, seated at his side, played her lute and sang, causing him such pleasure that his physicians considered it beneficial to his health. He could not bear her to leave his side. It was a fortnight before the royal party made it to St Denis.

Mary's state entry into the capital would be followed by the jousts the Dauphin was busily organising. Throughout Europe the prospect of this grand tournament had created a flurry of excitement. The English nobles who had attended the wedding had taken a proclamation back to England, inviting challengers.

Henry, predictably, fielded a formidable team, including the Marquis of Dorset and his four brothers, all champions, and Charles Brandon, Duke of Suffolk, the greatest champion of them all. Brandon, granted expenses to the tune of one thousand pounds, brought his own horses and equipment along to the occasion.

In late October, Brandon, Neville and Sir William Sidney crossed the Channel, travelling incognito in grey hooded coats, in accordance with romantic convention – even though few would have been fooled.

Brandon caught up with the royal party at Beauvais on 25 October. Intelligence he had received at Canterbury made him suspect that the dismissal of Mary's attendants had been part of a malicious attempt by Norfolk to sabotage Wolsey's policy of peace with France by causing trouble. Brandon urged Wolsey to work for the reinstatement of Lady Guildford, and also wrote to Henry from Beauvais, reporting that he had found the King lying in bed, with a dutiful Mary in attendance. Louis had embraced Brandon, clutching him warmly as an expression of the love he bore Henry, who had given him 'the greatest jewel ever one prince had of another'. Louis instructed Brandon to inform Henry that 'never Queen behaved herself more wisely and honourably'.[23] Brandon added that this opinion was shared by all the French aristocracy. Perhaps surprisingly, in the light of future developments, Brandon also repeated to Henry, man to man, a coarse jest Louis had made. Louis promised to send Henry a destrier and a set of saddlery, 'for he says your Grace has mounted him so well'.[24]

In a man more devious than Brandon, of course, repeating this lewd comment to his sovereign could be interpreted as a diversionary tactic, to distract attention from any romantic involvement of his own with the French Queen. He was clearly aware of Mary's interest in him, because he intimated to Henry that he was gratified and relieved that her demeanour was restrained and dignified.

Louis revelled in displaying his physical passion for his young Queen, hinting lasciviously at its reinvigorating effects, especially in the hearing of the Dauphin, whom it was calculated to annoy. Doubtless it had reached the King's ear that Francis was putting it about that Louis was incapable. Otherwise, Brandon discreetly made no mention of Mary. The rest of his letter dealt with sport and the grand tournament, his main reason for being in France.

Louis introduced Brandon to the Dauphin Francis, suggesting that Dorset and Brandon should be his aides at the tournament. Francis invited them to dinner and declared that they should be not aides but brethren, and assist in the organisation. Travelling to Paris ahead of the King and Queen, the three of them paused for a boar hunt in which Francis courteously allowed Brandon the kill. Brandon slew one boar with such a powerful thrust that he bent the sword, a portent of the remarkable prowess he would exhibit in the royal tourney.

An arch was erected in front of the Bastille bearing four shields, upon which contestants could register their names. Challengers wishing to fight on foot or in the mêlée signed up on the black and tawny shield, those intending to 'run at the tilt' inscribed their names on a silver shield, but major stars like Brandon and Dorset wrote their names on the gold shield. They would 'run with the sharp spears and fight with the sharp swords.'[25]

Louis was not so dazzled by the attractions of his young bride that he lost his head. The day before Mary arrived in France, Louis had taken Worcester aside. He displayed to the startled Ambassador the priceless jewellery he intended to bestow upon her. Worcester wrote to Wolsey that he had never seen such opulence; at least 55 pieces of superb quality, diamonds and rubies and seven of the greatest pearls Worcester had ever seen. He estimated the value of the cheapest stones at 2,000 ducats, the most valuable more than 100,000. But Louis said slyly that he had no intention of lavishing the whole hoard on Mary at once. She would have to earn them. He intended to dole them out piece-meal, and 'have many kisses and thanks for them'.[26] The court understood: when, on the day after the marriage, he gave her a 'marvellous great pointed diamond with a ruby about two inches long,' the next day another ruby even larger, valued at 10,000 marks, and on the third day a 'great diamond with a great round pearl hanging by it',[27] there was much banter and sniggering. The young Queen had clearly paid her dues for her baubles.

In late October, Louis having recovered from his illness, the royal couple resumed their journey, pausing at each town so that, as tradition dictated, all prisoners could be released on the Queen's command. As they travelled, Louis enthusiastically discussed his projected Italian campaign. Mary listened, enthralled. Louis had promised to take her to Venice after her coronation. The Venetian Signory's informant revealed that Louis, apparently enjoying a temporary relief from his gout, had slept with his wife two nights on the journey.

On 5 November, Mary's coronation at the abbey church was witnessed by a large crowd of nobles who had ridden out from the Court. The Bishop of Bayeux officiated at the simple ceremony. The Dauphin led Mary to the altar, where, after anointing her, the Bishop invested her with the ring, sceptre and rod of justice. The crown was then placed on her head and she was conducted to a throne erected in the sanctuary, where she heard high Mass and received the sacrament. During the Mass Francis held the heavy matrimonial crown above her head to relieve her of its weight. The Queen and the Dauphin then joined the King for dinner. Louis ignored the regime recommended by his doctors and dined at noon.

Louis left St Denis early in the morning to ensure that all was ready for his bride's triumphant entry into his capital. Sixteenth century Paris was Europe's chief city, a sprawling metropolis, five times bigger than London, seductive, dangerous, a nest of robbers, a haunt of assassins, a by-word for wickedness. Every echelon of late mediaeval society thronged these dog-leg alleyways; nobles and artisans rubbed shoulders with merchants, vagabonds, hustlers, hawkers, monks and students. At the heart of a city where thousands of paupers eked out a subsistence-level existence, the French Court feasted, each banquet featuring two to four dozen meat courses. Outside the sheltered Court, in a dog-eat-dog society where so many were scraping a living by fair means or foul, there was constant threat of violence. Murder was commonplace. Organised gangs like the 'mauvais garçons' systematically looted and terrorised more law-abiding inhabitants. In its filthy glamour and decadence, the great city fascinated and repelled in equal measure. The Venetian Contarini wrote 'it stinks of mud. There is much silk; the whole court dresses in silk; even the pages trail it on the ground.'

On 6 November, despite the chilly late autumn weather, Paris excelled herself to welcome the beautiful new Queen. The city was adorned with lilies and roses, some fashioned from silk, others painted on arras or on giant scaffolds lining the processional route. A large contingent of prominent merchants, dignitaries and 3,000 members of the French clergy, welcomed Mary at Porte Saint Denis, still the main gate of the walled mediaeval city, and conducted her to the Palais Royal where Louis awaited her. Arrayed in gold brocade, crowned with a diadem of diamonds and pearls, and riding in an open litter draped with white cloth-of-gold, Mary was the star of yet another magnificent procession. The Dauphin, also clad in gold studded with diamonds, escorted her, along with the French Dukes. Mary, radiant, was all smiles: in place of the insensitive Duke of Norfolk rode Dorset, and with him Charles Brandon, the charismatic Duke of Suffolk.

Passing through the gate, she witnessed the second in a series of seven *tableaux vivants*, an imaginative blend of heraldry, allegory and pantomime verse, designed to surpass even those which had celebrated Anne of Brittany's entry into the city in 1504. Three were sponsored by the municipality and four by private organisations. The first, presented at St Denis, had comprised a giant ship bearing figures of Ceres, Bacchus and, at the helm, Paris herself, symbolising the corn, wine and commerce of the city. Real matelots dressed the rigging, choirs sang songs of welcome, and the four winds of classical antiquity filled the sails. The leitmotif was Peace.

The mariners sang:

> Noble Lady, welcome to France,
>
> Through you we now shall live in joy and pleasure,
>
> Frenchmen and Englishmen live at their ease,
>
> Praise to God, who gives us such a blessing.

An orator addressed Mary as 'most illustrious, magnanimous Princess'. Mary was the symbol that war and hostility had been replaced by peace, alliance and friendship. The humanist and court poet Pierre Gringoire recorded that Mary's entry into the city was of unprecedented magnificence – perhaps there was a hint of self-congratulation in his enthusiasm, since he himself had composed the celebratory anthems. He presented Mary with a handwritten souvenir programme, illuminated with gold leaf.[28]

In the second tableau a marble fountain, bright with lilies and roses, played against a background of celestial blue, while three Graces danced in a garden. The third showed Solomon and the Queen of Sheba, a flattering allusion to Louis's popular title of 'Father of his People'. In the fourth, a platform erected before the Church of the Holy Innocents featured God the Father, robed as in the mediaeval mystery plays, holding aloft a huge pasteboard heart and a bouquet of red roses above the heads of figures representing the royal couple, wearing gold and ermine. The fifth pageant impressed even the illiterate, familiar with the tradition of the French courtly romances of Guillaume de Loris. The imaginative staging introduced a walled city enclosing a rose garden; a huge rosebud, raised by concealed machinery, approached a lily growing on a balcony, beneath a luxurious pavilion before a golden throne. When the rose reached the balcony, onlookers gasped when its petals opened, disclosing the figure of a living maiden, who now recited Gringoire's fulsome odes. Mary was identified with the fabulous 'rose vermeille', the symbol of peace which had bloomed in the gardens of Jericho and adorned the illuminated margins of a thousand romances. The Parisians declared her a goddess of love and an emblem of peace.

At the Chastellet de Paris, another lengthy paean was recited, in which Louis was compared to the Sun and Mary to the Moon. By the time the procession reached the Palais Royal at five-thirty, the young Queen had been on show since early morning. If she was flagging, she hid it well, continuing to enchant spectators and welcoming committees by her beauty and grace.

Her long day culminated in a reception by the dignitaries of the Sorbonne at Notre Dame de Paris, where, after High Mass, she was welcomed by the Archbishop of Paris. She then returned to the Palais Royal for a state banquet. Louis, no longer young, healthy or accustomed to late nights, retired long before the feast was finished. Several reports claimed that Mary, too, collapsed from exhaustion and was carried sleeping to her chambers.

Next day, the royal couple proceeded to the Hôtel des Tournelles, where they rested until the Grand Tournament began the following Monday, 13 November 1514.

Now Charles Brandon, more at home in the tiltyard than in the city or the corridors of power, came into his own. Instinctively wary of foreigners and their peculiar ways, he was beginning to dislike Paris as a 'stinking prison'. Weighing up his opponents, the French knights, he concluded that they wore their armour awkwardly, without the assurance of his compatriots. His confidence grew.

Originally, the tournament was to have consisted of a series of friendly jousts between the English and French knights, held at Abbeville immediately after the wedding; but the Dauphin's ambitions had taken wing. The event would now take place in Paris, having grown from relatively modest beginnings into the kind of vast glittering Renaissance spectacular that Francis delighted in masterminding. He was determined to outdo any show Henry VIII might put on, and also to humiliate the English nobles and steal their crown as Europe's premier jousters, by a dazzling display of personal prowess. Excitement was rife. Patriotic pride was at stake.

A huge stage had been erected in the Parc for the spectators, including the whole court. The Dauphin and his aides rode into the meadow to salute the King and Queen. Louis, once more crippled by 'gout', received their greeting reclining upon a couch. Mary, radiant with excitement, rose to acknowledge the cheers of the adoring multitude.

Among the most popular of the usual stunt riders and warm-up acts was Anthony Bownarme, who took to the field dressed as the emblematic porcupine, with spears in his hand, under his arm and sticking out of his stirrups. To rapturous applause, he rode before the Queen and shattered ten spears into the ground.

The English had carefully selected their champions from among the country's best lances, led by Thomas Grey, Marquis of Dorset, and Charles Brandon. The combat would be ferocious. The peace was only six months old. Although the tournament was officially a friendly sporting event, old animosities still smouldered, old scores still rankled.

The Dauphin Francis, spokesman for the French competitors, pledged to meet all 'answerers' both afoot and on horseback. Each contestant would run five courses over three days. The jousts proper comprised hand-to-hand combat on horseback with spears, and afoot with swords and lances, followed by the general tournament, or mêlée, at barriers, where groups of knights engaged simultaneously. In all, 305 men took part, some of whom, one chronicler commented laconically, were slain and not spoken of. From the outset, public interest centred on the stars, the Dauphin Francis, his brother-in-law the Duc d'Alençon, and the mighty English champions, Dorset and Brandon.

The knights were ceremoniously introduced individually, each galloping twice round the arena, pausing on the second lap to bow low before the royal stand, their plumes sweeping the saddle bow. On the first day the honours went to Brandon: he nearly killed one opponent, beat another to the ground, and broke his sword on a third with such force that the man's horse was too terrified to approach him again. Brandon knew his friend the King, that aficionado of the joust, would have applauded his efforts. He wrote to Henry that he only wished the King had been there to witness his triumph to the honour of his country.

What the Dauphin Francis lacked in the lists he compensated with sartorial glory. He sported a different set of armour and colour scheme each day, first silver and gold, then crimson and yellow velvet, and on the third day, as a compliment to the Queen, the Tudor green and white. The English knights wore the red cross of St George. The French were spectacularly costumed. However, their sportsmanship justified Brandon's modest expectations. Overshadowed by the daring and skill of the English knights, their praise was grudging. Francis, reluctant to court defeat, retired after injuring his little finger, substituting one of his seconds. Brandon, although injured, shamed him by fighting on, ignoring his wounds.

On the second day both Dorset and Brandon excelled, shivering many spears, but again Brandon overwhelmed all opponents, unhorsing his opponents in three successive rounds. Then the competition hotted up – Dorset later said the fighting was as furious as anything he had ever experienced. Horses and a French competitor were slain. On Tuesday 21 November, Francis, nursing his finger and his dented pride, sent in Dorset and Brandon, who had agreed to act as his aides, to fight alone against all comers. His secret agenda was to discredit Brandon, already enjoying the Queen's delighted approval and the approval of more open-minded members of the French Court, who realised that the English were being unfairly treated. Francis, resolved to salvage the remains of French prestige, replaced one of the French contestants with a massive unknown German mercenary, disguised, under secret orders to despatch the English champion.

Brandon, suddenly finding himself facing a furious onslaught from a towering hooded figure, paused briefly, then rallied and counterattacked, eventually, after the exchange of many savage blows, grabbing the giant by the neck; he 'pommeled [him] so about the head that the blood issued out of his nose'. The defeated Goliath, blood streaming, was quickly removed on the Dauphin's orders. His identity was never revealed.

The event was an English triumph. There were few injuries on the English side, and no deaths. Brandon made light of his own injuries. His account of his exploits was modest and matter-of-fact. He wrote to Wolsey on 18 November: 'The jousts are done and, blessed be God, all our Englishmen sped well as I am sure ye shall hear by others.'[29]

Dorset noted: 'The Queen continues her goodness and wisdom and increases in the favour of her husband and the Privy Council. She has said to my Lord of Suffolk and me that the King of France her husband said to her that my Lord of Suffolk and I did shame all France, and that we should carry the prize into England.'[30]

Besides defending British honour in the tiltyard, Brandon and Dorset had also been charged with a secret diplomatic mission, so confidential that it was never recorded anywhere, lest the despatches might be intercepted and the project become known in Spain and Italy. They were charged with arranging a meeting between Henry and Louis. Henry wanted friendship with France, with a particular view to obtaining French support in his projected war with Spain. He intended to make war on Spain to promote his claim to Castile by right of his queen, Katherine, daughter of Isabella. He hoped for French military aid to help him drive Ferdinand out of Navarre as punishment for reneging on the many promises he had made to both France and England.

The proposed meeting between the sovereigns had been much discussed, but there had been no agreement about its location, chiefly because Louis, hell-bent on his proposed Italian expedition, was all for travelling in an easterly direction towards Lyons. A tentative agreement was reached for a meeting in early April, at a venue to be decided later, but which would be somewhere between Boulogne and Calais. Louis tentatively agreed to support an invasion of Spain, in return for a loan of 200,000 crowns and Henry's assistance in enforcing French claims on Milan. There was a rumour doing the rounds in Venice that Brandon, the British martial arts champion, would himself join the Italian campaign at the head of 6,000 English troops.

More or less vague threats of war, like promises of marriage, featured widely in European diplomacy. There was no formal treaty between France and England. The two monarchs would discuss the details in person when they met. Neither could know that this would never happen: by spring 1515 Louis would be dead and his successor, Francis, would be unwilling to honour his predecessor's commitments.

Brandon was no skilled diplomat, having little interest in the intellectual challenge of international political intrigue, and disliking subterfuge. But with his straightforward, soldierly personality and considerable charm, and the immediate entrée of his ducal rank, he was able to make useful contacts among Francis's circle without a great deal of effort. Louis's councillors attempted to exploit Brandon's inexperience, but, at the bold suggestion that John Stewart, Duke of Albany, the possible claimant to the Scottish throne who had long been harboured at the French Court, might be given safe passage to Scotland to negotiate, Brandon dug his heels in. Louis, impressed with Brandon's open, agreeable character, appreciated his loyalty to Henry, traits he found sadly lacking in his own son-in-law and heir. 'That big lad will ruin everything', he had recently remarked, remembering all he himself had sought to achieve for France and how little Francis seemed to care about it. By the end of their time together, Louis was promising to conduct all negotiations with Henry through Brandon and Wolsey. He assured Henry that no monarch had such a good servant in times of either peace or war.

Brandon sent Henry gifts in token of friendship and reported to him directly on French matters. But, away from court, he had to rely on the goodwill of Wolsey to keep him informed about the King's intentions and reactions. He was reluctant to undertake diplomatic initiatives without direction from Wolsey. For the moment, Henry was delighted with Brandon, and Wolsey was happy to co-operate with him. But all that could change in an instant, and Wolsey never let Brandon forget it.

Behind the scenes, Mary contributed to the success of the negotiations with grace and skill, ensuring that her husband was good-humoured and in a receptive mood. She displayed a talent for tact and diplomacy far beyond her years and experience by seeking the advice of de Longueville and other leading French courtiers. Brandon reported to Wolsey that she asked them 'how she might best order herself to content the King, whereof she was most desirous...because she knew well they were the men whom the King loved and trusted, and knew best his mind.' The King and his Council were enchanted: Louise of Savoy and her circle remained aloof and sceptical.

Despite her demure demeanour, the beautiful teenage Mary, surrounded by chattering courtiers whose daily topic of conversation was romance, must have compared the vigorous and dashing Brandon with her frail husband, recumbent upon his couch. At the tournament held in her honour, Brandon was her champion, fighting for the glory of the Tudors and of England. Yet Mary's conduct remained impeccable, unlike that of the Dauphin. To the general embarrassment, Francis seemed to have fallen heavily for his glamorous stepmother. His infatuation quickly became public knowledge, hurtful and demeaning to his pregnant wife, the Dauphine Claude, and infuriating for the Dauphin's clever and ambitious mother, Louise of Savoy, who realised the dangers of his rash behaviour. Patient Claude suffered in silence, but Louise furiously reprimanded her son, commanding him to control his lustful impulses, and warning him that he was putting his throne at risk.

The last act of the coronation festivities was a banquet held in Mary's honour at the Hôtel de Ville by the University of Paris. As things turned out, this would be Mary's last ceremonial appearance as Queen of France. People flocked to glimpse her, causing such a throng around the main door that the official party had to enter by the back door through the porter's lodge, filing up a narrow staircase to the vestibule where the dignitaries awaited them. After more effusive oratory and toasts in praise of the union between England and France, Mary was congratulated for marrying a monarch whose throne was secure. The insinuation was that England was prone to revolutions, unlike the more stable European powers.

The future Cardinal Jerome Alexander reported that he had never seen such a *'repas pantagruélique'* or so many splendidly attired and distinguished personages at any one time. The Queen charmed everyone when, after enjoying a dessert especially prepared for her, she kindly ordered that a portion should be sent to the royal nursery at Vincennes for her four-year-old stepdaughter, Renée, the second surviving child of Louis XII and Anne.

The banquet brought the court season to a close. Their mission concluded, the English lords returned home for Christmas. Brandon alone lingered to complete his confidential assignment, although he itched to leave, weary of diplomacy for which he had little natural bent, and of penning endless reports and despatches. On November 27, 1514, the King and Queen travelled to St Germain en Laye to spend three weeks at the King's country palace. Perhaps Louis hoped to go hunting, although it was becoming increasing apparent that such strenuous activities were now beyond him.

In December the royal couple returned to Paris, where Louis took to his sickbed. Mary sat by his bedside, chatting with Francis, who, displaying little concern for Louis, made no secret of his obsession with her, and sat about making suggestive remarks.

Courtiers began to speculate whether the young Queen would soon share the honours of the Dauphin's bed with his official mistress, Madame de Châteaubriant. Francis, a year older than Mary, was considered charming and handsome, witty and affable. Already known at Court as a womaniser, he spiced his conversation with innuendos which Mary, she confided to Dorset and Brandon, found distasteful. Mary was determined to play the devoted wife so long as Louis lived. But she could not afford to alienate the heir to the throne, upon whom she would be dependent if Louis died. She recalled the fate of her friend Katherine of Aragon, widowed, left without means, in a strange land. Although she loved her brother, Mary suspected Henry would probably be as little help to her in such a situation as Ferdinand had been to his daughter.

Because of the difference in their years and physical health, Mary and Louis had already been the subject of lewd gossip, speculation and sniggering. Mary was accused of being dizzy and flirtatious – one author claimed she could be giddy in six languages – and deliberately irresponsible. Francis's old chum Fleuranges, now Marshal of France, wrote vividly of the ailing monarch valiantly struggling to satisfy his young bride:

> The King left the palace and took lodgings at Tournelles in Paris because it had the best climate and also he did not feel very strong because he had desired to be a pleasing companion with his wife; but he deceived himself, as he was not the man for it... he lived on a very strict diet which he broke when he was with his wife; and the doctors told him that if he continued he would die from his pleasure.[31]

Parisian gossipmongers ascribed Louis's decline to English trickery; they had sent him a lusty 'young filly' to hasten his demise, darkly reminding each other of the proverb 'an old man in love hugs death'.

Notwithstanding, as soon as Louis felt a little better, the round of banquets and diversions was resumed. Louis, abandoning his diet and early nights, plunged into pursuits suited to younger, fitter men – dancing, hunting, riding, indulging in copious amounts of food and drink. Louise of Savoy watched and waited; in her diary she recorded that these 'nights of love' hastened the King's end. But the King, having recovered his zest for life, continued in good spirits. Mellowed by age and illness, and the late flowering of happiness with his adored young wife, he lavished gifts on Mary and on his daughter Claude. When Marco Dandolo asked him on 22 December when exactly he planned to embark on his Italian campaign, he told him not to hassle him, as he was keener than anybody to get going, and the expedition was imminent. 'This gout rather troubles me,' he admitted, adding stoutly: 'By Candlemas I shall be at Lyons, send troops into Italy and have with me my guard of 8,000 foot at 1,000 men at arms'.[32]

Brave words. Louis would not see another Candlemas.

Although ill, the King wrote on 28 December to his 'good brother the English King', expressing his continued delight in his Queen, and commending the service of Brandon, whose 'virtues, manners, politeness and good condition' deserved that the King should hold him in even greater honour. Brandon would later have good use for this royal reference.

This letter was to be the last Louis would ever write. Three days later, on New Year's Day 1515, he was dead.

When they broke the news to Mary, she fainted.

7 - Notes

1. L&P Hen VIII vol l pt 2 3272
2. CSP Ven vol ii 500
3. L&P Hen VIII vol l pt 2 3344
4. ibid 3262
5. Contemporary descriptions of Mary suggest that she had fair hair. Certainly, the lock of Mary's hair held in Moyses Hall Museum in Bury St Edmunds is strawberry blonde, with a darker strand. Her tomb was opened in 1784, as mentioned by Samuel Tymms, *An Architectural and Historical Account of the Church of St Mary, Bury St Edmund's* [London: Simpkin and Marshall, 1854], p. 179. Tymms gives a transcription of an unpublished manuscript by Sir John Cullum that describes the disinterment. 'The hair was perfectly sound, retaining the original strength, and adhering very closely to the skull. It was of considerable length, some perhaps near two feet long, and of a beauteous golden colour, as was that of her mother at the time of her marriage.' Cullum adds that Mary's teeth 'were all entire and even, both above and below.'

6. CSP Ven vol ll 500

7. L&P Hen VIII vol 1preface

8. Du Bellay, *Correspondence*, vol vi, 183

9. Hall, ed. Ellis, 570

10. CSP Ven vol ii 207

11. ibid, 208

12. Du Bellay, vol vii, 208

13. CSP Ven vol ii, 208

14. ibid, 202

15. Du Bellay, vol vii, 187

16. CSP Ven vol ii, 211

17. Du Bellay, vol vii, 187

18. CSP Ven, vol ii, 496,507,535

19. ibid, 211

20. BL, MS Cotton Caligula DVI, f 257

21. ibid, f 146

22. L&P Hen VIII vol i pt 2 3416

23. ibid, 3387

24. ibid

25. Hall, ed. Ellis, 571

26. L&P Hen VIII vol i pt 2 3387

27. ibid, 3336

28. BL, MS Cotton Vespasian BII, f6

29. L&P Hen VIII vol i, pt 2, 3449

30. ibid; BL, MS Cotton Caligula DVI, f196v

31. Robert de la Marck, Seigneur de Fleuranges, *Mémoires du maréchal de Florange, dit le Jeune Aventureux,* published for the Société de l'Histoire de France by Robert Goubaux & P. André Lemoisne, Paris, H. Laurens, 1913-1924, 2 vol 'Comment le roy Lys XII, par ung jour de l'an, après avoir faict bonne chiere avec que sa nouvelle femme, morut à Paris. 1514, 146-168: Le roy Loys partit du palays et vint logier au Tournelles, à Paris, pour ce qu'il est en plus belle air que le palays et ne se sentoit pas fort bien, car il avoit vollut faire du gentilz compaignon avecque sa femme; Le roy Loys partit du palays et vint logier au Tournelles, à Paris, pour ce qu'il est en plus belle air que le palays et ne se sentoit pas fort bien, car il avoit vollut faire du gentilz compaignon avecque sa femme'.

32. CSP Ven vol ii 553

8   LA REINE BLANCHE

At nineteen, after just eighty-two days of marriage, Mary found herself a widow, and Queen Dowager of France. Before the news of Louis's death reached London, fate had dealt the Tudors another blow. Queen Katherine had been delivered of yet another premature stillborn child. The Tudor succession was still not secure. Now the future of the French monarchy, too, hung in the balance. Despite Mary's devoted vigil at his bedside, Louis had drawn his last tortured breath, not in the arms of his adored wife but of his successor, the Dauphin Francis.

Immediately after death, Louis's corpse was disembowelled, embalmed and laid in state in the great hall at Les Tournelles, with crown, robes and sceptre, befitting a worthy prince. Monks were paid to keep vigil as the public shuffled respectfully past for a last glimpse of their late monarch, the Father of his People. The next day, at the Church of St Denis, Louis was buried, as he had wished, beside his second wife, Anne of Brittany, whom he had loved so well, fought with so fiercely, and mourned so intensely, if so briefly.

The late King's lying-in-state and his funeral lacked nothing in ceremony, but the unseemly haste with which they were executed betrayed the Dauphin's impatience to mount the throne. Mourning cost money: Francis cut short the wake. On the eleventh day, the household ministers' staves were struck. The old reign was decisively over. The Dauphin's mother, Louise of Savoy, had consulted the stars, desperate to read the future. For nineteen years her whole life had centred on the hope of seeing her son on the French throne. She rejoiced as she heard the bells tolling the monarch's knell. Like Louis, Louise had long suffered from an agonising arthritic condition; now, in her hour of triumph, she defied her disability, riding the 100 miles to Paris within 48 hours, in time to witness her son's coronation.

Despite the impatience of Francis and Louise, Francis could not formally be crowned until it was certain that Mary was not pregnant with a male heir by Louis. According to ancient custom, Mary had to allow herself to be draped in the hideous white robes which earned a childless Queen Dowager of France the title of 'la Reine Blanche', the White Queen, and retire to the palace known as the Hôtel de Cluny, a former Benedictine Abbey on the left bank of the Seine, to await confirmation that she was not with child.

The term of isolation imposed on the Queen Dowager was an old safeguard in France dating back to the death of Philip the Fair in 1314, whose three successors had all died before their heirs expectant were born. This calamity had led to the introduction of the Salic Law and the vexed question of female succession.

Mary found her sojourn profoundly depressing. Her chamber, although handsomely appointed, was a cheerless, sunless cavern, virtually soundproof, airless and unheated, hung about with black cloth, its long windows heavily curtained. Flickering tapers cast weird shadows on the dark walls. Here, day after day, the vivacious Tudor Princess, so recently the petted and adored Queen, tossed and turned, fretting, on her bed, with no friend or confidante. The Dauphin Francis's controlling female relatives, Louise of Savoy and her daughter Marguerite, had stepped in the moment Louis was dead. As the self-appointed 'curators of the womb', still suspicious of Mary, they had made sure she was isolated. They had handpicked her few French attendants, and commanded them to monitor Mary's movements closely and report back anything that might be regarded as untoward. Unsurprisingly, Mary, lonely, spoiled, highly-strung and now in a state of emotional fragility, in a foreign land and surrounded by people who treated her with suspicion, grew irritable and anxious. She sent complaining messages to her brother that she felt desolate and bewildered. To make matters worse, she was suffering from toothache. She begged Henry to allow his chief surgeon John Verye to attend her, which he did.

Custom and prudence dictated that the heir presumptive should delay his coronation until all doubt about the succession had been removed. But Francis, impatient to forge ahead with his coronation, had already extracted assurances from Mary that she was convinced she was not pregnant. His mother, however, was more sceptical. Devious herself, Louise imputed similar duplicity to Mary. There had been whispers at the French Court that Mary was with child before Louis's death. For those first three weeks of January, Louise lived on edge. Dreading that her lifelong ambitions for her son might yet be foiled, she resented Mary, as she had secretly hated Anne of Brittany, concealing her emotions under a superficial veil of cordiality. When Anne had given birth to a son, Louise suffered a frenzy of frustration; the baby's death came as a huge relief to her. In her journal she exulted that the child would not *retard the exaltation of my Caesar, for he did not live.* [1]

At twenty-one, Louise's 'Caesar', Francis, was a tall, broad-shouldered youth with an athletic figure already inclined to corpulence. His portraits show a superficially handsome oval face, with dark curling beard and narrow black eyes, their louche and saturnine expression both calculating and cynical. Francis considered himself an Adonis, but his long Valois nose was so disproportionately large that behind his back he was nicknamed 'Le Roi Grand Nez'. When Mary knew him he was liberal, cultured and suave, but the signs were already there of the sly despot and voluptuary he would become. Ironically, while a great womaniser, convinced he was irresistible to the opposite sex, he was at the same time so dominated by his powerful and doting mother and sister that the earlier years of his reign were called a petticoat government. His mother, Louise and his sister, Marguerite, were the first beneficiaries of his new-found wealth and power. He bestowed upon Louise two counties, two duchies and a barony, and the title of Duchess. To his sister he gave the county of Armagnac and a lucrative monopoly in the appointment of guild officials. While Francis jousted, hunted and feasted, lavishing money freely on his princely lifestyle and apparently fulfilling the gloomy prophecies of those, including Louis, his predecessor, who had predicted that he would bankrupt the French Treasury, his mother gathered the reins of power into her own capable hands, ruling in all but name. While Francis indulged his artistic temperament, building châteaux, collecting art and playing at patronage, diplomacy and military campaigns, Brandon, who realised what was going on, advised Henry to address official correspondence directly to Louise.' Sir, [it is] she that rules all, and so may she well, [for I] never saw woman like to her.'

Already depressed by her tiresome sequestration at Cluny, Mary was irritated to receive a letter from Wolsey, warning her to exercise caution, and 'if any motions of marriage be made unto you, in no wise give hearing unto them'.[2]She thanked Wolsey for his wise counsel, promising not to do anything without the direction of 'the King my brother and his Council'. But in her few months as a King's consort and a feted Queen Mary had matured. She sharply reminded Wolsey that she was no longer a child. As she dictated the letter to a secretary, her indignation rose:

> I trust that the King my brother and you will not reckon in
> me such childhood. I trust I have so ordered myself, so since
> that I came hither, that I trust it hath been to the honour of
> the King my brother and me since I came hither and if here is
> anything that I may do [for] you, I would be glad for to do it.
> And no more to you at this time.

Written at Paris the 10th day of January 1515

Francis's relationship with Mary has provoked much speculation, including claims that Mary, even before her husband's death, was so desperate to shore up her situation that she was willing to take a lover to give her a male child – the same kind of suspicion that would later be levelled at her attendant, Anne Boleyn, when she became Queen of England. Francis was notoriously infatuated with Mary. According to the French historian Brantôme, Mary made a play for him, and the couple embarked upon an illicit affair which became the scandal of the court. Louise of Savoy and her circle, alarmed, ordered their spies to increase their vigilance. Francis was taken to task by concerned members of the nobility.

> In the name of Heaven, what are you about? Can't you see that this woman, who is a cunning and subtle creature, is merely trying to attract you so that you can impregnate her? And if she has a son, then you are then only Count of Angoulême for the rest of your life and will never be King of France as you hope. The King her husband is old and will never give her any children…You are young and hot, she is young and hot. Good Lord! She'll snare you, just like that; she'll have a child, and you're done for! After that, you may as well say: Goodbye to my kingdom of France. So think on![4]

The gossip-loving chronicler Brantôme inventively presents Mary as a manipulative minx who hoped to ensnare Francis in order to maintain her position as Queen of France. Francis realised the danger but, 'tempted time and again by the clever tricks and caresses of this fair Englishwoman, he rushed more than ever into it. For such is the ardour of love!' The scandal-mongering chronicler later claimed that Mary, during her seclusion at Cluny, paraded about padded with linen and sheets, 'linges et drapeaux', in a feigned pregnancy, until dramatically unmasked by a furious Louise.[5]

This is almost certainly all the invention of a malicious fantasy. Mary had already frequently complained to her brother and to Wolsey about the unwelcome importunities of Francis. She was inexperienced in the game of courtly love as practised at the French Court, and did not dare protest too much in case she appeared ignorant of their sophisticated customs. The French Court was larger, livelier and more cosmopolitan than she was used to. Francis had gathered about him a group of celebrities from the worlds of letters and diplomacy, garnished with young beauties, on the principle that 'A Court without ladies is like a year without springtime, or a spring without roses'. Whereas in England, the King set the tone at Court, in France the example was often set by the Queen. Allegedly, in the days of Anne of Brittany, who was lame, fashionable ladies affected a limp. During the few months while Mary was Queen, they had begun to adopt what they thought of as cool English reserve.

While Louis lived, Francis had to some extent restrained his passion for Mary, hoping through her to reach the ear of her brother, the King of England. He had always feigned approval of her marriage to Louis, even though he had secretly schemed to prevent it because it was a threat to his own ambitions.

Henry ordered an impressive memorial service to be held at St Paul's for the French King, his brother-in-law, creating work for many craftsmen on the royal payroll, chandlers, haberdashers, the court painter, and bell-ringers. Aware of Francis's reputation with women, Henry was concerned for his sister when he heard rumours that the new King was considering divorcing his pregnant wife, Claude, and marrying Mary instead.

Mary herself believed Francis's designs were less honourable. Some historians have dismissed this as unlikely, in view of the fact that he scribbled a disobliging comment on a drawing of her in the Album d'Aix [Bibliothèque Méjanès] some years later. However, it is entirely possible that Francis, a notorious philanderer, did genuinely hope to seduce Mary, to whom he had certainly felt attracted. His blatant flirting with her while she was his father-in-law's wife had incurred rebukes from his own mother. Now Mary was no longer the wife of the King, he could importune her with impunity, as he could not have done while Louis lived without jeopardising his own future aspirations. Moreover, scrawling the words 'more dirty than queenly' [plus sale que royne] on a portrait smacks of lust spurned and sour grapes...or possibly it was a reference to what Francis regarded as Mary's 'theft' of the Mirror of Naples.

Whatever Francis's intentions, Mary's brother Henry now took a fateful step. He appointed as his ambassador, charged with bringing the widowed queen home to England, together with what could be recovered of her dowry, none other than his trusty servant, Charles Brandon, Duke of Suffolk.

Meanwhile, on 28 January, Francis, having dispensed with prolonged mourning, went ahead with his coronation at the ancient cathedral of Rheims, where holy oil was said to have been miraculously brought down from heaven by a white dove on Christmas Day 496. Legend held that French Kings anointed from this sacred phial were thrice blessed. Francis was duly anointed, ceremoniously recognised, prayed for, enthroned and offered homage. By the authority of St Marcoule, he was now so thoroughly God's anointed that he could 'touch for the King's evil.'

The coronation had taken place so swiftly that the English ambassadors arrived too late to attend. Fortunately, however, they were in time for the celebratory jousts. Besides offering their condolences on the death of Louis and congratulations to Francis on his accession, they were under orders to take possession of Mary's jewels and plate, and make an inventory of all her English valuables in order to obtain compensation and restitution for the costs of her transport to France and her extravagant trousseau and equipment, and arrange for her return home. Francis for his part demanded the restoration of Tournai, conquered by Henry the previous year. This exchange was to form the basis of the negotiations. Wolsey had set his heart on the bishopric of the town. Throughout the negotiations between Henry and Louis XII, this office had been promised to him, despite the Pope's disapproval. There were other matters, too, had to be taken into consideration. There was the French debt of a million gold crowns, outstanding from the previous reign; the asylum offered by France to Richard de la Pole, the 'White Rose' contender for Henry's throne; and the nefarious activities and schemes of the Duke of Albany.

Despite his reluctance to undertake foreign assignments not of a military nature, embassies being both onerous and expensive, and offering opportunities during his absence for his enemies at court to stab him in the back, the chief burden of mediation fell on Brandon. Although the least experienced of Henry's three ambassadors, Brandon spearheaded the embassy by virtue of his rank and his closeness to the King. He possessed a further qualification in that he was acquainted with the new king, Francis and his services had been personally recommended by Louis. Now he needed to ingratiate himself and Wolsey with France's new sovereign, although Brandon was aware that this would be no easy matter. He knew Francis was as distrustful as his mother, and also both manipulative and venal. Brandon had no intention of making any concessions, even though his predecessor's councillors had only months previously signed documents confirming that, in the event of Louis's death, Mary would be free to return to England with her 'servants, jewels and effects.' Part of her dowry had been offset against the French debt of one million crowns. There was also the question of whether the spectacular jewellery bestowed upon her so liberally by Louis now belonged to Mary or reverted to the French crown. Henry expected his envoys to drive a hard bargain. Transporting Mary with all her retinue and baggage in September had cost an eye-popping sum, settled on 28 January at Greenwich. Compensation had also been paid out to the survivors of her ship the *Great Elizabeth*, wrecked off Sandwich in the storm during the crossing.

Henry certainly suspected that his sister was in love with Brandon, but he reassured himself that the couple had never contracted any formal understanding. Mary was inhibited by her upbringing and delicacy and Brandon by their difference in status. A letter, 'revealing a most extraordinary fact in the history of Suffolk's love for the Princess Mary, of which historians have been quite at fault', was sold in 1840. No trace of this vital document remains at time of writing. Brandon's attractiveness to women, his chequered marital record and his gallant affairs of the heart were well known in the English court.

But Henry guessed that Mary, homesick and depressed, might fling herself at Brandon. Consequently, in early January 1515, at Eltham, the King extracted a promise from Brandon that he would not propose marriage to her. Letters written by Wolsey later suggest that Henry would not have been unwilling, eventually, to honour his waterside promise, made as Mary was about to embark for France, and allowed her to marry Brandon. But for the present he wanted to keep his options open, retaining Mary as a bargaining chip on the European marriage market as long as possible. He also wanted to preserve the French alliance, especially in view of the new catastrophic turn of events in Scotland. Brandon's mission included the extraction of assurances from the new French King that he would not renege on Louis XII's promise to restrain the Duke of Albany and prevent him from rallying to the aid of the renegades.

Meanwhile, Mary, still chafing and fretting in seclusion in Cluny, had finally put her foot down and dismissed her unsympathetic French attendants. Vigilance had been so far relaxed that she had been allowed to have some of her English ladies to keep her company. But she was still confined to the 'chambre de la reine blanche', draped in the unbecoming nun-like white robes, when on 4 February Henry's other ambassadors, Nicolas West and Sir Richard Wingfield, visited her, accompanied by Brandon. The pressure of her onerous seclusion was lifted sufficiently for her to be permitted to receive the English ambassadors and accept their condolences. Their arrival cheered her immensely. Brandon passed Mary's thanks on to Henry for sending 'in her heaviness my Lord of Suffolk and others as well to comfort her as for obtaining her dower.'[6]

But Brandon found Mary in a highly nervous state. Immediately after Louis's death, Friar Bonaventura Langley and another friar had been sent from the English court to visit Mary at Cluny, presumably by Henry, or possibly by Katherine, who had previously used Langley's services, sending him to offer condolences to her sister in law, Queen Margaret of Scotland, after the battle of Flodden. It has also been claimed that Langley was in the service of the Duke of Norfolk, who constantly sought to undermine Brandon. Whatever the truth of the matter, Langley, appointed Mary's confessor, tried to extract from her a confession of her feelings for Brandon. He had been instructed to warn her against marrying Brandon by persuading her that Wolsey and Brandon were plotting to control Henry's mind through diabolical means. Brandon, according to Langley, was evil personified and in league with the Devil. In support of his extraordinary accusation, the Friar quoted the sinister affair known as 'Compton's leg'. Sir William Compton, like Brandon, had grown up at court as a companion to King Henry. Langley accused Brandon of having inflicted an ailment of the leg upon his rival by invoking satanic powers.

The friars also tried to intimidate Mary by warning her that her brother had no intention of keeping any promises she might have extracted from him. They hinted that Henry only wanted her home so he could marry her off again. Once again, the bridegroom envisaged was, they claimed, Prince Charles of Castile. Mary was appalled by what they told her.[7]

Brandon himself suspected that his enemy Norfolk and his supporters on the council were plotting to bring down both himself and Wolsey, and to destroy the Anglo-French alliance. He had already confided his suspicions to Wolsey months before, after the summary dismissal of Lady Guildford by Louis XII. Handwritten drafts of Mary's own letters, in the Cotton Manuscript, show Mary's desperate state of mind. The drafts are unevenly scrawled, filled with crossings-out and repetitions.

The friars were called off, recalled to England and severely reprimanded by Wolsey.

But the wolf pack was already eagerly eying the Dowager Queen of France, young, beautiful, royal, rich and available. All over Europe, prospective suitors were gathering. The English ambassadors advised Henry to bring her home as quickly as possible, for her own protection and to foil any plotting by Francis. Mary was no fool: she was well aware that neither

Henry nor Francis was motivated so much by a concern for her welfare as by mercenary and political considerations.

Francis entertained notions of marrying her off, his top contenders being Anthony the Good, Duke of Lorraine, or Charles III, Duke of Savoy, his twenty-eight-year-old uncle, who was at least the right age. Henry, however, thought Mary's hand could more advantageously be bestowed elsewhere. This was a cogent reason for bringing her home, together with whatever could be clawed back of her dowry.

Emmanuel the Fortunate of Portugal made a bid for Mary's hand on behalf of his son John. Germany put forward William, Duke of Bavaria, and Charles of Castile, after all his dithering, had the nerve to renew his suit, too. Even old Emperor Maximilian was stirred by rumours of Mary's beauty. He instructed his daughter the Archduchess Margaret to procure a portrait of Mary for his scrutiny. He was so captivated by the young Queen's image, his secretary informed the Archduchess, that His Imperial Majesty stared at the portrait for a full thirty minutes. Reassured that it was a good likeness, he wrote off to Henry expressing his eagerness 'to get the lady into his own hands,' warning Henry that if she were to be married in France and died without heirs his kingdom would be in jeopardy. As usual, Maximilian refrained from making a concrete proposal, but shilly-shallied until it was too late.

Brandon, in his late twenties, at the height of his physical powers, had known Mary for years. His charm, daring and skill in the tiltyard, as well as his close friendship with the King, were legendary. While a mutual attraction had been suspected, there had been no open suggestion of a romance. As a royal princess, no flirtatious behaviour had ever sullied Mary's name. A secret liaison would have been the riskiest of indiscretions for both. Their names had never been openly linked, even by the prurient gossip-mongers of Henry's court. But Brandon certainly suspected how Mary felt about him, because he wrote to Henry how pleased he was to note how well she controlled her feelings when he first met her again in France after her marriage to Louis. Her restraint 'rejoiced me not a little,' he wrote, adding 'your Grace knows why.'

Now, before Francis left for his coronation at Rheims, Mary threw caution to the winds and confessed to him her love for Brandon. On 3 February, after the English envoys brought Henry's official congratulations to the new sovereign, Francis summoned Brandon to a private audience in his bedchamber, at first feigning lofty indignation, declaring that he knew Brandon had come to France with the treacherous intention of wedding 'the Queen, his master's sister'. Brandon stoutly denied the allegations, sensibly pointing out that he could hardly marry the Queen Dowager of France without the permission of the present ruler of France or of his own King. But to Brandon's mortification, Francis then revealed how much he knew about the relationship between the French Queen and the handsome Duke, including a secret 'ware word' or endearment which he had imagined nobody else knew, and which, as he later confided to Wolsey, he know ' no man alive could tell' except for Mary herself. Seeing that Brandon had been completely taken aback by this revelation, Francis now changed his tactics. He adopted a chummy reassuring tone, and told Brandon not to worry. Brandon had found in him 'a kind friend and a loving, who would help them both as keenly as if it were for himself.' Later, Mary would reveal to Brandon that on 15 February she had written to Henry confessing that she had told Francis of 'the good mind I bear towards my Lord of Suffolk'. She had, she said, been forced to do this to stop Francis pestering her.

Seeing how the thought of Henry's fury paralysed the faithful Brandon, Francis promised that he and Mary would both write to Henry 'in the best manner that can be devised.' Brandon, honourable and straightforward himself, ingenuously believed Francis to be sincere, rather than craftily acting in the best interests of France. Mary had refused the suitors proposed by Francis. If she married an English subject, bringing no political advantage to England, this would deprive Henry of a potentially valuable foreign alliance.

After this meeting, Brandon wrote at once to Wolsey, who congratulated him on his discretion and at this stage raised no objection to a marriage at some future date. Wolsey advised Brandon to urge Francis to write to Henry in support of his suit. Moreover, Brandon was informed that the King had bestowed on him a further concrete and very welcome mark of favour, the whole of the de la Pole estates and the lordship of Claxton, worth a thousand marks in cash.

The next day was occupied with Francis's triumphant entry into Paris.

By 20 February there was open talk of a marriage between Mary and Brandon. On 3 March the couple were married in secret. As soon as the secret marriage had been consummated, Mary was sure she had conceived. Brandon, panicked at their recklessness, and correctly anticipating Henry's outrage, wrote to Wolsey 'with as heavy a heart as any man living', hoping the brilliant Archbishop of York would handle the King and solicit his forgiveness on Brandon's behalf. 'The Queen would never let me rest till I had granted her to be married,' he explained, 'and so, to be plain with you, I have married her heartily, and I have lain with her insomuch I fear me lest she be with child.' [8]

Wolsey was horrified by such rashness. In rushing into a marriage without the King's consent the couple had been foolhardy beyond belief. He felt obliged to cover his own back by showing Brandon's letter to the King, stating that 'he had secretly married the King's sister, and they have lived together as man and wife.' Hitherto, Wolsey had been a benign fatherly figure on Mary's horizon. Now was the time for severe talking. There followed an exchange of letters of greater formality. Wolsey attempted to make the best of things, pointing out that Brandon's description of the secret wedding made it sound like a contract *'per verba de praesenti'*, which could still be annulled. There followed the suggestion that a full public marriage ceremony might follow, but this could not take place in Lent according to English custom, whereas it could, according to French custom, by episcopal dispensation.

Brandon also wrote to the King that Mary had been told by Friar Langley that she would never be allowed to marry Brandon if they returned to England first. They would send her to Flanders to Charles. '… she said she had rather to be torn in pieces than ever she should come there, and with that wept. Sir, I never saw woman so weep.'[9]

Brandon tried his best to assure her the Friar was lying, but 'in none ways I could make her believe it.' He had gently suggested that Mary should write to obtain her brother's goodwill, and then he would have had an easy conscience. He explained that he had given Henry his word not to marry her without Henry's consent. But Mary was adamant. She had already confessed her feelings to Francis; if Brandon did not marry her forthwith he would never again have the chance.

Brandon, overwhelmed by her distress and entreaties, was persuaded against his better judgment into a precipitous action, risking his career and even his life. 'And so' Brandon wrote to Henry naively 'she and I was married.' Only ten witnesses were present at the Cluny Chapel in Paris. Neither Ambassador Wingfield nor West were invited to attend, in case – as Mary knew they would – they raised objections.

Posterity has chosen to view Mary's behaviour as that of the archetypical damsel in distress, overwrought, helpless and tearful, throwing herself on the chivalry of her beloved, and Brandon as the knight on the white charger, risking all to rescue her. But in reality both played their roles and their cards skilfully in the circumstances, in order to ensure the desired outcome – their union, eventually sanctified and generally accepted, and their future reconciliation with Mary's brother, achieved largely through the good offices of their friend Wolsey. That this goal was obtained without lasting damage to their reputations or inheritance – although the fine Henry imposed was crippling and the Suffolks remained in debt for most of their lives thereafter, this did not prevent them from living in some style, and the debt was never really called in – is a testament to the good sense they both displayed.

Initially, of course, Brandon's worst fears seemed about to be realised. Henry, incandescent, flew into a fine Tudor rage. The flagrant disregard for his express commands, displayed by the two people he loved most in the world, and, moreover, trusted, was a tremendous blow to his self-esteem. Marrying without his consent broadcast to the world that the King's sister and his favourite had no qualms about flouting his authority. In truth, Henry was more upset about Brandon's betrayal than Mary's, for women were notoriously weak creatures, a prey to fantasies and ruled by their emotions. But oath-breaking was a grave offence against the very core of the chivalric code. Brandon, 'the man in all the world he loved and trusted best', had promised not to wed Mary before they returned to England. Wolsey had been present at Eltham when Brandon gave the King his word. Wolsey, like Henry, was stunned that Brandon should so far forget himself. Wolsey also knew that it would be he who would have to pick up the pieces. But first he would say his piece: he berated Brandon, telling him he would have thought that rather than break his oath Brandon would be 'torn with wild horses', and cursed the 'blind affection' that had brought him to such a pass. Despite Wolsey's intervention, the nobles, especially Norfolk and the Howards, already smarting with jealousy over Brandon's meteoric rise to power and resentful of his influence over the King, fanned the flames of the King's wrath. The Privy Council, led by the Howards, were baying for blood. They urged the King to have Brandon imprisoned or executed for treason. Marriage to a blood relation of the monarch without royal permission was a capital offence. Moreover, they cried, was not Brandon vaguely understood to be betrothed to his thirteen-year-old ward, Lady Elizabeth Lisle?

From Montreuil, on his way back to Calais, in April, Brandon wrote to Henry, pleading for his life, gambling on the King's affection for him, and seizing the opportunity for a sideswipe at his enemies.

> Most gracious sovereign Lord, so it is that I am informed divers ways that all your whole council, my lord of York [Wolsey] excepted, with many other, are clearly determined to tempt your Grace that I may either be put to death or be put in prison, and so to be destroyed. Alas, Sir, I may say that I have a hard fortune, seeing that was never one of them in trouble but I was glad to help them to my power, and that

Your Grace knows best. And now that I am in this none little trouble and sorrow, now they are ready to help to destroy me.

He cast himself on Henry's mercy, humbly acknowledging his offence and calling himself a most sorrowful wretch. 'Punish me rather with prison, Sir, rather than you should have me with mistrust in your heart. Strike off my head, and let me not live.'[10]

Mary supported his plea for clemency, assuming all the blame: Brandon had not actively courted her. She it was who had persuaded him to break his promise. She reminded her brother of his promise, and spelled out their bargain to him:

'whereas for the good of peace and for the furtherance of your affairs, ye moved me to marry with my lord and late husband King Louis of France, whose soul God pardon, though I understood that he was very aged and sickly, yet for the advancement of the said peace and for the furtherance of your causes I was contented to conform myself to your said motion, so that if I should fortune to survive the said late King, I might with good will marry myself at my liberty without your displeasure.'

She reminded Henry that he had agreed to this,.

'as ye will know, promising unto me that in such case ye would never provoke or move me but as mine own heart and mind should be best pleased, and that whosesoever I should dispose myself ye would be wholly contented with the same...'[11]

Free again, she had remembered 'the great virtues which I have seen and perceived heretofore in my Lord of Suffolk, to whom I have always been of good mind, as ye well know, I have affixed and clearly determined myself to marry with him, and the same I assure hath proceeded only of mine own mind, without any request or labour of my Lord of Suffolk or any other person.'

Wolsey advised them that Brandon's diplomatic mission to secure the friendship of Francis needed to succeed, and also, as Mary and Brandon knew, they would have to make some financial sacrifice to appease the King. When Mary received

Wolsey's letter informing her of her brother's rage, she smuggled out as a peace offering the greatest treasure she possessed, the stupendous Mirror of Naples, which Louis had given her and which was the hereditary property of the Queens of France. Brandon alerted Wolsey to the imminent delivery of 'a diamond with a great pearl' to the King, and promised the King that he should have whatever remained of her jewellery. Mary could not write herself, he explained, because her toothache had flared up again. Optimistically, he added ' My Lord, she and I remit these matters wholly to your discretion.'

In March, Francis demanded the return of the Mirror of Naples. Henry's curt refusal, even when Francis offered to pay 30,000 crowns for it, triggered a diplomatic row. Venetian sources suggest Henry flaunted his ill-gotten gains, wearing the 'Mirror' in public, even, later, during his historic encounter with Francis at the Field of the Cloth of Gold, sporting it on his cap as a gesture of defiance.

Mary had calculated her brother's reaction astutely: Henry would fulminate and threaten, but he loved her, and he loved Brandon, and in the end she was confident he would accept the situation, especially if it were sweetened by financial gain. She also knew that Wolsey needed Brandon's help against Norfolk and his enemies on the Council, and would support them. She clung to Henry's promise that she would be free to choose her second husband, having complied with his wishes in marrying her first.

Paris was in uproar. Everyone knew that Mary and Brandon had technically put their lives in danger by marrying without Henry's permission. Francis, gloating secretly over Henry's discomfiture, wrote to Henry. Mary wrote, threatening, unless she heard 'comfortable words' from her brother, to enter a nunnery; even kindly Queen Claude, whose affection for Mary had survived her own husband's indiscreet attentions to her, wrote to the King.

On Saturday 31st March, during Lent, the second, public, marriage between Mary Rose and Brandon took place. This ceremony advertised their union and proved the legitimacy of their future offspring. It was impossible to conceal their relationship. Mary insisted on having Brandon at her side the whole time, at dinner and in her rooms. Louise of Savoy noted with ill-concealed satisfaction: 'On Saturday the last day of March the Duke of Suffolk, *homme de basse condition*, whom Henry VIII hath sent as Ambassador to the King, married Mary, sister of the aforesaid Henry, widow of Louis XII'. Sixteen days later she wrote with satisfaction that the Mary Tudor chapter was over so far as France was concerned. 'Marie d'Angleterre, widow of Louis XII, left Paris with her husband, the Duke of Suffolk, to return to England.'

During her last days in Paris, Mary's loss of political status was made subtly clear. A handsome gift from the Signory of Venice, a black silk hat in a jewelled black velvet box, with a pendant balas ruby and pear-shaped pearl attached to the band, had been intended as a wedding gift to mark her marriage to Louis but its delivery was delayed by the illness of the envoy. It was valued at £225. When Mary received the Ambassadors, they extended their condolences on Louis's death, but refused to take her hint that they might have a gift for her. Instead, they kept it, for presentation with other gifts, to Henry VIII and the English nobles.

Poignantly, Mary's last use of her official seal as Queen of France was to transfer everything she possessed to her brother. She was now penniless and completely dependent on her husband, if her incomes from France failed. She retained the courtesy title 'Queen of France' for the rest of her life, but she was now Duchess of Suffolk. The French seal was brought back with her and archived as a souvenir of her past glory as wife of a reigning monarch.

Mary Rose and Brandon left Paris for Calais, there to await Henry's permission to cross the Channel and return to England. Francis escorted them as far as St Denis. As a last gesture of good will he presented her with four rings.

Ambassador West noted coolly that these were 'of no great value'.

The little town of Calais, within Henry's jurisdiction,

entertained Mary and Brandon honourably; when word came from Henry, they were soon able to embark for England. Mary had been away from home exactly seven months, the most turbulent period of her life.

They reached Dover on 2 May. Henry's fury with the two people he loved most on earth had been violent but had soon evaporated. He sent Wolsey to meet them. Wolsey escorted them to the King where he was staying at Lord Bergavenny's house at Birling.

Henry rode out at the head of a great cavalcade to greet his sister. He graciously accepted her confession that she was entirely to blame for the secret marriage. On March 9 Mary signed a document agreeing to hand over all her jewels and plate to Henry. It was also agreed that the Suffolks should pay him a huge fine of £24,000 in annual instalments of £2,000 by way of compensation. Brandon, despite his rank, was not a man of means. The debt to Henry was a strain on his finances, and he would spend the rest of his life in debt, but that was not shameful; it was nothing out of the ordinary for a sixteenth century peer. Besides, although Henry could be a ruthless creditor, he was indulgent towards the Suffolks and allowed their indebtedness to increase year by year without foreclosure. Brandon would hand over to the King the lucrative ward-ship of Lady Elizabeth Lisle. Mary was also bound, against a penalty of £100,000, to surrender all her other valuables. By 11 May, the financial arrangements had been completed.

Many members of the Council, especially Brandon's enemies, who had been baying for blood and were foiled by the King's affection for the runaways, felt Henry had been unduly lenient. As the question of the succession became more acute, the threat posed by random marriages by princes and princesses of the blood intensified. After 1536 it was declared treason by Act of Parliament for royals to marry without the consent of the sovereign.

Henry VIII has in many quarters been viewed as a monster; his daughters were perhaps even more intractable. Henry forgave Mary Rose. But Mary and Brandon's grand-daughter,

Katherine Grey and her beloved husband the Earl of Hertford, would feel the full weight of Queen Elizabeth's vengeance when they defied her. The youngest Grey sister, Mary, would also bear the brunt of the Queen's disapproval. The descendants of Mary Rose's younger daughter, Eleanor, would not escape unscathed.

But in 1515 there was no real threat to the throne, despite the mutterings of Brandon's enemies. At the King's insistence, the couple now underwent a third marriage ceremony on 13 May in the Church of the Observant Friars at Greenwich, in the presence of the entire Court. Because of the climate of public disapproval, the celebrations were kept low-key. The guests included some of those nobles who had pressed for Brandon's execution. Public feeling was expressed in one of several copies made of a wedding portrait of Mary and Brandon: it showed a court jester whispering to the Duke:

> Cloth of gold do not despise
> Though thou be matched with cloth of frieze;
> Cloth of frieze be not too bold
> Though thou be matched with cloth of gold.

The motto is also attributed to Brandon himself, possibly embroidered on the caparisons of his horse at a tournament shortly after his marriage to Mary Rose, or at the wedding itself. There prevailed a keen perception at the Tudor court of cloth and colour as representative of status, much as purple was revered in the ancient world.

Wolsey, whose intervention had virtually saved Brandon's life, had made of Brandon a client seeking patronage. However, Brandon was now the King's brother-in-law: 'much honour and respect were paid him'. After Wolsey, he occupied the second seat on the King's Council, although he attended meetings only when matters of importance were at stake, spending most of his time looking after the royal interests in East Anglia.

The Venetian envoys, noting the general disapproval and lack of public celebration, prudently waited two months before congratulating Brandon on his marriage. Encountering him in the King's company at a public audience, they addressed him in

Latin. He answered 'very lovingly' in English. The chronicler Edward Hall recorded that many men 'grudged against the marriage', and said it was a great loss to the realm that Mary had not married Prince Charles of Castile, but wiser men were content, reflecting that another foreign marriage would have involved expenditure. As matters stood, Mary brought nine or ten thousand marks into the realm. And 'whatsoever the rude people said, the Duke behaved himself so that he hath both the favour of the King and of the people. His wit and demeanour was such.'[13]

The handsome Suffolks rode out the storm with their customary charm and dignity. Posterity has tended to regard Mary Rose as the beautiful Tudor Princess who became a Queen and then romantically married for love. Rarely is she given credit for intelligence or courage. It should not be forgotten that, had she not played her few cards well, keeping her bargain throughout her brief marriage to the King of France, and holding her clever, volatile brother to his word, she would not have managed it. She displayed determination, and an acute understanding of the character of the men with whom she had to negotiate, and who had power over her life. Although in many respects very different from them, she was, after all, the granddaughter of the formidable Margaret Beaufort and the granddaughter of Elizabeth Woodville.

8 - Notes

1.   Journal de Louise de Savoie, Petitot collection of *Mémoires sur l'Histoire de France*, Series I. t. xvi., 457

2.   L&P Hen Viii ed. Brewer, vol 2 pt 1.1 , BM Calig D vi 268

3.   BL, MS Cotton Vespasian FXIII, f 202 b, ed. Ellis.

4.   Jean Grignaux de Talleyrand Périgord, in Pierre de Bourdeille, Seigneur de Brantôme, *Oeuvres Complètes*, Société du Panthéon Littéraire, 1842, Andre de Bourdeille, Jean Alexandre Buchon, vol 4, quatriesme discours, 357

5.   ibid.

6.   L&P For&Dom Hen VIII vol ii 43-51

7.   BL MS Cotton Caligula DVI, 246-7

8.   L&P Hen VIII vol ii pt 1 222

9.   BM L&P Hen VIII Jan 1515 21-31, Calig. D VI 179, 80. Suffolk to Henry VIII

10. L&P Hen VIII vol ii pt l 225

11. ibid, *Preface*, section 1

12. Many English secondary sources given the more flattering adjective 'bonne' rather than the derogatory 'basse', which is probably more in keeping with Louise's views. 'Journal de Louise de Savoie, Duchesse d'Angoulesme', Petitot collection of *Mémoires sur l'Histoire de France,* Series I. t. xvi

13. Edward Hall, *Henry VIII*, an edition of Hall's *Chronicle*, 1904, ed. C Whibley, London

9 DUCHESS OF SUFFOLK

At twenty years old, having married the love of her life and patched things up with her powerful brother, Mary was still brimming with zest for life. Consequently, she found living in the country a little dull. She detested prolonged periods spent away from Court. However, her presence there depended upon two factors: her brother's whims, and the current state of her own precarious finances. After their marriage, she and Brandon spent the remainder of 1514 re-establishing their relationship with Henry. Other Court favourites were shrewder than Brandon, possessed a readier wit, shone with greater intellectual brilliance. Yet Brandon was soon reinstated as the King's favourite: brave, loyal and honest, his was a refreshing presence in a court teeming with sycophants and intrigants, and Henry valued him for it. Henry had had his Tudor tantrum over the lovers' disobedience, punished them, and quickly forgiven them. Within the year, Mary and Brandon were back in favour.

Mary had benefited from her brief experience as Queen of France. English fashions had always lagged behind the Continent. Mary now became the arbiter of taste at Court, introducing new fashions in dress and manners to the ladies, keeping herself *au fait* with trends by studying long accounts of banquets and balls held at sophisticated Continental courts.

In 1515, Brandon's life changed dramatically. Not only had he obtained the de la Pole estates, but his marriage to Mary meant that any children of their union would have a legitimate claim on the throne of England. This last was almost certainly not a distinction to which Brandon had aspired, or perhaps even reckoned with, when he entered the rash runaway marriage with the King's sister. Indeed, their royal blood would prove a curse rather than a blessing for the young Brandons and their descendants, with consequences at times heart-breaking, at others fatal.

The royal connection and royal godparents were certainly a privilege, but Brandon's marriage to Mary was problematic in many other respects. Her frail health distracted Brandon from other important enterprises. Moreover, Mary's financial links with France were a constant political liability, while Brandon's friendship with King Francis engendered suspicion n England.

It was rumoured that the Brandons' household harboured French spies. The gossip may not have been entirely without foundation: in 1517, the French Government paid Mary's treasurer, George Hampton, 300 crowns for an undisclosed secret mission. Hampton made numerous trips to France – he was arrested there in 1522 – while other of Brandon's agents were in Bordeaux allegedly engaged in purchasing wine. William Fellowe, Brandon's future herald pursuivant, was involved in a discreditable attempt to sell off some of the over 200 judicial offices at Mary's disposal, the most valuable of which would fetch £800.

Brandon constantly urged a meeting between the French and English sovereigns. In such a meeting, tournaments would play a major role. When the mighty summit meeting, attended by such opulence that it would go down in history as the Field of the Cloth of Gold, was finally arranged, it was decided that Brandon would be largely responsible for organising the attendant jousts.

Brandon felt indebted to Francis for his part in smoothing over the thorny issue of the Suffolks' clandestine marriage. He also rather admired the French King. He seemed to his detractors so in thrall to the French that he was virtually an additional ambassador for France at the court of England. He had severed his ties with the Low Countries, requesting the Archduchess Margaret to send home his daughter Anne from her court.

Mary too, needed the good will of the French sovereign. She owned no land except for her 'great properties in France', guaranteed to her by Francis before she returned home. Access to the annual income from these estates, some six or seven thousand pounds, was dependent on the whim of Francis. If war broke out between France and England, and this source of funds was cut off, Mary would be penniless.

Brandon himself was cash-strapped but land-rich, at least in theory. Shortly after their marriage, Brandon settled the customary property jointure on Mary, designed to give her financial independence in the event of his death. The jointure designated for her by Act of Parliament included all the de la Pole manors as well as 18 others, 47 in all, to revert to the Crown on her death. However, in those which formed part of the de la Pole lands, Brandon had only a reversionary interest. In the event, neither he nor Mary would survive long enough to acquire them in full.

Brandon urgently needed to establish a power base on his newly granted estates. Henry had been dispensing de la Pole possessions right and left right up to 1 February 1515 when he granted the lands to Brandon. Later that month, Margaret, Countess of Suffolk, widow of the executed Edmund de la Pole, died, freeing her jointure for Brandon, but some of the manors had reverted to her feoffees in 1513. Brandon's officers Oliver Pole and Humphrey Wingfield had to buy them back for £1,000. Consolidating his East Anglian properties meant repurchasing them from the Earl of Surrey at extortionate interest rates.

His own irregular income and Mary's fluctuating French pension provided an uncertain financial basis for their lifestyle;

Mary did not really have a country seat worthy of her status until 1527, when Brandon built Westhorpe.

When Brandon was granted the de la Pole properties, he was still having to borrow money to finance his stay in France, which was never reimbursed, so his acquisition of the estates was delayed. He never managed to secure the whole estate. The Brandons would fall deeper and deeper in debt as they struggled to repay Mary's huge debt to the King. Worried about the cost of keeping up appearances at Court, Mary remained on their East Anglian estates for long periods while Brandon was in attendance on the King. This economy reduced her dressmaker's and other bills, and the number of paid attendants she required when she needed to live up to her status as the 'French Queen' while at court, but she found life in the country dull compared to the excitement of the court.

Brandon, who needed officers he could trust, followed the example of other peers by employing his own relatives in key positions. Many of them had helped him during his troubled stay in France: Sir Richard Wingfield, his cousin, had written to Wolsey on his behalf, calling him 'the said unhappy Duke', and another cousin, Sir William Sidney, was despatched to Paris to persuade Francis to conceal the secret Parisian marriage, because it was potentially so damaging to Brandon and, by extension, to the House of Tudor. Another of Brandon's relatives, Humphrey Wingfield, a gifted lawyer, once had to plead Brandon's cause while riding alongside the Cardinal, advancing his arguments as their horses splashed through puddles.

Replacing the de la Poles as a major landowner in East Anglia required Brandon's presence. In the summer of 1515, he seized the opportunity to accomplish this, while accompanying the King who was hunting in the area. The Suffolks went on a grand progress round Norfolk and Suffolk. Mary, as Dowager Queen of France, outranking every woman at Court, except for Queen Katherine, stole the limelight. Brandon was content that it should be so, especially as the progress proved successful. They were both indulged with expensive gifts and regally entertained.

Brandon's efforts to establish himself in East Anglia suited both the King and Wolsey, both of whom were keen to see a strong, reliable magnate in the south-east to replace the de la Poles. The menace of the exiled but scheming Richard de la Pole was ever present. He and the French, who unscrupulously flaunted him as a threat to England, bragged that they could raise support among the remaining Yorkists. In 1523 Richard, primed with funds from his supporters, contemplated an invasion. East Anglia was the obvious target, being accessible by sea, and the site of the majority of the de la Pole lands.

Brandon had made huge efforts to establish himself in the area and to replace the de la Poles, altering his seal to include the Brandon lion rampant, *queue fourchée*, reminiscent of an earlier seal of the de la Poles. As well as his own relatives and connections, he diplomatically employed members of families who had been prominent in the de la Pole administration, thus ensuring continuity and defusing potentially treacherous conspiracies. By building Westhorpe in 1527, Brandon now had a residence close to his East Anglian heartland.

Outside East Anglia too, Brandon's sphere of power and influence continued to expand. In October 1515, Sir Edward Guildford handed over to him the stewardship of Sir Edward Burgh's estates in the south-east.

The same month, he and Mary attended the launching of another of the King's new ships, the *Virgin Mary*, (*la Pucelle Marie*) which would later become known as the *Princess Mary*. The vessel was huge, 6-800 tons, with 120 oars, 207 guns and the capacity to carry 1,000 men. The occasion was a merry one. Henry, wearing a sailor's suit of cloth-of-gold, piloted the ship down the Thames himself, to the great delight of his queen and his sister. Round his neck on a golden chain he sported a whistle, which, according to Wolsey, he blew 'as loud as trumpet.'

The *Princess Mary*, with the *Peter Pomegranate*, the *John the Baptist* and the *Katherine Pleasaunce*, would form the nucleus of

Henry's great navy, destined to become the most powerful maritime fleet in Europe. Other monarchs grew uneasy as they observed the massive sums Henry spent on his ships. Wolsey did his best to assure the French envoy that the great vessels had been built 'solely to give pleasure and pastime' to the two Queens. There was some truth in Wolsey's assertion: the dedication ceremony for the *Princess Mary*, 'the greatest cheer and triumph that could be devised', was chiefly designed to delight the King's sister, now fully restored to favour. But the French reaction was cool and watchful: they recognised the potential threat.

In reality, the glamorous Suffolks lacked the means to stay at Court for long periods without financial assistance from the King. At first this was not forthcoming, and they retired to Tattershall, one of their largest Lincolnshire manors, returning to Court in the autumn for the ceremony on November 15 1515, when the papal prothonotary entered London bearing the Cardinal's hat for Wolsey. Suffolk and Norfolk greeted the Cardinal at the door of Westminster Abbey the following Sunday after the ceremony and escorted him to York Place at Charing Cross, where a banquet awaited them. As French Queen Dowager, Mary sat at the top table with Henry and Katherine. Spirits were high. Both Mary and Katherine were pregnant.

At Christmas 1515, the King and Brandon amused themselves by running at the ring, Henry sporting a wreath of green satin embroidered with the Queen's pomegranate badge. He had kitted out the competitors at his own expense at a cost of £142. At the end of the day each man was told he could keep whatever he was wearing. In addition, Brandon was presented with the horse, armour and saddle he had been using. The courtiers watched the event from elaborate pavilions with chivalric names: White hart, Harp, Greyhound, Flower-delice, Leopard's head, Ostrich feather.

Thereafter, Mary remained in the country awaiting the birth of her child. Brandon wrote to Wolsey from Butley about their debts, and the couple agreed that he should send some of

Mary's jewels to Wolsey as an earnest of their intent to pay up. Brandon also sought to consolidate Henry's favour with the gift of a prized goshawk. He announced his intention of bringing Mary up to London for her confinement in March, adding plaintively that he had heard the King was planning 'some pastime' in May, but hinted that he himself was too hard up and ill-equipped to cut a dashing figure. They both assured the King that they desired nothing so much as the pleasure of his company.[1]

Mary was finally summoned in February for a joyous occasion: Queen Katherine had at long last succeeded in bearing Henry a viable child. Her labour had been an ordeal throughout which the Queen clasped the holy girdle of her patron saint, St Catherine. At age thirty-one, poor Queen Katherine, described uncharitably by one contemporary observer as 'rather ugly than otherwise', had already buried four children. The King, on the other hand, was only 25 and in full vigour. He had hoped for a son, but the longed-for child was a girl. However, the King was delighted to have a healthy child. 'The Queen and I are both young, and if it is a girl this time, boys will follow,' he told Giustinian, the Venetian Ambassador. The little Princess, the future 'Bloody Mary', was a tiny Tudor redhead who never cried.

She was named Mary for her beautiful aunt and baptised at Greenwich in the little Franciscan chapel of the Friars Observant, where her parents had married seven years before and where Henry himself had been christened. The ceremony followed the solemn time-honoured ritual established by Lady Margaret Beaufort in the Household Ordinances. The silver font had again been transported from Canterbury, the processional route was spread with rich carpets, the church was hung with tapestries. The baby, three days old, was divested of her robes and ermine-trimmed train of cloth-of-gold in a specially-constructed cabinet containing a brazier and towels, and then immersed naked in the font, set on a raised dais in view of the congregation. She was then anointed with holy oil and the white chrisom cloth was wrapped about her tiny head. Her little fist was closed around a lighted taper and she was borne to the high altar, where she was confirmed by Archbishop Warham.

Mary, far advanced in pregnancy, did not attend. It was an ice winter. From her windows she watched children sledging on the frozen Thames, and laden carts crossing the great river on a highway of solid ice. Brandon represented the family, presenting the infant with a New Year's gift of a golden pomander. This practical piece of jewellery was worn on the girdle by women of all ages. It contained perfume, usually based on ambergris, musk or civet or aromatic spices, to be delicately sniffed at when confronted by 'foule, stinkying aire'. Wolsey stood godfather, and the baby's great-aunt, Lady Katherine Courtney, Countess of Devonshire and daughter of Edward IV, and the Duchess of Norfolk were the godmothers.

On Tuesday March 11, late at night, at Bath Place near Temple Bar, Mary gave birth to her first child, a son. In an impressive ceremony the baby was given his uncle's name, Henry. The King and Wolsey stood as godfathers, Lady Katherine was godmother to this child too, highlighting Mary's links with the royal house of York. The font in the Hall at Suffolk Place was filled with lukewarm water for the baby's comfort. Fires blazed on the hearths in the corners, the light of 24 torches flickered on the wall hangings and bench cushions, embroidered with red Tudor roses and white Yorkist roses. It was a state occasion attended by everyone of importance except Mary herself. She waited in the nursery to receive her son and his baptismal gifts. The walkway from the nursery to the door of the hall had been newly spread with gravel and rushes, enclosed by an ornamental rail and lit by flaring torches. Outside the Hall a substantial timber porch had been erected, covered and lined with cloth-of-gold. The christening procession passed along this artificial aisle. After the ceremony, spices and wine were served by the peers, headed by Norfolk. The christening gifts were presented one by one. Lady Katherine Courtney gave two pots of silver and gilt, the King a saltcellar and cup of solid gold.

Those who resented Brandon's influence and despised his humble origins observed with ill-concealed envy the auspicious launching of this royal child. Obsessed with dynastic succession, people reflected that, if the ageing Queen continued to fail to produce a male heir, baby Henry Brandon might eventually inherit the throne.

The birth of a healthy Princess had brought out the sunny side of the King's volatile nature. He was equally delighted with his small namesake, Mary and Brandon's son. The whole month of May was devoted to revels and enjoyment, in celebration of the safe arrival of the baby cousins, and also the visit of Henry and Mary's older sister, Margaret. The costly christening had drained Brandon's coffers, but the Suffolks remained at Southwark for several weeks in anticipation of a reunion with the widowed Queen of Scots, and the attendant festivities.

Margaret, Queen of Scotland for ten years and Regent for two, widow of James IV and mother of three-year-old James V, was in trouble. Determined to retain the power in Scotland for herself and her son, her position as Regent was threatened when John Stewart, Duke of Albany, cousin and potential successor to her son, arrived in Scotland. Although usually courageous and resourceful, Margaret was also headstrong and reckless, and she now destroyed her own powerbase with one act of romantic folly. The handsome young Earl of Angus, Archibald Douglas, had been introduced into her Court by his grandfather, Lord Drummond, the Chief Justiciary of Scotland and the father of the murdered Lady Margaret Drummond, Margaret's late husband the King's favourite mistress.

On 14 August 1514, aged twenty-four, Margaret married Douglas in a secret ceremony at Kinnoul Church. This disastrous action alienated many clans who nurtured a deep hatred of the Douglases. The Scottish lords foregathered and solemnly voted to depose the Queen from the Regency. Sir William Comyn, Lyon Herald, who the previous year he had had to face Henry VIII with James's IV's declaration of war, now faced another unpleasant task. He had to inform Margaret of the lords' decision. Ushered into Margaret's Presence Chamber, he addressed her by her new title decreed by the Council: she was no longer 'the Queen's Grace' but 'My Lady the King's mother'. Enraged, Old Lord Drummond rose from his chair, squared up to Lyon Herald and slapped him across the face with his glove.

The Duke of Albany was chosen as Regent by the Scottish Parliament. He immediately took custody of young James. Scotland was on the brink of civil war.

By August 1515, Margaret realised she had lost both her Regency and her children. She fled from virtual captivity in Edinburgh, to live quietly in northern England. At Harbottle Castle in Northumberland on October 8, after a difficult labour in which she nearly died, Margaret bore her seventh child and third daughter, Margaret, the future Countess of Lennox.

On 3 May 1516, after resting up for a few days, Margaret rode out to Tottenham Cross to meet her brother Henry VIII. Margaret was now destitute and suffering from sciatica. Neither of her siblings had seen her since 1503 when she left London to become the bride of James IV, but they had followed her turbulent career with astonishment and alarm.

But she was received with all honour. Queen Katherine had sent a white palfrey upon which Margaret rode in triumph into London, followed by a large procession of courtiers and dignitaries. Later that year, Wolsey would arrange for her to occupy Scotland Yard, once the ancient London residence of the Kings of Scotland, but now incorporated into York Place. For the time being, she was to be accommodated in Baynard's Castle. Arriving there with her escort at six in the evening, Margaret must have remembered how she and Henry, two carefree children, had danced there, fifteen years previously, at their brother Arthur's wedding feast.[2]

Margaret was formally received by the King and Queen at Greenwich and reunited with her sister Mary. She appeared overawed by magnificence of her brother's court and overwhelmed by the gifts lavished on her. Margaret had inherited the Tudor taste for pomp and pageantry and luxurious living. It was reported to Henry that the gifts and gowns he had sent her in Northumberland after the birth of Margaret Douglas had cheered her wonderfully and done her more good than all the physicians in the world. After a state banquet at Lambeth in Margaret's honour, there followed a series of celebrations and jousts at Westminster or Greenwich. The climax was the Grand Tournament on 19 and 20 May, where the King, with Essex, Suffolk and young Nicholas Carew were the challengers. The three Queens, Katherine, Margaret and Mary, still often referred to as the Queen of France, surveyed the spectacular parade of gorgeously-apparelled contestants, tricked out courtesy of the Great Wardrobe in black velvet overlaid with a tracery of honeysuckle in 'fine flat gold'[3]so that the leaves and branches appeared to move and shimmer in the May sun.

Brandon was Henry's first aide. The King, Brandon, Essex and Carew were all dressed alike, but only the King's and Brandon's retainers were attired in yellow damask. The King's other attendants were clad in blue velvet fringed with gold. On the first day Henry won many accolades for his performance. Next day, Brandon outshone him in a series of thrilling contests in which all his opponents broke at least four lances on him in their eight runs. On this occasion, Henry and his attendants were resplendent in purple velvet embroidered with golden roses and foliage, the noblemen's mottoes picked out in gold on the borders of their trappings. The officers of the tiltyard wore yellow satin edged with cloth of gold. Their opponents wore white and gold.

But the King was out of temper. He felt the quality of his opponents did him little honour. He announced that in future he would 'never joust again except it be with as good a man as himself.' Thereafter he usually chose outstanding competitors, principally Brandon. At the end of the official programme, Henry and Brandon delighted the spectators by running 'volant at all comers' with a dazzling exhibition of freestyle jousting.

Shortly after the tournament, Mary and Brandon retired to the country. Mary's sister Margaret remained in England for just over a year. There was much speculation about her separation from her husband, and the possibility of a new marriage with the Emperor. One of the many people who reported back to

Louise of Savoy swore he had heard Wolsey say he would willingly renounce his cardinal's hat or 'lose a finger of his right hand', if he could bring about such a marriage.

Headstrong Margaret had no intention of being meekly married off to any elderly infirm monarch as her sister had been. She was still in love with Angus. Moreover, had the marriage been declared void, little Lady Margaret Douglas, for whom her uncle the King of England had conceived a great liking, would have been rendered illegitimate.

In June, Queen Katherine's favourite Lady-in-waiting, Maria de Salinas, left the royal service to marry William, Lord Willoughby d'Eresby, Master of the Royal Hart Hounds. The Queen provided Maria with a handsome dowry and frequently invited her to court after her marriage. She was probably a godmother to Maria's daughter Catherine, born in 1517 and named in her honour.

Fourteen years later, Catherine Willoughby would become Brandon's wife, succeeding Mary Rose as Duchess of Suffolk.

Wolsey, now in full command of the Council, was directing foreign policy. Brandon appeared to be temporarily out of favour. He spent the rest of the year in the country, unwilling to return to court unless the King sent for him. Mary, too, was in the country. She wrote a sad little letter to her brother from Letheringham, Suffolk, in September, saying she hoped soon to be with him again. She longed to be recalled to court. But Brandon was even more heavily in debt to the King than usual. By the end of 1516, he owed £1200.

Margaret, Dowager Queen of Scots, was in even worse financial straits. By Christmas 1516, she had to beg Wolsey for funds to enable her to make the traditional New Year's Day gifts to her servants and attendants, both for her brother's honour and her own. It would be a disgrace were she unable to honour her obligations. Wolsey delayed replying, so Margaret wrote him a note in her own hand, entreating him to advance her £200, against her expectations of receiving her promised income from Scotland. By the spring of 1519, Margaret would be reduced to pawning her jewellery and dismissing her household servants.

The Scottish lords had given her 'nothing but fair words'. She declared she would rather be dead than live among such people.[4] While she was in England her husband Angus seized her Scottish estates and rekindled his affair with his old flame, Lady Jane Stewart of Traquair. When she discovered that the adulterous couple were boldly cohabiting in Margaret's home and at Margaret's expense, Margaret's passion for Angus turned to black hatred.

Nonetheless, Christmas 1516 was celebrated with the usual immoderate sumptuousness at Greenwich, graced by the presence of the three Queens. There was a mood of moderate optimism: Wolsey had finally stumped up and saved Margaret's face by lending her £200 to pay for her Christmas gifts. Brandon was back in favour, having been chosen to command Henry's army in the event of the outbreak of war with France. Their reconciliation included a new financial arrangement whereby Mary's annual repayment could be made in kind – jewellery – rather than hard cash. Brandon was also granted an extension of the loan, to be paid off by instalments. Brandon managed to stall his other creditors, including the Earl of Shrewsbury, indefinitely.

In the spring of 1517 Brandon's financial difficulties were partially relieved by being granted the ward-ship of the two young sons of Sir Thomas Knyvet, bringing in lucrative resources from their estates in Norfolk and Wiltshire. Brandon tended to take a relaxed view of finances, and refused to allow his indebtedness to depress him. Nor did he curtail his lavish life style. Confident of the King's leniency, he imported expensive tapestries from the Continent and spent vast sums on his houses, building a fine brick residence in London on his ancestral estate by the Thames, Suffolk Place, in what is now known as Southwark High Street, and carrying out renovation and improvements on his country seat, Westhorpe Hall in Suffolk. Here Mary spent most of her time, attended by a staff of fifty, while Brandon was at Court. He also maintained five other properties in East Anglia, Berkshire and Oxfordshire.

It was now almost a year since the birth of the Princess Mary, and there was still no sign of the longed-for son and heir. Queen Katherine undertook another desperate pilgrimage to the renowned shrine of Our Lady of Walsingham at the Austin Priory. The Suffolks travelled to meet her at Pickenham Wade in Norfolk and accompanied her to the Priory. On the return journey, they entertained her 'with such poor cheer as we could make her Grace', Brandon recorded modestly, but so graciously that, fortunately for them, the Queen felt obliged to reciprocate by offering them hospitality the next month.

The Suffolks spent much of the rest of the year in the country as a necessary money-saving exercise. Brandon would have cash flow problems and remain in debt for most of his life. But the Suffolks much preferred the luxurious and exciting life at Court. Mary, loved by both the King and the Queen, was with her beauty and magnetism an acknowledged ornament, while Brandon was once more the King's favourite companion, in constant demand for jousts, pageants and other royal pastimes. Henry and Brandon often rode out to the lists together, their contests ending symbolically in renewed declarations of eternal brotherhood. Seventeenth century surveys of the Tower of London found complementary sets of arms and armour, one belonging to the King, the other to Brandon. Often, two equally splendid jousting suits were made for them. They invariably opened the tournament, running the first eight courses, always dazzling the spectators by their brilliance.

In late April 1517 the Suffolks visited Richmond, where Henry and Katherine were spending Easter. Henry always fled town at the slightest hint of an epidemic, and an outbreak of the plague was once again ravaging London. There was also growing social unrest in the city. Foreign merchants, French and Genoese, had begun to dominate trade through unfair practices, driving up prices and disregarding the rules of commerce laid down by the Mayor and aldermen. Eventually the English workforce revolted. On Easter Tuesday, they were inflamed by a sermon preached at St Paul's Cross by Dr Beal[e], a canon of St Mary's Hospital, who assured his audience that under God's law any man had the right to fight for his country against foreigners. England was for the English. 'This land was given to Englishmen, and as birds would defend their nest, so ought Englishmen to cherish and defend themselves and to hurt and grieve aliens for the common weal.' [5] Violence erupted. Artisans and apprentices rioted. During the night of April 30, a furious mob sacked the houses of foreign craftsmen. On 1 May 1517, always thereafter remembered as 'Evil May Day', hundreds of Londoners thronged the streets seeking out foreigners to attack. Wolsey and the Earl of Surrey rode to the gates of London only to find that the apprentices had locked the city gates. Surrey forced an entry and his father, the Duke of Norfolk, brought up reinforcements. The troops quickly suppressed the rising and rounded up the ringleaders. Forty rioters were hanged, drawn and quartered, hundreds more imprisoned. Gibbets were erected at the city gates where the grim remains of the victims of rough justice were displayed. On 22 May, in a choreographed piece of theatre, over 400 miscreants, including eleven women and many young boys, were brought to trial before Wolsey and the King in a packed Westminster Hall, hung with banners and arras of cloth-of-gold. The accused were paraded before the dignitaries, cutting a wretched a figure, in shirtsleeves, barefoot, with ropes about their necks.

In a long and impassioned address, Wolsey, as Lord Chancellor of England, reprimanded the culprits and the city authorities who had failed to keep the peace. With tears in his eyes, he urged future loyalty. Then first Wolsey and then Queen Katherine, weeping, begged the King to show mercy. The prisoners fell to their knees, taking up the cry: 'Mercy! Mercy!' The mighty Cardinal fell to his knees also, pleading for clemency. The King ordered the prisoners to be released. The prisoners leapt and shouted for joy and threw their halters in the air. There were tears of relief all round. 'Then were all the gallows within the city taken down and many a good prayer said for the King.'[6]

There was more cause for rejoicing. Both Mary and Katherine were pregnant again. On May 18, Margaret had set out to return to Scotland, to attempt a reunion with her wayward husband.

Henry had worked out her itinerary and rode north with her for the first four days. He had entertained her for over a year at a cost of more than £2,000 and she left England laden with his gifts of gold, valuable textiles and equipment and trappings for her horses. His generosity was based on the understanding that Margaret would promise to take no further part in government and administration in Scotland. But by September she had gone back on her promise and was plotting to take control. Predictably, given the amount of opposition, she failed. On 30 October Wolsey learned that she was 'badly treated and no promise kept to her.' [7]

But Henry was too preoccupied with his own affairs of the heart; he sent neither money nor troops to help Margaret. His Queen was expecting her fourth child, but Henry was deeply involved in his romance with young Bessie Blount, now one of the Queen's maids of honour. Bessie had first attracted the King's attention when he had partnered her in a Christmas pageant at Greenwich back in 1514. Bessie seems to have been a popular and lively young lady: in October 1514, Brandon, who was single at the time, and already in France, had added as a postscript to a letter to Henry, asking him to remind 'Mistress Blount and Mistress Carew' to reply to him when he wrote to them or sent them love tokens, the implication being that both the King and Brandon were on familiar terms with both ladies and possibly shared their favours.

Margaret now wrote to her brother, pleading to be allowed to return to England and live separately from her husband, although she did not mention the word 'divorce', nor did she mention Wolsey's notion of marrying her off to the Emperor. She did, however, meekly promise that she would never marry again unless Henry selected her bridegroom.

Henry's response demonstrated the double standard and arrant sexism of Tudor morality: at Margaret's suggestion of leaving her erring and faithless husband, despite his appalling behaviour, Henry declared himself outraged and sent Friar Bonaventure Chadworth to Scotland to lecture Margaret on moral values and wifely duty. Despite her pleas to be allowed to return to England, both Henry and Wolsey found it more expedient, as well as cheaper, to keep her where she was. Over the next few years Mary heard from her sister occasionally, but neither she nor Henry ever saw Margaret again.

Queen Katherine's son was born in February. The child did not live long and its name was never recorded. Bessie Blount, on the other hand, would eventually bear Henry a healthy illegitimate son, Henry Fitzroy, Duke of Richmond. Henry's disappointment over his lack of a legitimate male heir was tempered by his delight in this living proof of his ability to beget male children.

9 - Notes

1. L&P Hen VIII vol ii pt 1 1605 44

2. ibid, 1861

3. Hall, 584

4. BL MS Cotton Caligula BI f 275; L&P Hen VIII vol 3 pt l 1024

5. ibid, I, 57; also Brewer, I, 247, quoting Giustinian, the Venetian ambassador: 'From that day they commenced threatening the strangers that on the first of May they would cut them to pieces and sack their houses.'

6. Hall, 591

7. L&P Hen VIII vol ii pt 2 3712, 3713

In the summer of 1517, the dreaded sweating sickness returned, causing the inevitable panic. At the first sign of infectious disease, the Court left the city and fled to their country houses, seeking purer air and less congestion. The dreaded sweating sickness had first appeared in England in 1485, causing some to view it as divine retribution visited upon the Lancastrian Tudors for usurping the Yorkist throne. Europeans called it 'the English sweat', because it appeared to have originated in England and raged with great virulence there. Victims usually died within 24 hours, often succumbing within four or five hours. Brandon and Mary left town.

The permanently impecunious Suffolks needed a spell away from the expenses of court life, anyway, their finances being more precarious than ever. Brandon, so dependent on the King's favour that he dare do nothing to jeopardise their relationship, had reluctantly added his signature to a treaty of friendship with Spain. He was well aware that, if he alienated Francis, Mary's French income, unreliable at the best of times, could be terminated at any moment.

Notwithstanding, in July the Suffolks happily returned to Court in July to participate in the lavish reception of the envoys sent by Charles and Maximilian. From playing the military commander, Henry had now recast himself in the role of international peacemaker, intent on maintaining the balance of power between Francis and Maximilian. He modestly informed the Venetian envoy Giustinian that he had no international aspirations; he was content with what he had, and wished only to govern his own subjects.

The Imperial diplomatic mission arrived with an imposing retinue of a hundred horses and a twenty-four wagon baggage train. Henry responded by sending out 400 nobles to meet the ambassadors and escort them to Greenwich, where they were received in audience with great magnificence. Queen Katherine and Mary, Duchess of Suffolk, resplendent in cloth-of-gold, showcased their priceless jewellery. But the King outdid them, wearing a splendid garment 'in the Hungarian fashion' with a heavy collar of 'inestimable value' about his neck. The Venetian minster recorded that 'everything glittered with gold.' As Henry intended, the foreign delegates were duly dumbfounded by this display of English opulence and culture. They were lavishly wined and dined, and entertained with concerts, pageants, jousts and exhibitions. In these events the King always starred, demonstrating his many and varied talents at tilting or music-making.

On St Peter's Day, after Mass, the terms of the accord were discussed. The event culminated in a joust held before 50,000 spectators. A special walled tiltyard had been built, which the awed Venetians declared to be three times larger than the Piazza di San Pietro at Mantua. There were grandstands for guests, tented pavilions of cloth-of-gold for the contestants. Henry had at first declared his intention of challenging all comers single-handed, but he was persuaded, on time considerations, to content himself with a single opponent, Brandon. The pair 'bore themselves so bravely that the spectators fancied themselves witnessing a joust between Hector and Achilles', recorded Francesco Chieregato, the papal nuncio. In a four-hour contest, the champions tilted eight courses, shivering their lances, 'to the great applause of the spectators'. The King, mounted on a succession of splendid destriers, executed breath-taking caprioles. 'On arriving in the lists the King presented himself before the Queen and the ladies, making a thousand jumps in the air, and after tiring one horse, he entered the tent and mounted another...doing this constantly, and reappearing in the lists until the end of the jousts.'[3] Dinner was then served. Chieregato stated that the guests remained at table for seven hours by the clock.

After dancing till dawn, the business meeting was conducted. A defensive league comprising the Papacy, the Empire, Spain and England was proclaimed. The ambassadors left with a loan of over £13,000, to be repaid in instalments, and laden with gifts worth £3,000. Chieregato was impressed with the English and their King, their wealth, elegant manners, decorum and courtesy, blessed with a worthy and eminent sovereign. Nobody, he thought, could call the English barbarians.

Chieregato would find Wolsey's demeanour less decorous: the great Cardinal's usual affability concealed ruthlessness. On a later occasion, he cursed and struck the papal nuncio, and threatened to have him put to the rack.

Wolsey supervised Brandon's finances. None of the total debt for which Brandon had contracted in 1515 had been paid. In May 1517, Wolsey moved the goalposts and tightened the purse strings. The payments remained at 1,000 marks a year, but Brandon was now to pay off 500 marks a year towards his own debts, even when no dower was forthcoming from France for Mary. Instead of falling due within forty days, Wolsey reduced the time scale to fourteen days. In the event of Mary's death, all her personal jewels and valuables would revert to the Crown. She had to promise not to resign her dower to Francis. Jewels to the value of 2,000 marks were handed over, and the total debt was increased by more arrears on the Welsh lordships of which Brandon was the Receiver; additionally, in an unprecedented sideswipe, the Suffolks were charged £600 for their lodging at Court. In the end, calling in the debt remained merely a threat, just so long as Brandon retained the King's favour. The Suffolks remained the King's greatest debtors, after Francis himself.

After the departure of the Burgundian envoys, the Court dispersed. Mary, in the last stages of pregnancy, set off for Walsingham Priory, but when her labour started she was forced to accept the hospitality of her old acquaintance Nicholas West, Bishop of Ely.

Hatfield, 17 miles north of London, had been the seat of the bishops of Ely since the Middle Ages, but the palace had been leased to the King's farriers and was Crown property. In this idyllic and secluded mansion set amid orchards, early on 16 July, St Francis's Day, Mary gave birth to her first daughter. The baby was christened two days later at the local parish church before a congregation of 75. She was given the name Frances, ostensibly after the Saint but perhaps also in honour of the King of France. The ceremony was illuminated by 80 torchbearers. The godfather was the Abbot of St Alban's. The godmothers, Queen Katherine and the infant Princess Mary, were represented by Elizabeth Grey and Lady Boleyn, probably Lady Anne Boleyn, the wife of Edward Boleyn and a favourite of the Queen's. Katherine had little idea that Lady Anne's niece and namesake would one day cause her such grief. This christening was less formal than that of Mary's first- born, since the King was not present. Besides, Frances's birth was less dynastically important. The King already had a healthy legitimate daughter and a thriving illegitimate son, his child by Bessie Blount.

No-one could have foreseen that baby Frances Brandon's own daughter, Lady Jane Grey, would pay a terrible price for her royal Tudor descent.

The epidemic continued to sweep through England's cities, keeping many of the nobility away from London for the rest of the year. The Suffolks remained mostly at Westhorpe Hall, in the green heart of rural West Suffolk with its windmills and dovecotes. Westhorpe was a comfortable manor house nestling within its moat, boasting a cloistered court and a private chapel, the latter beautifully lit by high stained glass windows. Under Mary's influence, the gardens had been laid out in the elegant French fashion. The 14th century parish church was within walking distance. It still contains the royal pew, once occupied by Mary and Brandon on Sundays. Only 75 miles from London as the crow flies, the journey along meandering country roads usually took four or five days. The Brandons usually set out at dawn at a leisurely pace, their little cavalcade of carts and horses passing up the Great North Road – the Old Watling

Street of Roman times – to St Albans, where they would spend the first night. Mary and the children travelled in a small carriage with the nurse, the others on horseback; servants took care of the packhorses and baggage train.

Brandon had much to occupy and interest him in the country. His parks were well stocked with red deer, and he enjoyed hunting and took pride in his herds of valuable horses and mules. The Suffolks spent that winter quietly with friends and family. Both of Brandon's daughters by his wife Anne Browne were present, and possibly also Magdalen Rochester, the girl whose life he had saved in France, now aged thirteen. His older daughter, Anne, a good-looking sixteen-year-old, returned from the court of the Archduchess Margaret, kept Mary company during Brandon's frequent absences. Her sister Mary was only eight.

The sweating sickness continued its ravages in the cities. The Court was closed to all but those whose official business required their presence. Wolsey stoically remained at his post, fighting off four attacks of the disease. The King, terrified by any threat of epidemics, fled from one residence to another before the spreading infection. He ordered the numbers of visitors to be monitored and limited, in case they brought disease. Even Mary and Brandon were not often permitted to join Henry, except when he relented and sent for them out of boredom or anxiety.

The Suffolks had yet again narrowly avoided financial ruin, and were once more enjoying the King's favour. This was confirmed in March 1518, when to their delight they were invited to spend Easter with the King and Queen, who were currently staying in Abingdon. Henry wanted to celebrate Easter with his sister as he had done in 1516. When the Brandons arrived on April 1, the atmosphere was tense; rumours of plots to overthrow the King were circulating. Henry had intended to return to London, but had once again lost his nerve upon learning that the capital was still infested with disease. He decided he was better off in Abingdon, where there was less danger, and where people did not depress him by coming to him every day bringing news of yet more deaths. Buckingham and other members of the Council were dismissed, but the Suffolks stayed on, accompanying the King and Queen to the royal manor of Woodstock at the end of the month. Mary was loath to leave, and Henry found it difficult to deny his adored younger sister anything. She was an ornament to the court. Besides, she was not well.

That Easter brought the added strain of political concerns. Wolsey was in London negotiating a rapprochement with France. He frustrated Brandon by keeping the King, Sir Henry Marney and Sir Thomas Lovell informed of his progress, but excluding Brandon. Brandon's enemies claimed he had promised the French the restoration of Tournai, thus destroying Wolsey's main bargaining point. Brandon, eager to vindicate himself, bombarded Wolsey with assurances of good faith for two months. At the end of July he hurried from the Bury St Edmund's Abbey of Elmswell, where he was staying, to Enfield to confront Wolsey. He found Wolsey more relaxed than expected: the treaty was just about signed and sealed. Brandon sensed that the temporary coolness between them had evaporated. The King came to stay at Wanstead, where Brandon was still Keeper, and enjoyed Brandon's entertainment. At the end of July, Brandon attended Wolsey in Council at Westminster, having been commanded by Henry to be present. But Mary, laid low with repeated attacks of fever, remained longer at Woodstock than intended. Brandon apologised to Wolsey for the delay. 'The French Queen was unable to depart the Court so soon as was appointed, for, Sir, it hath pleased God to visit her with an ague, the which has taken her Grace every third day four times very sharp, but by the grace of God she shall shortly recover.'[4] He added that she was attended daily by the King's physicians, who were able to assuage much of her suffering, as was the kindness of her brother.

By late September, Mary had shaken off her indisposition and was sufficiently recovered to visit London for the reception of the French envoys, headed by her old admirer, Admiral Bonnivet. The French embassy had three objectives: to negotiate the return of Tournai, to sign a peace contract between England and France, and to celebrate the betrothal of King Henry's daughter, Princess Mary, to the Dauphin, the infant son of Francis and Claude, still a babe in arms. Princess Mary, aged two and a half, was brought in for their inspection. On catching sight of Friar Dionysio Memmo, the court chaplain, a skilled musician born in Venice, the little princess captivated the company by squealing 'Priest! Priest!', begging him to play for her. The King jovially swept his daughter up in his arms, and the musician obliged, to the general delight.

On 3 October a general peace, the Treaty of London, was proclaimed between England and France at St Paul's. The French regained Tournai, paying Henry compensation. The 323,000 crowns outstanding on Mary's dower was to be settled. Correct procedures were to be put in place to ensure that her income as Queen Dowager was duly transmitted to her. Bonnivet wrote to Francis that the King of England processed to Mass accompanied by a 'great train of gentlemen, richly dressed', and by the Cardinal, and the Ambassadors from Spain and Venice.[5] The Mass was celebrated by all the Bishops and Abbots of the Kingdom. In an atmosphere of 'solemnity too magnificent for description', Henry swore to observe the peace.

After the solemn proceedings, the King and his company dined at the house of the Bishop of London. In the evening it was Wolsey's turn to feast the dignitaries. He threw a banquet at York Place which overwhelmed the Venetian Giustinian by its opulence. 'We sat down to a most sumptuous supper, the like of which, I fancy, was never given either by Cleopatra or Caligula: the whole banqueting hall being so decorated with huge vases of gold and silver that I fancied myself in the tower of Croesus.' [6] After supper there was mummery, starring the talented Suffolks, then twelve masked gentlemen and as many gorgeously-dressed masked ladies took the floor. At the end of the dance, they removed their masks, revealing the identity of the two principal performers: the King and his sister, Mary. The dancers were plied with 'countless dishes of confections and delicacies'; great bowls were placed on the tables containing ducats and dice, for guests wishing to gamble.

In the excitement of the constant diversions – Masses, banquets, pageants and dancing – Henry even forgot his dread of illness and threw himself into the swing of things with his old gusto, his favourite companions, Brandon and Mary, ever at his side. Mary and the Queen were the centre of attention. Mary was in her element, delighted with everything. She smiled at the amazement of the Londoners when they saw the French capering about the streets mounted on mules, and at the gallant efforts of the French courtiers, who had been urged by Bonnivet to 'warm up these cold ladies of England.' The French brought the hottest fashion news from Paris. Modish gentlemen were now affecting the 'shemew', a gown 'cut in the middle', or worn loose and open. This garment was soon to gain popularity in England. Henry would wear one, the gift of the French King, at the Field of the Cloth of Gold.

Two days later the Court embarked for the barge trip along the Thames to Greenwich for the espousals of the two babies, Princess Mary, and the French infant prince. In the Queen's Great Chamber, the French Admiral stood proxy for the Dauphin. The Princess, a tiny figure in cloth-of-gold, and a little black velvet hat studded with jewels, stood in front of her mother Katherine, who was once again heavily pregnant. After an eloquent Latin oration in praise of marriage, the little Princess was lifted up so that Wolsey could slip onto her finger a ring with a huge diamond. As the Admiral pressed it into place, to everyone's amusement, the child looked up at the Admiral and demanded sagaciously: 'Are you the Dauphin of France? If you are, I want to kiss you!' – an indication that she had some inkling of the purpose of all the ceremonial. Sadly, probably in all her life, no man would return Mary's embrace with passion.

In the royal chapel, to which the company now proceeded, the scene was spectacular, the rich clothing of the courtiers being set off by the whole choir, draped in cloth-of-gold. Brandon, the Dukes of Buckingham and Norfolk, served the King when he washed his hands before the feast. The Queen retired early, but the splendid festivities continued until 2 am. A grand joust on 7 October was followed by another banquet and a pageant in honour of the peace and the betrothal. That evening, Henry wore a long robe of stiff gold brocade lined with ermine. When Admiral Bonnivet admired it, Henry, in one of those fits of impulsive generosity which formed part of his legendary charisma, threw it off and presented it to him.

He then invited the company to Richmond to hunt, and proposed that Wolsey should now entertain them all at Hampton Court, which he had been embellishing since 1514. While Henry and Bonnivet set off for Richmond, Wolsey's staff were thrown into a frenzy of activity, preparing the banquet. Wolsey's gentleman usher George Cavendish recorded that they were commanded 'to spare neither expense nor labour, to make the French such triumphant cheer that they might not only wonder at it here, but make a glorious report in their country to the King's honour and that of this realm.'[7]

Wolsey was a brilliant host. Costly delicacies were brought in by the cartload, the cooks toiled night and day to devise subtle dishes to surprise the eye and delight the palate. The rooms where the French envoys were to spend the night had beds of silk and walls hung with rich tapestries. When they were shown to their rooms they found roaring fires in the grates to welcome them, and fine wines on hand for their refreshment. At supper time they were escorted to banqueting halls draped with rich hangings. The first dining chamber was imaginatively illuminated by placing candelabra on polished silver salvers, thus diffusing and reflecting the light on all sides. The tables were spread with snowy damask, the sideboards groaned under an array of precious plate. In the Presence Chamber, where the most important guests would be seated, the tablecloths had been sprinkled with perfume. The gold plate on display was so precious that it was barricaded off. The best plate was for show only. The great Cardinal, in the course of his career as the star of European diplomacy and Henry's chief minister, had acquired so much plate that there was an abundance of gold and silver salvers and dishes left to serve the banquet.

A fanfare of trumpets greeted the guests, followed by music that entranced the French envoys. But they still glanced around, perplexed, looking for their host, who did not appear to be present. As they admired the second course, a triumph of the pastry-cook's art, a model of St Paul's cathedral, complete with steeple, dishes in the shape of birds and animals, edible models of English soldiers fighting with swords and cross bows, and a chessboard made of spiced sweetmeats, Wolsey rushed in, booted and spurred as though fresh from travelling, crying out a general welcome. He dropped into his seat, still in his riding clothes, 'laughing and being as merry as ever I saw him in my life', Cavendish reported. Wolsey offered the edible chessboard to one of the French guests, who declared it was too beautiful to eat. In a grand gesture, Wolsey ordered a special case to be made in which it could be carried back to France as a memento of the occasion.

The highlight of the evening was the loyal toast to the two Kings, proposed by Wolsey, lifting a golden bowl filled with spiced wine. The company joined in enthusiastically. A document was signed promising that the two Kings would meet face to face before 31 July 1519.

But the Queen, approaching the birth of the child that was to be her last, had much to ponder. For the first time, she found herself at odds with the Brandons, usually her close and supportive friends. Katherine's kinship with Spain and the Netherlands meant she secretly deplored the French alliance, and had been quietly working behind the scenes to further the cause of her nephew, Charles of Castile. As the proposed summit meeting approached, she felt her husband should not have been meeting with Francis I at all, but with the Holy Roman Emperor. With political intrigue preying on her mind, and desperate to produce the son and heir her husband and the whole country yearned for, in November 1518, Katherine bore her sixth child. The baby girl died before she could be christened.

Two months later, in January 1519, the Emperor Maximilian died. This required the election of a new Holy Roman Emperor, even though Maximilian's grandson, Charles of Castile, nephew of Queen Katherine and the former faithless betrothed of Mary Rose, was the obvious candidate for the office. Undeterred by this, Henry VIII put his own name forward, and awaited with impatience the outcome of the election, which took place on June 28 1519. He was playing tennis with the French hostages at the Duke of Buckingham's residence, Penshurst Place, when word came that his candidature had been unsuccessful. Henry took his disappointment very well: when he learned how much bribing the electors had cost Charles, Henry snorted that he was glad he had not bothered about it too much, after all.

After the Queen's disastrous confinement, Mary retired to the country, spending the winter and most of the summer of 1519 at Westhorpe. Sometimes she and Brandon stayed at Letheringham Hall, where they were occasionally visited by Wolsey, or at Butley Priory, near Westhorpe, which, with its annual income of £400, was well able to cater for distinguished guests. The Brandons were received into the Augustinian Order in 1518. If the canons of Butley hoped for financial patronage, they were disappointed –the Brandons enjoyed their hospitality but made no major donations. They were allocated an apartment within the main building where they could have privacy, although during the summer they took their meals with the canons on the sacrists' garden. They went fox-hunting in Staverton Park or Scuttegrove Wood until late afternoon, staying out for a picnic supper afterwards. On their last recorded visit, in 1530, they stayed for two months, hunting, riding and gaming. On excursions to Yarmouth or Norwich, they always enjoyed royal receptions. During these months they were also frequently at Court in the royal household, dining at the top table. When in London the King often dined with them and spent the evening at Suffolk Place. Brandon was granted various fees and annuities in Wales, and Henry made him the gift of a 'big bald black horse bought at the Hague'.

Brandon's relationship with Wolsey had also improved. Brandon wrote to tell Wolsey that Henry was dissatisfied with the French hostages left by the French delegation as earnest of their master's good intentions regarding fulfilment of the peace treaty. Henry did not think the hostages were of sufficiently elevated status, nor did he think their own sovereign held them in sufficiently high esteem. On a more practical note, they so often beat the King at gambling on dice and cards that he was reputed to be losing six to eight thousand ducats a day. These losses hardly endeared them to him.

Concentrating on the Imperial election, Henry had postponed his meeting with Francis I until the following year. By 1520, Queen Claude was pregnant and, as both Kings were insistent that their spouses should attend the occasion, the date for their encounter could not be safely be set much later than early June. The two Kings joked that such was their eagerness for this personal encounter that neither would shave his beard before it took place. Henry's beard grew golden, but Katherine so objected to it that she nagged him constantly to shave, and before long he gave in, breaking his promise. Francis's clever mother, Louise of Savoy, managed to avert an international incident by declaring that the love the two kings bore one another 'was not in the beards but in the hearts.'[8]

The Brandons now had three surviving children, Henry, born in 1516, Frances, 1517, and Eleanor, born in 1518. After Eleanor's birth, Mary's health, never robust, declined, keeping her away from court, but by 1520 she had rallied again and was in excellent spirits as she contemplated another exciting occasion. The Court was buzzing with the forthcoming summit meeting between the two monarchs. In March 1520, the enormous preparations began for the historic encounter, which would be immortalised as the Field of the Cloth of Gold. 6,000 workmen were despatched to start work on the English quarters. At this momentous event, Mary, her charm and beauty outshining all others, would yet again prove an inestimable political and diplomatic asset to her brother the King, scoring another public relations triumph.

10 - Notes

1. CSP Ven vol ii 396-410
2. L&P ii 4134
3. CSP Ven vol ii 396-410
4. L&P ii pt 2 4479
5. CSP Ven vol ii 1085 letter 192
6. ibid
7. Cavendish, 100
8. L&P Hen VIII Preface no. 514

11 FIELD OF THE CLOTH OF GOLD

The Field of the Cloth of Gold, the legendary summit meeting between Francis I and Henry VIII, would go down in history as the Eighth Wonder of the World. Its celebrity reposes upon its extravagance as spectacle and display of opulence rather than upon its political significance. In the spring of 1520, the preparations for this massive event were snowballing rapidly. Wolsey, his power approaching its zenith, personally selected those who would accompany the King and Queen of England. But Mary Rose, Duchess of Suffolk, was not only the King's sister, but the Dowager Queen of France. This was yet another headache for Wolsey: there was no precedent to dictate the number of a former Queen's attendants.

In March 1520, Wolsey contacted Brandon. Brandon replied that Mary had again fallen ill. He apologised for his absence from recent Council sessions, explaining that Mary had sent for him from her sickbed. 'The said French Queen hath had, and yet hath, divers physicians with her for her old disease in her side, and as yet cannot be perfectly restored to her health.'[1]

But at the prospect of another glorious occasion, Mary's spirits rallied. As Dowager Queen of France, she was Henry's trump card. During the spring she and her sister-in-law, Queen Katherine, threw themselves wholeheartedly into the preparations for their visit to France. Henry, resolved to dazzle the French, gave the two Queens *carte blanche* to order sensational finery. The meeting with Francis would cost Henry £15,000 altogether. As for the French, it would take them ten years to pay off their share of the expenses. Bishop John Fisher, scandalised by the extravagance, wrote: 'Never was seen in England such excess of apparelment before'. Courtiers in both countries spent fortunes, bringing their families to the brink of ruin.

The historic meeting was to take place six miles from Calais at the Val d'Or, the Golden Valley, on a great plain near the English-held town of Guisnes, where Henry would stay, and the French town of Ardres, where Francis would be based. It was a logistical and political nightmare. Five thousand people would need to be transported across the Channel. Calais, England's last remaining Continental possession, would be the storehouse and centre of operations. The English ambassador to Paris, Thomas Boleyn, would conduct the diplomatic negotiations. Both monarchs had entrusted the formidable operation to the capable hands of Wolsey, who also had to rule on matters of precedence and etiquette, and resolve the numerous arguments that arose. A lesser man would have quailed before the challenge.

Henry, determined to present a show of breathtaking magnificence, unprecedented, unparalleled, and unforgettable, dismissed Guisnes Castle as inadequate for his august purposes. So a temporary palace, the 'palace of illusions', was to be constructed from wood and canvas, designed like a banqueting house or one of the elaborate stage sets which featured in his court entertainments, 328-foot square, with an inner courtyard, gatehouse and battlements. Completed in less than three months, this triumph of Tudor ingenuity with its brick foundations and real glass windows staggered the French; the diamond panes were described by Fleuranges as the clearest and finest he had ever seen. An Italian observer remarked that even the great Leonardo da Vinci, who had died the previous year, could have created nothing finer.[2]

The *pièce de résistance* was a banqueting hall with a ceiling of green silk studded with golden roses and carpeted with patterned taffeta. There was a King's side, a Queen's side, and a suite for Wolsey, which became his operational headquarters, and another suite for Mary. Each suite featured spacious chambers furnished with costly tapestries, Turkey carpets, beds of estate, sideboards laden with precious plate. The whole edifice was a triumph of *trompe l'oeuil*. The pitched roof was of canvas painted to resemble slate. Pennants featuring the royal arms fluttered from flagstaffs carved with Welsh dragons, English lions, the white harts of the Angevin monarchs, not forgetting the legendary Beaufort yales, deer whose antlers allegedly swivelled round on their heads.

On the lawn before the palace, beside a gilded pillar bearing a statue of Bacchus, God of Wine, a fountain 'of ancient Roman work' flowed with wine of three types, white, Malmsey and claret. An invitation in Old French was carved in the stonework, welcoming all comers to partake of this munificence: 'Faicte bonne chere quy voudra.' Silver drinking cups were chained to the fountain. The French were astonished that nobody attempted to steal them.[3] Both Princes kept open house throughout the proceedings. Grand marquees were erected for entertainments and banquets. A nine-foot high rampart encircled the whole camp. Leading courtiers were to be accommodated in the Castle of Guisnes, others in the 2,800 gaudy pavilions set up at nearby Balingham, but there was not enough accommodation. Some of the aristocratic participants paid local farmers to put them up on a bed-and-breakfast basis; some even had to set up impromptu beds in hayricks.

The food bill came to £8,839, £440 spent on spices alone: 2,200 sheep, 800 calves, 1,300 chickens, 340 beeves, 26 dozen heron, 13 swans, 17 bucks, 9,000 plaice, 7,000 whiting, 700 conger eels, 4 bushels of mustard, mountains of sugar for the refined pastries that were to astound the French, gallons of cream for the King's cakes. The bill for wine and beer came to £7,400.

The King of England's retinue would comprise 4,000 persons, including a hundred peers and princes of the Church; Dukes, chaplains, the entire staff of the Chapel Royal, heralds, poursuivants, 200 guards, 70 Grooms of the Chamber and 266 household officers, each attended by his own household servants.

Queen Katherine's suite numbered almost 1200; her attendants included Mary Boleyn, who had served Mary Rose in France in 1514, staying on at the French court in the service of Queen Claude after Mary returned to England in 1515. Mary's reputation has been sullied both by contemporaries and history. King Francis ungallantly referred to her as 'my English mare.' It has been widely assumed that she was his mistress, although never 'maitresse en titre' like Françoise de Foix. Even 20 years later, he would refer to her as 'a great whore, the most infamous of all'. Certainly, Mary Boleyn had later become the mistress of Henry VIII, supplanting Bessie Blount, the mother of his son. Both parties conducted the affair with unaccustomed discretion. But in 1528 when Henry asked the Pope for dispensation to marry Anne Boleyn, he admitted that he had placed himself within the forbidden degrees of affinity by having sex with her sister. The secret was out. That Mary Boleyn had recently managed, despite her notoriety, to secure a respectable husband in William Carey was probably thanks to King Henry's interest in her. Now Mary, a decent married woman at last, would witness the meeting between her two old flames – if indeed she ever really had been the mistress of Francis, who was not above casting aspersions of this nature on women.

Besides personnel and provisions, there was a huge cargo to be shipped to France: tapestries and hangings, furnishings, equipment required for the tournaments which had been planned for 11-22 June, under the direction of Brandon and Admiral Bonnivet: 1500 spears from the Tower arsenal, 1,000 Milanese swords, many valuable horses, which could only be transported in favourable weather conditions. The armourers' steel mill was brought from Greenwich for the repair of weaponry.

The French eyed all this English bustle and extravagance askance. There would be no prefabricated palace for Francis: the French court would occupy a town of four hundred glittering tents. The French also constructed a spectacular tiltyard. Lest either King should lose face, it was agreed that neither would joust against the other. The terrain was levelled out to ensure neither combatant had the advantage.

The area was soon crowded with sightseers, lured by the promise of thrilling spectacles and free drink. When the tournament finally got under way, so liberally did the wine flow that Francis issued a royal proclamation forbidding access to unauthorised persons, on pain of hanging. His officers turned away 10,000 people, but not before the streets were littered with drunken ploughmen, labourers and vagabonds lying in heaps. Still the crowds poured in; the Provost Marshal of the Field appeared powerless to stop the flow.

Henry, leaving England in the hands of Norfolk and Bishop Foxe, set off, arriving at Canterbury on 25 May 1520, with Brandon, Buckingham, ten earls, five bishops, the great Cardinal, the Archbishop of Canterbury, Queen Katherine, Mary Rose, their ladies, and 3,000 horses.

But before he met with Francis, Henry had planned another important meeting. The death of the Emperor Maximilian had radically altered the political balance of power in Europe: three dynamic young monarchs, power-hungry, ambitious and wily, now directed the course of history. Both Francis I, at 25, and Henry VIII, almost 28, courted the favour of Mary Rose's former betrothed, the hatchet-faced nineteen-year-old Habsburg Charles, the new Holy Roman Emperor. While Francis and Henry were effusively assuring one another of mutual support and affection, behind the scenes, each was secretly manoeuvring to ingratiate himself with Charles. Henry, dismissing the fact that his only daughter was already betrothed to the Dauphin, and that Charles himself was pledged to the Dauphin's sister, offered Charles the hand of the Princess Mary.

Wolsey had arranged this hasty meeting between Charles and Henry to enhance Henry's firepower in his subsequent discussions with Francis. Henry, hoping to conduct his meeting with Charles on English territory in France, had suggested Calais as the venue. But Charles announced that he would land at Sandwich in mid-May, on his journey from Spain to his northern dominions for his coronation at Aachen. Charles was keen to meet Henry before the latter had a chance to sign any binding contracts with Francis. But his ship was delayed by contrary winds, so he only just made it to England by 26 May, the date Henry had set as the deadline for his own departure to France. The Emperor's ships put in at Dover to a thunderous salute from the English flotilla lying in the straits of Dover. Charles strode ashore beneath a canopy of cloth-of-gold emblazoned with his device, the black eagle. Wolsey welcomed him and escorted him to Dover Castle, where he spent the night.

The moment he learned of the Emperor's arrival, Henry galloped off to the Castle to greet him. One account claims that Henry arrived after Charles had retired for the night, and had at Henry's insistence to be roused from his bed. Another version reports that Henry reached the castle just after dawn, and the two men bumped into each other on the stairs as they hurried to greet one another. The departure of Henry's fleet was now delayed for a further five days while he conducted his business with the Emperor and entertained him and his suite. Henry escorted the Emperor to Canterbury, where the citizens welcomed him rapturously, having loathed the French since time immemorial.

After High Mass in Canterbury Cathedral, King and Emperor knelt in prayer at the shrine of St Thomas à Becket and were shown the martyred saint's hair shirt, his battered skull and the sword that had inflicted the fatal blow, all of which sacred relics they devoutly kissed. Afterwards, on the marble staircase of the palace, the Emperor encountered his aunt, Queen Katherine. Elegant in ermine-lined cloth-of-gold, exquisite ropes of pearls looped about her neck, Katherine, overjoyed to be united at last with her nephew, burst into tears.

To enhance the glorious spectacle with which he proposed to astonish the French, Henry had encouraged the royal ladies to devise sumptuous new wardrobes. As they processed to Canterbury Cathedral for Mass, Mary Rose, walking with Katherine immediately behind the Emperor, was resplendent in cloth-of-silver trimmed with gold cord and studded with pearls.

When Charles beheld the matchless beauty of the Princess to whom he had been betrothed for six years as a boy, it was said he shed bitter tears in contemplation of the prize he had rejected.

Charles brought with him in his train another famous beauty, Queen Katherine's stepmother, Germaine de Foix, Dowager Queen of Spain. King Ferdinand had married the young widow after Isabella's death. Germaine endured the same salacious rumour-mongering as Mary Rose: people whispered that her charms had hastened the demise of an ageing husband, debilitated by his efforts to beget an heir of her. When Ferdinand died in 1516, Germaine had married the Margrave of Brandenburg.

At the three-hour state banquet all three Queens graced the royal table, and enjoyed 'much revelry' till daybreak. The fun was fast and furious. According to the Venetian ambassador, one young visiting gallant, the Count of Capra, 'made love so heartily that he had a fainting fit' and had to be carried bodily from the chamber.[4] After a banquet lasting four hours, because of the large number of courses, the tables were removed and the ball was opened by the Duke of Alba, a sexagenarian, 'but still amorous.'[5] He danced with a lady who, while not handsome, was very graceful. Mary was in great form, dancing with her brother the King and her husband Brandon, but the Emperor ungraciously refused to take the floor, although his new little proposed bride, Princess Mary, was present, in her party dress. One romantic interpretation ascribed Charles's moroseness to his being mesmerised by Mary Rose's beauty and tormented by his repudiation of her. However, marriage or romance was probably the last thing on the Emperor's mind. He was desperate for an alliance with England that would guarantee him the military assistance he knew he would soon need.

The two monarchs parted on excellent terms. Henry rode five miles with Charles, satisfied with the outcome of their talks, and now looking forward with greater confidence to his meeting with Francis. Wolsey escorted Charles to Sandwich, while Henry proceeded to Dover, embarking on 31 May with 27 ships, after five vessels had swept the Channel to make sure no threats lurked anywhere.

Arriving a few days later at Guisnes, they were delighted to find that their orders had produced a monument to Renaissance splendour and ingenuity, a worthy backdrop for the intended display of late mediaeval pageantry. The gateway of the English headquarters was guarded by four huge golden lions, above which hovered a naked winged Cupid, symbolising the celebration of love and amity between the two nations. The English encampment, 28 brilliantly-coloured tents, gleamed in the June sun; on the Ardres side the French tented town flashed in gold and silver around the huge royal marquee, lined in blue to represent the heavens, set with gold foil stars. Here, Francis entertained Henry and Wolsey, beneath the golden statue of St Michael the Archangel, until the gales of the Picardy plain blew the tent away, occasioning much mocking laughter from the English workmen, and scathing comments about shoddy French workmanship. After this humiliating disaster Francis moved his headquarters to Ardres, borrowing money to provide new halls and pavilions and a Roman theatre.

On 7 June, to the thunder of cannon, the two monarchs, accompanied by a host of courtiers, rode out from their respective headquarters to their historic meeting on the plain. Despite the protestations of friendship, their two nations had so recently been sworn enemies that fear of an ambush lingered, and both sides came in battle array. Henry VIII, attended by the Yeomen of the Guard, glittered in cloth-of-gold and silver, heavily bejewelled, with a feathered black bonnet and his golden Garter collar. He had grown his beard again, and it glinted reddish gold in the scorching Picardy sun; as his great bay horse trotted out the gold bells on its harness jingled. The sun gleamed also on the apparel of Francis I, also in bejewelled cloth-of-gold. He sported white boots and a black cap, and was attended by his Swiss Guards. The two young Kings paused dramatically on the perimeter of the Val d'Or, and then, to a fanfare of trumpets and sackbuts, galloped alone towards each other, doffed their bonnets and embraced as brothers-in-arms, still mounted on their destriers. After dismounting, they linked arms in a physical parade of amity, and entered Francis's gold damask pavilion. Here they chatted cheerfully until evening, sipping hippocras, a spiced wine popular in Roman times.

Aware of the prevailing climate of unresolved hostility and continuing suspicion, the young kings took care to display no hint of rivalry. Henry diplomatically insisted that their shields should be placed side by side on the tree of honour, so that neither should appear dominant. During the tournament they ran an equal number of courses, breaking an equal number of spears.

On 10 June they rode out to visit each other's Queens. Henry, accompanied by Mary Rose, rode over to Ardres to pay his respects to the heavily pregnant Queen Claude. Francis, meanwhile, arrived at the English Headquarters at Guisnes mounted on a mule. During the banquet held in his honour he was entertained by the choir of the Chapel Royal. Francis was in gallant mode. When 130 English ladies were presented to him, he insisted on kissing each one – with the exception of four or five who were 'old and not fair'. Competition between the ladies was as fierce as the jousting between their lords. The English Ambassador Sir Richard Wingfield, having learned that Francis's staff had been ordered to scour the country for the 'the fairest ladies and demoiselles', urged that the English ladies should be hand-picked for their looks. The French leading ladies were Francis's mother Louise, said to have invested in a 'whole emporium of cloth-of-gold', his sister Marguerite, and his current mistress Françoise de Foix, Duchesse de Châteaubriant. Poor Queen Claude was no beauty. She was, however, a pious and dutiful wife, a King's daughter, and obviously fertile as she clambered into the carriage. Madame de Châteaubriant was a noted belle but she, like everyone else, was eclipsed by Mary, who led the procession of lords and ladies to the French camp 'scintillating in her saddle', wearing a Genoese costume of white satin with a headdress and flowing veil.

Italian observers admired the wealth of gold chains worn by the English, but found the French more elegant. The Mantuan

Ambassador thought the English ladies badly dressed and over fond of alcohol. The Venetians thought the English ladies well-dressed but ugly. The English clucked in disapproval over the daring gowns worn by the French ladies. Mary, however, had acquired cosmopolitan tastes during her brief time on the Continent, and wore French fashions herself to splendid effect. She invariably stole the show; always described as 'superbly arrayed', she was an invaluable asset to Henry and he knew it, not only because as Dowager Queen of France she was assured of an ecstatic welcome, and knew personally all the major players in both camps, but because her extraordinary beauty illuminated every occasion. Following Mary's example, the English ladies soon threw caution to the winds and embraced the daring French fashions, by which 'what they lost in modesty they gained in comeliness.'

On 11 June, the Dowager Queen of France was borne to the tiltyard in a litter of cloth-of-gold embroidered with *fleur de lis* and the late King's porcupine emblem, as well as monograms of the initials L and M intertwined. The French spectators went wild, seeing their own *Reine Blanche*, Louis XII's bride, so exquisite, widowed so heartbreakingly young, and lost to France. The three carriages that followed Mary's, draped with cloth-of-gold, crimson and azure, carried beautiful women, splendidly dressed. Queen Claude, wearing cloth-of-silver, followed, with Louise of Savoy, the King's mother, stylish in black velvet, accompanied by a large number of ladies in crimson velvet, their sleeves lined with cloth-of-gold. Even Queen Katherine attracted attention when she wore a Spanish headdress with her still lustrous auburn hair, her remaining beauty, hanging loose over one shoulder. But for sheer crowd-pleasing charisma, Mary was unsurpassed.

One morning she and Henry led a party of masquers into the French camp, Mary and her ladies mounted on palfreys caparisoned in white and yellow velvet. Francis went to dine with Katherine, attended by nineteen gentlemen in elaborate disguise. Outside the English headquarters the fountain continued to gush forth fine wines, one day claret, another malmsey. During the two weeks of entertainments, feasting, jousts, dancing and 'midsummer games', the two courts vied for supremacy. Superficially, all was amicable, but tensions remained between old enemies. Francis half-jokingly misquoted Virgil's Aeneid to Henry, remarking 'I fear the English, even when they bring gifts.'

The semblance of bonhomie did not fool the shrewd Venetian observers, who noted 'These sovereigns are not at peace. They hate each other cordially.'[6]

Between 11 and 22 June three hundred contestants competed in the tournaments organised by Brandon and Bonnivet in the great tiltyard. Only blunted swords and lances were permitted. Henry and Francis meticulously continued their charade of courtesy. When an English Herald began to read out a proclamation in the old style used by English Kings since they laid claim to the Kingdom of France in the 14th century, 'I, Henry, by the Grace of God King of England and France…'Henry interrupted, saying 'That I cannot be, for you are here!' For the rest of the visit he would be styled 'Henry, King of England' only.

But the old rivalry between the young monarchs soon resurfaced. On 13 June, after watching a wrestling match between the Yeomen of the Guard and Francis's Bretons, Henry challenged Francis to a similar contest. He was ignominiously thrown on his back. He should have asked for a return match according to the rules of chivalry, but Francis was persuaded to refuse, by the queens and by his own courtiers, who perceived that the incident could disrupt the harmonious atmosphere. Fortunately, Henry soon regained face by scoring victory in an archery contest. Francis was determined to show Henry that no offence had been intended, so, ignoring the counsel of his lords, on June 17, accompanied by only two gentlemen, he rode over to Guisnes at dawn, and crept into Henry's bedchamber. Henry awoke to find the King of France standing over him, offering to act as his valet, helping him on with his shirt. Henry, always delighted by diversions, was charmed by this original token of respect. 'Brother' he exclaimed, 'you have played me the best trick ever played, and shown me the trust I should have given you. From now on, I am your prisoner.' He presented Francis a priceless collar of rubies. Francis returned the honour with the gift of an even more valuable bracelet.

The last public event took place on Saturday June 23. The sun still glared down, it was said to be 'hotter than in St Peter's in Rome'. The tiltyard had been converted into a chapel, and here, at noon, Wolsey, assisted by five other cardinals and twenty bishops, celebrated a solemn Mass for both courts. The choir of the Chapel Royal sang, alternating with its French equivalent, La Chapelle de la Musique du Roi, and Richard Pace gave a Latin oration on peace. The dignity of the Mass was interrupted by an almighty crash. Everyone jumped in alarm, some suspecting it was a natural or supernatural manifestation, a 'comet' or a 'monster', and others – since the peace was so new and fragile, and the old undercurrents of suspicion and hatred so ingrained, feared a treacherous ambush. It turned out to be a huge firework, in the shape of a dragon ora salamander, Francis's personal emblem, which had been set off too early by accident. It had come from the English camp. Wolsey continued with the Mass once people had settled down.

There was another unforeseen moment, if not of drama, then of comedy, when each king tried to allow the other to be the first to kiss the Holy Gospel. Queen Claude and Queen Katherine were not backward in showing similar tact: when the Cardinal of Bourbon offered them the Pax to kiss, they kissed each other instead.

The two Kings had agreed to found and maintain a chapel to Our Lady of Peace on the site of their meeting, and after Mass Wolsey laid its foundation. The solemn proceedings were concluded by a jovial banquet *al fresco*, a final joust, and the official fireworks display. The next day the Kings again paid courtesy visits to each other's Queens and, after one last feast where the entertainment included mummers and dancing, Queen Katherine presented the prizes to the champions of the jousts. The jousts had not been an unqualified success: Brandon, who had injured his hand, felt he had underperformed. Francis had sustained a black eye, Henry had managed to kill his own horse, and one of the French contestants had lost his life.

On 25 June, after lingering and effusive farewells and the exchange of many precious gifts, including jewels, horses and a litter, the French Court departed for Abbeville, while the English contingent removed to Calais, where Henry intended another diplomatic rendezvous with the Emperor Charles. Their route was lined with the comatose bodies of drunken stragglers. Henry thanked his lords for their support and, realising that many had beggared themselves to do him honour at the Field of the Cloth of Gold, gave them permission to dismiss half their suites, and bade them live 'carefully' for the rest of the summer. Most had enjoyed the occasion; few harboured regrets over the massive expenditure.

Politically, the concrete achievement of the Field of the Cloth of Gold was negligible. Despite the superficial display of friendship and cordiality, the old tensions, mutual distrust and jealousy persisted. The chapel to Our Lady of Peace remained unbuilt, the splendid temporary structures were demolished and the marriage between Princess Mary and the Dauphin never took place. Within three years hostilities had once more broken out between England and France. To all intents and purposes, the event had been a costly masquerade. But Henry chose to regard it as a triumph. Many years later, around 1545, he would commission- probably for Whitehall Palace – two large commemorative paintings from artists, probably Flemish. In one painting, the King is depicted as a tiny figure embarking on the *Katherine Pleasaunce*. The other work presents a composite view of events, including Henry's arrival from Guisnes with Calais in the distance, the meeting of the two Kings, feasting in a pavilion, with a tournament in the background. The effects of the gallons of free wine are not omitted: figures are shown brawling and vomiting. Above, the sky is illuminated by the impressive firework salamander.

If politically, the outcome was insignificant, the costly exercise had not been futile. The two Kings had gained insights into each other's intentions and capabilities. Henry, by his show of magnificence, had enhanced his international prestige. Moreover, Henry's meeting with Francis had paved the way for his meeting with Emperor Charles, a low-key event which was, nonetheless, of much greater political significance. On July 10, Henry and Katherine, with their reduced retinue, left Calais for Gravelines in Flanders to meet Charles V and his indomitable aunt, the Archduchess Margaret, now Regent of Austria. Mary now met face-to-face her 'chère tante', to whom she had written when a young girl, as betrothed Princess of Castile. There had once been scandalous rumours of a match between the Archduchess and Mary's husband, Brandon. Moreover, had the high-spirited Margaret not flatly refused to marry the ageing King Henry VII of England, she might once have become Mary's stepmother.

Returning to Calais with Charles and Margaret, Henry had intended to entertain them in a temporary banqueting hall painted with heavenly bodies, constructed 'upon the masts of a ship, like a theatre'. But it was the turn of the English craftsmen to suffer the force of the Normandy gales. The pavilion was blown down, and Henry and his courtiers, still arrayed in their gorgeous masquing gear, were forced to attend upon the Emperor in his lodgings instead.

Charles was a political animal, not a prancing peacock like Francis. He neither desired nor encouraged great demonstrations of sociability, and baulked immediately if he sensed that he was being manipulated. Under the expert guidance of Wolsey, who understood the Emperor's temperament, matters passed off satisfactorily. Henry was enthusiastic, the ladies were charming, Charles was agreeable. A contract of friendship was signed, promising support in the event of war with France. The betrothal of little Princess Mary to the Dauphin was annulled, and her hand offered to her cousin Charles, subject to the necessary Papal dispensation. Charles had broken off his engagement to numerous ladies, starting with Mary Rose. He now showed no more compunction in breaking off his betrothal to Princess Charlotte of France than Henry did at reneging on the promise to the French.

Friendly relations with the Empire progressed, as cracks appeared in the Anglo-French alliance. The Emperor, desperate for an ally, enticed Henry with promises of a joint invasion of France, the partition of conquests and the recognition of Henry as King of France. The betrothal of twenty-two-year-old Charles to six-year-old Princess Mary Tudor was to set the seal on the new Anglo-Imperial alliance. On March 2 1522 Henry held more jousts in the traditional Shrovetide festivities. The theme of the entertainment was unrequited love. Henry, riding a horse caparisoned in silver, sported the motto *'elle mon Coeur a navera'* (she has wounded my heart). This mysterious message may well have been dedicated to Mary Boleyn, as some assumed, but according to the rules of the game of courtly love, and given Henry's character, it could have been anyone.

Two days later, the imperial envoys were guests at Wolsey's palace, York Place, where a grand pageant was staged, featuring a green castle occupied by ladies in white satin gowns, with their pageant names embroidered in gold on their jewelled head dresses. Mary Rose, as Beauty, led the dancers. Mary Boleyn was Kindness, Jane Parker, Lord Morley's daughter (later to marry George Boleyn, become notorious, and die on the scaffold), portrayed Constancy, while Mary Rose's former attendant, Anne Boleyn, about to launch her brief stellar career, represented Perseverance – a trait which many would come to recognise that she possessed. Anne had recently been recalled from the French Court because of the political situation. She had remained in France after Mary returned to England, serving as maid-of-honour to Queen Claude. Mary had never warmed to Anne Boleyn, once she came to know her. She soon had greater reason than ever to distrust and dislike her.

Mary and Brandon played a leading role in honouring the Emperor Charles, Mary's former fiancé, entertaining him to dinner at Suffolk Place, followed by a hunt in the park.

Mary and Emperor Charles would never meet again.

11 - Notes

1. L&P Hen VIII iii 684
2. L&P Hen VII vol III pt 1 869, 305
3. Descriptions found in Hall, 1904, I, 188-218; L&P Hen VIII, III, i 632,704, 826, 852, 870; L&P IV,I, 2159.
4. CSP Ven Sanuto diaries v.xxii 210-239
5. ibid
6. CSP Ven iii 50

After 1523, although her husband's career was at its peak, Mary found herself spending less time at court. When in London, the Brandons lodged and dined on the Queen's side of the Royal household. When Mary was in the country and he was alone, Brandon stayed at the 'King's house', where meals were served daily between ten and eleven, and from four to six. Like other members of the household, the Brandons benefited from the usual allowances for the 'King's honourable house', the weekly 'bouche', which provided materials for heating and lighting their residences, and extra food and drink for their private consumption. The size of the allowance varying according to rank: Dukes and Duchesses were regarded either as having greater need of food and heating than other people, or as being obliged to entertain more extravagantly: in addition to their regular meals, they received two coarse grey cheat loaves of wheaten bread and three manchets, fine white bread, three gallons of ale and one pitcher of wine per day. The King could withdraw his bounty at any moment.

After the outbreak of war between Henry and Francis I, Mary's French income ceased. Francis seized her 60,250 livres revenue, and the Brandons had to renegotiate their debt to

Henry VIII. Technically, Brandon was required to pay the King 2,000 marks a year, but by February 1521 only a small part of the total owing, £25,234 6s 9d, had been settled. In 1522, Brandon had courted the Emperor's favour and patronage during his visit to Canterbury, gaining Imperial pensions for himself and his followers, but these were not sufficient to make up for the loss of Mary's French revenues.

However, lack of funds had never dampened the Brandons' spirits. They entertained the Emperor lavishly at Suffolk Place, and probably named their second daughter, Eleanor, for his sister.

When the war with France broke out, Brandon took the field in command of one of the most impressive armies Henry VIII ever sent to war under a lieutenant. Doughty deeds were expected of Brandon, who had not seen action since 1513. This promised to be his greatest opportunity for military glory, and also his greatest test. Henry first ordered him to besiege Boulogne, but then his orders were changed, and instead, he was instructed to lead a bold march over the Somme into the heart of France towards Paris, and link up en route with a rebel French leader, the Duke of Bourbon. This plan foundered when Bourbon's revolt crumbled.

This was not the only setback which would bedevil Brandon's campaign. Charles V had pledged that the Archduchess Margaret would support Brandon with troops and supplies, but Margaret had difficulties in meeting these commitments, with the result that Brandon's departure from Calais was delayed long enough for many of his troops to succumb to disease.

Once in the field, Brandon commanded competently, but lack of support forced him to retreat. A freak spell of frost transformed his already disease-ridden army into a mutinous rabble. The Welsh warrior Elis Gruffydd, who would later make a career in the Calais garrison, described the calamity in his vivid *Chronicle* of November 1523:

Some said it was too much for them to be lying there on the earth under hedges and bushes dying of cold, another said that he wanted to be home in bed with his wife…and yet they had No reason to complain except of their own sluggishness and slovenliness. For there was no lack of food, or drink, or wood for fire or making huts, and plenty of straw to roof them and to lie on, if they only fetched it…

At last on Wednesday night there rose a noise and shouting amongst the host and especially around the tents of the duke, and some of the soldiers said they would stay there no longer, and that they would go home willy nilly the next day…against this some of their comrades said …that was no less than treason… to this these obstinate senseless men answered that it was no worse being hanged in England than dying of cold in France. My master, Sir Robert Wingfield, heard all this noise and talking, and made me get out of my bed, where I was as snug as a small pig, to listen to the talk, and to take note of those men who were making this noise…[1]

Next morning, the mutinous feeling had spread throughout the host; men began shouting 'Home! Home!' Brandon and his captains conferred about the best course of action. The men set off to march against the freezing wind all day – one of the worst days the oldest man in the army had ever seen, though many of them were veterans over sixty years old.

This day…many men on horse and on foot died from sheer cold. Others said that some had lost the use of their limbs from the force of the frost wind. And others said that they had lost the use of their waterpipes, and could not pass any water that way until they had got fire and warm water to thaw them…[2]

In December, Brandon saw that his campaign was doomed. Defying the King's order to stay put, he led his wretched demoralised army home. Henry demanded furiously how the great Anglo-Flemish alliance of two great armies which had sworn to win him the crown of France had disintegrated into a pathetic stream of sickly scarecrows drifting back into Channel ports. However, when he learned of the misfortunes they had suffered, he calmed down, and accepted that Brandon had followed his orders as best he could. The catastrophe did not diminish either the King's affection for Brandon or his faith in him. The campaign brought Brandon little material benefit, but at least his martial reputation remained undimmed.

A few months later, the whole court was thrown in shock when Brandon almost caused his monarch's death. As the chargers of the country's greatest jousters, Brandon and the King, thundered towards one another, the spectators' breathless anticipation turned into a gasp of horror. People screamed 'Hold! Hold!' The King, desperate to try out his latest invention, a new harness he had designed himself, had forgotten, in his enthusiasm, to lower his visor. Brandon's lance was pointed at the King's exposed face. But Brandon, behind his own heavy helmet, could neither see nor hear. As he crashed into Henry, his lance struck the King on the brow under the guard of the headpiece and shattered, filling the King's headpiece with splinters. The King crashed to the ground. Brandon, tearing off his armour, leapt off his horse and rushed to the King's side. Appalled, he swore that he would never run against him again.

Henry sought to calm the general consternation and Brandon's distress, assuring everyone that the accident had been his own fault. To prove he was unhurt, he defied advice, remounted and ran six more courses, to huge acclamation, although possibly to the detriment of his health. The severe headaches from which Henry VIII suffered in later life may have been a direct result of this heavy blow to the forehead.

The incident caused a panic. The King had almost been killed, leaving no son to succeed him, thus raising the spectre of a potential civil war over the succession. A handful of potential claimants descended from the Plantagenets were still around, shadows haunting the wings. It was five years since Queen Katherine's last pregnancy, and all she had produced was a daughter. There was a general feeling that many people would never accept the rule of a woman.

At thirty-eight, the Queen's child-bearing years would soon

be ending, and this weighed on Henry's mind. Since 1522, prompted by doubts raised by his confessor John Longland, Bishop of Wilson, the King had been pondering the validity of his marriage. Now Henry started asking himself in earnest why Katherine's sons had been stillborn or died in infancy. Seeking his answer in the Scriptures, he stumbled upon the fateful passage in Leviticus which would have such an impact on English history. The verse condemned a marriage between in-laws as impure, and childlessness as the penalty inflicted by the Almighty. Although Pope Julius II had granted a dispensation for his marriage to Katherine, the King began to suspect or feign that he suspected, that his lack of viable sons was God's judgment. But the Queen was popular, and he was fond of her. Moreover, she was the Emperor's aunt. Henry knew that to put her aside would jeopardise the Imperial alliance.

Meanwhile, the entertainments went on. Christmas 1524 saw another grand tournament, originally intended as part of a great pageant, for which a massive Castle of Loyalty was built to the King's design in the tiltyard at Greenwich. The Queen was seated in the model castle when two 'ancient knights' appeared before her, begging leave to 'break spears'. When Katherine praised their courage in performing feats of chivalry at their age, they threw off their masks to reveal the thirty-three-year-old King and Brandon.

This would be the last major tournament in which Henry would participate.

In February 1525, the Emperor inflicted a resounding defeat on the French at the Battle of Pavia, taking Francis prisoner. When he heard the news, Henry leapt from his bed, threw on his shirt, and enquired after Richard de la Pole, the troublesome last Yorkist pretender, who had been among Francis's officers.

'The White Rose is dead in battle,' the herald replied.

'God have mercy on his soul,' Henry said piously, adding 'All the enemies of England are gone'. He told the messenger he was as welcome as the Archangel Gabriel had been to the Virgin Mary, and called for him to be plied with wine. He ordered bonfires to be lit in the streets of London and free wine to be dispensed to the citizens.

Henry's old dream of replicating the glory of Henry V and reclaiming England's lost possessions flared into life again briefly. His military ambitions had seen the country taxed severely to pay for futile campaigns. The attempt to levy an 'Amicable Grant' to enable him to lead an invasion of France in person met with a refusal, and provoked a revolt in Suffolk, which the two East Anglian Dukes, Norfolk and Suffolk, united forces to suppress. Howard and Brandon were both concerned that Wolsey and the King did not seem to appreciate the depth of feeling against the projected campaign, and together demanded a Council meeting so they could make their views known to Henry. The Amicable Grant was abandoned and Wolsey made peace with France. Charles V had no intention of allowing England to regain Normandy, Picardy and Brittany, and the Treaty of More, signed at Wolsey's house on 30 August 1525, made more modest arrangements.

It also made provision for both Henry's sisters. The arrears of Mary's dower rents, some £2,000 a year, were paid retrospectively for the three years during which they had been interrupted by the war. Wolsey also negotiated a deal that left the Suffolks some 22,000 livres a year better off.

Brandon maintained a prominent ceremonial role at court; after 1526, the strengthening of the French alliance placed him once more at the centre of foreign diplomatic affairs. In late 1525 the French ambassadors travelled to Reading to thank Mary for her part in bringing about the new rapprochement, and her husband replied on her behalf that she would do her utmost to maintain it.

Mary's feelings for Francis I were equivocal. He had importuned her with his attentions in her youth, but her husband Brandon had experienced Francis from a different angle, and admired him. On 9 May 1526 he and Mary wrote a joint letter to Francis congratulating him on his release from captivity after the defeat at Pavia. Mary assured him that the ladies of England had been praying for his release, both those ladies who had met him and those who had only heard tell of his God-given grace and virtue. Brandon offered Francis all that a gentleman had in his power, namely, to die at his feet in his service.

Though Henry had gloated over the capture of the French King, he and his court were still in awe of French Renaissance culture, which Henry was bent on emulating and outdoing. Mary Rose, still widely known as the French Queen, remained the court authority on French style, following Paris fashions, and an important patroness of French cultural innovations. In 1530, she presented her brother the King with a French book of hours illustrated with classical architecture and playful putti. She was the leader of an inner circle of younger nobility and distinguished foreigners, one of whom was probably Anne Boleyn, recently returned to England, but distinguished by her French manners. At one of Wolsey's revels in 1522, Mary Rose, Anne and six other ladies were rewarded for their part in the entertainment by the gift of the gowns they wore, of yellow satin decorated with 24 'resuns' each, and cauls of Venice gold.

Long before her notorious relationship with the King, Anne had incautiously become romantically involved with a member of Wolsey's household, Lord Henry Percy, heir to the Earl of Northumberland. Percy would frequently 'resort for his pastime unto the Queen's chamber, and here would fall in dalliance among the Queen's maidens.' Percy was already engaged to Lady Mary Talbot, daughter of the Earl of Shrewsbury, a better match than a Boleyn. He had the effrontery to ask Wolsey if his betrothal could be broken off, earning a stern rebuke. The Cardinal, aware that the King had been Anne's sister's lover and had certainly noticed Anne, sent for Percy's father. Northumberland told his wayward son he was a 'proud, presumptuous, disdainful and very unthrift waster', dragged him back to the North and married him off to Mary Talbot forthwith[4].

The age gap between the King and Queen was becoming increasingly obvious. Katherine had lost her youthful bloom with the years of disappointment and repeated pregnancies, while Henry was still on fire with youthful energy and zest for life. Mary Rose's affection for the ageing Queen deepened. She helped her friend Katherine entertain Charles V's sister, the Queen of Denmark, on a royal visit in 1523. The German Ambassador noted with surprise that '*La Reine Blanche*' was given precedence over the Danish Queen at the dinner table.

Two years later, Mary and Brandon were excited to be in London again when a peerage was conferred upon their second son, Henry, aged nine. (Their first son, also Henry, had died at the age of six). Several other young boys were honoured at the investiture at the new Bridewell Palace on 18 June. But the event was overshadowed by the elevation to the Earldom of Nottingham and the Dukedom of Richmond and Somerset of Henry Fitzroy, the King's six-year-old natural son by the enchanting Bessie Blount, now safely married off to Gilbert Tailboys, the son of Lord Kyme, 'an lunatic' kept in the custody of the Duke of Norfolk. In a hot, stifling room packed with courtiers, Henry Fitzroy entered to a fanfare, knelt before his father and was robed in the mantle of crimson and blue, sword, cap of estate and coronet of a Duke, as the patent of creation was read out. He then took his place on the dais beside his father the King, taking precedence over every other peer in the room.

Katherine concealed her indignation, but she was mortally offended by the insult to her own daughter, the Princess Mary, and the threat to her position. Whether a female monarch would be welcome or not, England had no Salic law. Henry had shown no qualms about leaving Katherine as regent when he marched off to fight the French. Katherine had exhorted the troops as her mother, the heroic Queen Isabella, had done, rejoicing in her title of 'King' of Castile. Katherine distrusted Wolsey, blaming him for the advancement of Henry Fitzroy. In June 1525 his spies in the Queen's household informed Wolsey that three of Katherine's Spanish ladies were encouraging her to protest. The Cardinal engineered their dismissal. When Katherine urged Henry to rescind the order, he refused.

It was becoming apparent to Katherine that she no longer held much sway with her husband. She felt increasingly isolated. The Emperor had also jilted her daughter, deciding that the beautiful Isabella of Portugal with her million-pound dowry was a better bet. Katherine's dreams of a Spanish marriage for Mary seemed unlikely to be fulfilled. Mary Rose sympathised, but both she and Brandon kept their feelings to themselves. Their own son, now Earl of Lincoln, remained a potential heir to the throne.

In 1526, Mary Rose was principal guest at the spectacular banquet given at Greenwich in honour of the French and Italian Ambassadors. The Queen, meanwhile, was comforted by the presence of her favourite lady-in-waiting, Maria de Salinas, Lady Willoughby de Eresby, who had returned to Katherine's service after the death of her husband in October. Lord Willoughby's death meant that an eminently suitable heiress became available, the ideal match for young Henry, Earl of Lincoln. Brandon had known the now-widowed Spanish-born baroness since at least 1511, when she stood godmother to his daughter Mary. He had had further dealings with her over the years, and now, supported by Wolsey, quickly put in a bid in November 1527 for the wardship of her daughter Catherine. That Christmas and every following Christmas for eight years he was to pay 500 marks until he had paid off the debt of 4,000 marks. The price was high, but it would prove a worthwhile investment for the future.

In 1527, Mary Rose stayed for over a month in the peaceful surroundings of Butley Priory, visiting friends, and distributing largesse to the monks. Brandon joined her briefly, but could spare little time to hunt and picnic with Mary. His responsibilities in the counties had grown, and now, when in the country, he was very much on business, rushing from one appointment to the next, meeting his chief supporters, attending sessions, then speeding back to London for official receptions.[5.] In the late 1520s, after the death of Richard de la Pole at Pavia, and the elimination of the Yorkist threat, Brandon's chief role in the south-east was to quell popular unrest, in co-operation with the Duke of Norfolk.

Also in 1527 Mary returned to London to attend the

celebrations of yet another betrothal for the King's only legitimate child. Having been rejected by the Emperor Charles, Princess Mary was now being wooed by that notorious womaniser, Francis I. Widowed for less than a year, Francis was exploring every available matrimonial avenue, although he was most interested in an alliance with the Empire. Reports stated that he was so keen to cement his relationship with Charles V that he was willing to propose to any woman even if she were aged a hundred. He would even propose to Caesar's mule. Charles's sister Eleanor, Dowager Queen of Portugal, was available. Her brother peremptorily ordered her to 'cast off her widow's weeds'. Eleanor obeyed, and even began somewhat prematurely calling herself the Queen of France, although Francis made no secret of the fact that he found her unattractive. Francis swore as a monarch and a gentleman to keep the troth, and at the same time swore to the English that he was free of all ties and longed for nothing more earnestly than to wed the young Princess Mary, being aware of her 'manifold virtues and other gay qualities.'[6]

Wolsey, well aware of these double negotiations, pointed out that Madame Eleanor at thirty was too old for Francis, and lacked the malleable good nature and humility possessed by 'my lady Princess.' The monarch, Wolsey cajoled, deserved a lady of more tender years and nature, of better education, greater beauty and other virtues. If she was not to be the King's bride, he suggested that perhaps Princess Mary would suit the French King's second son, the Duke of Orléans. At the end of February 1527 an embassy arrived from Paris to discuss a Treaty of Eternal Peace, to be sealed by the marriage of the Princess Mary to Orléans. If Henry continued to lack a male heir, Orléans would one day rule England as Mary's consort. Not ideal, but a provisional solution. After much feasting and revelry, the treaty of betrothal was signed at the end of April 1527. Francis offered a bride price of an annual tribute of salt, two million crowns and a personal pension to Henry of 50,000 gold crowns.

The only fly in the ointment was a throwaway remark made at Bridewell, questioning the validity of the King's marriage and therefore the legitimacy of the Princess Mary.

At the time, Henry dismissed it: but he would remember it later, when he had decided to discard Mary's mother in favour of his new love, with whom he had become obsessed, the darkly sparkling Lady Anne Boleyn.

At the same time as conducting negotiations with France, Henry was eagerly planning yet another war, this time against the Low Countries. Brandon, Wolsey, Francis I and Henry discussed strategy. Brandon was commanded to purchase armour. He was the French King's choice for the task of attacking the Netherlands with 10,000 English troops in 1528, if the Emperor refused to return the French princes held hostage for their father's humiliating treaty of 1526. Brandon's importance increased as he and Wolsey prepared for war. Troops were mustered in London, word was sent to prepare Guisnes, and the co-operation between Wolsey and Brandon was closer than ever. However, in June 1528 economic concerns – disruptions to the cloth trade and the fishing industry – forced a truce with the Low Countries; Brandon's captains disbanded their troops.

On 5 May, after Mass, Mary Rose and Queen Katherine sat side-by-side watching when the French envoys were welcomed to the King's new banqueting house at Greenwich. In this splendid new construction, the hand of Holbein was evident in much of the sumptuous decoration. Next day there was a tournament, a recital, a banquet, and masques. In one of these the King and his daughter participated. As they danced, the proud father could not resist tugging off her netted caul and letting her 'profusion of silver tresses' tumble cascading about her shoulders for the admiration of the French envoys.[7] After the masque the dancing continued till dawn. Henry, who had injured his foot playing tennis, was wearing black velvet slippers, and every courtier did the same, so that he would not be made to feel conspicuous.[8]

The revels were rudely interrupted by terrible news. Mercenaries in the Emperor's armies, exasperated by lack of pay, had run amok and sacked Rome. The Pope had barely escaped with his life, and was now a prisoner. The atmosphere ruined, everyone plunged into sombre mood, the French envoys departed quietly.

That summer, the whisper that the King's marriage was unlawful began to circulate in the taverns and pot-houses of London. When Henry got wind of it he summoned the Mayor of London, Sir Thomas Seymour, and 'charged him to see people should cease this rumour upon pain of the king's high displeasure'.[9] Henry had confided his own doubts about his marriage to Katherine to Wolsey. As a preliminary to divorce, Wolsey and Archbishop Warham had convened a secret ecclesiastical court at Westminster on 17 May 1527, at which Henry was cited for living in sin with his brother's widow. This strategy would allow the original papal dispensation of 1503 to be further examined by experts in canon law. This was the first step. Henry was furious that news of it had leaked out to the court.

He had been toying with the idea of creating his illegitimate son Henry Fitzroy King of Ireland, to make him a more acceptable match for Charles V's niece, Maria of Portugal. Katherine protested, fearing this might be a subtle move towards Henry's naming the boy his heir.

Worse was to follow: on 22 June, the King marched into Katherine's chamber and announced that after 18 years their marriage was over. He had asked the Pope for an annulment. He himself would receive absolution for committing adultery through ignorance, Katherine could spend her remaining years in a nunnery, leaving Henry free to marry Anne Boleyn and sire a male heir.

Katherine, distraught, threw herself on the advice of Mendoza, the Spanish Ambassador, and the aid of her nephew, the Emperor Charles.

Henry and Wolsey realised that the Pope, currently the Emperor's prisoner, would be unlikely to antagonise his captor by annulling the marriage of his aunt. In July, therefore, Wolsey left for France with great pomp. When his men were seen loading huge chests at Dover, reputedly containing £240,000 of the King's money, intended as bribes, people's suspicions were aroused. Officially, Wolsey was on Church business, bound to attend a convention of cardinals at Avignon, and to solicit Francis's support for the restoration of Pope Clement. But he also intended to conduct private discussions with Francis about a possible marriage between Henry and the French King' sister-in-law, Madame Renée. Meanwhile, the plan to have Henry's sister Margaret's son, James V of Scotland, declared his heir, was dropped. Mary Rose's son, Henry, Earl of Lincoln, would be second in line to the throne – after the son Henry hoped to beget with Anne.

There was sufficient genuine doubt about the validity of Henry's marriage to Katherine for the theological debate to occupy the minds of European scholars. The Pope issued a bull in 1527 granting the King a dispensation to remarry when he was free to do so. The murky matter of Anne Boleyn's relationship with Percy had to be clarified. There was also paperwork, left incomplete when Brandon married Mary Rose, to be cleared up. Pope Clement VII, who had fled for his life from the rioting Imperial troops, first took refuge in the Castello Sant Angelo and later in Orvieto. Here on 12 May 1528 he signed the bull which recognised the legitimacy of the Brandon's three children, the Earl of Lincoln and the Ladies Frances and Eleanor Brandon.

One of the mysteries in the story of Mary Rose and Charles Brandon is why either Brandon or his lawyers never addressed the matter of Brandon's messy matrimonial status in 1516. In 1507, Brandon had obtained a dispensation to allow him to marry Margaret Mortimer, thus invalidating his previous contract with Anne Browne, and bastardizing his elder daughter. At the time of his marriage to Mary Rose, Brandon required another dispensation to repudiate Dame Margaret. A lawsuit brought by Margaret's daughter by another marriage, attempting to gain possession of her mother's properties, brought the oversight to Brandon's notice. Margaret, bewildered by the lawyers' jargon, appealed to Brandon for help, thus alerting everyone to the fact that he was bigamously married to

Mary Rose, and that in spite of the splendid wedding ceremony Henry had arranged for the couple at Greenwich, their children, designated heirs to the throne, were in effect illegitimate.

Perhaps, in the haste and emotional turmoil of his secret marriage to Mary, Brandon simply forgot to sort things out, or possibly he felt overwhelmed by the intricacies of canon law, and felt unable to proceed until he had the King's support. Now Henry, perceiving parallels between his own case and Brandon's, supported him, encouraged by the fact that the Pope had granted a divorce to his sister Queen Margaret of Scotland on even flimsier grounds.

Wolsey, as usual, fixed things for Brandon with his usual efficiency. He promptly sought a bull confirming that the dispensation to marry Margaret Mortimer had been founded on error. Lady Margaret had since died, so the issue was concluded as far as the Church was concerned. The Orvieto bull found that the dispensation to marry Dame Margaret had not been viable. This legalised Brandon's subsequent marriage to Anne Browne, who thus became his only previous legal spouse. Anne Browne was safely dead before Brandon married Mary. The bull was perfect: decisive in threatening with ecclesiastical sanctions anyone who challenged it, and at the same time suitably vague about two dubious points, the consanguinity which invalidated the Mortimer marriage, and the dates of birth of Brandon's two daughters by Anne Browne. It set the record straight in more ways than one: it confirmed the legitimacy of Anne Brandon, his elder daughter by Anne Browne; by March 1525, Anne had become the bride of Lord Powys. The marriage had been planned long before, and Brandon had contributed the £1,000 dowry. With a few strokes of the papal pen, all Brandon's children were rendered legitimate. The most important effect of this was to confirm his son Henry, the six-year-old Earl of Lincoln, in the line of succession.

Brandon's second daughter by Anne Browne, Mary, married Thomas, son and heir of Edward Stanley, Lord Mounteagle.

In youth, Thomas had been raised in Wolsey's household, where he had acquired a taste for luxury. He was heir to a major fortune and his wardship had been purchased by Lord Darcy and Sir John Hussey, on the understanding that he would marry Hussey's daughter. But before the summer of 1527 Brandon managed to secure the young man's wardship and within a year he married Mary Brandon. If Brandon congratulated himself on a dazzling match and the birth of a grandchild which followed, he would have cause to regret the match. Mounteagle was thrilled to come into his inheritance in summer 1528, but he was soon running up vast debts which his father-in-law would eventually have to settle. His creditors included the royal goldsmith and the royal shoemaker.

In May 1528, the satisfactory conclusion of the Suffolks' case encouraged the King to look for success in his own, but it also increased his sense of frustration that matters were not progressing faster. Wolsey, facing the greatest test of his career, was exerting all his powers of diplomacy and his skill in ecclesiastical law and politics to secure a papal annulment of the King's marriage to Katherine, but progress was slow. Frustrated, Henry now began to doubt Wolsey's commitment.

Throughout that summer while the sweating sickness once more ravaged the country, the court sought refuge in less dangerous area. Henry and Katherine went on progress to several religious houses but the tension between the royal couple made their sojourn less cheerful than the Brandons' pleasant holiday at Butley Priory. They were relaxing, enjoying the autumn sunshine under the oaks of Sholgrove Wood after an excellent morning's hunting, when suddenly their idyll was shattered. A messenger burst in upon the happy scene, summoning Brandon to Court to welcome the papal Legate.

Mary's mood changed from one of happiness to deep foreboding. Throughout the difficult summer Mary, who known and loved Katherine since childhood, had listened sympathetically to the Queen's increasingly despairing confidences. She was appalled by the thought of a royal divorce, and broke out into bitter lamentations. Katherine had stayed with the Brandons after making a pilgrimage to Walsingham after the birth of the Princess Mary. Mary Rose had commiserated with her sister-in-law's difficult births and her bitter disappointments. She was godmother to Princess Mary, she understood and sympathised with Katherine's anger over the elevation of Henry Fitzroy in 1525.

From now on, the upstart Anne Boleyn would take precedence over Katherine of Aragon, Queen of England, and Mary Rose, Dowager Queen of France. When Wolsey returned on 17 September from his Embassy to France, he realised with a horrible shock that he had lost ground. His monopoly on power had been gradually eroded.

That Christmas, the Brandons played their usual leading role in the revels and celebrations. Katherine went to Richmond at the beginning of December, and when she returned, after the season of misrule, she found Anne Boleyn comfortably installed in a suite of rooms in the royal palace. Katherine struggled for composure, but she was grim-faced, 'made no joy of nothing, her mind was so troubled'.[10] Katherine's private life would become common property, to be picked over salaciously and lewdly gossiped about. The King was hell bent on marrying Anne Boleyn.

Brandon kept quiet and did as his King bade him. But he would find many of the duties he would be called upon to perform over the coming months distasteful. The Imperial Minister, Chapuys, had no doubt where the Suffolks' sympathies lay.

'Suffolk and his wife, if they dared, would offer all possible resistance to the marriage,' he wrote to the Emperor.[11]

12 - Notes

1. Elis Gruffudd, *Chronicle*
2. ibid.
3. L&P IV.i.1511, 21594.
4. Cavendish, 1825, 62.

5. Butley Register, 51-55.

6. L&P For &Dom, 1526, 21-31

7. CSP Ven vol 4 1527-1533 56-66

8. ibid 105

9. Hall, 756

10. ibid

11. L&P For&Dom Hen viii vol 5 June 1531 287

13   THE GREAT WHORE

During the early months of 1529, the legates prepared for the hearing of the King's nullity suit. The Great Matter polarised opinion among the élite, leading to a vicious power struggle. By 1528, three distinct factions had emerged: those who supported Wolsey and the King; the aristocratic conservatives, who discreetly supported the Queen and hoped to break Wolsey's iron grip on power; and the Boleyns' supporters. Through Anne Boleyn's influence, Wolsey's power was declining. Yet Wolsey had left no stone unturned in his efforts to ensure that the King's case was watertight. When the legatine court opened on 31 May in the Great Hall of the Priory of Blackfriars, he was confident of a happy outcome.

After the Christmas celebrations at Greenwich, Mary Rose had slipped quietly back to her peaceful country estate, and the company of her own children and her stepdaughter Mary Brandon, soon to wed. Until Henry had begotten a living legitimate male heir, little Henry Brandon, Earl of Lincoln, remained high in the line of succession. Mary Rose had two daughters of her own and one stepdaughter to be matched and married, a large household to run, charitable enterprises to be fostered.

Westhorpe had been enhanced with a grand new wing, surmounted by battlements and decorated with terracotta figures, costing £12,000, a sum mainly derived from Mary's French revenues. In East Anglia, Mary was still revered as the French Queen. At the summer fair at Butley Abbey she held state in a cloth-of-gold pavilion. At Court, she had taken precedence over every lady but the Queen. Although Mary loved Court life and the exhilaration of London, the delights of court life had become tarnished by disputes, ill feeling and uncertainty. She welcomed the opportunity to retreat from a debate she found repugnant. In the country, she did not have to suffer the indignity of finding herself outranked by the woman now generally nicknamed 'the Concubine' or 'the Great Whore.'

Brandon was despatched on an embassy to France to canvas Francis I's support for Henry's planned marriage to Anne Boleyn. Although an unattractive mission, the trip provided a welcome escape: it meant that, even though he had been among Prince Arthur's attendants who witnessed hearing the young bridegroom's boasts the morning after his wedding, Brandon would be spared having to testify against Queen Katherine in the June hearing.

The case aroused huge public interest. No royal couple had ever been summoned to appear before a court, or to subject their private lives to public scrutiny. Eyes were popping when the Queen swept into the chamber, scorning the chair designated for her. She fell on her knees before the King, proclaiming loudly that she had been a true wife to him and had come to him as a virgin. She rose, curtseyed deeply, and left the court as swiftly as she had appeared, ignoring the shouts urging her to return.

There followed days of depositions and heated and unsavoury debate. Much of the evidence focussed on whether Prince Arthur had effectively consummated his marriage with Katherine. It was nonsense to claim that the prince had been too young to be capable, several noblemen proclaimed, boasting of their own sexual prowess at Arthur's age. The King clung to his position that Katherine's unsuccessful pregnancies were divine retribution for their incestuous marriage. Katherine repeated that Arthur had never 'carnally known her', and that Doña Elvira had spoken true when she insisted that her Princess had emerged from her bridal chamber each morning still a virgin.

But the courtiers had watched the young couple go off to bed each night, with the usual lewd nudges, and the squires of the bedchamber, now middle-aged men but then lusty young blades in their prime, had sniggered knowingly when they heard young Prince Arthur's adolescent bragging in the morning.

The Pope's representative, Cardinal Lorenzo Campeggio, listened impassively. Finally, on 23 July, he announced that he was referring the whole matter to Rome, as he had been secretly instructed to do by the Pope. A horrified silence greeted his announcement. As the King strode out in a fury, Brandon thumped his fist on the table and yelled 'By the Mass, now I see that the old said saw is true, that never cardinal or legate did good in England!'[1]

Wolsey, aghast, conscious that he faced ruin, replied with great dignity: 'Of all the men in this realm, ye have least cause to dispraise or be offended with cardinals. For if I, a simple cardinal, had not been, ye should have at this present no head upon your shoulders!'

This was a sharp reminder that he had saved Brandon's bacon in the matter of the secret marriage in Paris. He advised Brandon to behave himself and hold his peace, 'for ye know best what friendship ye have received at my hands, the which yet I never revealed, to no person alive before now, neither to my glory, nor to your dishonour.'

Henry had already stormed from the room. Brandon followed him in silence.

Brandon's outburst against Wolsey may well have been provoked by two characteristically high-handed actions of the Cardinal's: the first was the 'Amicable Grant', the forced loan of 1525 levied on property and goods to enable Henry to finance yet another military campaign. Brandon had resented having to impose the levy on his tenants and then endure obloquy for an unpopular policy not of his devising. Open resistance had obliged the use of force and soured relationships.

Secondly, Brandon was among those who had suffered for Wolsey's determination to leave a legacy of educational memorials. His desire to found a college at Oxford and a preparatory school for it in his native Ipswich had entailed the seizure of land in the area, including three valuable properties belonging to the Brandons: Snape Priory in Suffolk and the manors of Sayes Court and Bickling in Kent. The Brandons, now realising that Wolsey's assistance in securing Mary's French revenues had not been free of self-interest, had reminded Henry gently that, without Brandon's efforts and his cordial relationship with Francis, negotiations with France would be much more precarious.

Throughout August and September, no-one moved against Wolsey. There remained a faint hope that he would by some miracle succeed in outmanoeuvring the alliance of Pope, Emperor and Queen of England.

After his return from France, Brandon's usually robust health suffered a setback. Enforced rest allowed him to spend part of the summer in East Anglia with Mary and their family. Now that their daughters were of marriageable age, they at last took the necessary steps to have Brandon's own divorce papers notarially attested before witnesses. The bull, signed the previous year at Orvieto by Pope Clement VII, was presented to the Bishop of Norwich on 20 August. Now unquestionably legitimate, Mary's daughters, Frances and Eleanor, had suddenly become highly desirable brides on the aristocratic marriage market. In 1530, a marriage was discussed between Frances and the Norfolks' eldest son, Henry Howard, Earl of Surrey. It seemed the ideal arrangement, in view of the proximity of their estates. At this point the rivalry between the two dukes was in abeyance and their co-operation in council was relatively amicable. But although thirteen-year-old Frances was the King's niece, in Norfolk's eyes her royal birth was insufficient to compensate for her meagre dowry.

Brandon returned to court in the autumn to find Wolsey's

enemies in full cry. Anti-clerical feeling was running high. Against his own inclinations, through his loyalty to the King Brandon found himself drawn into the increasing circle of Boleyn supporters and in opposition to the Cardinal.

Wolsey's fall was sudden and dramatic. On 6 October he chaired the Council Meeting. On 9 October, he was charged in the Court of the King's Bench with the offence of praemunire: in allowing the legatine court to be set up he had broken the law of England by introducing an illegal foreign body into the land[2]. Wolsey knew his enemies had triumphed. He made no attempt to refute the charges. On 19 October, Norfolk and Suffolk called on him formally to remove the seals of office. Du Bellay wrote: 'Wolsey has been put out of his house and all his goods taken into the King's hands. Beside the robberies of which they charge him between Christian Princes, they accuse him of so many other things that he is quite undone. The Duke of Norfolk is made chief of the council, Suffolk acting in his absence and at the head of all, Mademoiselle Anne.'[3]

The great Cardinal was sent to a modest dwelling in Esher, and later in the autumn retired to his see of York. The moment he left York Place, Henry and Anne Boleyn, aware that Wolsey had ordered his officers to conduct an inventory of his goods, hurried over to pick over the spoils. The word on the street was that Wolsey would be sent to the Tower. Agog for drama involving their betters, the good citizens of London clustered at the riverside to witness the great man's arrest. A thousand craft were said to be scouring the river, but Wolsey foiled pursuit by embarking on his barge from his own private steps, surrounded by his own attendants. He sailed to Putney, where he had arranged to be met by his attendants, with horses to transport him to Surrey.

Wolsey was banished. Anne's star had risen. Henry was lavishing priceless gifts on her. On 9 December 1529, at the banquet held to celebrate her father's elevation to an Earldom, Anne, ablaze with jewels and radiant with triumph, occupied the seat of honour next to the King. She took precedence over Mary Rose, who, as Dowager Queen of France, had the right to be treated as a queen. On this occasion, Mary Rose forbore to comment but no doubt she was infuriated by the interloper's presumption, both on her own account and on behalf of her friend Queen Katherine.

Suddenly, in November 1530, the Earl of Northumberland – the former Lord Henry Percy whose affair with Anne Boleyn had been curtailed by Wolsey's intervention – appeared at Cawood and arrested Wolsey for high treason in the King's name. Wolsey travelled south with his captors. He knew he faced the block. He was to be spared this final humiliation. At Leicester Abbey, where the company were to spend the night, Wolsey collapsed and died. His recorded last words were: 'If I had served my God as diligently as I have done my King, He would not have given me over in my grey hairs'.[4]

When the news of Wolsey's death reached London, a troop of players funded by Anne Boleyn's father staged a distasteful comedy *'of the descent of the Cardinal into Hell'*. Norfolk, Anne Boleyn's uncle, ordered the text to be published, treating it as a huge jest.

Privately, the King registered the magnitude of his loss, sighing: 'Every day I miss the Cardinal of York more and more.'[5] Henry had good reason for his regret. For the next two years, he found ruling England alone a heavier burden than he had imagined possible. Initially, he tried to assign the blame to Wolsey for leaving affairs in a mess. But it soon became clear just how many and how diverse were the tasks that had been shouldered by the Cardinal, and how subtly and how brilliantly he had performed them.

Wolsey's fall was a political victory in which Brandon had played no significant part. Although he had not actively supported Wolsey and had gone along with the power play of the Boleyn faction, he had never actively joined the conspiracy against a minister who had never really harmed him and who, in respect of the secret marriage to Mary Rose, had shown him vital support. Nevertheless, he shared in the spoils when the great man fell: Wolsey's prize mules came to his stables, Wolsey's kitchen clerk entered his service, and the manor of

Sayes Court in Deptford was returned to him. The office of president of the Council was revived for him and for Norfolk, with whom he shared it.

Brandon had also been Henry's first choice as Lord Chancellor of England, but a jealous Norfolk opposed the appointment, protesting that Brandon was already too powerful: he objected to the Seal being given into 'such high hands'. Brandon himself may not have wished for such a responsibility. He had a realistic view of his own abilities, and knew his skills and interests lay elsewhere. In consequence, the post went to an initially reluctant Thomas More, who recognised that his views regarding the Great Matter differed from the King's, and anticipated the inevitable clash.

Meanwhile the Divorce trial proceeded seamlessly. Eager to curry favour with the King, most people fell into line and spouted prearranged testimony. Brandon, who had always shared Mary's respect and affection for the Queen, was outwardly courteous to Anne, suppressing his personal feelings out of loyalty to the King. It was for that unwavering loyalty that Henry so valued him. On the surface, their friendship remained unchanged. They continued to exchange gifts. Brandon gave the King greyhounds and a gold-bound book containing a clock. Henry visited Ewelme in 1531, 1532 and 1535, and the two men continued to play tennis and gamble together, and relax by listening to Mary Rose's sackbut players. When members of the Privy Council urged the King to seek reconciliation with Charles V, an indignant Henry snarled at them all except for Brandon.

But their relationship was complicated. The disinheritance of Princess Mary, which would eventually be followed by that of Elizabeth, reinforced the claim to the throne of the Brandon children. The Brandons' friendship with Katherine of Aragon was also problematic. Chapuys reported that the Brandons secretly deplored the divorce. At last one contemporary attributed Mary Rose's early death to her grief over the treatment of her friend, Queen Katherine. Lady Willoughby, prospective mother-in-law of the Suffolks' son Henry, Earl of

Lincoln, Katherine's former lady-in-waiting Maria de Salinas, remained devoted, rushing to Katherine's side when she lay on her deathbed. Maria's own daughter, Catherine, was second mourner at the ex-Queen's funeral in February 1536. The first mourner was the Brandons' younger daughter, Eleanor.

Brandon deplored the repeated missions to humiliate Katherine; so impressed was he by her dignity in May 1531 that for once he spoke out to his friend and sovereign, in an attempt to persuade the King to change his behaviour. Norfolk, Suffolk and 30 councillors held a conference with the Queen at Greenwich. Katherine insisted that she was Henry's lawful wife and that the case must be heard in Rome. Norfolk told the King what he wanted to hear, but Brandon told Henry that, although the Queen was ready to obey him in all things, she recognised two higher authorities. Henry was about to explode; he demanded to know who these two authorities were, thinking them to be the Pope and the Emperor. Brandon said bluntly: 'God and her conscience.' Chapuys, relating the incident to Charles V, said Henry received Brandon's remark in stony silence. 'Suffolk and his wife' the Ambassador added 'if they dared, would offer all possible resistance to his marriage.' Two days previously he had heard Brandon and the Treasurer saying 'The time was come when all the world should strive to dismount the King from his folly'.[6]

As time passed, the antagonism between Norfolk and Suffolk increased. They clashed both in council and back on their own turf over local issues. Their henchmen began to form bands. In April 1532 matters came to a head. The Lady Anne's dominance at court was now complete. Sharp-tongued, tough minded and clever, she flashed her black eyes, made cutting remarks in French or English, and flaunted the jewels lavished on her by the besotted monarch, in case anyone should dare to doubt that she held him in thrall. Henry planned to take his inamorata to France to meet Francis I, and had asked the Queen to hand over her jewels. Katherine indignantly declared that she would not give up what was rightfully hers to adorn 'a person who is a reproach to Christendom and is bringing scandal and disgrace upon the King, through his taking her to a meeting such as this in France'.[7] But, she added, if the King sent for her jewellery, she would surrender it. As soon as she had relinquished her jewels, most of them, including four bracelets set with rubies and diamonds, were reset for Anne.

Relations between Brandon and the arrogant Boleyns were increasingly strained. Anne was bitterly hostile to Brandon. In July 1531, in retaliation for disrespectful remarks Brandon had made about her, according to the Imperial Ambassador, she went to the lengths of smearing his name with allegations of incest with his own daughter.[8]

In April 1532, at last, Mary Rose gave rein to her feelings. Up in London on business concerning her dowry, she openly criticised Anne.

The Venetian Ambassador Capello reported of the fatal brawl: 'it was owing to opprobrious language uttered against Madame Anne by his Majesty's sister, the Duchess of Suffolk, Queen Dowager of France. The affair of the divorce becomes daily more difficult.'[9]

The King's sister's insults were gleefully repeated, first at court and then, bandied about in taverns by the followers of the two great dukes, throwing the Court into an uproar, and resulting in murder. Richard Southwell and his brother, Norfolk's henchmen, with a band of twenty heavies, goaded a group of Suffolk's supporters until violence broke out in Westminster Abbey. Sir William Pennington, one of Suffolk's gentlemen, sought sanctuary in the traditional way by throwing himself before the high altar. He was pursued and brutally cut down by Norfolk's people in the aisle. Brandon, furious, rushed to the Abbey 'to remove the assailants by force.' The King sent Thomas Cromwell after him, 'for the turmoil displeased him.'

Cromwell, Wolsey's former servant, was a self-made man of humble origins who was to rank among the greatest statesmen and politicians of the Tudor age. The King, having lost Wolsey, was coming to rely upon him increasingly. Richard Southwell, one of Norfolk's retainers, had been tutoring Cromwell's son. The quarrels and the murder of Pennington caused a furore at court. Brandon and Mary Rose, disgusted, retired to their estates, but their retainers were still spoiling for a fight. The King and Thomas Cromwell had to intervene to prevent further outbreaks of violence. Shortly afterwards, Henry himself called on Brandon. It took all his powers of persuasion to convince Brandon to return to court. The murderers, Norfolk's retainers, the notorious Southwell and his brother, were pardoned after paying a £1,000 fine.

Anne, who had played a clever waiting game and now felt sure of her triumph, continued to ride roughshod over everyone. Hell-bent on appropriating every honour and privilege of Queenship, she ordered her Chamberlain to seize the Queen's barge, repaint it in her colours of blue and purple, burn off its coat of arms and replace it with her own. For her proposed State visit to France, she ordered stacks of gowns, furs and nightgowns.

Unfortunately, it appeared that no royal lady at the French court was willing to receive her. To Henry's disgust, it was suggested that Francis's current mistress, the Duchess of Vendôme, should do the honours. In the face of this unspeakable insult, Henry decided that Anne would remain in the English enclave of Calais while he travelled on into French territory to meet Francis.

Notwithstanding, there was a holiday atmosphere on 7 October when Henry and Anne left Greenwich with a 2,000-strong retinue, including the King's bastard son, Richmond, the Duke of Norfolk, and an unenthusiastic Brandon. Mary Rose had flatly refused to participate in the charade. Even the deliberate snubbing by King Francis's sister, Marguerite d'Angoulême, and his second wife, Queen Eleanor, did not set a damper on the festive air of the excursion. More conservative members of court deplored the unedifying spectacle of the King of England, setting off to France accompanied by his bastard and by the woman referred to by London commoners and Marguerite d'Angoulême alike as 'the King's Whore.'

There was speculation among the courtiers whether the King would follow Mary Rose's example sixteen years earlier and simply wed secretly in France, returning to England to present the world with a *fait accompli*, and, if this happened, what the consequences of such a rash action would be for them all. When this rumour reached Anne's ears, she hotly denied it, declaring that she would have no hole-and-corner ceremony, but a proper state wedding such as all queens of England had. Her arrogance unabated, despite her ambivalent situation.

In April 1533, Brandon was given the bitter task of informing Katherine that she was no longer Queen. In December, he was commanded to dismiss some of her attendants and move her into an insalubrious residence at Somersham. Katherine refused to budge and locked herself in her room. Lady Willoughby later told Ambassador Chapuys that Brandon had been to confession and communion before he could man himself up to embark on this distressing mission, and had wished some accident might befall him to relieve him of the odious duty. His motto *'Loyaulte me oblige'*, by which he had conducted his life, had never been so hard to live up to.

13 - Notes

1. Hall, *Chronicle*, 1548, 758; Cavendish, 1557, 125
2. L&P Hen VIII vol 4 pt 3 5859
3. ibid.6019
4. Cavendish, 219
5. CSP Milan, 530
6. L&P Hen VIII vol 5
7. Martin A.S. Hume, *The Wives of Henry the Eighth and the Parts They Played in History*. 1905. Reprint. London, 1967
8. CSP Span vol iv pt I n. 302
9. CSP Ven vol iv 761

14 THE FATAL INHERITANCE: LADY JANE

In the early summer of 1533, Charles Brandon, Duke of Suffolk, shrugged off his perpetual indebtedness and splashed out £1,666 on the celebrations to mark the marriage of his and Mary Rose's older laughter, Lady Frances Brandon. The slim, good-looking sixteen-year-old daughter of one of society's most glamorous couples starred in one of the most sumptuous weddings London had ever seen. It was typical of Mary Rose that she should defy her own poor health, repress her anxiety about her sickly son Henry, in order to grace with her presence the festivities at Suffolk Place. But this would be her last public appearance.

The wedding was not only a joyful occasion, but also something of a coup. It was sharpened with an edge of triumph. Three years previously, Frances had been ignominiously rejected as a bride by the ambitious Norfolks, unimpressed by her paltry dowry – Brandon's finances, never very secure, having been yet further depleted by the demands of Lord Monteagle, the feckless husband of his daughter Mary.

Moreover, the Duke of Norfolk and Brandon, although they had co-operated when obliged to do so by circumstances and their shared respect for the sovereign, had never warmed to each other. Mary Rose had never cared for Norfolk. She had complained, when a young bride in France, that the Duke displayed a lack of empathy.

Now the spurned bride, young Frances, had made a dazzling match. Her bridegroom, Henry 'Harry' Grey, Marquis of Dorset, whose father the 2nd Marquis had died in October 1530, was six months older than France, 'young, lusty, well-learned and a great wit'.[1] Brandon had successfully negotiated the marriage with Harry's mother, the formidable and querulous Dowager Marchioness. Dorset's royal connections made him a suitable match for the King's niece: his grandfather the 1st Marquis was the son of Elizabeth Woodville, and therefore the half-brother of Henry VIII's grandmother, Elizabeth of York.

The wedding seemed to open up avenues for rapprochement with the King. The Brandons, accustomed to basking in the King's favour, had felt less welcome at Court since the King's marriage to Lady Anne. Mary Rose made no secret of her dislike of Anne. Once, she had requested the young Anne as her attendant. But now her loyalty to Queen Katherine and her suspicion of the Boleyns, as well as Anne's personality, had led to a mutual loathing. Mary had made disparaging remarks about her brother's new wife. Anne had retaliated by spreading slanders about Brandon. But now, the King graced Frances's wedding with his presence, while to everyone's relief, his new wife, conscious of the hostility of the bride's mother, had for once the good sense not to impose her presence on the festive gathering.

Harry Dorset's father, Thomas Grey, had, like Brandon, earned the King's approval in the lists. He had served with Brandon in the French war of 1513, and led the successful English team in the splendid Parisian tournament celebrating Mary Rose's marriage to King Louis. In 1529 he had borne witness for the King in his efforts to secure an annulment of his marriage to Queen Katherine.[2]

In gratitude, Henry VIII created young Harry Grey a Knight of the Bath at Anne's coronation. Self-willed Harry had exhibited a rebellious streak since boyhood. He had been previously betrothed (and quite possibly married) to the Earl of Arundel's daughter but had jilted her, buying himself free of the engagement by paying a large sum of money.

In 1523, the Brandons had another reason to feel well pleased: the future of their younger daughter, Eleanor, was also settled. She had recently become betrothed to Henry, Lord Clifford, eldest son of the Earl of Cumberland.

After the wedding, Frances left for her new home, the Grey manor of Bradgate in Leicestershire. Brandon, as Earl Marshal, was obliged to stay in London to carry out his duties. Mary Rose, accompanied by Eleanor, set out on the slow journey home. She had mustered her last shreds of energy to grace Frances's glittering wedding. She would never see London again.

Brandon managed a brief visit to his wife at Westhorpe in mid-May, but had to hurry back to London to finalise the arrangements for Anne's coronation, scheduled for 1 June. Brandon, appointed High Constable of England specifically for this occasion, stage-managed the great triumph of the woman whom her detractors called the King's 'goggle-eyed whore'.

And triumph it was to be: Anne, already proudly pregnant with the King's child, was determined to have no modest ceremony, but a breathtaking triumph. The celebrations lasted four days. The procession of barges on the Thames was said to stretch for four miles. Brandon, resplendent in pearl-encrusted doublet and robes of crimson velvet, mounted on a destrier similarly bedecked, supervised the whole proceedings, from the new Queen's entry into the Tower, her procession through London, and the banquet for 800 guests in Westminster Hall.

Despite the pomp and extravagance, Anne's reception by the people of London displeased her. Many despised her as an adulterous interloper who had ousted the rightful Queen Katherine, who had been revered as a virtuous, well-born and charitable lady. Few doffed their caps or cried 'God save the

Queen!' Anne's fool attempted to lighten the atmosphere by yelling at them 'I think you all have scurvy heads, and dare not uncover!' Unabashed by Anne's grim expression, at the sight of the royal couple's entwined initials, some wits burst out laughing, shouting 'HA! HA!'[3]

In the midst of the hullabaloo Brandon rode with a heavy heart, secretly aware that Mary Rose was dying. He managed another flying visit to her bedside after Anne's coronation, bearing with him a loving and conciliatory message from the King. Any temporary rift between brother and sister was healed. On 25 June Mary died. She was thirty-seven. Exhausted, Brandon hastened from Court back to Westhorpe. It was not the custom for a husband to attend his wife's funeral. The chief mourner was always of the same sex as the deceased. So, after paying his respects, Brandon returned to court.

Mary's body was embalmed and laid in a lead coffin. In the 16th century, the funerals of the great exuded pageantry and symbolism. Tradition demanded that the splendour of the deceased's obsequies must reflect their earthly status. The 'Orders of Precedence' drawn up by Mary's grandmother, Lady Margaret Beaufort, in 1503, dictated the protocol, detailing the correct dress for public mourning, even the length of train to be worn by ladies. Heralds, mourners and a pursuivant were despatched from France by Francis I to assist the English heralds with the complicated ceremonial befitting a Dowager Queen of France. The science of embalming was well advanced in northern Europe; Mary lay in state for three weeks at Westhorpe in the chapel, where daily masses were said. Beside her coffin, draped in blue velvet, her family and retainers kept vigil night and day by the light of flickering wax tapers. On 10 July the King ordered a Requiem Mass to be sung at Westminster Abbey. This official ceremony was a public gesture, conducted with all the ostentatious formality befitting royalty. (Three years later, when it was suggested that a service be held at St Paul's to commemorate Katherine of Aragon, the King refused. His sister Mary, he said, was a Queen. There was no need to go to the expense of commemorating Katherine...)

Brandon and the King were struggling to establish Henry's unpopular new Queen. Neither could spare the time to visit Suffolk. Mary's family gathered for the service on July 22. The lords, wearing black hoods and gowns, the ladies dignified with black trains, were led by Frances, the young Marchioness of Dorset, and her brother Henry, the frail seventeen-year-old Earl of Lincoln. Eleanor, their sister, and Lady Catherine Willoughby, Brandon's ward and his son's fiancée, followed in the procession, and after them Mary's stepdaughters, Lady Powys and Lady Monteagle. After early Mass, the family breakfasted together in the house that had been Mary's home.

The procession formed in the courtyard. Six gentlemen bore the coffin, draped in a black pall of cloth-of-gold with a white cross, from the chapel, setting it upon a hearse draped with black velvet embroidered with Mary's emblems and drawn by six horses. The coffin was surmounted by Mary's effigy, representing her as Queen of France, wearing a golden crown, and holding a sceptre brought specially from France. Above the hearse, a canopy was supported by four knights. The cortege proceeded at snail's pace along the narrow roads to Bury St Edmunds, preceded by a hundred poor countrymen in coarse black hooded garments, glad to earn a few pence by trudging through the leafy lanes bearing wax tapers to honour the French Queen, of whose status they had been proud and whose kindness and beauty they remembered. The chapel clergy followed, carrying the cross, then came Mary's household staff, heralds, officials, mounted knights and nobles, and the hearse itself, followed by another hundred taper-bearing yeomen. After them rode Frances, as chief mourner, her palfrey caparisoned in black velvet, flanked by her husband and Lord Clifford, her sister Eleanor's betrothed. In single file rode ten noble ladies who had served Mary, each attended by a running footman. Mary's gentlewomen rode in two carriages. Yeomen and servants followed on foot. Along the way through the Suffolk villages, more people joined the procession, and delegations met the cortège at various points to pay tribute to the dead Queen and to receive money and torches.

At Bury St Edmunds, the procession was ceremoniously received by the local clergy, the Abbot and monks, and the Bishop of London in his pontifical robes. A catafalque had been prepared before the high altar for the coffin, draped in black and embroidered in gold with Mary's arms and her modest motto '*La volonté de Dieu me suffit.*' Banners decorated with the symbols of Lancaster and York, the Tudor portcullis and the fleur-de-lis, were hung from the monastery gate up to the high altar. The mourners, their positions strictly governed by rules of etiquette, clustered about the coffin as the Dirge was sung and the French herald chanted: 'Pray for the soul of the right high excellent Princess and right Christian Queen, Mary, late French Queen, and all Christian souls.'

The company then moved to the refectory for supper. Free food was distributed to everyone who had followed the procession. Eight women, twelve men, thirty yeomen and several clerks and priests were appointed to keep the last overnight vigil beside the coffin.

Requiem Mass was sung early next day, and offerings of palls of cloth-of-gold were made by the chief mourners – the four Brandon daughters, Anne, Mary, Frances and Eleanor, and Catherine Willoughby and her mother. The Abbot of St Bennet's delivered a lengthy funeral oration, leaving Mary's daughters exhausted and emotionally drained. One tradition suggests that Mary's biological daughters had good reason to be upset beyond the ordinary transports of grief: their rowdy step-sisters, Mary and Anne Brandon, barged their way to the front of the funeral cortège just as the coffin was being lowered into the crypt, horrifying Mary's own children.

The household staves were broken, accompanied by a general outburst of lamentation. After the final funeral dinner, meat and drink were freely distributed. Paupers received 4 pennies as 'largesse of the grave'. On 23 July the funeral party dispersed. The catafalque remained in the church awaiting instructions from Brandon. The memory of Mary's beauty, grace and benevolence lingered long in the countryside even after the whirligig life of Court had moved on. Those who always sought a psychological reason for death rather than a medical one murmured that it was the shock of learning that her brother had secretly married Anne, and that she was pregnant by him, that hastened Mary's death.

After spending lavishly on Mary's funeral, Brandon found himself even deeper in debt, with a young ward and two unmarried children to support. Mary's death had diminished the prestige of the Suffolk household and put a further strain on Brandon's already precarious finances, causing him to reconsider his agreement to support Frances's husband Dorset at court until his majority. Frances's mother-in-law, the dowager countess, bombarded the new rising star at Court, Thomas Cromwell, with appeals against his decision. Underhand attacks by her lawyers forced Brandon to capitulate; he ended up supporting the Dorsets for almost five years.

His finances finally received a much-needed boost when he was granted the revenues of the vacant see of Ely, over 12,000 ducats, and a crown debt of 1,000 pounds was remitted. Within three years he had obtained remittance of all Mary's crown debts and refinanced his own. He and the King probably shared the cost of Mary's ornate alabaster monument at Bury St Edmunds. Both tomb and records were destroyed during the Dissolution, but the coffin itself was saved and quietly removed to the monastic church of St Mary's, its present location.

There were other strategies available to Brandon to increase his wealth. It was fully expected that a widower, still in the prime of life, should marry again. Brandon, at forty-nine, had mellowed from a handsome young athlete into a distinguished and still commanding figure. His muscles, honed in the field and in tournaments, might have started to bulk out, but his animal magnetism remained undimmed. Brandon had a further advantage over his friend the monarch in that none of his injuries, incurred by his recklessness in the hunting field and the tournament, had so incapacitated him as to prevent him from continuing to engage in violent exercise. He had thus been able to stave off the portly middle-aged spread which good living and enforced inactivity had occasioned in Henry VIII, with his headaches and suppurating ulcerated leg.

Brandon needed to remarry. He did not have to look far for the ideal bride. Lady Catherine Willoughby, his ward and the intended bride of his sickly son, Henry, was an attractive, intelligent, strong-minded girl of impeccable antecedents and impressive fortune. She had reached the marriageable age of fourteen. Catherine, the daughter and heir of Lord William Willoughby by his second wife, Maria de Salinas, the Spanish lady-in-waiting so beloved of her mistress, Queen Katherine, was a baroness in her own right with an annual income of 15,000 ducats. Brandon had purchased Catherine's wardship for £2, 266, 13s, 4d, five years earlier, intending to keep her fortune in the family by marrying her to his son Henry, as soon as the boy was old enough. Henry's fragile health had been a constant worry to his parents. His older brother had died in childhood.

It seemed to Brandon a shame to lose Catherine's fortune, when his son could so easily make another advantageous match. Accordingly, on Sunday, 7 September, 1533, a few hours before Queen Anne Boleyn was delivered of a baby girl, the future Elizabeth I, Charles Brandon and Catherine Willoughby were married.

Mary Rose had not been in her grave seven weeks, but the hasty remarriage raised few eyebrows and received comment only from those, like Anne Boleyn, who bore Brandon ill will. Marriage among the great had less to do with romance than with power, politics and economics. It was a fact of life that a man needed a wife with a dowry and sufficient youth and robustness to produce sons. But Ambassador Chapuys, reporting on the union to Charles V, noted not only the age gap between bride and groom, but also the speed with which Brandon hastened 'from the bier of one spouse to the bed of the next.'[4]

Within six months of his father's remarriage, in March 1534, young Henry Brandon died. Spanish chroniclers, who delighted in ascribing sudden death to emotional anguish, remarked that the young Earl, jilted by his betrothed in favour of his own father, 'was so sorry he died'. Anne Boleyn reputedly commented acidly: 'My Lord of Suffolk kills one son to beget another.'[5]

Despite malicious whispers and the age difference, Brandon's last marriage proved a success. Catherine, the new Duchess of Suffolk, was attractive, intelligent and witty. Although she was younger than any of Brandon's four daughters, she had more good sense than either Mary or Anne, and enjoyed more robust good health than Eleanor.

To his credit, Brandon had succeeded in maintaining relations with the husbands of his wayward older daughters. It had not been easy. In 1538 Mary's husband, Lord Monteagle, complained in vain to Thomas Cromwell about his wife's bad behaviour. Cromwell, the arch fixer, now becoming a major influence at Court, was often called upon to intervene in family matters. Monteagle was incompetent as well as querulous, and Brandon had to enlist Cromwell's intervention in his inept administration of his estate.

Two years later, Brandon's older daughter, Anne, caused a scandal by deserting her husband to cohabit openly with her lover. Her husband, Baron Grey of Powys, petitioned Henry VIII's Privy Council to punish Anne for adultery and for conspiring with her lover to murder him. Nothing came of the latter allegations.

One contemporary source remarks that though 'handsome women, they took to evil courses, and became common women, the father, however, taking no notice of it'.[6] The last comment was a little unfair: in reality, Brandon showed great concern for his daughters in addition to supporting them financially. He asked Cromwell to mediate between Lord and Lady Powys, and to favour Anne only if it could be proved that her behaviour had been honourable. Following the violent removal of Anne's lover in a night raid on their lodgings by Lord Powys, Cromwell renegotiated a maintenance agreement preparatory to a legal separation. Lady Powys was a survivor, and she was soon back in court circles. Whenever she needed cash she had no compunction about borrowing, either from Cromwell or her father.

Catherine, the new Duchess of Suffolk, was just fifteen when their first son, Henry, was born. Brandon proved a loving husband to Catherine for the last twelve years of his life. When he died in 1545 he left her and their two sons, neither of whom would survive to adulthood, both material and landed wealth, and strong alliances within the ranks of the English aristocracy. To Frances and Eleanor, Mary Rose's daughters, he bequeathed £200 worth of plate bearing the ducal arms. He had helped their husbands, buying lands for Cumberland and guiding Dorset through his military apprenticeship in France. In time, Brandon having no living male heirs, his son-in-law Harry Dorset assumed the position of head of the family. In 1551, after the deaths of Catherine Willoughby's young sons, Harry was created Duke of Suffolk.

Charles Brandon would be long remembered for his military leadership and superb horsemanship. Even cold-hearted Charles Wriothesley lamented the death of 'so valiant a captain in the kings warres'.[6] The grizzled, cynical old warrior Elis Gruffydd, who remembered Brandon from the 1523 campaign in France, claimed the King grieved for the Duke 'with reason, because of his courtesy and ability, for he was the flower of all the captains of the realm and had the necessary patience to control soldiers.'[7] Brandon was remembered as heartily beloved of both high and low, rich and poor. The most affable, least devious and ambitious, of men at the Henrician court, this was the secret of his success and political survival. Shortly after Brandon's death, the King stated in open Council meeting that Brandon had never betrayed a friend nor taken unfair advantage of an enemy. Doubtless aware that his rosy view was not shared by all his Council, Henry glared round at them and warned them to hold their tongues, for which of them, he challenged, could say as much?

As the King grew disillusioned, with the nostalgic sentimentality of increasing age, he frequently recalled the loss of his last true friend, and of his beloved younger sister, who had loved him and shared his most carefree moments. Young and beautiful, while dancing, jousting, making music, dazzling with their gaiety and grace, the three of them had seemed to bear charmed lives. Where had it all gone wrong?

Brandon was scarcely cold in his grave when Henry VIII took a step that would prove disastrous for Mary and Brandon's descendants. He sought to safeguard England's future security by means of a peaceful and uncontested Succession. One legitimate male heir – Prince Edward, son of Anne Boleyn's less conspicuous successor, Jane Seymour – was not enough. (Jane's reputation has suffered by comparison with the feisty and doomed Anne Boleyn, yet she was no mere non-entity: to her credit she tried to speak up in defence of Robert Aske and the leaders of the Pilgrimage of Grace and of the monasteries.)

Henry knew the succession could not depend on one fragile boy and two unmarried daughters whose legitimacy had been thrown into question more than once. The first in a series of Henry's Succession Acts came in 1534, a year after Mary Rose's death. In the 2nd and 3rd Succession Acts of 1536 and 1543, the Will received parliamentary sanction. In 1546, the Will bequeathed the crown to the descendants of Henry's two sisters, should his own three children die without issue. Henry swept aside the tradition of primogeniture. Preference was to be given to the Suffolks, the descendants of his younger sister and Charles Brandon, over the Stuarts, the descendants of his older sister, Margaret. There were complex reasons for this. Politically and instinctively, Henry distrusted the Scots; besides, there was the common-law rule that foreigners could not inherit English land. John Strype, however, may have been closer to the truth when he wrote that Henry was influenced by personal feelings, because he loved Mary and Brandon and their children better than he had loved Margaret. The First Edwardian Treason Act of 1547 confirmed that to attempt to alter Henry's Will was decreed to be treasonable.

This lent support to the Suffolk claim for another fifty years, effectively blighting the lives of several of Mary's descendants. Their closeness to the throne and Henry's affection for his younger sister would lead to grief, imprisonment and violent death.

Despite the bad blood between the Suffolks and the Boleyns, when Queen Anne Boleyn had borne the King a daughter, Frances's husband Harry Dorset had carried the salt at little Princess Elizabeth's christening. A pinch of salt was placed on the baby's lips to drive out the devil. Salt had been used in Christian baptism since the 4th century. [8]

But this living royal child had been followed by several miscarriages. Opinions vary about the number of stillbirths and miscarriages suffered by Anne Boleyn. Several authorities believe that Henry's second Queen underwent at least four pregnancies. Anne's reign had not lasted long. She had been executed on charges of adultery and treason, and her marriage to the King had been annulled. Both his daughters, the Princesses Mary and Elizabeth, had been declared illegitimate, Mary when the King's marriage to her mother, Katherine of Aragon, had been annulled, Elizabeth when her mother Anne was executed on 19 May 1536. This raised the importance of Mary Rose's children and grandchildren in the line of succession, although the King was still determined to sire a son of his own to succeed him. He had quickly replaced Anne with Lady Jane Seymour.

At the end of May 1537, Frances Grey entered the twilit seclusion of the traditional dark, bland chamber for her lying-in. She and Harry Dorset hoped, no doubt, that this child would be male, and that this time the baby would survive, as previous infants had not. But Frances was delivered of a daughter, who at least appeared in good health. Infant mortality was a fact of life, so the baby's christening was arranged immediately, as was customary. Frances, like many new mothers, did not attend the occasion, which belonged more to the godparents than to the parents. Frances chose as godmother the new Queen, Jane Seymour, for whom the little girl was named. King Henry VIII had announced his betrothal to the calm, pallid Lady Jane, the greatest possible contrast to his last Queen, sharp-witted Anne of the flashing black eyes, the day after Anne's execution.[9]Jane had played a cool and prudent waiting game, returning gifts from Henry when he sought to court her while still married to

Anne, refusing to dine alone with him.

Now Queen Jane Seymour was already with child: the Dorsets had hitched their wagon to the Seymour star, and their confidence was to prove justified. The two families would remain linked for many years. Frances's pushy step-sister, Lady Monteagle, was a favoured Lady-in-waiting. Queen Jane bestowed jewellery on her, and ordered the Flemish artist Hans Holbein the Younger, King's Painter to Henry VIII, to sketch her portrait.

On October 11 1537 word came that Queen Jane's baby was on the way. Dorset galloped off to London. After a difficult and protracted labour, at 2 in the morning, Henry's third Queen delivered his only legitimate son. The city exploded in an outburst of joy. Bells pealed, cannon were fired, the usual hogsheads of wine were distributed to a jubilant populace, the Te Deum was sung, mayor and clergy processed through the streets crowded with cheerful people. Dorset, together with the French Ambassador, and Thomas Cromwell, now promoted as Lord Privy Seal and Baron Cromwell of Wimbledon, and Lord Thomas Audley, the Lord Chancellor, who had witnessed the execution of Anne Boleyn and recommended to Parliament the new Act of Succession, and a crowd of other notables, attended services of celebration and thanksgiving in St Paul's.[10]

At Prince Edward's christening, Gertrude Blount, Marchioness of Exeter, bore the infant prince on a cushion. This important role had originally been intended for Dorset's mother, the dowager marchioness, but she cried off: there had been an outbreak of plague in Croydon, near her home. She wrote: 'as many thanks as her poor heart can think, that it hath pleased his grace to appoint me, so poor a woman, to so high a place as to have borne my lord prince to his christening, which I should be so glad to have done as any poor woman living: and much it grieveth me that my fortune is so evil, by reason of sickness here, in Croydon, to be banished your grace's presence. Written at Croydon, the 14th day of October'. (State Papers.)[11] If, as some suspected, the parsimonious Marchioness was secretly loath to pay out more money for yet another costly royal christening gift – she had presented a golden goblet at the christening of the Princess Elizabeth – and advanced the plague as a convenient excuse, it was a good one. Henry would never question it. His first legitimate son was a pearl beyond price and he himself was always terrified of infection.

Twelve days later, on 24 October, Queen Jane suffered a massive haemorrhage, possibly caused by partial retention of placenta, or by puerperal sepsis, certainly exacerbated by poor contemporary knowledge of hygiene and medicine. She had attended the lengthy celebrations when she was exhausted, had lost a lot of blood and desperately needed rest. The myth than she had undergone an enforced caesarian section at the insistence of the King, a malicious rumour which sprang up soon after her death and was perpetuated in folk ballads, is highly unlikely to have had any factual foundation.

Frances had missed the christening, but she and Dorset played leading parts in Jane's state funeral in November.

Away from court, the Dorsets resided at their family seat, the magnificent Bradgate Old Manor, a U-shaped Tudor mansion constructed of expensive red brick, set in the extensive Bradgate deer park with its parterres and terraces, its avenues and fishponds complete with water lilies and ornamental fish. This palatial residence had been built by Dorset's grandfather, Sir Thomas Grey of Groby, the eldest son of Elizabeth Woodville, the beautiful widow who later married King Edward IV. Bradgate was one of the first unfortified mansions in England, and both Dorset and his father had added to it. The House with its elegant proportions and mullioned windows represented in many respects the cutting edge of Tudor rural residential design. Brick had scarcely been seen in England since Roman times. But the design of the manor was also traditional, with a central courtyard open on one side, flanked by two wings and joined by a great hall. There were summer and winter parlours and three towers. The family's apartments were in the East Wing, along with the chapel. The west wing housed the servants' hall, the bakery, brewery and the great kitchen. In these idyllic surroundings Frances and Harry Grey brought up three daughters.

Recent research suggests that Lady Jane, the eldest, was not born at Bradgate but at the Dorsets' London residence, on a date somewhat earlier than the usually suggested date of October 1537. The few verifiable contemporary comments on her appearance note that she was slight, and pleasant-looking. The prevailing perception was certainly that she was formidably intelligent and well-educated. The Dorsets appear to have been determined that their girls should develop practical and intellectual skills.

That Jane was also spirited and had a mind of her own even at a young age is evident from the correspondence of her learned tutor, John Aylmer, of whom she spoke fondly, with the Swiss reformer Henry Bullinger, who had sent to Jane and her father 'a little volume of pure and unsophisticated religion', with a dedication. Aylmer wrote to Bullinger that young people's minds needed the counsel of older people and serious influences, thanking Bullinger for his contribution to Jane's 'improvement'. Tellingly, he employed the metaphor of 'bridles for restive horses'.[12]

Katherine, the Dorsets' second daughter, traditionally considered the beauty of the family, is shown in the miniatures by the Flemish-born miniaturist to the English court, Levina Teerlinc, as a fair-complexioned, golden-haired young woman, almost the stereotypical English rose.

The third daughter, although uncharitably depicted as 'dwarfish in stature' – Lady Mary was only four feet in height – was disparagingly described by the Spanish Ambassador Guzman da Silva, writing to King Philip, as 'little, crook-backed, deformed, and very ugly', freckled and red-haired, like her sisters. Mary was undoubtedly intelligent, yet her career followed the fateful pattern set by others in her family. She not only fell in love but was determined to marry her beloved, despite the awful example of the retribution which befell her sister Katherine.[13] e

The Grey sisters' father, Harry Grey, Marquis of Dorset, was generally considered weak but ambitious. The combination of these qualities was to prove his downfall. In youth he had been a member of the group around the King's illegitimate son by Bessie Blount, Henry Fitzroy, Duke of Richmond, who had died at the age of seventeen. Some writers have dismissed Dorset as a man of little scholarship, but in reality he was sufficiently well-educated to enjoy renown in his own time as a patron of learned men. He and Frances certainly provided an impressive education for their daughters, modelled on the curriculum devised by the scholarly Sir Thomas More for his own daughter, Margaret.

Both the Dorsets were Protestant sympathisers of the Reformation, so-called Evangelicals. The term 'Protestant' first became current in 1529 to designate Christians who separated from the Roman Catholic Church. Around the same time, the term 'evangelical' came into vogue. The 'Evangelicals' based their faith on scripture. Their beliefs were regarded by religious conservatives as dangerously radical and advertising them was ill-advised, as even the King's sixth and last wife, Katherine Parr, would find to her cost. Frances was among the ladies serving Queen Katherine at the glamorous, dangerous court, a hotbed of gossip and intrigue. Disappointed in those he had loved, suspicious, ailing, irascible, in constant pain and worried about the succession even though he had secured the crucial male heir, Henry VIII was no longer the splendid young sun king of yore, and the mood and character of the monarch dictated the atmosphere at court. Katherine Parr would prove a benign influence, but even her life and person were not proof against plotting and mistrust.

It is possible that Frances's oldest daughter, Jane, occasionally visited her at court. Certainly, Jane was the chief mourner at Queen Katherine's funeral in 1548, although this role may well have been dictated by her rank rather than her personal involvement with the deceased. A portrait of Queen Katherine Parr was discovered among the possessions of Frances's second husband, Adrian Stokes, after his death. It seems probable that this once belonged to Frances, who predeceased Stokes. Janel Mueller states that the British Library MS Harley 2342, known as 'Lady Jane Grey's prayerbook', which Jane carried with her to the scaffold, is written in the hand of Katherine Parr. Mueller believes that the small volume was given to Jane by Katherine on her deathbed in Sudeley, where she had gone for her lying-in, and where she succumbed to puerperal fever after the birth of her only child, Mary Seymour.[14] At fifty-five, Henry VIII no longer represented the picture of masculine beauty so celebrated in his younger days. Wan and obese, lumbering awkwardly on legs permanently damaged by hunting and jousting injuries, he remained increasingly secluded in his private apartments. When he did emerge, he was wheeled about on custom-made invalid chairs, rather like sedan chairs, with shafts and footrests. One was covered with tawny velvet, the other with golden velvet and silk. The chairs were kept in the King's private study, which became known as the 'chairhouse'.[15]

His new bride, Queen Katherine, was of a 'lively, pleasing appearance'.[16] Graceful and of cheerful countenance, she was widely praised for her virtues.[17] She was sufficiently caring to allow her new husband to rest his ulcerated leg on her lap. But Katherine was no unworldly blue-stocking: she loved scent, especially juniper and civet, and enjoyed music and dancing as keenly as she did humanist and theological discussion. She purchased, among other items, from the royal apothecary, cinnamon comfits and liquorice pastilles.[18] She dressed in silks, placed large orders for black velvet and blue satin, and delighted in her large collection of fashionable shoes.[19] She was 'quieter than any of the young wives the King had, and as she knew more of the world, she always got on pleasantly with the King, and had no caprices'.[20]

Good-natured and intelligent, Katherine, still only in her late twenties, had previously undergone two arranged marriages, first to the young but sickly Sir Edward Borough, and, after his death, to the twice-widowed John Neville, Baron Latimer, who was twice her age. Neville was a committed Catholic, and it was perhaps the intemperance of the Catholic mob during the Lincolnshire Rising that had shocked Katherine and inclined her strongly towards the Reformed religion. She invited Reformist preachers like Nicholas Ridley, Hugh Latimer and Nicholas Shaxton to preach to the members of her circle, and there would ensue lively theological discussion. [21]

Despite the disapproval of the more conservative elements at court, Queen Katherine refused to be deterred in her efforts to spread the new teaching in universities. But her enemies feared and resented her influence over the King and the young Prince of Wales. Chief among those who were suspicious of her were Stephen Gardiner, Bishop of Winchester, and Henry Wriothesley, the Lord Chancellor. They appointed spies who were instructed to scrutinise the Queen's activities closely for evidence of heresy. Many tenets of the Reformed faith, such as the denial of transubstantiation, the miracle of the Eucharist, were still illegal under English law. King Henry himself, although he had been responsible for engineering the break with Rome, and for introducing some measure of religious reform, had remained a religious conservative.

In July 1546, unable to find concrete evidence against Katherine herself, the Privy Council tried another tack to incriminate her. They selected their victim and pounced. Anne Askew, a gifted young advocate of reform from Lincolnshire, had dared to embrace evangelical views and to argue with her husband about theology. She was arrested on the orders of Wriothesley. Anne, a gentlewoman and a poet, was brutally tortured on the rack. As the ghastly business proceeded, it became increasingly clear that the chief motivation of Anne's torturers was not to convict her of heresy but to persuade her to betray others, especially the Queen, and Frances Grey's young stepmother, the Duchess of Suffolk. But Anne Askew refused to allow her spirit to be broken or to implicate anyone else.[22]

The plot emerged later with all necessary clarity. In his treatise, *Three Conversions of England,* published in 1604, the Jesuit Robert Parsons stated that Askew had sought 'meanes to enter with the principall of the land, namely with Queene Catherine Parr herself, and with his nieces, the daughters of the Duke of Suffolke', by which Parsons meant the Grey sisters. Chapuys, Ambassador of Emperor Charles V of Spain, wrote to Mary of Hungary that the Queen had been 'infected' with the Reformation virus by her friends, including the Duchess of Suffolk. '... the Duchess of Suffolk, the daughter of Doña Maria Salinas, who was a lady-in-waiting on Queen Catherine. She is one of the worst heretics in England.'[23]

Catherine Suffolk was not only attractive and intelligent, but high-spirited and not afraid to make her adversary, Bishop Gardiner, the butt of her wit. Asked at a banquet to choose the man she liked best, she said could not choose, but would instead select the one she liked the least. She chose Gardiner. She also called her pet spaniel 'Gairdner' and delighted in shouting commands and reprimands at him.

When the constable of the Tower, Sir Anthony Kingston, sickened, walked out of the torture chamber in disgust, refusing to continue Anne Askew's torments (it was, anyway, illegal to torture a woman, but the noble gentlemen had not let that stop them), Wriothesley and his sinister assistant, Richard Rich, took over the ratcheting up of the rack themselves. They continued to demand the names of fellow believers, probably on the orders of Gardiner, in the hopes of implicating the Queen. So terribly was Anne 'racked of Wriothesley, the Chancellor, and Rich, that the strings of her arms and eyes were perished'. Unable to walk or sit after the agonies she had suffered, Anne Askew had to be carried to the stake at Smithfield, where she was tied on a chair and burned alive, along with three male martyrs. Nicholas Throckmorton, whose mother was aunt by marriage to Queen Katherine Parr, had joined the Queen's household along with two of his brothers, George and Clement. The three brothers attended Anne's martyrdom as sympathisers, and stood on the sidelines, shouting encouragement to her.[25]

John Foxe the martyrologist was not alone in suspecting that the real target of this hideous inquisition was the Queen, whose enemies were becoming bolder and closing in. Rumours were spreading throughout Europe that the King's roving eye had fallen upon the alluring young widow, Catherine Suffolk, and that it was this attraction rather than the Queen's dubious connections with the New Faith and her Reformist zeal which motivated the King's tacit support of efforts to prove her conveniently guilty of heresy. In February 1546, the Imperial Ambassador Francis van der Delft wrote: 'I hesitate to report there are rumours of a new queen... Madame Suffolk is much talked about and is in great favour, but the King shows no alteration in his behaviour to the Queen – although she is said to be annoyed by the rumour.'[26]

On the other hand, Wriothesley, Gardiner and the other conservative forces were determined to prevent the Reformists from gaining an even greater foothold at court and increasing their influence over the King, irrespective of whether such influence were exercised by the present Queen, or even more powerfully by a putative seventh Queen, in the person of the strong-willed and outspoken Duchess of Suffolk.

In the event, clever Katherine Parr managed to soothe her increasingly unpredictable lord, and was soon restored to his good books. He was not to live long thereafter, dying in January 1547. He was fifty-six.

His successor, nine-year-old Prince Edward, was described by Chapuys and the Catholic ambassadors as 'one of the prettiest children you could see anywhere'.[27] He is usually depicted as a pale, fair-haired, rather solemn boy, sometimes rather incongruously adopting for the portrait the same macho stance as that favoured by his father, legs apart, hand reposing upon on the pommel of sword or dagger.

Edward was young, but the succession was secure. This was cause for rejoicing. On 19 February, on the eve of his coronation, Edward rode through enthusiastically cheering crowds on his way to Westminster, pausing along the official route to enjoy the traditional pageants and entertainments. Outside St Paul's, the young prince burst into delighted laughter when a Spanish tight-rope walker bent to kiss his foot. The city reverberated to cannon fire from land and from the ships moored in the harbour. The next day, Edward travelled by barge to Whitehall, there to don his coronation robes, and process to Westminister.

Every tradition was observed, but in some respects Edward's coronation represented a departure from the norm, and not only because the ceremony had been shortened slightly, some aspects being no longer relevant since the Reformation, and also out of consideration for the king's youth, 'lest the tedium weary him or do him harm.' Thomas Cranmer, the Archbishop of Canterbury, had rewritten the coronation oath in a manner which revised the notion of sovereign power. The monarch's traditional promise to uphold the liberties and privileges of the clergy was omitted. Instead of the monarch swearing to accept laws presented by his people, the people were now obliged to accept Edward's laws – in reality, the laws of the Council, presented under the seal of the royal authority. The Reformation of the church could now be enabled by the royal prerogative. At one stroke, the King of England had thereby declared himself to be above the authority of the 'Bishop of Rome', and also above the law of the land.

In his sermon, Cranmer stressed the boy king's role in the reforming of religion: 'Your Majesty is God's vice-regent – to see, with your predecessor Josiah, God truly worshipped, and idolatry destroyed; the tyranny of the bishops of Rome banished from subjects, and images removed'. Three swords were brought to Edward, and he demanded where the fourth was, the Bible, the sword of the spirit.[28] That evening, Edward presided at a banquet at Westminster. The young boy king recorded in his own Chronicle that he ate his meal wearing his crown on his head.

Before he sailed for Boulogne in summer 1544, Henry VIII had made his will, and also firmly established his recent Act of Succession. In an effort to avoid a descent into factionalisation, he had decreed that sixteen executors, all Reformists, should serve on a Council of Regency until the young King reached his majority.[29]

On the day on which the King's death was finally announced, three days after he had actually expired, these sixteen men constituted themselves the Privy Council. They elected Edward's evangelical elder uncle, Edward Seymour, a successful soldier-politician, on whom Henry VIII had come to rely heavily towards the end of his reign, as Lord Protector of England. Seymour was also created Duke of Somerset.

There was little love lost between Somerset and Harry Dorset. Somerset's elevation and arrogance annoyed Dorset. In turn, the 'good Duke', as Somerset delighted in being known, despised Dorset. Meanwhile, Somerset's younger brother, the dashing Thomas Seymour, jealous of his brother's advancement and his influence over their nephew, the young king, was already pondering a political alliance against his brother.

Thomas Seymour was charismatic, ambitious, and allegedly the handsomest man in England. Somerset was aware of his younger brother's feelings and had sought to appease him by appointing him to the Privy Council, creating him Lord Admiral and bestowing upon him the title of Baron Sudeley. But Thomas Seymour's resentment was intensified when, a month after Edward's coronation, Somerset consolidated his own power by assuming the post of Governor of the King's Person.

Having at various times contemplated a union with either of the late King's daughters, Thomas Seymour, now Baron Sudeley, set about rekindling his romance with the Queen Dowager, Katherine Parr. The virtuous Queen Dowager had fallen for the handsome Thomas Seymour long before her marriage to the King. Katherine herself would admit as much in her correspondence with Sudeley. 'I would not have you think that this mine honest goodwill towards you to proceed of any sudden motion of passion; for, as truly as God is God, my mind was fully bent, the other time I was at liberty, to marry you before any man I know.'[30] Among the handful of Katherine's friends who had long been aware Katherine Parr's affection for Thomas Seymour was her friend the Duchess of Suffolk, Catherine Willoughby, who owned a stable of fine horses. Once again, in a spirit of mischief, she used the names of her animals to hint at a secret relationship: having dubbed a dog 'Gardiner', to annoy the cleric, she now named one of her mares 'Parr' and one of her stallions 'Seymour'.

Henry VIII had died at the end of January. By March, his hitherto demure, intellectual widow was living recklessly for perhaps the first time in her life. She and Sudeley had become lovers. Sudeley galloped across country to enjoy trysts with Katherine at her manor house. Through the intermediary of trusted messengers, they exchanged wildly indiscreet and passionate love-letters. Katherine knew they were playing with fire and attempted to urge her lover to proceed with caution: 'Ye must take pain to come early in the morning, that ye may be gone by seven o'clock. And then I suppose ye may come without suspect. I pray you, let me have knowledge overnight at what hour ye will come, that your fortress may wait at the gate of the fields for you.'[31] Sudeley wrote that the weeks he spent away from her were 'four days longer in everyone of them than they were under the plumet at Chelsea'.[32] After weeks of dangerous clandestine assignations and a romantic correspondence, the couple were secretly married in May 1547. They knew they were courting disaster and the news of their marriage, so soon after the death of the King, caused scandal.

But marriage to the King's widow did not assuage Sudeley's ambition. He needed another string to his bow. He now became increasingly determined to obtain the wardship of the Dorsets' oldest daughter, Lady Jane Grey.[33] The Greys' significance had increased with the accession of the young King, because, like him, they were Reformists. They were also close to the throne because of their royal blood, and their high position in the line of succession. Sudeley sensed a kindred spirit in their father, Dorset, who was feeling alienated and embittered, his nose having been put out of joint by Somerset. This made him a natural ally.

Sudeley now set about courting the friendship of the Dorsets. Sudeley was aware that time was of the essence. He suspected that his brother, Somerset, also had dynastic designs on Dorset's oldest daughter, Jane Grey, and hoped to see her married to his own son, eight-year-old Edward Seymour, Earl of Hertford, two years Jane's junior, in due course. If Sudeley obtained Jane's wardship, he could effectively block his brother's power play.[34]

He involved as intermediary someone who had long been his confidential agent, go-between and spy, his gentleman John Harington. Harington had studied music under Thomas Tallis and was said to have married an illegitimate daughter of King Henry VIII. Harington now visited the Dorsets' Westminster residence, where he earnestly encouraged the Dorsets to embrace Sudeley's proffered friendship. He offered an irresistible incentive: he assured them that, as the young King's uncle, his master Sudeley had the prospect of achieving great power in the land.

Sudeley expressed his concerns about his brother's plans to his own brother-in-law, William Parr, Marquess of Northampton. Parr would state in his deposition: 'When the sayd Lord Admirall came laste to London, he tolde me in hys owne Gallerye, that ther wolde be moch ado for my Lady Jane, my Lorde Marques Dorsett's dowgther; and that mi Lord Protector and my Lady Somerset wolde do what they colde to obtayne hyr of my sayd Lord Marques for my Lord Hertforde.' Sudeley added that his brother was not going to win this particular battle, ' for my Lord Marquess hath given her wholly to me.'[35]

In his own later deposition to the Council, Jane Grey's father Dorset famously described his conversation with Sudeley's envoy, Harington: 'The said Harington advised me to be contented that my daughter Jane might be with the said Admiral; whereunto if I would agree, he said he durst assure me that the Admiral would find the means she should be placed in marriage much to my comfort.

"With whom" said I "will he match her?" "Marry," quoth Harrington, "I doubt not but you shall see him marry her to the King." Sudeley had publicly stated that he considered Jane 'as handsome as any lady in Christendom'.[36]

The Dorsets' qualms being eventually overcome, Sudeley got his way.

Posterity has dealt harshly with the Dorsets. They have been accused, on flimsy evidence, of being exploitative and ambitious, and even brutal, parents. Yet both physical punishment and aspiration were normal at all levels of society, and not considered either remarkable or reprehensible. Since, for the vast majority of females, the only opportunity life offered was to marry well, parents of all classes were eager to see their daughters advantageously matched. It was customary for the young daughters of the aristocracy to spend time in another household to broaden their horizons, increase their prospects and complete their education, a kind of seventeenth century 'finishing school.'

The prospect of an alliance, through his uncle Thomas, with the young King proved too alluring for Dorset to resist. In his deposition, Dorset would state that, talking with Lord Sudeley, in the garden of Seymour's house at Seymour Place, he discovered that Sudeley 'showed himself so desirous and earnest, and made me such fair promises, that I sent for my daughter, who remained in his house from that time continually unto the death of the Queen.'[37]

Sudeley and Katherine Parr managed to live down the scandal occasioned by their hasty marriage. The Princess Elizabeth became a member of their Chelsea household, which soon also included young Jane Grey. Ten-year-old Jane found the company of Katherine Parr congenial, and shared many interests with the young King, into whose company she now came with increasing frequency. Jane's range of interests was expanding, and she was growing less priggish. So much so, that in December 1551, Jane's 'kindly' tutor, Aylmer, suggested to their mutual correspondent, the Swiss Reformer Henry Bullinger, that a few words of advice might be appropriate in respect of Jane's awakening interest in fashion and finery. 'It now remains for me to request that, with the kindness we have so long experienced, you will instruct my pupil in your next letter as to what embellishment and adornment of person is becoming in young women professing godliness.' Jane's cousin, the Princess Elizabeth, who at this stage of her life was circumspectly reining in her own monstrous vanity and playing the role of the demure Protestant maid, was to be upheld to Jane as an example of what was becoming in a young woman.

Nor was Jane to devote herself to music at the expense of her academic and religious studies. 'Moreover, I wish you would prescribe to her the length of time she may properly devote to the study of music', Aylmer beseeched Bullinger. [38]

Jane's interest in religious matters had been kindled at an early age, and, as is the case with many young girls, it intensified as she approached her teens. Under the example of the Queen Dowager, whose piety and intellectual achievements were legendary, Jane's Reformist zeal gained momentum. Katherine Parr had become a strong advocate of church reform, and had supervised the best-selling translation of one of the earliest Protestant religious works, Erasmus's *Paraphrases of the New Testament*, (1545), and two years later published *The Lamentation of a Sinner,* an account of her personal spiritual journey in her quest for salvation. Because of its Lutheran overtones, she had not dared publish it in the King's lifetime, Henry having denounced Luther as a heretic. Katherine's household continued to observe prayer times several times a day. Not every member of the household shared Katherine's zeal: the future martyr Hugh Latimer, chaplain to Catherine Suffolk, complained that Katherine Parr's husband Sudeley, the High Admiral, avoided daily prayer sessions by any excuse, 'like a mole digging in the dirt'.[39]

But Katherine, despite her pleasant and amenable personality, her religious devotion and conciliatory reputation, was no plaster saint. Whatever the truth about the alleged wrangle with Lady Somerset over precedence at court and the royal jewels – much of which has been exaggerated or indeed invented – there was clearly little mutual affection between these two great ladies. Katherine's uncle, brother and brother-in-law were all awarded titles and dignities after her marriage with the King, but this development was relatively predictable, not to say inevitable – after all, honours had been heaped on the rambling Rivers clan after King Edward IV's marriage to Elizabeth Woodville, Jane Grey's ancestress – and the advancement of the Parrs may or may not have owed much to Katherine's direct intervention and influence. Katherine may certainly have borne much of the responsibility for the downfall of Thomas Cromwell, usually ascribed to the antics of Catherine Howard. It was certainly Katherine who had alerted King Henry to the rapaciousness and unpopularity of his trusted chancellor. Although Katherine was intellectual, spiritual and deeply religious, she was neither naive nor unworldly. Not only had she displayed her susceptibility to romantic love and an alarming lack of caution in secretly marrying Sudeley but she was a woman who loved elegant apparel and delighted in music. Katherine and her cultured brother, Northampton, were the greatest patrons of musicians at court. Under the tutelage of the Queen Dowager, Jane Grey's own interests in these areas developed until she incurred her tutor's disapproval.

Jane may have been enjoying the companionship and widening horizons of her new life, but her father was chafing at the bit. Despite his promises to her parents, Sudeley did not appear to be actively promoting a marriage between Jane and the young King. This undertaking had become more complicated since Sudeley had also quarrelled bitterly with the

Protector, his brother, making him persona non grata at a court dominated by Somerset. Sudeley was doing his best to undermine Somerset by manipulating the affections of the boy king with surreptitious gifts of money, and encouraging him to 'bear rule, as other kings do'. He hinted that his brother, the Protector, kept the boy in a state of poverty ill-befitting a monarch. He also tried to persuade Edward to write a document in favour of his own marriage with Katherine Parr, but Edward refused, and told him to leave him out of it. 'I desired him to let me alone,' he stated in his deposition. Yet both the late monarch's orphans, the Princess Elizabeth and Edward VI, felt great affection for their stepmother Katherine, even though they may have disapproved of her swift remarriage.

Now, at the age of thirty-six – perilously late in life to be a first-time mother for the times – Katherine found herself expecting her first child. Despite her joy at the prospect of motherhood, Katherine suffered a nagging anxiety. She and everyone else was aware that, before she and Thomas Seymour revived their romance and eventually married, he had set his sights on the Princess Elizabeth, Katherine's lively, clever stepdaughter. Fourteen-year-old Elizabeth now lived in Katherine's household, and Seymour's indiscreet flirtation with the young princess was disquieting. Katherine's imagination ran riot; she envisaged herself dying in childbirth, as so many of her contemporaries did. Would she be replaced in her beloved husband's affections by the young flame-haired Princess?

Katherine had displayed extraordinary tolerance towards the horseplay indulged in under her own roof by her adored Sudeley and the teenage Princess. After three previous, probably loveless, marriages, and after weathering interminable wrangles with her sister-in-law, Lady Somerset, and other leading figures, including the conservatives at court who had plotted against her, she had become a consummate expert at handling difficult situations. She even indulged her husband's robust frolics with the teenage Princess, joining in with him to tickle Elizabeth as she lay in bed. On one extraordinary occasion in the garden at Hanwell, pretending it was all innocent merriment rather than a romp with highly sexual overtones, she helped hold Princess Elizabeth down, while Sudeley slashed her gown 'being of black cloth' into 100 pieces.[40] When Kat Ashley, Elizabeth's beloved governess and life-time friend, attempted to remonstrate with the young Princess about this unseemly episode, Elizabeth replied that she 'could not strive with all, for the Queen held her while the Lord Admiral cut the dress.' As Ashley would later testify, Sudeley was in the habit of entering Elizabeth's chamber 'in his night-gown and bare-legged in his slippers', and would 'strike hir upon the bak or buttocks famylearly'[41]

But when she was six months pregnant, Katherine discovered her husband and the princess in an embrace that even she, thus far complaisant, could not interpret as innocent. She packed the teenage Princess off to stay with her friends Sir Anthony and Lady Denny, at Cheshunt. This was not only an attempt on Katherine's part to make sure she retained her husband's affections, but, perhaps more importantly, to protect Elizabeth's reputation.

So far as it went, this course of action was successful. Sudeley focussed his attention on Katherine's baby. He had made lavish preparations, having persuaded himself that the child would be a son. Katherine, with Jane Grey and other members of her household, moved to golden Sudeley castle in Gloucestershire, nestling in a dip in the Cotswolds.

In August, when Dorset visited the expectant father, Sudeley confided cheerfully that his brother the Protector had begun to make enemies. Sudeley painted for Dorset a picture where, having come of age, the King rejected the unpopular Protector. Knowing his brother would not relinquish power without a fight, Sudeley predicted a struggle. He enlisted Dorset's help in recruiting the support of the yeomanry. Dorset was to call on them in their homes, taking with him 'a flagon or two of wine and a pasty of venison', chatting with them in an unassuming, affable manner, to win their confidence. [42] After this conversation, Dorset returned home to Bradgate deep in thought.

On 30 August 1548 Katherine was delivered of a baby girl, but she quickly succumbed to delirium, the first sign of puerperal fever, and on 5 September she died, leaving everything she possessed to her husband, and expressing the wish that she had had a thousand times more in value to bequeath to him. She was buried at Sudeley, in the first royal Protestant funeral in England. She was the only English Queen to be buried in a private house.

The care of baby Mary Seymour was handed over to a somewhat reluctant Catherine Suffolk. She would resent the expense and inconvenience, but not for long. Within the year baby Mary would be dead.

After performing her first public role walking in Catherine's funeral procession from the house to the chapel at Sudeley, Jane Grey had returned to the care of her parents at Bradgate. But Sudeley was reluctant to let her out of his clutches and lose the potential advantage her wardship represented. Ten days after Katherine's death, he wrote to the Dorsets to say he hoped Jane would be returned to his custody. In an attempt to reassure the Dorsets of the propriety of his household, he said he had retained the services of all his late wife's gentlewomen and other attendants, and that his own mother, Lady Seymour, would love her like a daughter. But Dorset replied that Jane would be better cared for by her own mother, and Frances thanked Sudeley for his concern but asked him to trust her with the care of her own daughter.[43]

Sudeley was not to be fobbed off. He arrived at Bradgate with two convincing arguments against which the Dorsets had no defence: the first was the reiteration of the initial incitement, the possibility of a royal marriage. The second was the promise of a financial sweetener of £2,000, the first instalment of which he handed over immediately. He was accompanied to Leicestershire by his friend the unscrupulous Sir William Sharington, Under-Treasurer of the newly-established Royal Mint at Bristol Castle. The deal was sealed.

Sharington was bankrolling Sudeley out of obligation. Not only did he probably owe both his knighthood and his seat in Parliament to Sudeley's influence but the main reason for his indebtedness was that he had approached Sudeley when he began to fear that his lucrative abuse of his position at the mint had been discovered. He desperately needed Sudeley's protection.[44]

At last, after 'long debating and much sticking', Frances conceded. Jane would be returned to Sudeley's care. Another £500 changed hands. This decision sealed Jane's fate.

Sudeley, now widowed, set about pursuing his courtship of the teenage Princess Elizabeth in earnest. He was aware that to marry the Princess without the consent of the Privy Council amounted to treason. But his overwhelming ambition made him reckless. At the same time as he was contemplating renewing his pursuit of the young Princess, he was planning a direct attack on the parliamentary power base of his hated brother Somerset, the Protector, probably using some of the ill-gotten gains of his associate Sharington to arm his retainers.

Sudeley had also approached Wriothesely about his project of wresting the Protectorship from his brother and obtaining it for himself. He declared that he had the support of Pembroke and Dorset. Wriothesley had impassively overseen the torture of numerous people, but this suggestion filled him with horror, and he warned Sudeley: 'It were better for you if you had never been born, nay, that you were burnt to the quick alive than that you should attempt it'.[45] Dorset, however, as usual enthusiastically backing the wrong horse, promised Sudeley his allegiance.

Sudeley was finally trapped when the luck of his partner in crime, the devious fraudster Sharington, ran out. On the orders of the Privy Council, Sharington's home, Lacock Abbey in Wiltshire, was ransacked and incriminating evidence of the rackets he had run while employed at the Royal Mint came to light. In a desperate bid to save his own skin, Sharington revealed all he knew. Sudeley now made a reckless move. Accompanied by two servants, he entered the Privy Garden and burst into the royal bedchamber brandishing a pistol, possibly intending to kidnap the King. The King's little pet spaniel started yapping in alarm. Sudeley shot it. The gunshot roused the household.

Somerset was aware that his enemies at court were already using his brother's transgressions to tarnish his reputation. He had summoned his brother to a meeting to discuss Sharington's revelations, but Sudeley had not attended. Pushed too far, Somerset moved against his brother. On 17 January 1549, Sir Thomas Smith, Clerk of the Privy Council, and Sir John Baker, Privy Councillor and lawyer, arrived at Seymour Place with orders for Sudeley's arrest. Baker, an uncompromising grey-haired fifty-year-old, would come to be known as Butcher Baker. During the reign of Mary Tudor, he would renounce his own Evangelical past and send his former co-religionists in droves to the fires of Smithfield.

Sudeley was accused both of conspiring to overthrow Somerset and of having designs on the Princess.

The question now arose of whether Elizabeth's reputation, also, was tainted. To her dismay, two of her favourite retainers, Kat Ashley, her governess, and Sir Thomas Parry, her cofferer, or treasurer of her financial affairs, were both arrested and interrogated by Sir Robert Tyrwhit and others. Ashley had previously expressed her concerns to Parry regarding the boisterous and indecorous horseplay in which Sudeley and the teenage princess indulged, while Katherine Parr was still alive. William Wightman, a servant of Sudeley, stated that Sudeley had met secretly with Parry to discuss the Princess's estates and financial affairs.[46] Princess Elizabeth, distressed and alarmed that this trusted pair had been arrested, conceded that Parry had asked her, hypothetically, whether she would agree to marry Sudeley if the Council were to consent to the match. Elizabeth replied that she had no intention of answering that question, and 'demanded who bade him ask that question'.[47] Parry said nobody had put him up to it; he had just perceived an inclination that way on the part of the Lord Admiral. Sir Robert Tyrwhit, who conducted the examination, was unable to trap Elizabeth into any damaging admission. He concluded that Elizabeth 'hath a very good wit, and nothing is gotten of her but by great policy', and he despaired of being able to convict Elizabeth of impropriety with Sudeley, because the princess,

Parry and Ashley 'all sing one song,' as though they had co-ordinated their version of events and had agreed beforehand what line to take.

As two young girls in the household of the Queen Dowager and Sudeley, Jane Grey and Princess Elizabeth had been thrown together, although there is no evidence that their relationship was ever close. The Princess's feelings towards Katherine Parr, for whom she had previously felt affection, had become ambivalent. Katherine had showed her kindness and affection, yet her hasty remarriage had filled Elizabeth with moral outrage, tinged, perhaps, with jealousy. The attentions of the dashing Thomas Seymour had flattered her teenage ego. One day, Elizabeth would hold the destiny of Jane Grey's sister Katherine in her nervous white hands. Elizabeth's half-sister, Queen Mary, would, albeit reluctantly, sign Jane's death warrant.

Without confessions or more evidence, Ashley and Parry were released, and the interrogation of the Princess was terminated, although she remained under a cloud. But Sudeley was condemned to death for high treason. His undoubted charisma and popularity caused anxiety among the authorities lest the verdict and sentence should arouse strong emotions. Consequently, Bishop Hugh Latimer was instructed by the Privy Council to justify the decision to execute Sudeley by systematically denigrating him. In his subsequent sermon, Latimer denounced Sudeley as 'a man the farthest from the fear of God that I knew or heard of in England.' He said that the High Admiral died 'very dangerously, irksomely, horribly'.

While imprisoned in the Tower, Sudeley had written notes to Princess Mary and Princess Elizabeth, urging them 'that they should conspire against my Lord Protector's grace; surely, so seditiously as could be.' Just as he was about to lay his head on the block, he turned to the Lieutenant's servant and told him to order his own servant to hurry up and do 'the thing he wot [knew] of.' The aside was overheard, the servant was interrogated, and Sudeley's last-ditch attempt was revealed. Secret messages were discovered, which had been hidden by being sewn between the soles of a velvet shoe. They were written in secret ink made with 'cyfre of an oriege'[orange juice], 'made...so craftily, and with such workmanship, as the like hath not been seen'. Latimer added, almost admiringly: 'I was a prisoner in the Tower myself, and I could never invent to make ink so. It is wonder to hear of his subtilty. He made his pen of the aglet of a point which he plucked from his hose'.[48]

Others dismissed this dramatic turn of events as a malicious rumour, invented by Sudeley's tiresome sister-in-law, Lady Somerset. There certainly seems to have been an undignified scuffle before Sudeley was finally wrestled to the block and his head hacked off. He was said to 'die most unwillingly'.

Princess Elizabeth's comment has entered into history as Sudeley's epitaph. She said he died 'a man with much wit and very little judgement.'

Harry Dorset had escaped the consequences of his embroilment with Sudeley by the skin of his teeth, but his relief was to be short-lived. He and his three daughters would soon occupy the centre stage. After Sudeley's downfall, Jane returned again to Bradgate, having spent three years away from home.

Sudeley's brother Somerset was still the most important of the three noblemen, the 'Mighty Tres-Viri', who made up the triumvirate of the Protectorate. The other two were John Dudley, the powerful and ambitious Earl of Warwick, and Sir William Herbert. Somerset's credibility had suffered because of his brother's execution and his own mishandling of the rebellions that had racked the country that summer. Triggered by the forced introduction of the new Prayer Book, written in English, protests had developed into a widespread revolt against the ruling elite. The wealthy nobility had bought up farms and enclosed the common land, causing hardship and even starvation among landless peasants. By the end of May, rebellious mobs had been looting the estates of unpopular landlords, including those near Bradgate, tearing down fences and slaughtering deer in the parks.

Somerset, well aware that big landowners were greedy, had flown in the face of advice from colleagues on the Privy Council and tried to negotiate with the rebels, instead of sending out troops and crushing them by force, as Henry VIII would have done. His enemies had interpreted this as weakness. England teetered on the brink of civil war. The King of France, Henri II, seized the opportunity to exploit England's domestic crisis to declare war. Calais, England's last remaining bastion on the Continent, would soon be lost. Somerset was forced to abandon his policy of negotiation and deal with the crisis at home as brutally as any of his predecessors. The Government imported foreign mercenaries to quell the rebels in a series of bloodbaths. Two and a half thousand men fell valiantly in Devon. In Norfolk, Warwick led an army of 12,000 professional soldiers and German mercenaries against farmboys who hoped only for 'an equal share of things.' On 27 August, at Dussindale outside Norwich, 3,000 died.

Now, on 5 October 1549, Somerset felt the net cast by his own enemies tightening about him. As a last resort, he despatched his son, young Edward, Earl of Hertford, whom he had once hoped to see married to Jane Grey, with an urgent message to Sir William Herbert at Wilton. Herbert, with Lord Grey and Lord Russell, and Welsh troops, reinforced by Italian and German mercenaries, had been suppressing the Western Rising with brutal efficiency. The rough warrior chieftain Herbert, described by John Aubrey as a 'mad fighting fellow', who may well have been illiterate – although possibly only in English, since his native language was Welsh – had been one of Somerset's cronies and close associates. Now, Somerset was appealing for his aid, in the name of the King.

After sending his son off to Wiltshire, Somerset informed the eleven-year-old King that he needed to leave Hampton Court, because Somerset's enemies might seek him out and murder him. Edward carried a little sword to defend himself, and they set out after nightfall for gloomy, unwelcoming Windsor, where they found little cheer and few provisions. The nocturnal flight in the chilly autumn air did little to improve the young King's health.

When young Hertford reached the army in Wiltshire, he

recognised Sir William Herbert by his lofty manner and red hair. Foreign ambassadors had sneered that Herbert, Welsh-born, knew no English 'nor any other civilised language.' He had a fearsome reputation for violence. Not only was he a fugitive from justice, having allegedly murdered a man in Bristol in his youth. It was also said that when rebellious peasants overran his estate at Wilton that summer, he had personally attacked them and hacked some people to pieces. But, despite his thuggishness, Herbert was cunning and ambitious. He had managed to secure the hand of Queen Katherine Parr's sister, Anne Parr, in marriage. By extension, he could thus claim association with the royal family.

Despite their co-operation in the ruling triumvirate, Herbert bore Somerset a grudge. His wife's brother, William Parr, had been removed by Somerset from the Privy Council for divorcing his wife, the adulterous Lady Anne. But now, learning that the King himself might be in danger, Herbert ordered his army to hurry back to London. They set off on a series of punishing forced marches, through a land which was clearly in turmoil. When Herbert discovered that the person in danger was in fact Somerset and not the King, he and his associates sent young Edward back to his father with a gruff message saying that they deplored Somerset's attempts to rouse up the people, and warning him that bloodshed was to be avoided at all costs.[49]

Somerset, seeing that no help was forthcoming from that quarter, knew he was cornered and had no option but to step aside. He threw himself on the mercy of the Council. Two days after his twelfth birthday, King Edward was obliged to order his uncle's arrest. On 14 October 1549 Somerset was taken to the Tower. It was less than seven months since his brother, Sudeley, had been executed

The Grey sisters and their mother, Frances, joined took the Princess Mary at Beaulieu. Princess Mary, at 33, was still, astoundingly for a woman of her rank, single. The Venetian Ambassador, Giovanni Michieli, described her as of low rather than middling stature, 'spare, of delicate frame, quite unlike her father, who was tall and stout; or her mother, who, although not tall, was bulky.' Anxiety and stress had given her wrinkles which made her look older than her 33 years. Her myopic eyes were so piercing that they made people uneasy. Her voice was 'rough and loud, almost like a man's, and carried to a distance.' She was intelligent, spoke several languages fluently, and was a good musician. She was without imperfections, except for being, 'like other women, sudden and passionate, close and miserly'. Her demeanour was grave and dignified, and she had considerable personal courage. She had suffered depression, exacerbated by her constant menstrual problems, and attempts to cure her of these ailments meant that she often had to be bled, 'either from the foot or elsewhere, which keeps her always pale and emaciated.'

Her father had had men killed for aspiring to obtain her hand for their sons. He wanted no dangerous rivals to threaten his son Edward. Now Edward's Privy Council screened potential applicants for Mary's hand. They could exercise a legal veto on any choice she made. Mary watched her youth ebb away, devoting her affection to God. She treated the Grey girls kindly, giving them gifts of clothing and beads, gambled at card games with their mother – the Dorsets were so addicted to card-games that James Haddon, the chaplain at Bradgate, had complained of their lax lifestyle to Henry Bullinger – [51] and played her lute for them.

The young King loved his sister Mary, although he deplored her taste for frivolous foreign dances and had tried to persuade Katherine Parr to discourage it. Despite their differences over religion, Frances remained close to Mary. This kind of subtle networking was one of the inconspicuous but essential, functions of female courtiers. They managed to sustain links across religious and political divisions and warring factions. But things were about to become much more complicated.

By February 1550, the Grey sisters had returned to Dorset House on the Strand. It appeared, for the moment at least, that their father had for once managed to back the winning side, attaching himself to the new Protector, the last man standing of the erstwhile Triumvirate, the ruthless old warrior, John

Dudley, Earl of Warwick. Dorset was already reaping the advantages of this allegiance. He was made a Privy Councillor on 11 December 1549, and in 1550 he was appointed Justice Itinerant of the King's forests, Steward of the King's Honours and lordships in Leicestershire, 'parcel of the Duchy of Lancaster' for life, and Constable of Leicester Castle, with all the profits: an annual fee of 5/- and 2d a day; he had been granted extensive lands in five counties.[52] Warwick's dominance at Court was now almost complete. Forceful, intimidating and controlling, he introduced a rigorous training programme for the young King, and monitored access to the royal presence.

Warwick even explored the possibility of reviving his co-operation with Somerset, newly released from the Tower, and invited him on to the Privy Council. There was a suggestion of a dynastic marriage between Lady Anne Seymour, Somerset's clever, literary daughter, and Charles Brandon's older son, fourteen-year-old Henry Brandon, Duke of Suffolk, who was the King's study companion. When Catherine Suffolk demurred, saying she deplored the practice of forcing children into marriages that might prove unsuitable, Warwick promptly married Anne Seymour off to his own son and heir, John Dudley, Viscount Lisle, on 3 June 1550.[53]

Now a free man again, Somerset resurrected his plan for a marriage between Jane Grey and his son, young Hertford. But Dorset continued to cherish higher ambitions for Jane than Hertford. As for Jane herself, her independence of mind was becoming evident. There now occurred an encounter which was to assume key importance in the historical perception of Jane Grey. It was the autumn of 1550. Princess Elizabeth's former tutor, Roger Ascham, arrived at Bradgate, 'intending to take my leave of that noble Ladie Jane Grey, to whom I was exceeding much beholden.' Jane had written him a reference for his new job, and Ascham had long considered thirteen-year-old Jane a paragon. Finding Jane at Bradgate, he had with her the famous conversation that he reported twenty years later in his posthumously published book *The Schoolmaster*. 'It was the last time ever beheld that sweet and noble lady', Ascham noted.[54]

This incident has formed the cornerstone of later analyses of Jane's temperament and historians' perception of the characters of her parents as unpleasant and domineering bullies indifferent to her welfare.

Ascham claimed that when he came upon Jane she had been reading Plato's *Phaedo*, which describes Socrates' courage in the face of death, 'with as much delight as gentlemen read a merry tale in Boccaccio.' He inquired why she was not out in the park disporting herself with the rest of the household. Jane smiled, and remarked rather smugly that all their sport in the park was but a shadow to the delight she found in Plato. 'Alas! Good folk, they never felt what true pleasure meant!' She then seized the opportunity of a sympathetic listener to pour out her grievances against her parents.

> I will tell you, and tell ye a truth which perchance ye will marvel at. One of the greatest benefits that ever God gave me is that he sent me so sharp and severe parents and so gentle a schoolmaster. For when I am in presence of either father or mother, whether I speak, keep silent, sit, stand or go, eat, drink, be merry or sad, be sewing, playing, dancing or doing anything else, I must do it, as it were, in such weight, measure and number, even so perfectly as God made the world, or else I am so sharply taunted, so cruelly threatened, yea, presently sometimes with pinches, nips and bobs, and other ways (which shall not name, for the honour I bear them), so without measure misordered, that I think myself in hell till time come that I must go to Mr Aylmer, who teaches me so gently, so pleasantly, with such fair allurements to learning, that I think all the time nothing whilst I am with him. And when I am called from him, I fall on weeping, because whatever I do else but learning is full of grief, trouble, fear and wholly misliking unto me. And thus my book hath been so much my pleasure, and brings daily to me more pleasure and more that in respect of it, all other pleasures, in very deed, be but troubles and trifles unto me.[55]

Jane appears to have adopted a stance of self-imposed austerity, in which abstaining from vigorous outdoor pursuits in favour of study may have played a part. She also followed the advice that she should adopt the Princess Elizabeth's plain style of dress. This even led to her snubbing the Princess Mary, who had sent her a splendid gown of 'tinsel cloth of gold and velvet, laid over with parchment lace of gold.' Jane demanded scornfully 'What shall I do with it?'

'Marry,' her gentlewoman replied, 'wear it'.

'Nay', snapped Jane, 'that were shame to follow my Lady Mary against God's word, and leave my Lady Elizabeth who followeth God's word'.[56]

In the summer of 1551, both Frances Grey's half-brothers, Henry, Duke of Suffolk, and Charles, Brandon's sons by Catherine Suffolk, died of the killer disease, the 'sweating sickness.' Harry Dorset was elevated to his father in law's title as Duke of Suffolk. Dorset owed his promotion to his support of Warwick, who had now been created Duke of Northumberland and no longer envisaged an alliance with Somerset, but was plotting the former Protector's downfall by having him accused of planning to murder Northampton and Warwick himself. Dorset gladly signed the warrant for Somerset's arrest. He had learned of Somerset's aspirations for his daughter Lady Jane Seymour, as a bride for the King, a position Dorset still hoped to achieve for his daughter Jane. If Somerset fell from grace again, that problem would be solved.

Jane Seymour would become the best friend and confidante of Dorset's second daughter, Katherine Grey.

Somerset was condemned to death by his judges, the two new Dukes, and was executed.

Jane Grey, who turned 15 in May 1552, now had no serious rivals as a prospective bride for her cousin the young king, a few months her junior. Lady Jane Seymour, as the daughter of an executed criminal, was now out of the picture. Plans for Edward to marry the daughter of the French King Henri II had fallen through. As an adherent of the Reformed religion, Jane Grey was regarded in many quarters as eminently suitable. Clever, committed, like her cousin the King, to Protestantism, of considerable personal courage, thoroughly self-willed, with a youthful tendency to self-righteousness, she was in reality more determined and less malleable than those about her supposed. Jane had the psychological constitution and strength of mind of a martyr rather than a hapless victim, although she was certainly the victim of circumstances.

In August, cheering crowds in the southern towns of Southampton Salisbury and Portsmouth turned out to greet their teenage King. Small and slight, the bejewelled figure exuded the assurance and presence of a Tudor monarch. But this was illusory: the boy was fatally ailing. He was probably suffering from tuberculosis, contracted in summer 1551 and reactivated when he contracted measles in April 1552. On 6 February, his older half-sister Mary Tudor, fully aware that under the terms of her father's will, and the last Act of Succession of 1544, confirmed in Edward's Treasons Act of 1547, she was Edward's heir, arrived in London with 200 attendants to visit the King's sickbed. Northumberland, convinced that the young King could not long survive, announced the betrothal of his fourth son Guildford to Lady Jane Grey.

When this match was first suggested Jane would have none of it. She pointed out that she had been previously contracted to Lord Hertford, son of the ill-fated Somerset, and hence this proposed union would be bigamous in law. No written records of this prior contract have survived, possibly because they were deliberately destroyed.

Some historians have claimed that the thwarted Suffolks reacted violently to their daughter's disobedience: Harry allegedly cursed and raved, Frances beat Jane up. Between them they persuaded her. Frances would later claim, however, that she had vigorously opposed the match. Certainly, it is on record that she had previously stated that she did not wish Jane to marry too young. But the matter had become urgent. The King was dying. The Imperial Ambassador noted that 'the matter he ejects from his mouth is sometimes coloured a greenish-yellow and black, sometimes pink, like the colour of blood.' [57] The physicians were at a loss. Ambassador of the Holy Roman Empire Jehan Scheyfve noted also that the devious

Northumberland was now hedging his bets by insisting on the Princess Mary's rights to full arms as a 'Princess of England'. 'This all seems to point to his desire to conciliate the said Lady and earn her favour, and to show that he does not aspire to the crown.'[58] He added that the betrothal of Jane and Guildford looked suspicious, and was causing loose talk in the taverns. Several people of both sexes had their ears cut off for spreading rumours.

But Northumberland got his way. On 25 May 1553, a triple wedding was celebrated with great magnificence at Durham House, Northumberland's London residence. The three happy young couples were Guildford Dudley and Jane Grey; the sickly young Lord Herbert and pretty twelve-year-old Katherine Grey; and Guildford's sister, twelve-year-old Catherine Dudley, and Henry Hastings, son of the Greys' neighbour, the Earl of Huntingdon. The bridal couples and mothers-in-law Frances Grey and Jane, Duchess of Northumberland, made a dazzling appearance robed in gowns of cloth of gold and cloth of silver, with which they had been issued by the master of the King's wardrobe. The bulk of this costly material had been obtained from possessions forfeited by the disgraced Somerset and his widow, Lady Anne, still imprisoned in the Tower. Northumberland, orchestrating events, had commanded the Master of the Revels, Sir Thomas Cawarden, to provide entertainment in the form of two masques, one with an all-male cast, the other all-female. He had stipulated that the costumes must be rich and rare. There were celebratory games and jousts. Northumberland, who had the previous year unsuccessfully attempted to marry his son Guildford to Lady Margaret Clifford, Jane's first cousin, the daughter of Eleanor Brandon, was triumphant. Jane was an even greater prize than Margaret and, more importantly, closer in the line of succession.

The only discordant note was struck when Guildford and several of the guests went down with a bout of food-poisoning, caused, allegedly, because a cook had 'plucked one leaf for another'.

There was a great crowd of foreign dignitaries who were all

suitably impressed by the splendour of the event. Young King Edward was already too ill to attend, although he sent handsome gifts.

Within the space of a few months, one young bridal couple and both their fathers would be dead, as would the King. The marriage of Herbert and Katherine Grey would be annulled. Of the three coupes, only Henry Hastings and little Catherine Dudley would enjoy a long, harmonious but childless union.

Jehan Scheyfve, the Imperial Ambassador, who had an informant in the royal household, had been sending regular bulletins to his royal master about the progress of the King's illness. On 12 May, he reported that Edward had a tumour on the lung and had broken out in ulcers. By the end of the month, the doctors had confirmed that he was not expected to live. His limbs were so swollen that he had to lie on his back. It was at this point that Edward produced a will which he had drafted some time previously. As his father's will had done, it excluded the descendants of his aunt Margaret, the Queen of Scots. But Henry VIII's will had included Edward's half-sisters, Mary and Elizabeth. Edward, on the contrary, made it clear that he contemplated only a male heir. Frances Brandon had already been passed over in Henry VIII's will, which had stipulated 'the heirs of the body of the Lady Frances', rather than Frances herself. This putative heir had to be born before the death of Edward himself. Failing this, the throne would pass to the offspring of the Lady Jane Grey. If this course of events were to come to pass, then the new monarch would be a Dudley, the grandson of the ambitious Northumberland.

But now it seemed there would be no time for this long-term plan to come to fruition. The precipitous decline in the King's health made it imperative to identify an immediate successor. Desperate times, desperate measures: the matter was solved with a stroke of the pen. The words 'to the L. Jane's heires masles' was changed to read: 'to the L. Jane AND her heires masles.' The letter 's' was crossed out but remains clearly visible, and the words 'and her' were added above the line. In the Letters Patent, although not in the King's 'Devise', the names of the Ladies Katherine and Mary Grey were added.

The dying teenage King summoned his senior judges to his bedside to ratify his will. He explained why he had disinherited his half-sisters in favour of Jane Grey, and instructed them to prepare the necessary documents. But the judges had qualms. Some anxiously expressed concern before the Council that the will could not be enforced before the Act of Succession of 1544 was rescinded. Northumberland, furious at the potential thwarting of his ambitions, threatened to strip to his shirt and physically challenge anyone who opposed the King's wishes. He managed to browbeat fourteen of the judges into submission, but several refused to change their opinion.

Frances was then summoned to meet with Edward to ensure she agreed to being passed over in favour of her daughter. On June 21 the nobility and chief officers of the Crown were commanded to sign the legal document: Edward had pondered the question of the succession for a long time, even before the disastrous decline in his health. He had come to the conclusion that his sisters were only his 'half-blood'; they were illegitimate; and there remained the dire possibility that they would marry foreigners, whose dominion would have a catastrophic effect on the country. (In the case of Philip of Spain, the husband of his sister Mary, Edward's foreboding was to be fulfilled.)

By contrast, his married and betrothed cousins, the Grey daughters, were a much better bet. They were legitimate, had been honourably brought up and 'exercised in good and Godly learning, and other noble virtues' – in other words, they, like Edward, belonged to the Reformed religion.

Frances has not been recorded as objecting to her nephew's decision, but her husband Suffolk was furious that his wife had been passed over, and convinced that Northumberland lay behind it all and planned to see his own son crowned as Jane's co-ruler. This suspicion was well-founded.

Edward was now desperately ill. In one last endeavour to keep the King alive until Parliament could be called in September, an old crone who enjoyed a reputation as a healer was summoned. She dosed him with potions laced with arsenic, which only aggravated the poor boy's suffering. The whole country was in uproar, groaning under the boot of Northumberland. Rumours sprang up: Northumberland was poisoning the King. Northumberland was plotting to hand the whole country over to the French.

Edward made his last public appearance on June 27, showing himself at a window. It was an attempt to reassure the people, but the sight of the boy's pale wasted figure scarcely bolstered their confidence. That same night, Northumberland was spotted entering the residence of the new French Ambassador, Antoine de Noailles. To Northumberland's fury, when the people got wind of this, gossip spread like wildfire. Two citizens were chained to a post and whipped for uttering 'opprobrious and seditious words' against Northumberland and his allies.

On 6 July Edward VI died. The next morning, the Mayor of London and City Magistrates, along with the guard, swore an oath of allegiance to Queen Jane at Greenwich. Next day, Northumberland, as President of the Council, informed her officially that the King was dead and that she was Queen. Jane fell to the ground, weeping. This dramatic collapse contributed to the perception of Jane as the unwilling young victim of the manipulations of others.

However, Jane soon recovered her customary composure, got to her feet and delivered a gracious speech in which she modestly accepted her kingdom, expressing the hope that God would grant her the grace to enable her to govern, with his approbation and to His glory.

On 9 July, Nicholas Ridley, the Bishop of London and Westminster, preached at St Paul's Cross that Jane was the rightful sovereign and declared Mary and Elizabeth bastards. The mood among the crowd was sullen. They were 'sore annoyed by his words, so uncharitably spoken of him in so open an audience.' [59]

On Monday 10 July, accompanied by her parents, her husband and his mother, Jane travelled by barge along the river from Richmond to Westminster, and then to the Tower, where she processed in great state, her mother Frances, the Duchess of

Suffolk, bearing her train. However, the number of spectators was felt to be disappointing, and there were few cheers.[60]

As the great gates swung shut behind them, the heralds-at-arms and a company of archers rode forth into the city. Proclamations were read out at the Cross in Cheapside, Paul's Cross, and Cheapside; heralds proclaimed that the Lady Mary was 'unlawfully begotten' and that Jane was Queen. The omens were bad. The news was greeted with stunned silence. Only the heralds cried: 'God save the Queen', and at Cheapside, Gilbert Potter, a teen-age 'drawer' or potboy, who worked at the St John's Head in Ludgate, briefly became a folk hero overnight when he shouted out what most people were thinking, namely, that 'the Lady Mary has the better title'. He was denounced to the guard by his own master, Ninian Sanders, either because Sanders feared for his business, or because he was a supporter of Jane. The lad was seized and placed in the pillory. By an ironic trick of fate, Sanders, who had denounced the boy, lost his own life that very night, when he and another man, Owen, were drowned when shooting London Bridge in a wherry.[61] Next morning at 8 a.m. Potter's ears were nailed to the pillory and later sliced off with a knife. Machyn records that his savage punishment was attended by a herald and a 'trumpeter blowing'. By July, a propaganda sheet was circulating, entitled 'Epistle of Poor Pratte to Gilbert Potter.' Copies were thrown about in public places where the writers could be sure they would be picked up by the curious, ensuring that the views express would achieve maximum circulation. Two copies were even smuggled into the camp of the 'Ragged Bear' – the army of the hated Northumberland.

Mary's defiance also continued undaunted. The Tudor name was a rallying-point for some, while for others, their resentment of Northumberland was sufficient motivation.

On 12 July, the great Lord Treasurer, William Paulet, Marquess of Winchester, brought Jane the Crown. She wrote: 'he told me that another wold also be made to crown my husband as King; this suggestion aggrieved me, and after my Lord had left, I talked the matter over with my husband until he agreed that in case of he being made king, that would be by me and by act of Parliament.' Almost immediately, Jane felt she needed to modify this statement, so she sent for the Earls of Arundel and Pembroke, and told them 'if the Crown pertained to me, I should be pleased to make my husband a Duke, but I should never make him King'.[62]

When Guildford's mother, Lady Northumberland, heard what Jane had said, she flew into a rage and forbade her son to sleep with Jane or have anything to do with her. Guildford flounced about pettishly, shouting that he did not want to be a Duke, he wanted to be King. Jane had to send the two Earls after him to force him back to her side 'otherwise I knew that the following morning he would have gone to Sion. Thus I have been deceived by the Duke, by the Council, and by my husband, and ill-treated by his mother.'[63] In her letter Jane accused her in-laws of poisoning her twice, so that her hair fell out – almost certainly a false accusation, especially since her death would hardly have been in the interests of the Dudley family– but she also stated that, 'as Sir John Gates has confessed,' it was her father-in-law, the Duke of Northumberland, who persuaded King Edward VI to make her his heir. The extent to which the dying King's mind was influenced by those about him remains unclear. [64]

Meanwhile, the Imperial Ambassadors, Scheyfve and Renard, added fuel to the flames of suspicion surrounding Northumberland, claiming that he had made a secret deal with the French to place the French King Henri II's ward, Mary, Queen of Scots, aged eleven, on the throne of England if Jane should prove uncooperative.

On 12 July, word was brought to Jane and her Council in the Tower that the Lady Mary had rallied a large number of nobles to her cause at Kenninghall Castle in Norfolk. It was quickly decided that a force under the command of Jane's father, the Duke of Suffolk, should be sent to capture Mary, but the decision was changed because it was felt that Suffolk was not up to the challenge. In his stead, the Council appointed Northumberland, on the grounds that, having successfully suppressed the rebellion in Norfolk four years previously, he was uniquely qualified. Not only was he the greatest of warriors, but his reputation for brutality preceded him in Norfolk, inspiring such terror that 'none durst once lift up their weapon against him'.[65] The Duke undertook this commission with a certain reluctance, all too aware that the Council were unreliable. Not only might they prove vacillating once his back was turned, but they might also welcome the opportunity to stab him in the back. However, to Jane's relief, he agreed to lead the operations in East Anglia.

Next day, carts were laden with munitions and 'artillery, and field pieces prepared for the purpose'.[66] The armaments were moved after nightfall; Machyn records: 'On 12 July by night were carried to the Tower three carts full of all manner of ordnance, such as great guns and small, bows, bills, spears, Morrish pikes, armour, arrows, gunpowder, stakes, money, tents, a great number of cannon balls, a great number of men at arms.'[67]

Northumberland and his troops set out on 14 July for East Anglia, watched in icy silence by the crowds. As they passed through Shoreditch, Northumberland noted the lack of sympathy in the crowd who observed them ride out, and recorded bitterly: 'The people press to see us, but not one sayeth God speed us.'[68]

Amidst these ominous events, Jane stood godmother to the infant son of Edward Underhill, a radical evangelical cleric. Although too busy to attend the ceremony in the church on tower hill, she chose the names as tradition dictated. The baby was named for her husband Guildford and her father, Harry Suffolk. Her co-godparent, Pembroke, her sister Katherine's father-in-law, was already preparing to betray her.

On Tuesday, 18 July, the Council, now unsupervised by Northumberland, met at Pembroke's grim fortress, Baynard's Castle, where, just as Northumberland had feared, they switched allegiance, declared Northumberland a traitor, and proclaimed Mary Queen. Next day, they announced their decision to Jane's father. He panicked, knowing the game was lost, and rushed to the chamber where Jane sat at supper. He tore down her canopy, crying that she had no right to use it. Jane remained calm. 'When the Lady Jane heard of the Council's determination, she said she would give it [i.e., the royal dignity] up as gladly as she had accepted it.'[69] She said that this news was more welcome to her than being told she was queen, a role for which she felt inadequate. The throne was Mary's by right, and the part she had played had been prepared for her without her knowledge.

Perhaps this was an indication that the traditional view of Jane as the innocent pawn in other people's cynical power play was, after all, correct; on the other hand, since Jane's superior intelligence would appear to be a matter of record, it may well have been an attempt to pre-empt events, to disassociate herself from the illegal aspirations of others, and throw herself on Mary's mercy in the hope of obtaining a pardon. In view of the provenance of this particular primary source, it is small wonder that the rights of Queen Mary, and the popular acclamation with which her proclamation was received by the public, feature so prominently.

Mary was duly proclaimed as Queen, bonfires were lighted, church bells rang and men ran through the streets shouting the glad tidings. There was an air of jubilation in the city.

When Northumberland and two of his sons, Ambrose and Henry, all now prisoners, were escorted at sunset through London to the Tower on 25 July 1553, the Earl of Arundel, who had treated them with every courtesy and a genuine concern for their welfare, was alarmed by the angry mood of the mob. The citizens began hurling stones, rotten eggs and excrement at the prisoners, yelling 'Traitor!' and 'Heretic!' Arundel urged Northumberland to remove his distinctive cap and red cloak to make him less identifiable to the jeering multitude, who seemed in a mood to lynch him. The haughty Ragged Bear was reduced to begging for pity. His son Henry wept in terror. As Northumberland entered the Beauchamp Tower, his son, John, also wept, for the shame of it.[70]

On 27 July Jane's father, Suffolk, was brought to the Tower.

Scheyfve and Renard insisted that releasing Jane would risk 'scandal and danger'. Reluctantly, Mary decided to detain Jane, but pardoned Suffolk the next day. He remained in the Tower for a fortnight, too ill to be moved. Jane was charged with treason, for which the usual penalty was death.

On 3 August, Mary entered London to a fanfare of trumpets with 800 men and her sister, Elizabeth.[71] She was determined to make a splendid entrance, and had chosen a purple velvet gown in the French fashion, richly embroidered with gold and pearls, accessorised by a neckpiece of gold encrusted with gems. Her horse was accoutred in gold right down to its hooves.[72]

On 8 August her half-brother's funeral took place according to the rites of the reformed religion, which he had so enthusiastically embraced. Mary, who had wanted a full Requiem Mass, had been persuaded by the Imperial Ambassadors that this would cause confrontation, so she contented herself by having a Mass said for him in private.

Then the trials of the traitors began. Northumberland cravenly recanted his Evangelical views and re-embraced Catholicism in an effort to appease the Queen. He scribbled a desperate letter to Arundel at the last hour, in which he pathetically entreated him to beg the Queen to spare him and grant him 'the life of a dog, that I might but live and kiss her feet.' [73.]

No pardon came. Northumberland and several other leading figures were beheaded. When Jane heard of her father-in-law's pusillanimous eleventh-hour renunciation of the Reformed faith in hopes of obtaining a pardon, she was outraged: 'Pardon?' she cried. 'Woe worth him! He hath brought me and our stock in most miserable calamity and misery by his exceeding ambition.'[74] She wondered how he dared ask for a pardon when he had taken the field against Mary's forces. But his life was 'odious to all men, and as his life had been wicked and full of dissimulation, so was his end'. Jane declared she herself would die rather than renounce her faith, young though she was. She quoted the Scriptures, concluding that Northumberland was damned.

Mary's counsellors urged her to have Jane executed without delay, but she had long resisted their exhortations. So long as she remained alive, they argued, Jane was a potential threat to Mary's realm and to the re-establishment of the Old Religion. The validity of this apprehension became evident when it was learned that Mary had accepted a proposal of marriage from Philip of Spain. A group of noble Evangelicals, including Sir Thomas Wyatt and Harry Grey, Duke of Suffolk, led an unsuccessful popular rebellion. This sealed Jane's fate, even though the intention of the rebels had been to replace Mary with Elizabeth, rather than Jane. The rebel leaders were captured and executed. Suffolk hid in an oak tree and was run to ground with tracker dogs.

The date for the execution of Jane and her husband was set for 9 February 1554. Many 'traitors', including, to Jane's disgust, the greatest, Northumberland, had recanted their faith under the shadow of the axe. Now Mary's concern was for her cousin's immortal soul. Accordingly, in a final attempt to persuade Jane to be reconciled with the Queen's faith, a stay of execution of three days' duration was decreed. The Queen sent her own chaplain, Dr John Feckenham, the new Dean of St Paul's, to convince Jane to embrace the Catholic faith and save her soul. Feckenham, trained in the Benedictine tradition, was a fine man and a good theologian who had been imprisoned for his faith under Henry VIII.[75]

Jane remained friendly but resolute. Among her writings in the Tower is her prayer for courage: 'Lord, thou God and father of my life, hear me poor and desolate woman. Arm me, I beseech Thee, with thy armour, that I may stand fast.'[76] Feckenham found her cool and composed as ever. He complimented her on bearing up so bravely. Jane replied that far from regretting her situation, she regarded it as a 'manifest declaration of God's favour towards me.' She welcomed the occasion to repent of her sins. The two now engaged in a lengthy discussion of the path to salvation and the Real Presence of Christ in the Host and the wine. Jane did not hold back. She attacked the Catholic Church as the 'spouse of the

Devil, for its idolatrous interpretations.'[76]

Jane was left to compose her last letters, two of which, to her father and her sister Katherine, survive, although the first is suspicious. It did not surface until 1570. In it she reminds Suffolk how she was placed under pressure by him and by others to accept the crown. No letters to Frances or Mary Grey survive, although Michelangelo Florio claimed that Jane also wrote to Frances. To her sister Katherine, Jane wrote that she must not attempt to save herself by accepting the Catholic faith.[77]

At ten o'clock on Monday 12 February, Guildford Dudley was taken from his rooms in the Tower to the place of public execution on Tower Hill. Jane watched from the window as he was led out from the Beauchamp Tower. He died without benefit of clergy, but asked those gathered around to pray for him. After spending some time in prayer, he gave the signal, and the headsman severed his head at one blow. According to one anonymous primary source, his body was tossed upon a cart and his head was wrapped up in a cloth, and his remains were then taken into the chapel. From the window Jane had seen him walk out alive, and had seen his dead body, before she set off on her own last walk, to the scaffold which had been erected for her on the green by the White Tower. Surrounded by her weeping ladies, Jane approached her death with dignity, her eyes glued to the book she held. She mounted the scaffold, made the expected speech, saying she had come there to die, admitting 'the fact indeed against the quene's highnesse was unlawfull, and the consenting therunto by me; but touching the procurement and desire therof by me, or on my half, I doo wash my hands therof in innocencie.'

She wrung her hands and asked them to pray for her. Kneeling down, she asked Feckenham, who had failed to convert her, but whom she had, out of her regard for him, permitted to accompany her to the scaffold, whether she should recite a psalm. 'Yea', he replied. She then recited the *Misere mei Deus*, in English. Then, rising, she handed her gloves and 'handkercher' to Mistress Tilney, her 'maiden mistris' and her book to Master Thomas Bruges [Bridges] the brother of the Lieutenant of the Tower, and untied her gown, brushing aside the headsman's offer of assistance. She turned instead to her gentlewomen, who helped her, and handed her a 'fayre handkercher' to bind her eyes. The executioner then knelt to beg her forgiveness, which she gave him readily. He asked her to stand on the straw, and at that moment her eye fell upon the block, a rough beam of unhewn wood. 'I pray you despatch me quickly', she said. As she knelt, she was struck by the thought that perhaps he would misinterpret her request and strike before she was ready. 'Will you take [my head] before I lay me down?' 'No, Madam,' replied the executioner.

Jane tied her own handkerchief about her eyes and stretched out a hand, groping blindly for the block. Panicked, she demanded: 'What shall I do? Where is it?'

Appalled, someone, possibly Feckenham, guided her to the block. (This was a courageous action, since in theory at least it could be regarded as aiding and abetting a condemned criminal.) Jane laid her head upon the beam, stretched out her arms and said: 'Lord, into thy hands I commend my spirit'.[78]

14 - Notes

1.   J.S Brewer, ed., CSP, For & Dom, Henry VIII vol xiii, 280

2.   L&P, iv, 5773-4

3.   A source hostile to Anne, possibly Chapuys to Granville

4.   CSP Span

5.   Crónico del rey Enrico

6.   'Whose death all true Englishmen maie greatlie lament, which had been so valiant a captain in the Kinges warres...to the great dammage and losse of the Kinges enemies, whose bodie was honourably buried at Windsor at the Kinges costs', Charles Wriothesely, ed. William Douglas Hamilton, *A Chronicle of England during the Reigns of the Tudors: From AD 1485 to 1559.* Camden Society New Series XI, London, 1875, '18th August 1545'.

7.   Elis Gruffudd, *Chronicle*

8.   L&P: For & Dom Henry VIII iv 111

9. CSP Span. Marino Sanuto, *Diaries*, 1466-1536

10. L&P, XII, ii, nos. 889, 905,1053; Wriothesley , 1875-7, I, 66-7

11, Strickland, *Lives*, vol 5, 1902, 20-21

12, John Aylmer, 'Letter to Henry Bullinger, May 1551', in: *Original Letters Relative to the English Reformation,* 2 vols., Robinson, Hastings, Cambridge University Press, 1856-1857

13. Richard Davey, *The Sisters of Lady Jane Grey and their wicked grandfather,* Chapman & Hall, London, 1911, 257-8

14. Janel Mueller, 'Prospecting for Common Ground in Devotion: Queen Catherine Parr's personal prayerbook', in : *English Woman, Religion and Textual Production, 1500-1625,* Micheline White, ed. Farnham UK Asgate, 2011

15. PRO Inventory; Edward Hall, Henry VIII, Chronicle, ed. C. Whibley, London, 1902

16. L&P

17. CSP Span

18. PRO; Fraser

19. CSP: Spanish; L&P; PRO.

20. Crónico del Rey Enrico CSP Span; L&P; PRO

21. L&P

22. *Foxe's Book of Martyrs,* 209, John Day, 1563

23. L&P vol 2 485, ed. Hume; L&P Jan 29 1547; CSP For 1547-53 101

24. *Writings of Edward VI, William Hugh, Anne Askew, Lady Jane Grey, Hamilton, and Balnaves et al.,* Religious Tract Society, London,1831

25. John Bale, *The Examinations of Anne Askew,*1546

26. L&P, 21, pt 1, 1027, Francis van der Delft

27. CSP Span

28. *Writings of Edward VI, William Hugh, Queen Catherine Parr,:* author unknown. vol 3 of British Reformers, London, The Religious Tract Society, 1836, 4

29. Hall; Foxe; CSP Span.

30. Letter of Catherine Parr to Thomas Seymour, February 1547

31. Ellis, 2, 152

32. Patrick Fraser Tytler, ed., *England under the Reigns of Edward VI and Mary*, London, 1839, 65

33. DNB. GEC, Peerage, 4.420-22 ·CSP Dom, *1547–58* ·Nichols, *The history and antiquities of the county of Leicester*, 4 vols. 1795–1815 ·Nichols, *Chronicle* ; SP Dom Edward viTNA; PRO SP 10/6/7.

34. Haynes , 163-4; SP 10/6/13; SP 10/6/16;*Orig. Letters*, ed. Ellis, ii, 154-5; HMC Hatfield i, 55-56, 61-73; A.F. Pollard, DNM GEC**javascript:;** Peerage.420-22 · CSP Dom, *1547–58* ·Nichols, *The history and antiquities of the county of Leicester*, 4 vols. (1795–1815) · J. G. Nichols, ed., *The chronicle of Queen Jane, and of two years of Queen Mary*, CS, old ser., 48 (1850) · S P Dom Edward VI, TNA: PRO, SP 10/6/7 · exchequer, king's remembrancer, lay subsidy rolls, TNA: PRO, E 179/69/54, 75 · H. Robinson, ed. and trans., *Original letters relative to the English Reformation*, 1 vol. in 2, Parker Society, [26] (1846-7)

35. Deposition of the Marquess of Northampton; COLL. STATE PAPERS. ed. Haynes, 163-4; E. Dent, ANNALS OF WINCHCOMBE AND SUDELEY, 173; SP 10/6/13, f. 36; SP 10/6/16; ORIG. LETTERS, ed. Ellis, ii. 154-5; HMC HATFIELD, i. 55-56, 61-73; A. F. Pollard, ENGLAND UNDER PROTECTOR SOMERSET, 185

36. David W Bartlett *The Life of Lady Jane Grey*, Miller, Orton & Co, New York, 1857, 1886, 106

37. Haynes, 82, 84; Tytler, 138

38. *Original Letters Relative to the Reformation (Zurich Letters)*, H. Robinson, ed., vol I, Parker Society, no 23, 1846, 278-9

39. Hugh Latimer, *Observants*, 231

40. SP 10/6/21

41. SP, ed Haynes, 98,99

42. Tytler, *Original Letters*, vol i, 140

43. SP ed. Haynes,78-9

44. ODNB; 'Confession of Sir William Sharington, Vice-Treasurer of the Bristol Mint, February 11, 1548/9,' in Richard Arthur Roberts & Montague Spencer Giuseppi, eds., *Calendar of the manuscripts of the Most Honourable the Marquess of Salisbury,*1883, 68

45. Davey, *The Nine Days Queen, Lady Jane Grey and her Times*, 1909. CSP Hen VIII, Haynes, ed., Jan 20 1548/9

46. ibid, Jan 23 1548/9, 71

47. ibid; CSP Dom *1548–53* · CSP Span*1558–67* HoP, Commons, 1509-58, 3.63–5

BL, autograph, Add. MS 33924, fol. 3 · BL, autograph, Add. MS 34079, fol. 5

48. G E Corrie,(ed.) *Sermons and Remains of Hugh Latimer*, Parker Society, 16, 20, 1844-1845, 161-164; Sir John Godsalve; HoP 1509-1558, II, 221-222

49. J A Froude, *History of England from the Fall of Wolsey to the Death of Elizabeth*, 1860, 241.

50. CSP Ven 1557

51. Robinson, *Original Letters*, vol I, 277

52. Strype, *Memorials*, Clarendon Press, 1822, vol ii, pt 1, 435

53. CSPD Vol i

54. Roger Ascham, *The Scholemaster*, 1570, bk 1, no 7

55. Ascham, *The Whole Works*, vol III, 118, 119

56. Strype, *Memorials*, 1822, 167

57. CSP Span vol 11 28 April 1553

58. ibid.

59. Foxe, vi, 389

60. CSP vol 111553 [1916]68-69

61. Froude; Machyn; Nichols, *Chr. of Queen Jane*, Appendix V, 'The Epistle of Poor Pratte to Gilbert Potter', 1801, 115

62. Jane Grey, *Letter to Queen Mary I, 10 July 1553*

63. ibid.

64. J M Stone, The *History of Mary I, Queen of England*, Sands & Co, 1901, 487-498

65. Froude, *History of England* chapter xxx, 195

66. Nichols, *Chr. of Queen Jane*, 1850; Wingfield, *Vita Mariae Reginae*, tr. McCullough, Camden, XXVVIII 4th series

67. Machyn, *Diary*, ed. Nichols, London, Camden Soc, 1848, 34-40

68. John Stow, *The Annales of England faithfully collected out of the most autenticall authors, records, and other monuments of antiquitie,* London 1592, 611

69. CSP Span Vol II 1553, [1916] 109-12

70. Machyn, *Diary*, 1848, 37: *Greyfriars Chronicle*, 80-81; CSP Span 267 July 1553

71. Machyn, *Diary*, 38

72. CPS Vl xi; Rolls House MSS Renard to Charles V; Wriothesely, *Chronicle*

73. Northumberland to Arundel, 19 August, 1554

74. Froude, *History*, vol 5, 247

75. Nichols, *Chronicle*, 54;CSP Span, xxii

76. N H Nicolas, *The Literary Remains of Lady Jane Grey*, London, 1825, 49-51

77. ibid, 34

78. Nichols, *Chr. of Queen Jane,* 1850, 54-59

15 THE FATAL INHERITANCE: THE STANLEYS

When Mary Rose's second daughter, Eleanor, married Lord Clifford, eldest son of the Earl of Cumberland, the Earl was so delighted to have acquired a daughter-in-law of the blood royal that he gave orders for a 'great gallery for the accommodation of his high-born daughter-in-law' to be built in the tower at Skipton Castle. [1] Brandon endeavoured to help the young couple by enlisting Cromwell's support. In 1540, he managed to increase the Cliffords' fortunes by winning a major lease for them. But he felt Cumberland underestimated the real cost of maintaining his son at court. He was also unimpressed with Eleanor's country residence, which he feared was insalubrious. He wrote to ask the Earl to let the young couple reside at Brougham. He was also worried about his daughter's safety as well as her health, and with good reason. The most dramatic event in the life of Eleanor occurred in October 1536. Her husband and his father had refused to support the most serious rebellion against Henry VIII's rule, the Pilgrimage of Grace. This popular rising in Yorkshire was a protest against the King's religious reforms and the policies of Thomas Cromwell, his chief minister. The rebels laid siege to Skipton Castle. Eleanor was staying with her sisters-in-law at Bolton Priory. The insurgents threatened to kidnap them, take them hostage and, if Skipton Castle continued to resist the siege, 'to violate all the ladies and enforce them with knaves under the walls.' [2] Christopher Aske, the Earl's man of business, enlisted the aid of the vicar of Skipton, a groom, and a boy. They stole out of the castle at dead of night, leading their horses, through the camp of the besiegers and crossed the moors 'by unfrequented paths'. They managed to rescue the intended hostages and smuggled them back into the castle without arousing suspicion.

The siege of Skipton Castle lasted from October 21 or 22 to October 27, when the rebels abandoned their attempt on its sturdy stone walls. On November 7, 1536, Brandon, horrified to learn of the danger Eleanor had been in, wrote to the Earl of Cumberland, asking him not to risk her wellbeing but to send her to him at home if this could be done safely.

In 1542, Eleanor's father-in-law died and her husband succeeded to the Earldom. In 1545, Eleanor's own father, Charles Brandon, died, leaving to Eleanor and her sister Frances two hundred pounds' worth of plate. The two sons she had borne, Charles and Henry Clifford, both died in infancy. In 1546, Eleanor was at court, attending her uncle King Henry's sixth wife, Katherine Parr. She and Frances were 'ladies ordinary', probably lodged in the palace. On Valentine's Day she wrote the only letter that appears to have survived, a loving letter to her husband, describing her ill health and symptoms. Her water was red, leading her to believe she was suffering from both the ague and jaundice. She had no appetite and complained of pains in her back and side. She asked her husband to send a physician to attend her. She also mentioned that her half-sister Anne Brandon, Lady Powys, had been to visit her. That autumn, Eleanor, only in her twenties, died. Lady Anne Clifford offers a dramatic account of the effect of his wife's death on Cumberland.

> [H]e fell into an extreame sickness, of which he
> was at length laid out for a dead Man, upon a
> Table, & covered with a hearse of velvet; but some

of his men that were then very carefull about him perceiveing some little signs of life in him, did apply hot cordials inwardly & outwardly unto him, which brought him to life again, & so, after he was laid into his bed again, he was fain for 4 or 5 weeks after to such the milk out of a woman's breast and only to live on that food; and after to drink asses milk, and live on that 3 or 4 months longer.[3]

The woman who performed this somewhat bizarre but restorative service for the Earl was not named.

According to the terms of her uncle Henry's will, Eleanor had been eighth in line to the throne. After his own children and the heirs of her sister Frances, the crown was to pass to Eleanor's offspring. Through her daughter, the headstrong Lady Margaret Clifford, born in 1540, Eleanor's descendants continued as possible claimants to the throne of England long after Eleanor's death, and after her sister Frances's line had died out.

In 1552, the dynastically ambitious Northumberland had planned to marry fifteen-year-old Margaret Clifford to his own son, Lord Guildford Dudley. Margaret was the heiress to her father's vast northern estates, where Northumberland cherished aspirations of establishing himself as a magnate. But Cumberland was reluctant to see his only surviving child married to a mere fourth son, and fobbed Northumberland off, by hinting that there were impediments, perhaps a precontract.

Northumberland, arrogant and persistent, urged the young King to intervene on his behalf. Other members of the court were appalled that, while Northumberland was leading the army against rebels in the Northern Marches, the king should have consented to act as his marriage broker: Edward sent an extraordinary letter to Cumberland on 4 July, desiring him to 'grow to some good end forthwith in the matter of marriage between the Lord Guildford and his daughter; with the licence to the said Earl and all others that shall travail therein to do their best to the conducement of it'.[4] People began to whisper that Northumberland was pressing for the marriage because it was becoming apparent that he harboured designs on the throne for himself and his family. Having rejected Guildford Dudley as a suitor for Margaret's hand, Cumberland, rather strangely, now consented to marry her to Northumberland's ageing older brother, Sir Andrew Dudley, in 1553.[5] Possibly he felt pressured into this unlikely match, fearing Northumberland's ruthlessness and increasing power; but at the last minute Cumberland reneged on the marriage contract and in 1553 Sir Andrew was arrested and condemned to death for his part in his brother's attempt to establish Lady Jane Grey as Queen of England. He was later pardoned and released.

Margaret was thus fortunate to escape becoming embroiled with the Dudleys and thereby escaped the fate of her cousin Jane Grey, often regarded as an innocent victim sacrificed on the altar of her father-in-law's ambition and her own father's vanity.

Although neither projected marriage to members of Northumberland's family had taken place, Margaret Clifford retained the sumptuous cloth Sir Andrew had sent for her bridal gown, and had it made up for her wedding dress when she married Henry Stanley, Lord Strange, the future 4th Earl of Derby. With a legitimate claim to the succession not only by virtue of her descent from Mary Rose, but by the written testament of King Henry VIII, Margaret would never escape the spotlight, and she certainly never shunned it. She took appalling risks.

For Margaret's spectacular wedding, Queen Mary I laid on a full lavish programme of feasting, jousting and a tournament on horseback with swords, and a contest of the Spanish *jeu de cannes* organised by Queen Mary's husband, Philip of Spain. In this competition, combatants carried targets and hurled rods at one another. Although to English spectators, accustomed to the bloodthirsty jousts, the gallant entertainment appeared tame compared with the thrills and spills of tilting on horseback, King Philip participated so enthusiastically that the Queen, anxious for his welfare, begged him to desist.

Margaret's wedding took place in a country still reeling from the shock of the first of the notorious burnings that would earn the Queen the epithet Bloody Mary. John Rogers, a prebendary of St Paul's, had been executed at the stake only three days previously.

Margaret went on to bear Derby five sons; three survived to continue the line. As Queen Mary declined, debilitated by age and depression, becoming a pale, shrivelled figure, and her chances of bearing a child appeared increasingly remote, Margaret cherished the hope that Mary would nominate her as her heir.

Margaret's claim to the throne was inferior to that of her cousin Lady Jane Grey, since Margaret was descended from Princess Mary Rose's younger daughter. However, her mother Eleanor having died in 1547, it had the advantage of directness. Her claim appeared solid. If Princess Elizabeth were excluded on the grounds of illegitimacy, the same must apply to another claimant, Lady Margaret Douglas, the Countess of Lennox, daughter of Henry VIII's older sister. Lady Margaret's father had had a wife living at the time of his 'marriage' to her mother. Mary Queen of Scots, as the bride of the Dauphin, was clearly out of the running. That left the heirs of the French Queen, Mary Rose. The two surviving Grey sisters, Margaret's first cousins, although the daughters of Mary Rose's older daughter, were now ineligible, tainted by the treason and execution of their sister Jane Grey and of their father, Suffolk. Margaret, who feared and loathed the Grey sisters, never failed to point this out to anyone who cared to listen.

The subject of the succession certainly had its fascination. The question preoccupied the minds of not only the potential claimants and their adherents, but all the leading families and factions in the realm. Margaret's husband, Lord Derby, wisely never advanced his wife's claims; their sons displayed comparable discretion, but even this was not always effective.

Although several children were born to them, the relationship between Margaret and her husband was stormy.

The Earls of Derby were immensely rich and influential. The basis of the power of the great nobles was their ability to raise and maintain armed retainers, and their readiness to employ them in disputes. At times of crisis Queen Elizabeth, Mary's successor, was forced, however reluctantly, to seek their assistance, although she and her influential advisers, the Cecils, strove to develop some strategy that would reduce the power of the nobility and also forestall any Catholic insurrection. Accordingly, Margaret's husband, Lord Derby, was commanded to send his son and heir Ferdinando to Court 'to be fashioned in good manners', a euphemism for intense indoctrination in Protestantism and unquestioning loyalty to Queen Elizabeth. (So successful was this training process that, when Ferdinando acceded to the Lordship of Man in 1594, legislation was swiftly passed in the Island against the 'reliques of popish superstition.')

However, after his father's death in 1593, Ferdinando, now 5th Earl of Derby, briefly became the unwilling focus of a Catholic scheme to revive the family's pretension to the throne. The fact that Derby was one of the richest peers in England raised the hopes of exiled English Jesuits. The formal grounds advanced were that 'through propinquity of blood' the Stanleys were next in line to Queen Elizabeth. In the Derby heartlands in the North and West, Catholicism had survived, presumably with the connivance of Ferdinando's father and grandfather. The Cecils reported that Ferdinando was, in the view of leading Catholics, 'the fourth competitor in the road [i.e., claimant to the throne], *but if he be a Catholic, the first*'. [6]

The exiled Jesuits' agent on English soil was Richard Hesketh, an English adventurer who, having sought refuge in Spain, was sent back to operate in England on the promise of Spanish aid. When Ferdinando learned of the Catholic plot, Hesketh was captured and executed. Perhaps Ferdinando hoped to deflect suspicion: under the terms of Henry VIII's will, Ferdinando could claim to be Queen Elizabeth's successor. The throne was then to pass to Ferdinando's oldest daughter, Lady Anne Stanley.

But Ferdinando died suddenly in mysterious circumstances after a violent fit of vomiting. It was rumoured that he had been poisoned by his Master of the Horse, possibly on the orders of the Cecils, or even the Queen herself.

Ferdinando predeceased Queen Elizabeth by nine years. He was succeeded as Earl of Derby by his brother William, a less colourful character, who knew better than to emphasise his claim to the throne. His mother, however, was less cautious. Although Margaret Clifford had been granted the royal permission to marry, she had been kept under close surveillance; retribution for any indiscretions she committed was immediate and severe. With all three Grey sisters dead, Margaret became Elizabeth's heir under the terms of Henry VIII's will, a claim she incautiously trumpeted, with disastrous consequences.

In her youth, Margaret's grandiose pretensions had been dismissed as the vapourings of a fanciful chit of a girl. But when she continued to air her ill-advised aspirations after Elizabeth had succeeded to the throne, Margaret found herself in deep trouble. Her boasting that, in the eyes of many people, she was the heir presumptive to the crown, twice landed her in the prison in 1579.

Unrepentant, she was then accused of seeking by means of sorcery to discover when Queen Elizabeth would die, allegedly employing the supernatural skills of Dr Randall, a well-known physician, to cast spells to harm the Queen and to predict her death. [7] This was a capital offence. Despite her protests that she had hired him only to cure her toothache and to massage ointment into her aching, rheumaticky limbs, Randall was convicted and hanged. Lady Margaret was imprisoned in various houses under house arrest until her death in 1596.

After the failure of the Lady Jane Grey plot, it became clear that the Suffolk claims were doomed to failure. It was even questionable whether Henry VIII had had the right to bequeath the crown as he pleased, albeit with the authorisation of Parliament. Moreover, the Will had not been signed by his own hand, as required by statute, but merely by dry stamp. There was much quibbling over the phrase 'and if it so happen that the said Lady Eleanor die without issue, then we will that the said Imperial Crown shall come to our next rightful heirs,' not 'right heirs', as stated in the first Act of Succession.

Under Elizabeth, the legality of Mary Rose's marriage to Brandon and hence the legitimacy of their children was thrown into question. With each succeeding generation, their connection with the throne grew increasingly remote.

15 - Notes

1. Williamson, *Lady Anne Clifford, Letters* 19
2. Examination of Christopher Aske, Rolls House MS, first series, 840
3. Williamson, *Lady Anne Clifford, Letters,* 21
4. Strype, *Memorials*, vol 3 bk ii, London, 1816182
5. CSP Span 1553 vol ll 51
6. Hatfield House Papers, pt iv, 461ff
7. Peck, *Desiderata Curiosa*, London, 1779, 141

16   THE FATAL INHERITANCE: LADY KATHERINE

By 1554, London had become a place of nightmare. Across the city, rebels and traitors hung screaming in chains. Prisoners were hung, drawn and quartered. Rotting corpses and severed heads were displayed in public places as a warning. On 12 February, at every gate in the city, a new gallows had been erected, two pairs in Cheapside, two in Fleet Street, one in Smithfield, one in Holborn, Leadenhall, St Magnus, and Billingsgate. At Hyde Park corner three were hanged in chains. Two days later, six were hanged at Cheapside, one quartered at Aldgate and one at Bishopsgate, and three at Leadenhall. Seven were quartered at Fleet Street and their bodies and heads set upon the gates of London. The official purpose of this terror was twofold: to punish treachery in the most dramatic and public manner possible, and to discourage rebellion by intimidation.[1]

On 16 February, four days after Jane's death, the Greys' father, the Duke of Suffolk, was taken to Westminster Hall, where a scaffold had already been built, as though in anticipation of the outcome. He set out 'stoutely and cheerfully enough',[2] but on his return it was noted that he landed at the Watergate with a heavy and pensive countenance, and asked the bystanders to pray for him. He had been arraigned for treason, and condemned to death. As a traitor, all his property would be confiscated, and his family would be left penniless. Luckily for them, Queen Mary remembered that Mary Rose had been kind to her own mother, Catharine of Aragon, in the dark days of her repudiation. Although she could not pardon Suffolk, she commanded her chaplain Dr Weston, to accompany him to the scaffold and proclaim that the Queen forgave him. This meant that his family would not be entirely dispossessed, and that, should the Queen consent, Frances and her younger daughters could remain at court.

On 23 February, 1554. Suffolk left the Tower under guard for Tower Hill, accompanied by Weston. Suffolk resented Weston's presence, and twice, when Weston made to follow him up the steps to the scaffold, he gave him a shove. The priest lost his footing and grabbed at Suffolk, and the two scuffling men tumbled indecorously to the foot of the scaffold. Weston shouted out that he was only there on the Queen's orders. Suffolk relinquished his grip. Recovering his dignity, he addressed the crowd in the traditional manner, saying he had offended the Queen and was justly condemned. He asked for the Queen's forgiveness. Weston replied loudly: 'My Lord, Her Grace has already forgiven you.'[3] Some of the bystanders muttered that they hoped God would forgive Weston too. Suffolk then recited a psalm – either *Misere mei Deus,* or *In te Domine speravi.* After Suffolk had handed his cap and scarf to the executioner and formally forgiven him, another unexpected incident occurred: a man stepped forward, demanding: 'My Lord, how shall I do for the money that you do owe me?' Suffolk replied 'Alas, good fellow, trouble me not now.' He told him to apply to his officers. The execution then proceeded without further interruption.[4]

The same day, some 200 prisoners were paraded through the city streets with halters about their necks, indicating that they had been pardoned by the Queen. This piece of Tudor theatre was designed to show that the new monarch was capable of clemency as well as severity. But on 24 April, Suffolk's brother Lord Thomas Grey, sentenced to death in early March, was executed, and his head left on public display. The killing had begun to sicken people.

In April, some of the Grey manors in Leicestershire were restored to Frances Grey, including the lease of Beaumanor, near Bradgate, 'with free warren and chase of deer and wild beast'.[5] In July 1554, Frances was invited to join the Queen's Privy Chamber. Only six months after the execution of their father and sister as traitors, Katherine and Mary Grey were back at court as maids of honour.

Physically, the sisters were a contrast: pretty Katherine had happily resisted the efforts of her studious older sister, Jane, and her tutors to turn her into a scholar. Katherine preferred pets and entertainment to book-learning. Mary was stunted and plain. At only eight years old, she had been betrothed to a middle-aged kinsman, Lord Grey of Wilton. A valiant warrior and veteran of campaigns in France and Scotland, and originally a fine looking man, Lord Grey had been hideously disfigured in 1547 at the battle of Pinkie, having had a Scottish pike thrust 'the length of three fingers' through the roof of his mouth. The blow had smashed his teeth, pierced his tongue and almost killed him.

Katherine knew and liked her bridegroom, fifteen-year-old Henry, Lord Herbert, son of the Earl of Pembroke, to whom she had been married at the age of twelve.

The childhood marriages of both sisters were now officially dissolved. Mary may have been relieved, but for a while, Katherine's romantic fantasy was busy weaving dreams about the juvenile romance blighted by the cruel world of politics. Ironically, her life would be blighted by politics, but not in connection with her first 'husband'.

The atmosphere at court was dictated by the mood of the monarch, and Queen Mary's spirits were unusually buoyant. Elated at the prospect of marriage to the Emperor's son, Philip, she hoped she would soon be blessed with heirs to secure the throne and the future of her religion in her father's realm. The Queen's mood infected everyone with a new sense of optimism, despite the general misgivings about marriage to a foreign, and

Catholic, King. Philip's father, the Emperor Charles V, had ceded to him the crown of Naples and the claim to the throne of Jerusalem, so that he might equal Mary in royal rank. Philip, sacrificing his youth, good looks and virility on the altar of international politics, arrived in England on 20 of July confidently expecting that he would soon manage to be crowned King of England, despite an unsatisfactory marriage treaty.

Philip struck observers as slim and elegant and, despite his prominent Hapsburg lip, was considered attractive.[6] He clearly did not feel the same enthusiasm about his new bride or the circumstances attendant upon their union. The marriage treaty gave him no authority in England, and he was shocked when he first beheld his intended. Over ten years Mary's junior, he had been prepared for the age difference but not for the Queen's scrawny person and careworn appearance. Mary wore a black velvet gown in the French fashion, embroidered with pearls and girdled with diamonds. Philip's Spanish entourage found it unflattering. The English, on the other hand, were delighted with Philip's youth, good looks and confident swagger. He might be a foreigner and a Catholic, but they felt they had the best of the bargain, so far as that went. At least he was not French, and, more importantly, he looked capable of begetting heirs to ensure the succession. That was all that mattered.

The Grey sisters attended the royal wedding, celebrated at Winchester Cathedral on 25 July 1554. The decorations were splendid, and the Queen's person dazzling. During the ceremony, when the celebrant asked who gave away the bride, the Marquess of Winchester, the Earls of Derby, Bedford and Pembroke responded that they gave her, in the name of the whole realm. There was a great shout of joy.

While rallying her subjects in February against Wyatt's rebellion, Mary had made a speech at the Guildhall in which she referred to her coronation ring as her 'spousal ring', indicating that she was wedded to England, but not as a submissive wife, rather as 'prince and governor'. She has not always been credited by posterity with having anticipated the concept of the queen being wedded to her realm, which is usually attributed to her successor, her half-sister, Elizabeth.

The ring was placed on the book, to be blessed, and Philip placed three handfuls of fine gold upon the book, according to custom. Lady Margaret Clifford, Mary Rose's granddaughter and the Queen's cousin, opened the Queen's purse, and the Queen, smiling, placed the gold in it.

Philip's smile was strained. Not only did the marriage contract not give him equal power, but he found outer trappings symbolising his status insulting. Contrary to custom, during the service, he was placed ignominiously on the left. Mary was placed on the right, in the position of greater prominence. It also riled Philip, sensitive to such things, that Mary was seated on a larger and more imposing throne.

At the wedding banquet in Bishop Gardiner's palace, the bridal couple dined in splendid isolation beneath the canopy of state. Lord Herbert, Katherine Grey's former husband, now a Gentleman of Philip's Privy Chamber, was seated at the top table with the honoured guests. Herbert had been appointed on the recommendation of Philip's envoy, the Marquis de las Navas, who had been impressed with the young man's discreet manner.

The Greys' friend, the daring man-at-arms and 'hot gospeller' Edward Underhill, father of their sister Jane's godchild (the infant christened 'Guildford' on her instructions on the last day of her brief reign), took part in waiting on the guests, bearing golden platters of meat and game. After an initial rebuff, Underhill had managed to become one of the 'gentlemen pensioners', although the Chief Usher, Norris, had tried to block his appointment, calling him a heretic.

Underhill noted the embellishments of the Hall and the fact that the Queen was seated in the place of supreme precedence, and (another element calculated to annoy Philip) that the Queen was served on gold plates, Philip on silver. After the feast, observing the dancing, he mischievously relished the annoyance of the Spaniards, especially King Philip, at finding their terpsichorean skills surpassed by those of the English. When the party broke up, Underhill appropriated an enormous venison pie, which the replete and over-indulged diners had left untouched, and which other servers had refused to carry because of its weight. He despatched it to London for his wife and their friends to enjoy.

Underhill was a great survivor. Abandoning his youthful dissolute life and the gambling which had almost ruined him, he embraced radical views and began proselytizing in a way which he himself admitted made him 'odious to most men, and many times in danger of my life.' [7] He had rashly produced a ballad against popery on the very day after Queen Mary was proclaimed in London. He was released from Newgate only through the influence of his friends. Later, when the persecution of Protestants began in earnest, he relocated to Warwickshire, after ensuring the safety of his precious library by having it bricked up in a wall.

In September 1554, Mary's always intermittent and painful menstruation ceased. She experienced nausea, and appeared to be gaining weight. Everyone at court, including her physicians, assumed that the eagerly anticipated had happened, and that the Queen had conceived. For perhaps the first time in her life, Mary was grasping at happiness. But there were ructions in paradise: her adored young husband was chafing with ill-suppressed irritation. His Spanish attendants encountered hostility at court, Spanish clergy were openly insulted in the streets. Pamphlets of Protestant origin were being distributed, their contents calculated to inflame passions against Catholics and foreigners. At court, too, the atmosphere was strained. There was constant bickering, and occasional outbreaks of violence. Although joint monarch in name – coins had been issued, showing Philip and Mary with a joint crown hovering over them – Philip had been so far denied a coronation and there were severe limitations on his powers.

Nonetheless, for a while, the royal couple embraced whole-heartedly the Tudor notion of extravagance and spectacle. There was lavish spending on costly fabrics – damask, sarcenet, gold buttons. For a series of elaborate outdoor processions and other events, heraldic devices, streamers, banners and standards were commissioned. Religious houses were refurbished and equipped. Valuable horses and a new royal barge were acquired, furnishings were renovated. The outgoing Venetian Ambassador, Giovanni Michieli, estimated that, by March 1557, Philip had spent more than one million gold ducats in England.[8]

For a while, despite the tense undercurrents, court life took on a glamorous and dazzling aspect, and the atmosphere was upbeat.

Meanwhile, Lady Jane Grey's Dudley brothers-in-law, John, Ambrose, Robert and Henry Dudley, were still imprisoned in the Tower, attainted and under sentence of death. The upper chamber of the Beauchamp tower contains the most striking of all Tudor graffiti, the intricate carving of the Dudley coat of arms, showing oak leaves and acorns for Robert (Quercus robur, Latin for oak); honeysuckle for Henry, roses for Ambrose, gillyflowers for Guildford. John was released in autumn 1554, and died soon afterwards. There were several carvings of the name 'Jane.' The widowed Duchess of Northumberland, and Sir Henry Sidney, who had married her daughter Mary Dudley in 1553, campaigned tirelessly to obtain the release of the three remaining brothers by ingratiating themselves with prominent members of Philip's entourage at court. Sidney christened his new son 'Philip' and invited the King to stand godfather. Philip, for his part, had a strong motive for seeking to improve his relations with the English aristocracy. He hoped that young nobles might later be persuaded to enlist in his father's wars. The Dudley brothers were pardoned on January 23, 1555, the day after their mother died. In a tournament, perhaps intended as an acceptable outlet for rivalry, they participated with distinction, and, as Philip had hoped, in 1557, they joined his campaign against the French, in the course of which Henry Dudley was killed.

Members of the Privy Council had been suggesting a possible marriage between Frances and the personable but conceited and unreliable Edward Courtenay, a Plantagenet descendant, the great-grandson of King Edward IV. Courtenay had spent most of his young life in prison, much of it in solitary confinement. In 1538, he had been imprisoned in the Tower. His father, accused of plotting to marry Courtenay to Princess Mary, had been executed.

On her accession, Mary ordered Courtenay's release and showed him favour by creating him Earl of Devon and a Knight of the Bath. At her coronation, he carried the sword of state. Bishop Stephen Gardiner fanned the flames of Courtenay's ambitions, rekindling the notion of a union with the Queen herself, before Mary decided on Philip of Spain. Courtenay was delighted with the idea of himself as prince consort, and for a while strutted about in his household as though it were a minor royal court.

After Mary's marriage with Philip put her out of Courtenay's reach, there remained the possibility of a union with the Princess Elizabeth. The leading statesman Sir William Paget openly expressed his support for a marriage between the two second cousins. Paget had been reconciled with Queen Mary despite having signed King Edward VI's 'Devise' which excluded her from the succession. The Queen reinstated him as a Knight of the Garter and member of the Privy Council, and in 1556 appointed him Lord Privy Seal. When Paget suggested a marriage between Courtenay and Elizabeth, Courtenay loftily rejected it, declaring that it would be unbecoming for one of his unblemished lineage to contract such an unworthy alliance.

But then Courtenay, ever the prey of his own ambition, had become involved in Wyatt's rebellion, most of the details of which he betrayed under skilled examination by Bishop Gardiner.

Frances, for her part, had been married to one reckless and ambitious man. She had no intention of marrying the unstable and vainglorious Courtenay. As for Courtenay, he unchivalrously declared to the Queen that he would rather leave the land than marry Frances. By May, when he left England for the last time, Frances had already married her second husband, Adrian Stokes, probably in 1554 or possibly 1555. If there had been any suggestion that, if Elizabeth, still considered illegitimate, were excluded from the succession, Mary might consider making Frances her heir, her marriage to Stokes made it out of the question.

In spite of Elizabeth's pronounced resemblance to Henry VIII, Mary was not above spitefully insinuating to her ladies that Elizabeth was not Henry VIII's daughter. She feigned credence to the unfounded rumour that she was the bastard of the handsome young musician Mark Smeaton whom Anne Boleyn was reputed to have kept in a 'sweetmeat cupboard', calling for 'marmalade' whenever she required his personal services (a fanciful invention by a fairly unreliable primary source). Had the scandal been true, of course, in Mary's eyes Elizabeth would have been a 'double bastard', if such a thing were possible, since Mary and her supporters had never recognised the legality of Anne Boleyn's marriage to the King in the first place.

In reality, Mary had indicated that, despite the doubts about the Countess's legitimacy, her preferred heir would be her Catholic cousin Margaret Douglas, Countess of Lennox.[9]

Margaret had attended Mary as her chief lady at her wedding. In December 1558, she would be chief mourner at the Queen's funeral.

Elizabeth I's biographer, William Camden, spoke disparagingly of Frances Grey's second husband, Adrian Stokes, who was not of noble birth, intimating that Frances had married beneath her 'forgetting the nobility of her lineage, to her dishonour, but yet for her securitie.'[10] Stokes, her junior by just over a year, was a former soldier, well educated and a Protestant. Above all, Camden, for all his sniping, was correct in one thing: Stokes was a safe choice. Frances's stepmother and friend Katherine Suffolk, after losing her husband, Brandon, and both her young sons, had chosen to wed a social inferior, her Gentleman Usher, Sir Richard Bertie. Frances, in choosing Stokes, married a man whose station in life would forever preclude her from any aspirations to the throne. She would not be thrust into the dangerous role of a figurehead for rebellions or manipulated by ambitious third parties. Anne Somerset followed the same route to peaceful obscurity by marrying Newdigate, her Steward.

After her marriage, Frances largely retired from Court. Her health problems increased; some may have either occasioned, or been caused by, failed pregnancies. She bore Stokes at least one child, but no children of the marriage survived.

Frances's youngest daughter, Mary, now aged ten, remained in her care, while Katherine, still at court, was enjoying what may well have been the happiest period of her life. Her more serious sister, Jane, had exhorted Katherine to lead a 'life of grace', but Katherine's was a very different temperament from Jane's. Katherine had her own apartments at court, where, to the despair of her attendants, her pet dogs and monkeys ran riot. Katherine was by no means unique. Simian animal companions were in vogue: Princess Elizabeth also had a pet monkey.

Katherine's closest confidante remained her childhood friend, Lady Jane Seymour, whose father, the Protector, had also lost his life to the headsman's axe. Both girls had been proposed as brides for King Edward. Jane Seymour and her sisters, Margaret and Anne, were literary and gifted women who had produced a collection of 103 Latin distichs, *Hecatodistichon*, published in 1550, for the tomb of their fellow author, Marguerite of Valois, Queen of Navarre.

The temporary good cheer at Queen Mary's court evaporated as the clouds of paranoia and intrigue gathered. The Queen was becoming increasingly demoralised by her poor health and failure to produce an heir. In 1551, when she was thirty-five, she had written sadly: 'My health is more unstable than that of any creature.' Headaches, depression, anorexia, amenorrhea, combined with frequent medication and bleeding, had undermined a constitution that had never been robust.

In January 1556, Philip's father, Charles V, abdicated and Philip became King of Spain, the Netherlands, and all the Spanish possessions in Italy and America. Appalled by the spread of Protestantism in Europe, he promptly reinstated the Spanish Inquisition. After Mary's phantom pregnancy, Philip flounced off, refusing to return unless his wife granted him a full coronation. The House of Commons had unanimously rejected it, and Mary, aware of the strength of opposition in her Council and Parliament, did not press for it. Philip's position was weaker than it had been when it appeared that the Queen was expecting his child. He returned in March 1556 briefly to enlist English support for his war against the French. Despite the reluctance of the Privy Council to engage in expensive foreign campaigns, Mary allowed her foreign policy to be largely dictated by Philip, whose sole concern was for the cause of Spain, with little regard for the detrimental effect his aggressive policies were having on England.

Philip realised that if Mary named the Catholic Mary Queen of Scots as her heir, this would disadvantage Spain, since Mary of Scots was married to the Dauphin. He persuaded Mary to name Elizabeth as her successor, and wrote demanding that Elizabeth, as Mary's heir, should be married off to an Imperial ally or to a Spaniard. Upon reading this letter, Mary hurled her mirror across the room in a fury. Elizabeth also flatly refused.

In December 1555, anxiety that Mary intended to have Philip crowned triggered another rebellion against her rule. Sir Henry Dudley, a cousin of the executed Duke of Northumberland, hatched a plot to mobilise English Protestant exiles in France, invade England and overthrow Mary, replacing her with Elizabeth, who was to be married to Courtenay. The discovery of the plot in March 1556 alarmed both the Queen and her Council. Courtenay avoided arrest by remaining in Italy, where he died the same year, in dubious circumstances. Conspiracy theorists claimed he was poisoned by Philip's agents: Peter Vannes, Queen Mary's representative to the Republic of Venice, stated that Courtenay had caught a fever having been caught out in a storm when flying his beloved hawks, on an island near Venice, getting drenched but refusing to change into dry clothing; others claimed that Courtenay had died of syphilis.

Distressed by conspiracies against her regime, her religion and her life, ailing, unable to conceive, scorned and periodically abandoned by her beloved husband, Mary's religious fanaticism and her obsession with heretics and their intrigues deepened.

Between 1555 and 1558, despite the efforts of the Lord Chancellor, Bishop Gardiner, to limit the numbers of Spanish advisers and grandees in civil appointments, Spanish domestic policy on religious affairs was enforced. Smithfield's grisly fires smouldered where Protestants burned to death. The French Ambassador noted that John Rogers, Prebendary of St Paul's and the first martyr to be named, went to be burned 'as to a marriage.' An Italian Catholic, Aloisio Schivenoglio, described, in May 1556, watching a man of seventy hobbling to the stake on crutches, followed by a young blind boy, who was also burned to death. The following Saturday, four women were burned, going to their deaths without shackles or other restraints, as if they were going off to be married.

Despite the religious terror, the Greys maintained discreet friendships with Protestant friends, but religion figured less in the preoccupations of pretty Katherine than matters of the heart. She longed for romance, and confided to her friend, sixteen-year-old Lady Jane Seymour, how she pined for the love that might have been, the boy she had been married off to two years before, and her hopes that the Queen might someday relent and permit them to remarry.

Once again, political developments scuppered Katherine's teenage dreams. In March 1557, Philip had returned to England, but there was to be no return to the glamorous days of masques and feasting. In April, a second plot against Mary came to light. Protestant exiles, backed by the French, 'invaded' Scarborough from a French vessel. The rebels, led by the imaginative but bungling Thomas Stafford, who had decided that, since he was descended from royalty on both sides of his family, he was the rightful heir to the throne, were quickly rounded up, and the ringleaders, including Stafford, executed on 28 May.

Stafford's sister Dorothy, a staunch Protestant, prudently sought refuge in Geneva during Mary's reign. She would not return to England until January 1559, upon the accession of Queen Elizabeth, whom she would serve for forty years. As Mistress of the Robes, she would exercise considerable influence at court. Dorothy became a close friend of Mary Grey, who would leave her a gold tablet with an agate in her will.

Stafford's invasion, possibly engineered by an agent provocateur in the person of William Paget, with or without the connivance of the King of France, Henri II, certainly had the effect of dragging England into Philip's war with France, to which most of the Council had previously been opposed. Queen Mary, unduly influenced by Philip and her Spanish advisers, now formally aligned herself with the Imperial cause. In June, England declared war on France. Lord Herbert, Katherine Grey's first bridegroom, went off to fight in what proved to be a disastrous engagement. A pandemic of influenza meant that it was difficult to muster sufficient numbers of fit fighting men. In January 1558, England's last foothold in France, Calais, which had been an English possession since the conquests of Edward III, fell to the French. A devastated Queen Mary was said to have declared: 'when I am dead and chested, you will find the words "Philip" and "Calais" written on my heart.'

Philip had left his wretched Queen again, for the last time. Queen Mary, now a pathetic huddled figure, draped in black, hugged her swollen belly, which she now knew was not great with child but with disease. Elizabeth and her faithful William Cecil, Surveyor of her Estates, were already planning their next move in the event of Mary's death, which appeared increasingly imminent.

The English, debilitated by war and famine resulting from a succession of disastrous harvests, now succumbed in their thousands to the epidemic which continued to sweep through the land. When it reached the Court, among its victims was Lady Jane Seymour. Jane was sent away to convalesce at her mother's house, Hanworth in Middlesex, and Katherine Grey accompanied her. That summer, while Jane recuperated, Katherine quickly forgot her romantic adolescent fantasies about the boy who had been her first husband, and became passionately and recklessly infatuated with the love of her life.

Pretty Katherine, at almost eighteen, could hardly fail to catch the eye of Jane Seymour's brother, nineteen-year-old Edward, Earl of Hertford. If, when these two attractive young people were thrown together, a romance between Katherine and 'Ned' Seymour was perhaps inevitable, it was also political dynamite because of the lethal combination of two driving forces, royal blood and religion. Through his mother, Anne Stanhope, Ned was descended from Edward III and Philippa of Hainault. He was also the heir of Somerset the Protector who had brought the 'true religion' to England. If Ned and Katherine Grey married and produced a legitimate male heir, this Protestant claimant to the throne would constitute a concrete threat to Elizabeth. The Protestant view that female rule was contrary to the will of God was rapidly gaining credence.

The young couple's initial dalliance soon became serious. Ned Hertford asked his sister Jane, who passed secret messages between the lovers, to broach the subject of marriage. [11] As soon as Ned's mother found out what they were up to, she moved to put a stop to it. Lady Somerset had recently remarried, and, like Frances and Katherine Suffolk, had prudently chosen a man inferior to her in rank, her Steward, Francis Newdigate. Anne Somerset told Ned Hertford to forget Katherine Grey. As is customary with young people receiving such admonitions from their parents, this only served to harden Hertford's resolve. The young Earl retorted arrogantly that he intended to see Katherine whenever and wherever he pleased, so long as he had not been expressly forbidden to do so by the Queen.[12]

After the summer, the couple's opportunities to meet were automatically curtailed when Katherine returned to court. By October, it was clear the Queen was near death. On 17 November, she died. She was succeeded by her half-sister Elizabeth.

Elizabeth, determined that there should be no lack of honour accorded to a Tudor monarch, accorded Mary a Requiem Mass. Mary was buried in Westminster Abbey. Elizabeth had

not forgotten that Katherine Grey was the daughter and sister of traitors. Katherine was demoted from the Privy Chamber to the Presence Chamber, a more public space to which all major notables had access.

On 14 January 1559, as snow fell softly over London,

Elizabeth's eve of coronation procession set out from the Tower. Coronations required the new monarch to take possession of the Tower, thereby assuring London. The second stage was the monarch's procession from the Tower to Westminster, for the coronation itself. Elizabeth, affable and dripping with jewels, reclined in a golden litter drawn by two mules. The dramatic spectacle had been expertly choreographed. The attendant lords and ladies, as well as their mounts, were accoutred in crimson velvet, red-liveried trumpeters sounded the fanfare, following the heralds in their coat armour.[13]

A succession of pageants along the route depicted Elizabeth's illustrious ancestors, her personal graces and virtues, her devotion to the true religion. The presentation at Fleet Street portrayed her as the valiant Deborah, who had rescued the Israelites from the power of Canaan. The Queen herself won all hearts, even impressing Philip's envoy, Count Feria, who had initially resented her, because the days when Philip's envoy had the power to transmit his master's orders were over, and who had said scathingly that Elizabeth was 'very much wedded to the people and thinks as they do and therefore treats foreigners slightingly'.[14] He also described her as very clever, and extremely vain. He soon changed his tune to one of grudging and rather apprehensive respect, noting that she commanded more reverence than her sister, and issued commands with the same authority as her father. But now, Elizabeth was out to win hearts and minds, and she achieved it with consummate efficiency. She waved and smiled 'with merry countenance' to the cheering multitude, 'so that on eyther side there was nothing but gladness, nothing but prayer.'[15]

She wore the same ermine-trimmed mantle and kirtle of cloth-of-gold and silver, with a pattern of Tudor roses, that had been worn by Mary in 1553. In the style traditionally worn by queens at their coronation, her bright hair tumbled loose about her shoulders, symbolizing her youth and virginity.[16]

The surviving sons of the executed Duke of Northumberland, Ambrose and Robert Dudley, were given leading roles in the event. Ambrose led one of the mules.

Handsome Sir Robert, son, grandson and brother of executed traitors, and now Master of the Horse, and perhaps more besides, to Elizabeth of England, rode directly behind the Queen. Mounted on a magnificent charger, he led the Queen's grey palfrey as the procession moved ponderously through the gorgeously draped and decorated streets, lined with frantically cheering crowds. Along the streets from Fenchurch to Cheapside the city companies lined the way, in their liveries and furs. The city's gift was presented to her, a crimson satin purse with a thousand marks in gold. Elizabeth was the mistress of the quick-witted extempore speech. Her eloquence and sententious observations delighted everyone.

Next day, splendidly gowned, to pealing bells and the fanfare of organs, fifes, trumpets and drums, Elizabeth processed into Westminster Abbey.

As the euphoria subsided, the question of the Queen's own marriage became paramount. Only a royal heir, it was felt, could ensure political stability. The husbands of the two previous female monarchs had been disastrous: Guildford Dudley, son of the ambitious, overweening and ruthless Northumberland; Philip of Spain, the foreigner who embroiled England in his foreign wars and encouraged religious persecution. Yet it was whispered that Elizabeth was scandalously infatuated with the dashing Robert Dudley. She had set tongues wagging by moving him into a room close to her own at Hampton Court palace. She tried to reassure the Council by saying that if she did not marry, she would make sure to select a worthy successor. But this merely triggered rumours that she was barren, and, inevitably, focussed attention on Katherine Grey.

Elizabeth was having none of it. She at once set out to diminish Katherine's potential powerbase and separate her from potential allies by slighting her. Courtiers sycophantically followed suit. Now Katherine felt cold-shouldered. She complained to the Count of Feria that the Queen disliked her. Katherine, never as circumspect as she might have been, on one occasion was so irritated that she lost her temper in the presence

Chamber, using 'very arrogant and unseemly words in the presence of the Queen'.

The outburst did her no good at all. Feria reported these snippets of gossip to his master, feeling they might prove useful. Elizabeth had quickly disengaged her country from involvement in the Imperial war with France. Feria had been impressed with the new Queen's crowd-pleasing skills, but neither he nor King Philip trusted her. She had rejected King Philip's offer of marriage. He feared she might be contemplating an alliance with Henri II of France. Feria himself had married the Catholic Jane Dormer, Queen Mary's favourite, who had served in her Privy Chamber with Katherine Grey. Feria found Katherine Grey a sweet girl, a refreshing contrast to the 'vain and clever' Elizabeth.

But Katherine was less sweet and innocent than Feria assumed, and much more manipulative. She confided to him that she was a secret Catholic, and that her family hated her for it. She was spinning him a yarn, of course, but Feria swallowed it wholesale. Feria had also gleaned that Katherine was no longer mooning over her (largely imagined) romantic attachment to Lord Herbert, to whom she had been married as a child. But Katherine was cunning enough never to mention her new love, Ned Seymour, Earl of Hertford. Feria, assuming she was free of romantic entanglements, at once suggested she might consider marrying a Habsburg. But Katherine, as devious as she was charming, was merely exploiting the opportunity to make Hertford jealous and spur him into a declaration.

But in Spain the notion took root; plans were made to get Katherine out of the kingdom and marry her off to a Spaniard, possibly Philip II's inbred and unstable son, Don Carlos.

> 'Lady Catherine will probably be glad to go, being most uncomfortably situated in the English Court with the Queen, who cannot well abide the sight of her, neither the duchess, her mother nor her stepfather love her, and her uncle cannot abide to hear of her, so she lives as it were in great despair. She has spoken very arrogant and unseemly words in the hearing of the

Queen and others standing by. Hence it is thought that she could be enticed away if some trusty person were to speak with her,' Feria suggested.[17]

After Feria was recalled, or possibly invented his recall, sensitive to the dislike of Queen Elizabeth, his Countess, the former Jane Dormer, took over the role of go-between in the Imperial intrigues. The plan began to take form. Spanish ships were to drop anchor in the Thames and Katherine was to be smuggled aboard. Subsequent events indicate that Elizabeth was abreast of developments, kept up to date by her spies, and was merely biding her time.

On 30 June 1559, however, another dramatic incident scotched the Spanish scheme.

In 1524, Katherine's grandfather, Charles Brandon, had almost killed her great-uncle, King Henry VIII, in a jousting accident. King Henri II of France was riding against his young Scots Captain of the Guard, the Comte de Montmorency, when he neglected to close his helmet correctly and his opponent's lance pierced his eye. A large splinter penetrated through the King's right eye to the temple. The King swayed but managed to stay on his horse until spectators rushed forward to assist him as he swooned into their arms.

The celebrated royal surgeon, Amboise Paré, caused several condemned prisoners to be executed in a gruesome reconstruction of the King's wound. Henri, fatally injured, lay fighting for his life for eleven days. His wife, Catherine de Medici, forbade his adored mistress, Diane de Poitiers, from attending his deathbed. The King's death would thrust Catherine into the forefront of politics.

Henri II's throne passed to his heir, the sickly fifteen-year-old Francis II, the husband of Mary, Queen of Scots. The threat of a French invasion having evaporated, the Imperial plot to smuggle Katherine Grey to the Continent fizzled out. Katherine made ready to accompany the Queen on her summer progress.

Queen Elizabeth, clever, diplomatic and superficially conciliatory, never forgot a grievance. When her progress reached Eltham, where Katherine's grandmother Mary Rose had spent much of her childhood, Jane Dormer, Countess of Feria, arrived with a train of Spanish nobles to take her leave of the Queen before travelling to Spain to join her husband. Elizabeth had not forgotten that Jane's grandfather had sat on the jury that sent Anne Boleyn to the scaffold. Jane's father, Sir William Dormer, had been Elizabeth's jailer when Mary placed her under house arrest in 1554. Elizabeth deliberately kept Jane, now seven months pregnant, waiting, standing in the heat. The Spanish attendants, anxious about the Countess's well-being, urged her to sit down, but she proudly refused, although she appeared just about to faint.

Ned Hertford joined the court at Eltham, to Katherine's joy. When they moved to Henry VIII's fabulously ostentatious Palace of Nonsuch in Surrey, there was a constant round of entertainment. Love was in the summer air, not only for Hertford and Katherine, but also for the Virgin Queen, whose attachment to Robert Dudley, her 'sweet Robin', was causing anxiety to her friends, including Kat Ashley, her governess. When the royal party left Nonsuch on 10 August, Dudley remained close to the Queen's side at Hampton Court.

Hertford had had his titles restored by Queen Elizabeth. Had she been aware of his feelings and intentions towards her cousin's daughter, she might have been less generous.

Hertford now made up his mind to ignore his mother's advice to forget Katherine. In early October 1559, Frances Grey was at Sheen when he rode from Hampton Court to ask again for Katherine's hand in marriage. Although apprehensive about possible consequences, Frances was in favour of the match and promised to draft a letter to the Queen, requesting her permission.[18] Frances, although only 42, had been ailing for over seven years. In 1552 she was described as having a constant burning ague and stopping of the spleen. She was still composing her letter to the Queen towards the end of November when she died. Four years later, her widower erected a fine alabaster monument to her in Westminster Abbey. The monument, which bears the date 1563, has been attributed to the sculptor Cornelius Cure. Frances, a figure with clean, handsome features, is shown in effigy, coroneted, wearing an ermine-lined mantle, and with a lion at her feet. The inscription in English reads:

> Here lieth the ladie Francis, Duches of Southfolke, daughter
> to Charles Brandon, Duke of Southfolke, and Marie the
> Frenche Quene: first wife to Henrie Duke of Southfolke and
> after to Adrian Stock Esquier.

Shields and lozenges around the base of the tomb show the coats of arms of the families of Brandon, Stock or Stokes, Bruyn and Rokele. Frances's youngest Grey daughter, Mary, would be buried with her in 1578 but her tomb has no marker. The Latin inscription on the south side may be translated:

> Dirge for the most noble Lady Frances, onetime Duchess of
> Suffolk: naught avails glory or splendour, naught avail titles
> of kings; naught profits a magnificent abode, resplendent
> with wealth. All, all are passed away: the glory of virtue
> alone remained, impervious to the funeral pyres of Tartarus
> [part of Hades or the Underworld]. She was married first to
> the Duke, and after was wife to Mr Stock, Esq. Now, in
> death, may you fare well, united to God.

Queen Elizabeth, mollified by the fact that Frances's second marriage had eliminated her from the ranks of potential pretenders to the Crown, showed her appreciation by awarding Frances in death an augmentation to her arms of the royal quartering as 'an apparent declaration of her consanguinity unto us', 'lineally descended from our grandfather King Henry the Seventh'. [19] She promised to pay for the funeral of her 'beloved cousin'.

Her mother's death set Katherine's wedding plans back. She was still in mourning when Ned Hertford wrote a poem comparing his feelings to those of the Greek hero Troilus, separated from his beloved Cressida by political imperatives. [20]

Elizabeth, alert to potential threats, and aware of the Spanish plot to spirit Katherine away, responded by drawing Katherine closer rather than cold-shouldering her. In 1560, Katherine found herself transported into the Queen's inner circle. Nonetheless, she and Hertford pursued their romance, using his siblings Henry and Jane Seymour as intermediaries. The Queen's able Secretary, William Cecil, was exasperated by these Court amours, principally the Queen's disgraceful relationship with Robert Dudley. The smouldering scandal erupted into volcanic proportions when Dudley's wife Amy Robsart was discovered dead at the foot of a flight of eight stairs. Research indicates that Amy, who was in her late twenties, had been suffering from breast cancer, which can cause brittle bones. But the inevitable rumours of foul play motivated Cecil to extract a promise from the Queen that she would never marry Dudley. The Queen had planned to ennoble Dudley. When she realised that she could not fly in the face of the opinion of her great nobles, Elizabeth, enraged, allegedly slashed the patent for Dudley's earldom with a knife. In September 1564, she would create him Earl of Leicester in order to make him a more suitable bridegroom for the widowed Queen of Scots – a bizarre but politically expedient notion which was rejected by both members of the proposed bridal couple.

After Amy Robsart's death, the Queen prudently banished her favourite from court for a period. Disaster averted for the time being, Cecil now turned his attention to the vexatious Hertford-Grey relationship. He reinforced to Hertford the admonitions of his mother and friends about the potentially destabilising effects of a marriage between them. Katherine heard that Hertford had been flirting with a girl called Frances Mewtas and sent him a furious letter, which prompted him to propose that they marry at the first opportunity.

Frances Mewtas later married Henry Howard, 2nd Viscount Howard of Bindon, who was not only aggressive and a pirate but also mad. He was briefly imprisoned and Frances was rescued from his clutches by Queen Elizabeth, who took her on as a lady-in-waiting. When the Queen's messengers came to collect Frances, Bindon became abusive and said he was glad to see the back of his wife, who was a 'porky and filthy whore'.

When the court returned to Westminster, Hertford and Katherine secretly plighted their troth, swearing to marry at Hertford's London home the moment the Queen left the palace.

He gave Katherine a pointed diamond ring,[21] which she would keep all her life.

Their opportunity came in the late autumn when the Queen left Whitehall for a few days' hunting. Katherine, pleading toothache, was permitted to remain behind, with Jane Seymour for company. Katherine and Jane Seymour left Whitehall by the orchard stairs and walked along the sandy riverbank to Hertford's house on Cannon Row.[22] Hertford greeted them warmly, and Jane fetched the priest, who had been waiting nearby.[23] The couple spent the next few minutes billing and cooing 'such as passes between folk that intend as they did.'[24] Satisfied that the couple were free to marry, the priest proceeded with the ceremony. Hertford gave Katherine the five-linked gold wedding ring he had commissioned. Four of the links were engraved with a line of a verse he had composed.

> As circles five by art compact shewe but one ring in sight,
> So trust uniteth faithfull minds with secret know of might;
> Whose force to break but greedie death no wight possesseth power
> As time and sequels well shall prove. My ringe can say no more.[25]

Katherine and Hertford now embarked on a new intrigue, conspiring to indulge their physical passion as frequently as possible, whilst preserving outward appearances in order to keep the news of their marriage from the Queen.

Jane Seymour remained their 'beard' and confidante. Then, in March 1561, Katherine sustained three blows: Jane Seymour, her rock, fell ill again. This time, it was soon clear that she was dying; the Queen decided that Hertford should go on a European tour, to be joined by Thomas Cecil, eldest son of William Cecil, to broaden their minds; and Katherine thought she was pregnant. Jane advised her to confess all to the Queen, and throw herself on her mercy.[26] Hertford agreed that this was the only option. A few days later, on 29 March, aged only nineteen, Jane was dead. Hertford told Katherine that if she expressly told him she was with child, he would stay, but otherwise he was going on the proposed European trip. [27] Katherine, inexperienced and anxious, said she was still unsure. Hertford decided to go. Before he left he wrote his will, bequeathing lands worth £1,000 a year to Katherine. He gave her a signed parchment and some money, and said if she really was pregnant he would 'not long tarry from her'. [28]

Hertford arrived in Paris on 13 May and plunged into a ferment of activity. When Thomas Cecil joined him, his father's instructions about prayer, Bible study and confession were thrown to the winds as the two young men toured around various French cities, visiting the chateaux of the Loire, parting, making friends and generally enjoying themselves. [29] Cecil, when he found out, was outraged by their extravagant lifestyle. [30]

Meanwhile, Katherine, now in her eighth month, lived in dread of facing the Queen. Since Hertford had left, she had sensed that the Queen was showing 'a great misliking with her'. [31] She had sent reams of letters to France, addressed to her loving husband, but had received no reply. The only witness to their marriage, Jane Seymour, was dead. The priest was probably a Protestant exile whom it would be almost impossible to trace. Katherine, frantic with worry and feeling abandoned, conceived a desperate plan. Her former father-in-law, the Earl of Pembroke, had approached her in June with the suggestion that her marriage to his son, Lord Herbert, might be revived. At the times, Katherine, newly wed and in love with Hertford, had given him the brush off. But now her mind seized on the possibility as a way out. She wrote to Lord Herbert saying that she considered they were still married. [32] Herbert took the bait and began sending her gifts. When he realised that Katherine had been using him, he furiously denounced her and demanded that she should return his presents. In July, he sent her a bitter letter, insulting and repudiating her and calling her a whore. [33] Katherine still did not dare face the Queen herself, so she appealed to the Queen's favourite, Robert Dudley, once her sister Jane's brother-in-law, hoping he might soften the Queen's fury. But when Dudley broke the news to Elizabeth the next day, she flew into one of her notorious screaming rages. Katherine was arrested at once and taken to the Tower under armed guard. The Queen ordered the Lieutenant of the Tower, Sir Edward Warner, to interrogate Katherine rigorously about her relationship with Hertford, and find out who knew about it. To Elizabeth, who never forgot how her own mother had lost her life because of through slander and intrigue, any hint of plots and conspiracies was a red rag to a particularly volatile bull. Consequently, on 22 August 1561, Katherine was relentlessly grilled by professionals. Despite her appalling situation, Katherine steadfastly refused to confess. The Queen sent to Paris ordering Hertford to return immediately. At first he whined that he was sick in bed with fever, and told Nicholas Throckmorton, the Ambassador, that he had no idea why the Queen had summoned him. This was a lie. He knew perfectly well that Katherine was about to give birth, and that she had been arrested and imprisoned in the Tower. On 24 September Katherine gave birth to a son, Edward Seymour, Viscount Beauchamp, heir to Elizabeth under the will of Henry VIII, following his mother in the line of succession. The male Protestant succession was secure. Cecil was delighted. The Queen was incandescent. In May 1562 Warner was ordered to produce the two young people before the Archbishop at Lambeth for further interrogation about 'the infamose conversation and pretended marriage betwixt the Lady Katherine Grey and the Earl of Hertford.'[34]

Although it had been a clandestine, huddled affair, lacking in the usual formalities, according to canon law, a marriage was valid if vows were exchanged in the presence of witnesses. The problem with the Hertfords' marriage was that there were no available witnesses: Jane Seymour was dead, and the random priest had vanished.

Hertford bribed two guards to allow him to spent time with his wife, even though they were imprisoned in the Tower in separate apartments. When these romantic assignations were curtailed again by tightened security after the lovers had managed to meet just two or three times, Katherine knew she had fallen pregnant again. Nobody would be able to declare this child a bastard. Katherine and Hertford had declared their marriage before the Archbishop of Canterbury and other dignitaries. Nobody could now contend that they were not legally married.

Katherine and her little boys were still in the Tower in summer 1563 when the plague ravaged London, killing a thousand people a week. Eventually, the Queen agreed that they should be moved to protect them from the disease. However, they were to be separated, and their relatives were to foot the bill. Katherine's older son, Edward, was to be sent to her mother-in-law, the Duchess of Somerset, at Hanworth, with his father. Katherine and baby Thomas were to be sent to her uncle, Lord John Grey, at Pirgo in Essex. Elizabeth informed Lord John that he was now his niece's jailer, and that Katherine was not being released, simply moved for her own protection. She was forbidden to contact her husband or her sister Mary, who remained at Court. Katherine left her rooms in the Tower wrecked, the bed of changeable damask and the furniture 'torn and tattered by her monkeys and dogs.'[35]

Within the month, her relative and gaoler, Lord John was so concerned that he wrote to William Cecil, telling him that Katherine was hardly eating. When he urged her, she burst into tears and went to her room and declared that, if it were not for her husband and children, she wished she were buried, so intolerable was it to live 'in the Queen's displeasure'.[36]

At Cecil's suggestion, Katherine wrote a humble letter in which she cast herself on the Queen's mercy, admitted that she did not deserve it 'for my most disobedient and rash matching of myself, without your highness's consent'.[37]

Elizabeth was unbending. Katherine despaired and took to her bed.

Efforts to promote Katherine as her rightful heir enraged Elizabeth. Katherine and baby Thomas were removed from Pirgo and placed under close arrest, first at Ingatestone, and later at Gosfield Hall, and then at Cockfield Hall, Yoxford, Suffolk, the house of Sir Owen Hopton. Katherine kept up her desperate efforts to contact her beloved Hertford but they would never meet again. In January 1568, Katherine knew she was dying. Perhaps it was consumption. Others thought she might well have starved herself to death.

She had two last requests. The first was a message to the Queen, begging her forgiveness and pleading for her own children, and for her husband, Hertford. Katherine hoped that he would now be freed, 'to glad his sorrowful heart withal'[38]. She then asked for her jewellery box. Inside were the pointed diamond that Hertford had given her when they were betrothed in his sister's chamber at Whitehall, and the wedding ring with its five gold links engraved with Hertford's verse, and a *memento mori* ring mounted with a death's head. As she handed the last of the rings to Sir Owen, Katherine said: 'This shall be the last token unto my Lord that I shall ever send him. It is the picture of myself.' The ring was engraved for her husband: 'While I lyve, yours.'[39]

Elizabeth never truly forgave Katherine for marrying Hertford. She ordered Hopton to make the funeral arrangements for 'our cousin the Lady Katherine, lately deceased, daughter of our entirely beloved cousin, the Lady Frances, Duchess of Suffolk.' Katherine had been too dangerous to be 'entirely beloved.' Elizabeth put on the expected public show of mourning, but the Spanish Ambassador, for one, felt her grief was feigned. 'She was afraid of her,' he added.[40]

There were a herald and seventy-seven mourners at the choral service but 'nobody of note'. Hopton's account stated that there was but a meagre display of banners usual at state and semi-state funerals, although there were escutcheons of coloured paper and metal to decorate the house and the church. Hertford was not even permitted to send a proxy. There was no memorial to Katherine in Yoxford Chapel, although a small black stone in the chancel is said to mark her resting place.[41] Reyce's manuscript in the College of Arms suggests that her viscera remained at Yoxford after her grandson, William, had her remains transferred to Salisbury Cathedral to be buried with those of her husband. A local legend claims that one of

Katherine's pet spaniels pined to death upon her grave, as the Skye terrier of Mary Queen of Scots would also be reputed to do.[42]

Her son, six-year-old Viscount Beauchamp, still in the care of his paternal grandmother the Duchess of Somerset, was considered heir presumptive by the Council. Six years later, both Katherine's sons were declared illegitimate, although the Protestant party still supported their claim.

Hertford continued to work to establish his sons' legitimacy and reinstate himself in the Queen's favour. In 1603, when Queen Elizabeth herself was dying, her counsellors implored her to name her successor. She said: I told you my seat had been the seat of kings, and I will have no rascall to succeed mee; and who should succeed me but a king?' Asked to clarify what she meant, she replied 'who but our cosen of Scotland', and told them to trouble her no more.[43] Other accounts state that the Queen said 'I will have no rascal's son to succeed me,' and that she was thinking of Beauchamp.[44] They were her last coherent words.

The following year, Hertford won the battle for his sons' rights. Beauchamp was proclaimed his heir by Parliamentary statute. In 1606, the clergyman who had married Hertford and Katherine emerged from the shadows, gave his account of the ceremony and vouched for its validity. Once, this would have been inflammatory stuff. Now, it occasioned hardly a ripple. The new occupant of the throne, King James I, lost no sleep over the descendants of Mary Rose. The Grey girls were gone: Lady Jane on the scaffold, Lady Katherine dead, Lady Mary too, widowed, childless and obscure.

But politically dangerous secret marriages remained a family trait. In 1611, Katherine's grandson, Lord William Seymour, would secretly wed and attempt to elope with Lady Arbella Stuart, great-granddaughter of Margaret Tudor, Queen of Scotland. There would be the usual dire consequences.

16 - Notes

1.   Henry Machyn, *A London Provisioner's Chronicle*, 1550-156312 02 1554, folio 28v, 290

2. Nichols, *Chronicle*, London 1850 60-61

3.   John Foxe, 'The Duke of Suffolk's Behaviour on the Scaffold', *Martyrs*, Hart and Lewis, London, 1732 85

4. ibid, 545

5. CPR,1553-1554 106

6. Nichols, *Chronicle*, 166

7. Leland, *Collectanea*, 1774, vol. ii

8. Giovanni Michieli, *Relazione d'Inghilaterradel Clarissimo Giovanni Michieli Detta* in Pregadi i di 13 Maggio 1557, 344, 359

9. CSP Span [1916] 393

10. William Camden, *The History of the Most Renowned and Victorious Princess Elizabeth Late Queen of England*, Flesher, London, 1688 70

11. BL Add MSS33749 f 47

12. ibid

13. Machyn, 189, 201

14. Count de Feria to King Philip, 21 November 1558; Frank Mumby, *The Girlhood of Queen Elizabeth; A Narrative in Contemporary Letters*, New York, 1910, 252 253

15. *The passage of our most drad souereigne Lady Quene Elyzabeth through the citie of London to Westminster the daye before her coronation*, 1559, Mulcaster 790

16. CSP vol vii; Bayne, 1907, 'The Coronation of Elizabeth I'

17. CSP For vol ii pt 2

18. CSPD Add MSS 37749f74

19. Joseph Edmondson, Robert Glover, Sir Joseph Ayloffe, *A Complete Volume of Heraldry*, vol l Spilsbury, 1780, 181; Harris, *Literary Remains*, cxvii n

20. HMC Bath vol iv 178

21. BL Harl 611 f 1A

22. Add MSS 37749 f40 F

23. ibid, f 52

24. ibid, f 43

25. Ellis, *Letters*, 1827, 290n

26. Add MSS 37749 f 59

27. ibid, 42, 50

28. ibid, ff 63

29. CSPF vol iv 113

30. ibid, 299

31. ibid, 159

32. ibid, 160

33. Tanner MSS 193 f227

34. Cecil Papers, Hatfield House, vol i, 1561/2 Feb 10

35. Strickland, *Tudor Princesses*, 225, 226

36. Ellis, *Letters*, vol ii 279 – 282

37. ibid

38. Cotton Titus MS no 107 ff 124, 131

39. Ellis, vol ii, 289

40. Harris, *Literary Remains*, cxx

41. SP Dom Eliz., vol. xlvi., fols. 23, 24, 48, 49

42. Reyce's MS relating to Suffolk, College of Arms;

43. BL Cotton MS Faustina F III, f212

44. John Nichols, *The Progresses and Public Processions of Queen Elizabeth*, London, 1828, 'Elizabeth Southwell's Manuscript Account of the Death of Queen Elizabeth', 486

17 'THE LEAST OF ALL THE COURT': LADY MARY

At the Tudor Court, appearances were important. Royalty needed to look the part. In his own splendid youth, Henry VIII had established the tradition whereby royal blood was equated with an imposing physical presence. The King's grandmother, Elizabeth Woodville, had owed her position as Queen largely to her physical beauty – despite the accusations that she had won the heart of King Edward IV through sorcery, most people were aware that Edward, ever susceptible to feminine charms, had fallen for her lovely face. As a young man, Henry had impressed by his handsome person and physical prowess, and the older Henry continued to dazzle through sheer splendour of attire and stance. [1]

His daughter, Queen Elizabeth, who had once been recommended to Lady Jane Grey as an example of modest demeanour and apparel, now set about underlining her own regal status by means of magnificent raiment and dazzling jewellery. Any portrait of the Queen was examined thoroughly for any hint of physical imperfection; any flaws detected were eliminated before the works were displayed. The Queen's youngest Grey cousin, however, little Lady Mary, hardly met the requirements in respect of physical allure commensurate with her royal descent as far as the Tudor mindset was concerned. Although amiable and well-educated, and possessing the same rash emotional courage as her sisters, Mary Grey was tiny and misshapen. She further disqualified herself by falling in love with a commoner. He was much older, much larger, and they married without the Queen's permission. It was bound to turn out badly, and indeed it did. Big Thomas Keyes stood 6ft 8, with a correspondingly robust frame. The son of minor Kentish gentry, he was a widower over twenty years Mary's senior, with grown up children from his first marriage. He had been appointed Serjeant Porter, probably at the Watergates, by Mary's great-uncle, King Henry VIII, but had been considered sufficiently powerful and reliable to be entrusted with dealing with disputes and brawls among other servants, and with many other responsibilities and duties. Queen Elizabeth's vengeful fury when the clandestine marriage between Keyes and Lady Mary came to light may have owed something to the fact that Keyes, through his mother, may have been able to claim relationship with the Queen through a descendant of the sprawling clan of her great-grandmother Elizabeth Woodville, thus potentially reinforcing the claims of any offspring of the union. An alternative genealogy sees Keyes descended from the Knollys family, into which Anne Boleyn's sister Mary had married. It was certainly rumoured that when his clandestine marriage with little Lady Mary was discovered, Elizabeth declared: 'I'll have no little bastard Keyes laying claim to my throne!'[2]

The couple married in secret in the summer of 1565, (probably on 16 July, although alternative dates – 10 and 12 August – have also been suggested) while the Queen and the Court were attending the magnificent wedding of the Queen's kinswoman, (and some said, half-sister, since Henry VIII had been her mother's lover) Catherine Carey, daughter of Mary Boleyn, to Sir Henry Knollys. Some authorities state that, after the formal part of the wedding, members of the wedding party, including the famous beauty Lettice Knollys, repaired to the apartments of the convivial Keyes to continue the celebrations.

Lettice, who had married Walter Devereux, Viscount Essex, was pregnant with her first son but that had not stopped her from flirting with Robert Dudley, the Queen's favourite. The Queen was furious. Thirteen years later, Dudley would marry Lettice, and she would be banned from Court permanently.

After most of his guests had left, Thomas Keyes, emboldened by wine, married Mary by candlelight at an ad hoc ceremony witnessed by, among others, his brother Edward and one of his own sons, and three of Mary Grey's cousins, and conducted by a random priest, a 'little fat old man in a short gown', whose name nobody bothered to discover. [3]

This was exactly the same cavalier attitude to the formalities that had made it so difficult for Hertford and Katherine Grey, Mary's sister, to establish the legitimacy of their offspring.

After the final toast had been drunk and the guests had departed, Keyes carried Lady Mary up to his bed. Their bliss would be short-lived.

On 29 July, a marriage of even greater moment was celebrated: Mary, Queen of Scots, having refused to marry Dudley, strengthened her dynastic claims by marrying her cousin, the prancing popinjay Henry Darnley, in her private chapel in Edinburgh. Darnley was a grandson of Henry VIII's sister, Princess Margaret Tudor. The marriage annoyed and disquieted Elizabeth and was, moreover, a rebuke. In steadfastly refusing to choose a husband, Elizabeth had displayed an unnatural reluctance to accept the role divinely allocated to members of her sex, subservience, domesticity and child-bearing. Mary, also a Queen, had shown herself willing to embrace the role of a 'normal' woman. Moreover, she was now potentially in a position to produce a legitimate male heir to the throne.

On 21 August gossip reached the Queen's ears about Mary Grey's marriage. Cecil, appalled, denounced the affair as 'monstrous'. 'The Sergeant Porter, being the biggest gentleman of this court, has married secretly the Lady Mary Grey. The least of all the court…the offence is very great.' [4]

For Mary herself, and her new husband, the consequences would be immediate and grim.

Elizabeth, incensed, ordered them to be thrown into separate prisons, like Katherine and Hertford. Elizabeth's problem with the Greys was that Parliament's support of their claims as Protestant claimants to the throne threatened Elizabeth's absolutist belief in the divine right to rule and the authority of the monarch. Dynastic legitimacy was all; it must prevail over the secular power of parliamentary statute.

Mary was placed under house arrest at Chequers, the home of Sir William Hawtrey, High Sheriff of Buckinghamshire. During her two-year stay, until July or August 1567, when she was handed over to the care of her step-grandmother, Katherine Willoughby Brandon, the former Duchess of Suffolk, she was confined in a twelve foot square room. Her window overlooked trees and gardens, but she was permitted to stroll there only on rare occasions. She was not allowed visitors or excursions. Her attendants were limited to one groom and one waiting woman, and her food, for which the Queen was paying, was far from lavish. Both Keyes and Mary now began bombarding Cecil with letters, entreating him to plead with the Queen for forgiveness.[5]

Keyes paid even more dearly for his love than his bride. He was a man, not a naturally feckless woman, and he had enjoyed a position of trust. Accordingly, his betrayal was adjudged the more abhorrent. Where Mary was confined in a country house, Keyes was thrown into the dreaded Fleet, the ill-reputed prison built in 1197 on the eastern bank of the Fleet River in Farringdon. He was placed in single confinement in a tiny, cramped cell, agonising for a man of his stature. After Mary was moved to Buckinghamshire to the care of her step-grandmother, Katherine Suffolk, the unfortunate Keyes continued to linger in the Fleet.

When she arrived on 7 August 1567, Katherine Suffolk, who had herself seen her possessions diminished during her years out of favour under the reign of Queen Mary, could not believe how impoverished Mary was or the deplorable and dilapidated condition of her few possessions. She had asked Hawtrey to send on Mary's 'stuff' on in advance, so the accommodation could be made ready for her – Mary was to have one room, which she would share with her maid. But Katherine quickly realised that Mary had been obliged to borrow equipment from the Hawtreys, because she was practically destitute.

'She hath nothing but an old lyverie feather bed, all to torne and full of patches, without either bolster or counterpoint, but two old pillows, one longer than the other; an old quilt of silk, so old as the cotten of it comes out, such a little piteous canopy of sarsnett, as was scant good enough to hang over some secret stool [lavatory], and two little pieces of old, old hangings.'[6] Katherine was reduced to begging Cecil for a few pots and cups for Mary to drink out of, not daring to ask for a basin and ewer, 'for all these things she lacks, and hath nothing.'

Katherine added that she was deeply worried about Mary, who was so distressed and burdened with guilt and shame that she was refusing to eat, 'not so much as a checken's leg.'[7]

In 1569, Mary was transferred to the charge of Sir Thomas Gresham. Her presence was burdensome, especially to Lady Gresham, who complained constantly, and again Cecil was subjected to a barrage of requests from the Greshams to remove Mary. Gresham rather melodramatically referred to her unwelcome presence as 'bondiage and harte sorrow'. Gresham was willing to go to any lengths to preserve the peace of his household. He may well have exploited the impecuniousness of Edward de Vere, the illustrious but impoverished Earl of Oxford, who was betrothed to Cecil's daughter, Anne, to buy his way out of his predicament by offering Oxford a loan on very favourable terms. Gresham had gone to great lengths to ingratiate himself with the Queen, establish his already considerable fortune on a firm financial basis, and possibly get rid of his unwelcome house guest.

Inspired by the Bourse in Antwerp, where he had been Royal Agent for both Edward VI and Mary, he had invested part of the vast wealth he had acquired by his dealings in that city in building the new London Bourse on land acquired by the

Corporation between Cornhill and Threadneedle Street in the City of London. The aim was to create a trading floor, but the crafty Gresham intended to ensure a sound a steady income from the development by wooing the retail sector and building two more floors to house about a hundred shops. Essentially, this would be England's first shopping mall.

The trading floor combined Flemish and Italian features. It stood open to the elements, but, as a concession the English weather, it had covered piazzas for wet weather. Its bell-tower, crowned by a huge grasshopper, Gresham's emblem, stood on one side of the main entrance, from which the bell summoned merchants at 12 noon and 6pm. Its bell-tower, crowned by a huge grasshopper, stood on one side of the main entrance, from which the bell summoned merchants at 12 noon and 6pm.

Gresham's progressive notion was slow to catch on at first, but the Queen's visit in 1571, provided his project with a much-needed boost. Delighted with her visit, the flattery and entertainment, the wide and wondrous variety of goods on show, and ever alert to opportunities for exploiting commercial potential, Elizabeth granted Gresham's Bourse the title of the Royal Exchange and also, crucially, granted it a licence to sell alcohol. The licensing of landing quays for goods on the banks of the Thames ensured that the Crown also profited. The beauty of the Royal Exchange enterprise from everyone's point of view was that it linked the crown with the commercial success and prosperity of the city.

However, if Gresham had hoped that the Queen's delight in his new enterprise would result in the relief of his household from the burden of the presence of its unwanted guest, the Queen's cousin the Lady Mary, he would be disappointed. Mary would not be allowed to leave the Gresham household until 1572.

Meanwhile, Thomas Keyes, broken by the ill effects of his confinement in the Fleet, and despairing of ever seeing Mary again, died. When the news was broken to Mary, she was so distraught that she became ill and was sent to one of Gresham's country houses to recuperate. She entreated Gresham to write to

Cecil, pleading again for her freedom and the Queen's pardon. Grief had inspired a new resolution in Mary, and a sting in her words. She wrote: 'God having now removed the occasion of her Majesty's justly conceived displeasure towards her' and, for the first time, she signed herself Mary Keyes.[8] A portrait of Mary dated 1571 shows her proudly displaying her wedding ring.

With her new steadfastness, Gresham found Mary's presence even more of a trial. Determined to be rid of her, his efforts to get her removed became manic. He wrote to Cecil twice in one day in November 1571, and again in January he begged Cecil to bring about her removal because Mary and Lady Gresham quarrelled incessantly.

In May 1572, the Queen finally agreed to release the last Grey sister. But Mary had no income and no friends to take her in. The situation at the Greshams' residence was now intolerable for all parties. Finally, in desperation, Gresham suggested that Mary should go and stay with her step-father, Adrian Stokes, and his new wife. Early in 1573, to everyone's relief, she left the Greshams', 'with all her books and rubbish', as Gresham recorded contemptuously.

Mary was twenty-seven. After seven years as a prisoner, she enjoyed the welcome offered her in the lively household of her stepfather, Adrian Stokes, and his new wife, Anne Carew, the widow of Nicolas Throckmorton, who had brought into her new marriage a daughter and six sons, the oldest of whom had mental problems. Mary was embarrassed to feel she was adding to her stepfather's financial commitments.

Fortunately, by February 1573, the Queen relented. Mary was established in her own modest household in the London parish of St Botolph's Without Aldgate. By the end of 1577, Mary was sufficiently reinstated in the monarch's favour to be invited to court as one of the Queen's Maids of Honour. Childless, not wealthy or regarded as physically attractive, never having given the slightest indication of any ambition to ascend the throne, Mary clearly represented nothing like the danger to an unmarried female sovereign that her fecund and headstrong married sister Katherine had done.

Mary would not be Queen; nor did she wish to be, any more than Katherine had done.

She spent a merry Christmas at court. Her gift to the Queen was a gold cup, faithfully recorded. On New Year's Day 1577 she presented the queen, then at Hampton Court, with 'four dozen buttons of gold, in each of them a seed pearl, and two pairs of sweet [i.e. perfumed] gloves,' a gift acknowledged by Elizabeth. The Queen gave Mary a silver cup and cover, weighing eighteen ounces.[9]

This happiness was not to last. In 1578 the plague swept through the land again. By 17 April, Mary knew she was dying. As the plague approached London, Mary had not joined in the general panic-stricken exodus of the court who always headed for the country at the first hint of an epidemic. Perhaps after all the vicissitudes of her life, Mary had grown fatalistic, or perhaps she trusted in the mystic properties of the carbuncle she had been given by Keyes. Mystic rubies or carbuncles, believed to develop at the base of the horns of unicorns, were said to protect their owners against poison and disease. Unicorn horn, or alicorn, would continue to be taken for a century or more for its supposed medical and magical qualities. The alicorn so lucratively marketed by apothecaries during this period probably originated as the horn of the narwhal.

Although her carbuncle failed to save her life, Mary valued it sufficiently to mention it in her will, which she drew up three days before she died. In her testament, she referred to herself as Lady Mary Grey – the name she used at court – yet acknowledged her marriage to Keyes by describing herself as 'widowe, of wholl mind and of good and perfect remembraunce.'[10] She asked to buried 'wherever the Queen's Majesty shall think most meet and convenient'.

She offered her step-grandmother, Katherine Suffolk, the choice between her late mother's gold bracelets or her mystic ruby, the item not chosen by Katherine to go to Lady Susanna, Countess of Kent. She bequeathed her tankards, her horses, her bed, other jewellery and her money to friends and cousins. Her stepmother, Anne Throckmorton Stokes, whose guest she had briefly been after her release from house arrest, received a silver and gilt covered bowl. The bulk of her modest fortune went to her late husband's daughter and granddaughter. She had begged to be allowed to play the role of caring stepmother to Keyes's children.

While Mary lived, the Queen had turned a deaf ear to her pleas, but now that she was safely dead, the Queen could acknowledge her and pay her respects. She ordered an impressive funeral at Westminster Abbey. Mary was buried beside her mother.

Mary died at only thirty-three, but unlike her older sisters and her father, she died free.

With all three Grey sisters dead and Katherine's boys pronounced illegitimate, their cousin Margaret Clifford, now Countess of Derby, became Elizabeth's heir under the terms of Henry VIII's will.

Within weeks, partly thanks to her own rash behaviour, Margaret was placed in various people's houses as a prisoner. She died eighteen years later, without ever tasting freedom again.

17 -Notes

1. Pasqualino, CSP Span 158-67 468
2. Davey, 1911, *The Sisters of Lady Jane Grey*, Chapman & Hall, London, 262-3
3. ibid
4. Ellis, *Letters Illustrative*, Vol II, 229
5. Florence Molesworth Hawtrey, *The History of the Hawtrey Family*, I, 1903, London. George Allen, 30-31;

J W Burgon, *The Life and Times of Sir Thomas Gresham*, London, Robert Jennings, 1839, 409f

6. CSPD Vol I 425
7. Katherine Suffolk to Cecil, Dom. Cor. Sp Off. ; *Life and Times of Sire Thomas Gresham*, J W Burgon, 1839, London, 402ff
8. CSPD vol i 425
9. Davey, *Sisters*, 1912
10. Lansdowne, BL, 27, no.31, ff 60, 61

18   ALAS!

Although he had helped declare Katherine Grey's older son, Edward, Viscount Beauchamp, illegitimate, there was little doubt about the views held by William Cecil, now Lord Burghley, and still Elizabeth's closest adviser, as regards the succession. He continued to cast about for a Protestant heir, preferably male. Beauchamp, or his younger brother, Thomas Seymour, about whose legitimacy there could be no doubt, were his favoured candidates. He had supported Beauchamp's claim since 1562, when Elizabeth had caught smallpox and it had been feared that she would die without an obvious successor.

However, the great statesman's hopes were blighted by the headstrong Tudors' proclivity for unsuitable romantic liaisons and consequent disastrous marriages. In 1581, nineteen-year-old Lord Beauchamp became infatuated with his relation Honora Rogers. Honora's brother Andrew had married Hertford's sister Lady Mary Seymour. In 1581, Beauchamp and Honora, nominally supervised by 'two old hags', were thrown together in the summer holidays, as Hertford and Katherine Grey had been, in the idyllic setting of Hanworth Palace in Middlesex, and duly became infatuated. Beauchamp allegedly presented Honora with a ring and dallied with her in the orchard. Honora reputedly was a high-spirited hoyden, given to such adolescent larks as stealing the keys to the sweetmeat cupboard when her ineffectual attendants were dozing. Hertford disapproved of her, and appointed George Ludlow, himself rather a rough diamond, to approach Sir Richard Rogers to discuss the relationship between the two young people. Ludlow dismissed Honora as a 'baggage' and her father as a fool, who through his inaction was passively encouraging the affair. All Beauchamp had wanted, Ludlow said, was a night of two of pleasure with the girl.

Beauchamp's father Hertford, who had not relinquished his dreams of dynastic glory, thought Honora an unsuitable wife for a future King of England. He nicknamed Honora 'Onus Blowse' – 'that tiresome tramp', and ordered his son to drop her. Beauchamp promised to obey, but he was his parents' son. Just as Hertford had ignored his own mother's advice to leave Katherine Grey well alone, Beauchamp secretly continued to shower Honora with love letters, in which he bitterly lamented their separation. In August 1585, the exasperated Hertford ordered some men to kidnap his son and imprison him in one of his houses. Beauchamp threatened suicide if he were forced to part from his beloved, and sent a desperate message to the Queen, begging her to intervene on his behalf.

His entreaty played into Elizabeth's hands. Recognising the chance to permanently disqualify Beauchamp from the royal succession on the grounds of an unsuitable marriage, the crafty monarch graciously gave her permission for the marriage. When the Queen stepped in, Hertford knew he had been outmanoeuvred and had no choice but to accept Honora as his daughter-in-law.

As a sop to Cerberus, Elizabeth granted Hertford himself permission to marry his mistress of the past ten years, Frances Howard, daughter of Lord Howard of Effingham. Frances was accomplished and much admired, and was a favourite Maid of Honour to Queen Elizabeth. Hertford, now 46, had been a widower for twenty years or more by the time he and Frances married. (They may have been clandestinely married years before he was able to acknowledge her in public. Quite possibly, the Queen had withheld her permission out of spite.)

Hertford later attempted to have this marriage set aside in 1595, hoping to establish his sons' claim to the throne by clearing them of the slur of illegitimacy once and for all. He was arrested again, and Frances reputedly went mad with fear for his life, until she received a personal reassurance from the Queen that her dear 'Franke' need have no care, the Queen had no intention of executing Hertford.

Hertford's second wife, Frances, died in 1598 and was buried in St Benedict's Chapel in Westminster Abbey. She is commemorated by a large alabaster wall monument, 28 feet in height, with Corinthian columns, surmounted by a recumbent effigy of the Countess dressed in a red fur lined cloak, with a lion *couchant* at her feet.

In May 1601, now over sixty, Hertford secretly married once more; his new bride was Frances Prannell, confusingly also born Frances Howard, a penniless but beautiful descendant of two royal Dukes, Norfolk and Buckingham. She had been married off in extreme youth to Henry Prannell, a wealthy London vintner, to the annoyance of William Cecil, who, as always, had his own agenda for ladies of royal descent.

Henry Prannell wrote a humble letter to Cecil, explaining that he had not married Frances without being actively encouraged to do so by her friends. In fact, he said, he had loved her for a long time and had thought he was doing a good deed, since 'she had litle or nothing to maineteine and preferr herself; she being destitute of freindes and abilitie I thought it a most frindlie parte (with her good acceptance) to present her my selfe, and therbie to make her partaker of all wherwith God hath blessed me'.[1]

Lovely, rich, and popular, twenty-one-year-old Frances had many suitors, but selected the ageing Hertford, on the advice of her astrologer, Dr Simon Forman, celebrated occultist and herbalist, and on the promise from Hertford that he would settle a jointure of £4,000 on her at his death. The couple were married in a clandestine ceremony at his home in Canon Row on 27 May 1601, without banns or licence. When Archbishop Whitgift found out, the celebrant, Thomas Montfort, who had officiated at the wedding, was suspended from office for three years.

One of Frances's disappointed admirers, Sir George Rodney, in despair at her sudden marriage to Hertford, wrote her a sonnet in his own blood, threatening suicide. In her 'Answer', a witty verse-epistle of 160 lines, Frances drew on various literary sources, including Munday's *Hecatonphila* and Shakespeare's *As You Like It*, mocking Rodney's Petrarchan posturing:

No, no, I never yet could hear one prove
That there was ever any died for love.[2]

Upon receiving this, the unfortunate Rodney wrote a farewell note and fell on his sword.

After all the hullabaloo it caused, it was rumoured that the marriage between the second Frances and Hertford was far from idyllic. Frances gave herself great airs about her noble birth. When it became too much for Hertford, he would tap her cheek and ask 'Franke, Franke, how long is it since you married the vintner?' But as he declined into old age, Hertford grew so jealous of his bride's allure and popularity at court that he kept her sequestered in the country, where her principal entertainment was hunting rabbits. (A mere two months after Hertford died in 1621, at the unusual age, for the time, of eighty-two, Frances married Ludvick Stuart, Duke of Richmond, and her life became much more cheerful. She died in 1639).

Cecil, now Lord Burghley, and a white-bearded sage, retained undiminished faculties. He had quickly rallied from his disappointment over Beauchamp's disqualifying marriage in 1582, and concentrated his energies on Beauchamp's brother, Hertford and Katherine's younger son, Thomas Seymour, the boy conceived in the Tower when his amorous parents defied their jailors to be together. Burghley had another reason for his buoyant spirits: he was at last making progress with his plot for the ultimate destruction of Mary, Queen of Scots. The previous year, he and Walsingham had drafted the Bond of Association, whose members pledged to arrange Mary's murder in the event of any palpable threat to Elizabeth's life.

In February 1587, Mary was executed.

Two years later, in 1589, twenty-four-year-old Thomas Seymour, Hertford and Katherine's younger son, appealed against the decision that rendered him illegitimate. Although the appeal was again rejected, Thomas remained undeterred, conscious that the veneration the older generation felt for the Virgin Queen was not shared by his compeers. Among members of the younger generation he sensed a restless longing for change. Society traditionally marginalised old women, and the Queen was visibly ageing. Moreover, resentment against female rule had long festered in the country, England's multiple ills being widely ascribed to the gender of her sovereign.

In 1591, Thomas's father, Hertford, scored an immense propaganda coup when he entertained the Queen during her summer progress at one of his manor houses, Elvetham in Hampshire, to a spectacle rivalled in scope and expense only by that held in her honour in 1575 by her favourite, Robert Dudley, at Kenilworth. Hertford laid on a magnificent pastoral neverwhere for the royal visit, including the creation of an artificial lake – shaped like a half moon, symbolic of the Queen's virgin status – with an island crowned by a wood and canvas palace. There were monsters, wildfire, mock battles. The costumes were dazzling, the banquets lavish, the gifts extravagant. Hertford was not only seeking to ingratiate himself with a monarch who harboured a profound and well-justified mistrust of him and his family. The pageant's themes, Winter and Spring, ostensibly a celebration of the Queen's beauty – Elizabeth's vanity had remained undiminished with her advancing years – had a subversive subtext. Gloriana was old, childless, a withered elderly virgin.

A few months after his father's extravaganza, Thomas Seymour reinforced his appeals concerning the validity of his parents' marriage and his own legitimacy. He was playing a dangerous game. In 1594, Ferdinando, 5th Earl of Derby, the son of his incautious cousin Margaret Clifford, would die in suspicious circumstances.

In the autumn of 1595, Sir Michael Blount, Lieutenant of the Tower, was caught secretly stockpiling arms for Hertford.

Hertford found himself once more a prisoner in the Tower. He was released on the intervention of Burghley and his son, Sir Robert Cecil. But Hertford's dynastic ambitions received another blow in 1600 when Thomas predeceased him, aged only thirty-seven.

Thomas was dead, Beauchamp's marriage had disqualified him as a claimant to the throne, yet Hertford, undaunted, still fancied his family's chances. He clung to the hope that the clan's aspirations could be revived by a brilliant match for his grandchild, Edward Seymour. This dynastic union would involve Arbella Stuart, granddaughter of the redoubtable Bess of Hardwick, now Countess of Shrewsbury. In 1574, Bess, a former lady in waiting to Hertford's mother-in-law Frances Grey, had married her daughter Elizabeth Cavendish – Katherine Grey's godchild – to Charles Stuart, younger son of the Countess of Lennox, brother to the murdered Henry, Lord Darnley, husband of Mary Queen of Scots. This match, arranged by the mothers, resulted in the birth in 1576 of Arbella Stuart. 'My jewel Arbell', the darling of her ambitious grandmother Bess, was thus a great-granddaughter of Margaret Tudor, Queen of Scotland. Since Arbella and both her parents had been born in England, many considered her claim superior to that of James I.

Increasingly, murmurings against female rule continued to gather momentum in the country. People began to mutter more loudly than ever that the country's recent social problems and political unrest had come about because England was ruled by a woman; the weakness of character traditionally ascribed to females was reflected in all that was wrong in the country. Hertford hoped that a marriage between Arbella and young Edward Seymour, uniting as it did the Tudor lines of Henry VIII's two sisters, could create a joint candidacy which would attract widespread support. Any male child of the union would seal the deal.

Arbella had been a favoured lady in waiting to the Queen when she was discovered incautiously engaged in flirting with the Queen's favourite, Robert Devereux, Earl of Essex. The

Queen, furious, reacted by packing Arbella off to her grandmother's estate in Derbyshire. Elizabeth, suspicious to the point of paranoia, for reasons of personal jealousy and politics, ensured that Arbella was kept well out of the public gaze from the age of eighteen to twenty-eight, sequestered in the country.

Arbella, like Jane Grey, was highly educated, but she was trapped in a cocoon of dependence and maidenhood, with no prospects of marriage. In her enforced seclusion her overheated imagination ran riot, fuelled by notions of romantic liaisons and elopements. She and her powerful and vigilant grandmother, Bess, irritated one another. Arbella felt trapped. Life was passing her by. She made up her mind to spread her wings and break free of her enervating situation.

Out of these circumstances grew the plot to marry her to Hertford's grandson, Edward. Arbella embraced the idea enthusiastically and, with the aid of her chaplain, Starkey, planned her escape. When the plan miscarried, the disgraced chaplain killed himself.

But Arbella was undeterred. She had never met Edward, Beauchamp's son, but she now sent a message to his grandfather, Hertford, through one of her grandmother's servants.

Hertford had certainly at one point contemplated a union between either his grandson or possibly his younger son, Thomas, with Arbella, but when the man arrived with her message for him, he scented danger and lost his nerve. In marrying Katherine Grey, he had paid too high a price for his own secret unauthorised marriage into the Tudor dynasty. Having heard the servant's message, he sent the man under guard to Cecil, who informed the Queen. When the Queen learned of Arbella's scheme, the terrifying spectre which had consumed her forty years before, upon learning of Hertford's marriage to Katherine, resurfaced. The Queen's fury knew no bounds. Elizabeth was already in poor health and in no state or mood to deal with upsetting news.

Such was the Queen's anger that her death a few months later was ascribed to her rage and stress over the behaviour of

Arbella and the realisation that she was still being plotted against, as she had been all her life.

Arbella became hysterical, refused to eat, and wrote reams of letters in which she wildly accused the Queen and the Cecils of conspiring against her and plotting her downfall.

Next year, in 1603, the Queen died. She had repudiated the Protestant descendants of Mary Rose Tudor, her aunt, despite the prompting of Cecil. The way was clear for the Stuart succession. Representatives of the peers, gentry and Councillors signed the proclamation of 25 March. The next year, laws were passed that set aside Henry VIII's will.

Arbella Stuart was invited back to court, but remained unmarried and without estate. She rallied her forces for one final desperate act of defiance, marrying Mary Rose's descendant, Katherine Grey and Hertford's grandson, twenty-two-year-old William Seymour, the younger son of Edward Beauchamp. Recklessly, like other members of the family, she did so without royal permission.

As soon as the secret marriage became known, the lovers were thrown into separate prisons, Arbella in Lambeth and William in the Tower. They were not strictly guarded, and managed to plan their escape to France. Arbella, disguised as a young man, rode thirteen miles to the Thames where she boarded a French ship by prearrangement. William missed the boat and took passage on a collier. They were headed for the French coast and the vessels were approaching one another when a storm blew them apart. The lovers would never meet again. Arbella was arrested aboard the French ship by the crew of an English frigate and taken back to captivity. William waited in Ostend for her in vain.

Arbella was sent to the Tower, where she sank into an emotional decline and died in 1615. It was rumoured that she went mad, or possibly starved herself to death, as Katherine Grey is said to have done in 1568.

Arbella's bridegroom fared slightly better. William Seymour remained in exile until 1616, supported by his grandfather, Hertford, on the orders of James I, who had learned that

William was ill with smallpox in Paris. The King commanded Hertford to pay off William's debts and grant him an annuity of £400. However, William was not permitted to return to England until after Arbella's death.

Under Charles I, William, now Earl of Hertford, was gradually rehabilitated at Court. Before he died in 1621, William's grandfather Hertford had managed to seek out the clergyman who had married him to Katherine Grey almost fifty years previously. The children of their union could at last be unequivocally declared legitimate.

William now set about re-establishing the family reputation. He ordered the remains of his grandmother Katherine Grey to be disinterred from her grave in Yoxford, Suffolk, and had her transported to Salisbury Cathedral, where she was re-interred with her husband in a magnificent marble tomb in the Italian style, in the easterly corner of the south choir aisle.

The Latin inscription celebrates the lovers, united at last.

> *Incomparable Consorts,*
>
> *Who, experienced in the vicissitudes of changing fortune*
>
> *At length, in the concord which marked their lives,*
>
> *Here rest together.* [3]

The figures of their sons are shown, kneeling on either side. Edward is dressed in armour. unusually, Katherine is positioned higher than her husband, in deference to her royal descent.[4]

Although William had been an opponent of Charles I in the House of Lords, and had supported the Petition of Right in 1628, he later parted company with radical Parliamentarians. In 1641 he was created Marquess of Hertford by the King. Now a moderate Royalist, he was a trusted supporter of the King, who made him guardian of the Prince of Wales. During the King's imprisonment, William remained at his side, and in January 1649 he had the doleful task of witnessing the monarch's execution.

Along with three other peers, William was later given the task of helping entomb the monarch's decapitated body, the King's severed head roughly tacked on, in St George's Chapel,

Windsor. The site had been chosen by Parliament as remote and comparatively inaccessible, with a view to discouraging a flood of pilgrims to the shrine of the 'Martyr King'. William and his three companions in the burial party discovered that the unmarked tomb in the vault under the quire of St George's contained the coffins of William's great-great aunt, Queen Jane Seymour, and another massive coffin, which could only be that of William's great-great uncle, Henry VIII himself.

In Henry's will of 1546 he had given instructions that he was to buried with Queen Jane in the quire, half way between the high altar and Sovereign's Garter stall, until a more permanent tomb had been constructed for them both. Jane, alone of his six wives, had produced a son who survived infancy. The planned tomb was never completed because the money ran out.

Henry's Will had confirmed his wishes for the succession. His own children, Edward, Mary and Elizabeth, were to be followed by the Greys, the descendants of his sister, Mary Rose.

But things had moved on. A Stuart bestrode the throne. The turbulent story of the Tudor succession was over at last, and the curse of their royal blood was finally lifted from Mary Rose Tudor's descendants.

Her niece, Queen Elizabeth 1, a woman not given to sentimentality, had once commented:

'You know them all: Alas! What power or force has any of them, poor souls!'

18 - Notes

1. Ellis, *Letters*, vol 4 1846endorsed 8 Feb. 1591
2. 'The answer of the Countess of Hertford', Bodl. Oxf. MS Rawl. poet. 160 [lines 1-115 only] ff 118v-119v
3. Davey, *Sisters*, 1912, 244-5
4. *Salisbury Cathedral: A Pocket Tour*, Reef Publishing, 9

List of Abbreviations

BL British Library

Bodl Bodleian Library, Oxford

Cal/CSP Milan Calendar of State Papers, Milan 1385-1618, ed Hind, London 1912

Cal /CSP Span Calendar of State Papers, Spanish vols 1 & 2 ed G A Berneroth

Cal/CSP Ven Calendar of State Papers, Venetian ed Rawdon Brown, London 1864

CPR Calendar of Patent Rolls, Henry VIII 19-14-16, London

CSPD Calendar of State Papers Domestic1547-1625 ed Robert Lemon, 12 vols, 1856-1872, London

CSPD Calendar of State Papers Domestic1547-53 of the Reign of Edward VI, ed C S Knighton, 1992, London

CSPD Calendar of State Papers Domestic1543-58, of the Reign of Mary I, ed C S Knighton, 1998, London

CSPF Calendar of State Papers Foreign vols I-VIII, 1865, London

CSPD Calendar of State Papers Rome, vol I 1558-71, 1916, London

CSPD Calendar of State Papers Spanish, vol I, 1558-67, 1971, London; vol IX, 1547-49, 1912, London; vol IX, 1550-52, 1914, London; vol XII, Jan-Jul 1554, 1949, London; vol XIII, Jul 1554-Nov 1558, 1954, London

CSPD Calendar of State Papers Venetian, vol V, 1534-5, 1864-98, London; vol LVii,1556-7, vol LViii, 1557-58, vol VII, 1578-80, 1873-1890, London

CWE *The Complete Works of Erasmus*

DNB *Dictionary of National Biography*

HMC Bath Historical Manuscripts Commission, Calendar of the Manuscripts of the Marquess of Bath – Longleat, Wilts.

HMC Middleton Historical Manuscripts Commission, Report on the Manuscripts of Lord Middleton, Wollaton Hall, Notts.

HMC Salisbury Historical Manuscripts Commission, Calendar of the Manuscripts of the Most Honourable the Marquess of Salisbury, Hatfield House, Herts.

L&P Hen VII *Letters and Papers Illustrative of the Reigns of Richard III and Henry VII*, Rolls Series (1861-3) ed J Gairdner Rolls Series, 2 vols, London, 1861-3

L&P Hen VIII *Letters and Papers Foreign and Domestic of the Reign of Henry VIII 1509-47* (1862-1932) ed J S Brewer *et al*

Leland John Leland, *De Rebus Britannicis Collectanea* 1770, London

Memorials of King Henry VII, ed J Gairdner, Rolls Series, 1858, London

PRO Public Records Office

State Papers of Henry VII, 11 vols, London, 1830-52

Tudor Royal Proclamations, vol 1, *The Early Tudors 1485-1553,* New Haven &
London, ed P Hughes and J F Larkin

The College of Arms

Arundel 35 ff 5-9

Longleat MSS Portland Papers I ff 92,93

Bibliography

Adams, S, 'Eliza Enthroned? The Court and its Politics', in C Haigh, ed, *The Reign of Elizabeth I*, 1985, London

Adams, S, 'The Dudley Clientèle, 1553-1563', in G W Bernard, ed, *The Engish Nobility in the Sixteenth Century*, 1991, Leicester University Press, Leicester

Alford, Stephen, *Kingship and Politics in the Reign of Edward VI*, 2002, Cambridge University Press, Cambridge

Alford, Stephen, *Burghley: William Cecil at the Court of Elizabeth I*, 2008, Yale University Press, New Haven, CT

Alford, Stephen, 'The Political Creed of William Cecil', in John F McDiarmid, ed, *The Monarchical Republic of Mediaeval England*, 2007, Aldershot

Alford, Stephen, *The Early Elizabethan Polity, William Cecil and the British Succession Crises, 1558-1569*, 1998, Cambridge University Press, Cambridge

André, Bernard, *Historia Regis Henrici Sept (in: Memorials of King Henry VII* ed. J. Gairdner, 1858, London

Anglo, S, *Spectacle, Pageantry and Early Tudor Policy*, 1969, Oxford

Anglo, S, *Images of Tudor Kingship*, 1992, Seaby, London

Archer, Ian W, ed, *Religion, Politics and Society in Sixteenth-Century England*, 2003, Cambridge University Press, Cambridge

Archer, Jayne Elisabeth, Elizabeth Goldring and Sarah Knight, eds, *The Progresses, Pageants and Entertainments of Queen Elizabeth*, 2007, Oxford

Aristotle, *History of Animals*, tr D'Arcy Wentworth Thompson, 1907, London

Ascham, Roger, *The Whole Works*, ed Rev Dr Giles, vols i-iii 1864, London

Ashdown, Dulcie, *Tudor Cousins: Rivals for the Throne*, 2000, Gloucestershire, Sutton Publishing

Aylmer, John, *An harborow for faithfull and trewe subjects against the late blown blast concerning the gouerment of wemen*, 1559, London

Bacon, Francis, *The Historie of the raigne of King Henry the Seventh, and other works of the 1620s*, Michael Kiernan, ed, 2011 Oxford University Press, Oxford

Baker, Richard, *A Chronicle of the Kings of England from the Time of the Romans' Government unto the Death of King James*, 1670, London

Baldwin Smith, Lacey, *Treason in Tudor England*, 2006, London

Bale, John, *Select Works*, ed Henry Christmas, Cambridge University Press, 1849

Bartlett, David, *The Life of Lady Jane Grey*, 1857, 1888, Miller, Orton Mulligan, New York

Bateson, Mary, *Records of the Borough of Leicester*, vol iii, 1905, Cambridge

Bayley, J, *The History and Antiquities of the Tower of London, with Memoirs of Royal and Distinguished Persons, deduced from Records, State Papers and Manuscripts*, 2 vols, 1821, London

Bayne, C G, 'The Coronation of Queen Elizabeth I', *English Historical Review* 22 and 25 , 1907

Beaufort, Lady Margaret, *The Mirror of Golde for the Synfulle Soule*, 1506, London

Becon, Thomas, *Works*, 1843, Cambridge

Becon, Thomas, *The Catechism of Thomas Becon*, 1844, Cambridge

Becon, Thomas, *Prayers and Other Pieces*, 2004, Cambridge

Beer, Barrett L, *Northumberland, the Political Career of John Dudley, Earl of Warwick and Duke of Northumberland*, 1974, Kent State University, Kent, Ohio

Bernard, G W, 'The Downfall of Sir Thomas Seymour', in G W Bernard, ed, *The Tudor Nobility*, 1992, Manchester University Press, Manchester

Bernard, G W, *The King's Reformation: Henry VIII and the Remaking of the English Church*, 2005, Yale, New Haven and London

Bernard, G W, *The Power of the Early Tudor Nobility: A Study of the Fourth and Fifth Earls of Shrewsbury*, 1984, Harvester Press, Sussex

Bernard, G W, *War, Taxation and Rebellion in Early Tudor England: Henry VIII, Wolsey and the Amicable Grant of 1525*, 1986, Macmillan, London

Bindoff, S T, 'A Kingdom at Stake 1553', in: *History Today*, vol 3, 1953

Bindoff, S T, *Tudor England*, 1950, Penguin, London

Bindoff, S T, *The House of Commons, 1509-1558*, 3 vols, 1982, History of Parliament, London

Bower, Roger, 'The Chapel Royal, The First Edwardian Prayerbook, and Elizabeth's Settlement of Religion, 1559', *Historical Journal*, 43, 2, 2002, pp 317-44

Brewer, J S, ed, *Calendar of Letters and Papers, Foreign and Domestic, of the Reign of Henry VIII*, vols vi, vii, xii (pt 2), xiii (pt 1) xv, xvi, ix, xx (pt 2) xxi, 1894-1910, London

Brooke, Ralph, *A catalogue and succession of the kings, princes, dukes, marquesses, earles, and viscounts of this realme of England, since the Norman Conquest, to this present yeare*, 1619, London

Brown, R, Four Years at the Court of Henry VIII: Selection of Despatches Written by the Venetian Ambassador, Sebastian Guistinian, and Addressed to the Signory of Venice, January 12ᵗʰ 1515 to July 26ᵗʰ 1519, 2 vols, 1854, London

Bullinger, Heinrich, *The Decades of Heinrich Bullinger, Fifty Sermons divided into Five Decades Containing the Chief and Principal Points of Christian religion*, vol iv, 1587, tr 2004, Grand Rapids, MI

Burgon , J W, *The Life and Times of Sir Thomas Gresham*, vols i and ii, 1839, London

Burnet, Gilbert, *History of the Reformation of the Church of England*, new edn, 6 vols, 1820, London

Bush, M L, *The Pilgrimage of Grace: A Study of the Rebel Armies of October 1536*, Manchester University Press, Manchester, 1996

Caius, John, *A boke, or conseill against the disease commonly called the sweate, or sweatyng sicknesse*, 1552, London

Camden, William, *The History of the Most Renowned and Victorious Princess Elizabeth Late Queen of England*, Flesher, London, 1688

Carmelianus, Petrus, *Honorificia gesta solemnes cerimonii & triumphi habiti in suscipienda legatione pro sposalibus et matrimonio inter principem Karolum & Dominam Mariam*, 1508, London, tr. 1509, Camden Miscellany vol 9 ed J Gairdner

Carmelianus, Petrus, 2013, 36-7. *The Spousells of the Princess Mary, Daughter of Henry VII, to Charles Prince of Castile, 1508*. London: Forgotten Books. (Original work published 1894)

Carter, A, 'Mary Tudor's Wardrobe', Costume, 18, 1984, pp 9-29

Cavendish, George, *The Life and Death of Cardinal Wolsey*, Samuel Weller, ed, 1825 and Folio Society edn, 1962, London

Chapman, Hester, *The Thistle and the Rose: The Sisters of Henry VIII*, 1969, Coward, McCann & Geoghegan, Incorporated, 1969, London

Chapman, Hester, *Lady Jane Grey*, Jonathan Cape, 1962, London

Childs, Jessie, *Henry VIII's Last Victim, the Life and Times of Henry Howard, Earl of Surrey*, 2006, Cape, London

Clifford, Henry, *The Life of Jane Dormer, Duchess of Feria*, 1887, Burns & Oates, London

Colvin, H M, *The History of the King's Works*, vol III, pt 1, 1975, HMSO, London

Cook, Faith, *Lady Jane Grey*, 2004, EP Books, New York

Corrie, G E, ed., *Sermons and Remains of Hugh Latimer*, Parker Society, 16, 20, 1844-1845,

Davey, Richard, *The Sisters of Lady Jane Grey and their Wicked Grandfather*, 1911, Methuen, London

Davey, Richard, *The Nine Days Queen: Lady Jane Grey and her Times*, 1909, Methuen, London

Dent, Emma, *Annals of Winchcombe and Sudeley*, 1877, J Murray, London

Dewhurst, J, 'The Alleged Miscarriages of Catherine of Aragon and Anne Boleyn', Cambridge Journals, *Medical History*, 28, 1984, pp 49-56

Dickens, A G, *Clifford Letters of the Sixteenth Century* ,Durham and London, Surtees Society, 1962

Dickens, A G, *The Register or Chronicles of Butley Priory, Suffolk, 1510-1535*, 1951, Warren & Son, Winchester

Doran, Susan, *Monarchy and Matrimony, the Courtships of Elizabeth I*, 1996, Routledge, London and New York

Doran, Susan, and Thomas Freeman, eds, *The Myth of Elizabeth*, 2003, Palgrave, Macmillan, Basingstoke

Dowling, M, 'William Latymer's Chronickille of Anne Bulleyne', *Camden Miscellany*, 30, 1990, Camden Society, 4th Series, vol 39, pp 23-65, 501-1

Dyer, A, 'The English Sweating Sickness of 1551: An Epidemic Anatomized', Cambridge Journals *Medical History*, 41, 1997, pp 362-84; 42, 1998, pp 96-98

Edmondson, Joseph, Robert Glover, Sir Joseph Ayloffe, *A Complete Volume of Heraldry*, vol l Spilsbury, 1780

Ellis, Henry, *Original Letters Illustrative of English History*, 1824, Harding, Triphook & Leonard, London

Elton, G R, *Reform and Renewal: Thomas Cromwell and the Common Weal*, 1973, Cambridge University Press, Cambridge

Elton, G R, *The Tudor Constitution*, 2nd edn, 1982, Cambridge

Erasmus, Desiderius, *Adagiorum*, 1508, Basle; *Moriae Encomium Opus Epistolarum*, ed P S and H M Allen,

1906-58, Oxford; *The Complete Works of Erasmus,* tr R A B Mynors and D F S Thomson, 1974, Toronto

Evenden, E and T S Freeman, 'Print, Profit and Propaganda: The Elizabethan Privy Council and the 1570 Edition of Foxe's "Book of Martyrs"', *English Historical Review*, 119, 2004, 1288-1307

Feuillerat, Albert, ed, *Documents Relating to the Revels at Court in the Time of King Edward VI and Queen Mary*, 1914, Louvain

Fiddes, R, *The Life of Cardinal Wolsey*, 1724, London

Fisher, John, *The English Works of John Fisher*, ed J E B Mayor, 1876, Early English Text Society

Fletcher, A J, and D MacCullough, *Tudor Rebellions*, 1997, London

Fleuranges, Robert de la Marck, Seigneur de Fleuranges, *Mémoires du maréchal de Florange, dit le Jeune Aventureux*, published for the Société de l'Histoire de France by Robert Goubaux & P. André Lemoisne, Paris, H. Laurens, 1913-1924, 2 vols printed in Du Bellay *Les Mémoires de Martin et Guillaume du Bellay et les Mémoires du Maréchal de Fleuranges et le Journal de Louise de Savoye*, 7 vols, Paris, 1753

Florio, Michelangelo, *Historia de la vita e de la morte de l'Illustrissima Signora Giovanna Graia, gia regina eletta a publicata d'Inghilterra*, 1607, Ricardo Pittore, Venice

Fox, A, and J A Guy, *Reassessing the Henrician Age: Humanism, Politics and Reform*, 1986, Blackwell, Oxford

Fox, Julia, *Jane Boleyn, The Infamous Lady Rochford*, 2008, Phoenix, Orion, London

Foxe, John, *Actes and Monuments of these latter and perilous days touching matters of the Church, wherein are comprehended and described the great persecutions [and] horrible troubles, that have been wrought and practised by the Roman prelates, specially in this realme of England and Scotland*, 1563, London

Fraser, Antonia, *The Six Wives of Henry VIII*, 1992, Weidenfeld, London

Friedman, Alice, *House and Household in Elizabethan England*, 1989 University of Chicago Press, Chicago

Friedman, P, *Anne Boleyn: A Chapter of English History, 1527-1536*, 2 vols, 1884, Macmillan, London

Froude, J A, *History of England from the Fall of Wolsey to the Death of Elizabeth*, 1860, 1893, Longmans, London

Fuller, Thomas, *Church History of Britain*, vol iv, ed J S Brewer, 1845, Oxford

Gairdner, James, ed. *Letters and Papers, Foreign and Domestic of the Reign of Henry VIII*, vols 1-xxi, 1886, London

Gairdner, James, *The Paston Letters, A. D. 1422-1509* . London: Chatto & Windus, 1904, 6

Gairdner, James, 'Mary and Anne Boleyn', *English Historical Review*, 30, pp 53-60, 299-300

Goff, Cecilie, *A Woman of the Tudor Age*, 1930, John Murray, London

Green, M A E, *Lives of the Princesses of England*, 1849, Longman, Brown, Green, Longman & Roberts, London

Gruffudd, Elis, *Cronicl o Wech Oesoedd (Chronicle of Six Ages)*, National Library of Wales, MS 5276D &3054D

Guaras, Antonia de, *The Accession of Queen Mary*, ed Richard Garnett, 1892, London

Gunn, S. J., *Charles Brandon, Duke of Suffolk*, 1988, Blackwell, Oxford

Gutierre Gomez de Fuensalida, embajador en Alemania, Flandes é Inglaterra (1496-1509), *Correspondencia*, Duke of Berwick and Alba, ed, 1907 Madrid449

Guy, John, *Tudor England*, 1990, Oxford Paperbacks, Oxford

Guy, John, ed, *The Tudor Monarchy*, 1995, Cambridge University Press, Cambridge

Guy, John, *'My Heart is my Own'*, *The Life of Mary, Queen of Scots*, 2004, Houghton Mifflin Harcourt, Boston

Guy, John, *Thomas More*, 2000, Arnold, London

Hall, Edward, *The Union of the Two Noble and Illustre Famelies of York & Lancaster*, ed H Ellis, 1809, London

Hall, Edward, *Henry VIII* [an edition of Hall's Chronicle], ed C Whibley, 2 vols, 1904, London

Halliwell, J O, *Letters of the Kings of England*, 2 vols, 1848, London

Hallowell Garrett, Christina, *The Marian Exiles*, 1938, repr. 2010, Cambridge University Press, Cambridge

Hankinson, Maggie Mae, 'William Thomas, Italianate Englishman', unpb. PhD thesis, 1967, Columbia University

Harbison, E Harris, *Rival Ambassadors at the Court of Queen Mary*, 1940, Oxford University Press, Oxford

Harbison, E Harris, 'French Intrigue at the Court of Queen Mary', *American Historical Review*, vol 45, no 3, 1940 April, pp 533-551

Hardwicke, Lord, Hardwicke, *Miscellaneous State Papers*, vol1. 1778, London

Harington, Sir John, *Nugae Antiquae*, vol II, 1804, London

Harris, Barbara J, *English Aristocratic Women 1450-1550*, 2002, Oxford University Press, Oxford

Harris, Nicholas, *The Literary Remains of Lady Jane Grey*, 1825, Harding, Triphook & Lepard, London

Hawtrey, Florence Molesworth, *The History of the Hawtrey Family*, I, 1903, George Allen, London

Haynes, Samuel, ed., *A Collection of State Papers Relating to Affairs in the Reigns of King Henry VIII, King Edward VI, Queen Mary and Queen Elizabeth from the Years 1542-1570, Left by William Cecil Lord Burghley*, vol vi, 1740, London

Hayward, Sir John, *Annals of the First Four Years of the Reign of Queen Elizabeth*, ed John Bruce, Camden Society, MDCCC.XL, London

Herbert of Cherbury, Edward, *The Life and Raigne of King Henry the Eighth*, 1649, London

Hoak, Dale E, 'The Coronations of Edward VI, Mary I, and Elizabeth I, and the Transformation of the Tudor Monarchy', in C S Knighton and Richard Mortimer, eds, *Westminster Abbey Reformed*, 2003, Aldershot

Hoak, Dale E, *The King's Council in the Reign of Edward VI*, 1976, Cambridge University Press, Cambridge

Hoby, Thomas, A Booke of the Travaile and Lief of Me, Thomas Hoby, 1902, Camden Miscellany X, London

Houlbrooke, R A, *The English Family 1450-1700*, 1984, Longman, London and New York

Houlbrooke, R A, *Death, Religion and Family in England 1480-1750*, 1998, Blackwell, Oxford

Houlbrooke, R A, ed, *English Family Life, An Anthology of Diaries 1576-1715*, 1988, Blackwell, Oxford

Hoyle, R W, *Letters of the Cliffords, Lords Clifford and Earls of Cumberland, 1500-c. 1565*, 1992, Camden Miscellany XXXI, London

Hudson, Winthrop Still, *The Cambridge Connection and the Elizabethan Settlement of 1559*, 1980, Durham NC

Hume, D, *The History of England, from the Invasion of Julius Caesar to the Revolution in 1688*, 5 vols, 1796, London

Hume, Martin A., *The Wives of Henry the Eighth and the Parts They Played in History*. Nash, London, 1905. Reprint. London, 1967

Ives, Eric W, *The Life and Death of Anne Boleyn*, 1986, Blackwell, Oxford

Ives, Eric W, 'Tudor Dynastic Problems Revisited', *Historical Research*, vol lxxxi, no 212, May 2008

Ives, Eric, *Lady Jane Grey: A Tudor Mystery*, 2009, Wiley-Blackwell, Oxford

Jackson, J E, 'Wulfhall and the Seymours', *Wiltshire Archaeological and Natural History Magazine*, vol XV, 1875, pp 140-207

James, Susan E, *Kathryn Parr, The Making of a Queen*, 1999, Ashgate Publishing Limited, Aldershot

James, Mervyn, *Society, Politics and Culture, Studies in Early Modern England,* 1986, Cambridge University Press, Cambridge

Jones, Norman, *The Birth of the Elizabethan Age,* 1995, Wiley-Blackwell, Oxford

Kelly. H A, *The Matrimonial Trials of Henry VIII,* 1976, Stanford University Press, Stanford, CA

Kingsford, C L, *Chronicles of London,* 1905, Clarendon, Oxford

Knafla, Louis A, 'Stanley, Henry, Fourth Earl of Derby, 1531-1593', 2004, *Oxford Dictionary of National Biography,* Oxford University Press

Knecht, R J, *Renaissance Warrior and Patron: The Reign of Francis I,* 1994, Cambridge University Press, Cambridge

Latimer, Hugh, *Observants,* 1832, Hilliard, Gray, Massachusetts

Leland, John, *De Rebus Britannicis Collectanea,* 1770, London, ed. T Hearne

Lettenhove, M. le Baron Kervyn de, *Rélations politiques des Pays-Bas et de l'Angleterre,* 1883, F Hayez, Brussels

Levine, Mortimer, *Tudor Dynastic Problems 1460-1571,* 1973, Unwin University Books, London and New York

Lloyd, C, and S Thurley, *Henry VIII: Images of a Tudor King,* 1990, Phaidon Press, London

Loach, J, 'The Function of the Ceremonial in the Reign of Henry VIII', *Past and Present,* Oxford Journals, 142 Feb,1994, pp 43-68

Loach, J, *Edward VI,* 1999, Yale University Press, New Haven and London

Loades, David, *Mary Tudor: A Life,* 1989, Blackwell, Oxford

Loades, David, *Politics, Censorship and the English Reformation,* 1991, Pinter Publishers, London and New York

Loades, David, *John Dudley, Duke of Northumberland, 1504-1553,* 1996, Oxford University Press, Oxford

Loades, David, *Intrigue and Treason, The Tudor Court 1547-1558,* 2004, Pearson Longman, London

Loades, David, *The Dudley Conspiracy,* 2001, The Davenant Press, Oxford

Loades, David, *Two Tudor Conspiracies,* 1965, Cambridge University Press, Cambridge

Lovell, Mary S, *Bess of Hardwick,* 2005, Little Brown, London

Lovejoy, Arthur O, The Great Chain of Being, 1936, Harvard University Press, Cambridge MA,

MacCaffrey, Wallace, *The Shaping of the Elizabethan Régime 1558-72,* 1969, Cape, London

MacCullough, Diarmuid, *Reformation, Europe's House Divided 1490-1700*, 2004, Penguin. London

MacCullough, Diarmuid, *Suffolk and the Tudors, Politics and Religion in an Elizabethan County, 1500-1600*, 1986, Clarendon, Oxford

MacCullough, Diarmuid, *Thomas Cranmer, A Life*, 1996, Yale University Press, London and New Haven

MacCullough, Diarmuid, ed and tr, 'The Vita Mariae Angliae Reginae of Robert Wingfield of Brantham', *Camden Miscellany*, Fourth Series, vol 29, 1984, Royal Historical Society

D.MacCullough, ed.,*The Reign of Henry VIII: Politics, Policy and Piety*, 1995, Palgrave Macmillan, London,

McConica, James K., *English Humanists and Reformation Politics under Henry VIII and Edward VI*, 1965, Clarendon, Oxford

Malfatti, C V (tr) *The Accession, Coronation and Marriage of the Princess Mary*, 1831, London

Merriman, R B, *Life and Letters of Thomas Cromwell*, 2 vols, 1902, Clarendon, Oxford

Miscellanea Genealogica et Heraldica, 4th Series, vol 2, 1908, London

Moorhouse, Geoffrey, *The Pilgrimage of Grace*, 2002, Weidenfeld and Nicolson, London

Mueller, Janel, 'Prospecting for Common Ground in Devotion: Queen Catherine Parr's personal prayerbook', in *English Woman, Religion and Textual Production, 1500-1625*, Micheline White, ed., Farnham UK Ashgate, 2011

Mulcaster [Mulcahey], Richard, *The passage of our most drad souereigne Lady Quene Elyzabeth through the citie of London to Westminster the daye before her coronation*, 1559. London. in John Nichols, *Progresses*

Mumby, Frank, *The Girlhood of Queen Elizabeth; A Narrative in Contemporary Letters*, New York, 1910,

Murphy, V M, 'The Literature and Propaganda of Henry VIII's First Divorce', in *The Reign of Henry VIII: Politics, Policy and Piety*, ed D MacCullough, 1995, London, pp 135-58

Murphy, V M, and E Surtz, *The Divorce Tracts of Henry VIII*, 1988, Moreana, Angers

Neale, J E, 'Parliament and the Succession Question in 1562/3 and 1566', *English Historical Review*, Jan-Oct 1921, pp 497-519, Oxford

Nichols, John Gough, ed, *Narratives of the Days of the Reformation*, 1859, Camden Society 77

Nichols, John, *The Progresses and Public Processions of Queen Elizabeth, vols 1 & 2*, 1828, London

Nichols, John, *The History and Antiquities of the County of Leicester*, vol iii, pt 2

Nichols, John Gough, *The Chronicle of Queen Jane and Two Years of Queen Mary*, 1850, London

Nichols, John Gough, ed, *The Chronicle of the Grey Friars of London*, 1852, London

Nichols, John Gough, ed, *The Literary Remains of Edward VI*, vols 1&2, 1857, London

Nichols, John Gough, ed, *The Diary of Henry Machyn*, 1848, London

Nicolas, Nicholas Harris, *The Literary Remains of Lady Jane Grey*, 1825, London

Nicolas, Nicholas Harris, *Privy Purse Expenses of Elizabeth of York*, 1830, London

Nicolas, Nicholas Harris, *Privy Purse Expenses of Henry VIII from November 1529 to December 1532*, 1827, London

North, Jonathan, ed, *England's Boy King, The Diary of Edward VI 1547-53*, 2005, Ravenhall Books, Welwyn Garden City

Notes and Queries, 5[th,] 7[th,] 8[th,] 11th series, vol v, vii and viii, vol 240, vol 245,1877-2000

Parsons, Robert, *A Treatise of Three Conversions of England, from paganisme to Christian religion*, 3 vols, 1604, François Bellet, St Omer

Paul, J Balfour, ed., *The Reference of the Great Seal of Scotland*, Edinburgh, 1882, 1602, 553

Peck, Francis, *Desiderata Curiosa*, 1732-1735, London

Pegge, Samuel, *Curalia: Or an Historical Account of Some Branches of the Royal Household*, 5 pts, pts iv & v ed John Nichols, 1784 London

Perlin, Estienne, *Description des Royaumes d'Angleterre et d'Ecosse 1558*, 1775, London,

Perry, Maria, *Sisters to the King*, André Deutsch, 1998, London

Planche, J R, *Regal Records, or a Chronicle of the Coronations of the Queen Regnants of England*, 1838, London

Plowden, Alison, *Lady Jane Grey*, 2003, Sutton, Stroud

Pollard, A F, *England under the Protector Somerset*, Kegan Paul, Trench, Trübner & Co, 1900, London

Pollard, A F, *Thomas Wolsey*, London, 1929, Longman Green & Co

Pollard, A F, *Henry VIII*, 1902, Longman, Green & Co, London

Pollard, A F, *Tudor Tracts, 1532-1588*, 1903, Constable & Co, London

Pynson, Richard, King's Printer: '*The Solemnities and triumphs doon and made at the spousells of the King's daughter*', printed by The Roxburghe Club, Donee MSS, No 198 Bodleian.

Read, Conyers, *Mr. Secretary Cecil and Queen Elizabeth*, 1955, Alfred A. Knopf, New York

Read, Evelyn, *Catherine, Duchess of Suffolk*, 1962, Cape, London

Rex, Richard, *Henry VIII and the English Reformation*, 1993, Macmillan, London

Richardson, W, *Mary Tudor: The White Queen*, 1970, Peter Owen, London

Ridley, Jasper, ed, *Love Letters of Henry VIII*, 1988, Cassell London

Roberts, Richard Arthur& Montague Spencer Giuseppi, eds., *Calendar of the manuscripts of the Most Honourable the Marquess of Salisbury*,1883-9, HMSO, preserved at Hatfield House, Herts.

Robinson, Hastings, *Original Letters Relative to the English Reformation*, vol i, 1846-7, Cambridge

Roca de Togores Molíns, Mariano, Marquìes de, *Crónico del Rey Enrico Otavo de Inglaterra*, 1874, Madrid

Rosso, Giulio Raviglio, ed Luca Contile, *Historia delle cose occorse nel regno d'Inghilterra, in material del duca di Notomberlan dopo la morte di Odoardo VI*, 1558, Venice

Sadlack, Erin, *The French Queen's Letters*, Palgrave Macmillan, New York, 2011

Sanut[d]o, Marino, *Diarii*, 1879-1903, F. Visentini, Venice

Savoie, Louise de, *Journal*, Petitot collection of *Mémoires sur l'Histoire de France*, Series I. t. xvi.,

Scarisbrick, J J, *Henry VIII*, 1968, Eyre and Spottiswoode, London

Scarisbrick, J J, *The Reformation and the English People*, 1984, Blackwell, Oxford

Sil, N A, *Tudor Placemen and Statesmen*, 2001, Farleigh Dickinson University Press, London

Skidmore, Chris, *Edward VI, The Lost King of England*, 2007, Weidenfeld & Nicolson, London

Snow, Vernon F., *Holinshed's Chronicles, England, Scotland and Ireland*, 1965, AMS, New York

Spence, Richard T, 'Clifford, Henry, Second Earl of Cumberland' (1517-1570), 2004, *Oxford Dictionary of National Biography*, Oxford University Press

Starkey, David, *Six Wives: The Queens of Henry VIII*, 2004, Harper Perennial, London

Starkey, David, ed, *Henry VIII: A European Court in England*, 1991, Vintage, London

Starkey, David, *The Reign of Henry VIII: Personalities and Politics*, 1991, Grove Weidenfeld, London

Starkey, David, ed, *Rivals in Power: Lives and Letters of the Great Tudor Dynasties*, 1990, London

Stone, J M, The *History of Mary I, Queen of England, as found in the public records, despatches of ambassadors in original private letters, and other contemporary documents*, Sands & Co, London, 1901

Stow, John, *The Annales of England faithfully collected out of the most autenticall authors,, records, and other monuments of antiquitie*, London, 1592,

Strickland, Agnes, and Elisabeth Strickland, *Lives of the Queens of England*, 1852, Carey, Lea & Blanchard Philadelphia; London, 1868

Strong, Roy, *Artists of the Tudor Court, The Portrait Miniature Rediscovered, 1520-1620*, 1983, London

Strype, John, *Ecclesiastical Memorials Relating Chiefly to Religion*, 1822, Oxford

Talleyrand Périgord, Jean Grignaux de, in Pierre de Bourdeille, Seigneur de Brantôme, *Oeuvres Complètes*, Société du Panthéon Littéraire, 1842,André de Bourdeille, Jean Alexandre Buchon, vol 4, quatriesme discours

Tanner, Bodleian Library 193 f.224,227

Throckmorton, Sir Thomas, *The Legend of Sir Nicholas Throckmorton*, 1740, London

Thurley, Simon, *The Royal Palaces of Tudor England*, 1993, Yale University Press, New Haven and London

Thurley, Simon, *Hampton Court, a Social and Architectural History*, 2003, Yale University Press, New Haven and London;*The Reign of Henry VIII: Politics, Policy and Piety*, ed D MacCullough, 1995, London, pp 135-58, New Haven and London

Thwaites, G, M Taviner and V Gant, 'The English Sweating Sickness, 1485-1551,' 1997, *New England Journal of Medicine* 336, 580-2

Thwaites, G, M Taviner and V Gant, 'The English Sweating Sickness, 1485-1551: A Viral Pulmonary Disease?' *Medical History*, 42, 1998, 96-8

Tillyard, E M W, *The Elizabethan World Picture*, 1942, Donne & Milton, repr. 1976, London

Tymms, Samuel, *An Architectural and Historical Account of the Church of St Mary, Bury St Edmund's*, 1854, Simpkin and Marshall, London

Tytler, P F, ed, *England under the Reigns of Edward VI and Mary*, 1839, London

Weir, Alison, *Children of England, The Heirs of King Henry VIII*, 1996, Random House, London

Williamson, G C, *Lady Anne Clifford, Countess of Dorset, Pembroke and Montgomery, Her Life, Letters and Work*, Kendal, Titus Wilson and Son, 1922

Wingfield, R, *Vita Mariae Reginae*, tr D MacCulloch, Camden Miscellany xxviii, 4th series, 29 1984 London

Wagner, Sir Anthony, and Anglo, S, ed, *The Great Tournament Roll of Westminster*, 1968, Clarendon, Oxford

Wood, M A, *Letters of Royal and Illustrious Ladies of Great Britain*, 3 vols, 1846, London

Wriothesely, Charles, *A Chronicle of England during the Reigns of the Tudors, from AD 1485 to 1559*, 2 vols, ed William Douglas Hamilton, Camden Society, vols II, 20, New Series XI, 1875-7, London

Wyatt, Michael, *The Italian Encounter with Tudor England*, 2005, Cambridge University Press, Cambridge

Yorke, James, 'A Chest from Cockfield Hall', *Burlington Magazine*, London, vol 128, no 995, Feb 1986, pp. 84, 86-91

Young, Alan, *Tudor and Jacobean Tournaments*, 1987, Hamlyn, London